A Touch of the Poet

&

More Stately Mansions

Eugene O'Neill

Edited and Introduced by
Martha Gilman Bower

YALE NOTA BENE

Yale University Press New Haven and London

First published as a Yale Nota Bene book in 2004.

Introduction copyright © 2004 by Martha Gilman Bower.

A Touch of the Poet
Unpublished dramatic composition copyright © 1946 by Eugene O'Neill.
First published in 1957 by Yale University Press, copyright © by Carlotta
Monterey O'Neill.
Copyright © renewed 1973 by Oona O'Neill Chaplin and Shane O'Neill.

More Stately Mansions
Copyright © 1967 by Carlotta Monterey O'Neill.
Copyright © renewed 1995 by Yale University.
This edition copyright © 2004 by Yale University. The unexpurgated version
of the play was first published in 1988 by Oxford University Press.

For information about this and other Yale University Press publications,
please contact:
   U.S. office   sales.press@yale.edu
   Europe office sales@yaleup.co.uk

Set in Adobe Garamond type by Tseng Information Systems, Inc.
Printed in the United States of America.
Library of Congress Control Number: 2003111053
ISBN 0-300-10079-5
A catalogue record for this book is available from the British Library.

10 9 8 7 6 5 4 3 2 1

A Touch of the Poet

AND

More Stately Mansions

Contents

Introduction by Martha Gilman Bower   vii

A Touch of the Poet   1

More Stately Mansions   155

Introduction

MARTHA GILMAN BOWER

A Touch of the Poet and *More Stately Mansions,* the only of Eugene O'Neill's cycle plays to survive the flames when Carlotta O'Neill, at her husband's request, burned all the cycle manuscripts, represent two of the most provocative, psychologically revealing, and timeless of O'Neill's masterpieces. In O'Neill's early plans for the long cycle on America's history of corrupted opportunity and insatiable greed, *A Touch of the Poet* was to be the first play and *More Stately Mansions* the second. Both plays are fraught with parent-child jealousy and resentment and with familial sexual tensions that epitomize America's unique and contradictory personality—a duality that confuses innocence with evil and dreams of legitimate success with material greed. Therefore, it is most appropriate that the two plays appear together here in one volume.

O'Neill's cycle was originally called "Calms of Capricorn Series" and later "A Touch of the Poet Cycle." Eventually O'Neill settled on the title "A Tale of Possessors Self-Dispossessed." The grand saga was to begin in 1755 with arrival of the Harford ancestors to the New World, and to end in 1932 with the inventions of the automobile and the airplane. As more plays were added to the top and bottom of the cycle, *Poet* became the third play of the nine-play cycle and later the fifth play of the eleven-play cycle. O'Neill finished the play in 1939, although he made revisions on the typescript as late as 1942, and it was first produced on Broadway in 1958. *Poet* tells the story of the conflict between the Irish peasant Melody family and the patrician Protestant Harford family. The play underwent several plot revisions, from Sara and Simon Harford's life on the Melody farm to the conflicts, in the final version, between Sara Melody and her father, Cornelius (Con) Melody, over her engagement to Simon Harford. Simon, who is in love with Sara, lies ill in an upstairs bedroom of the Melody Inn, a room that was originally part of the set, until O'Neill in 1942 deleted all scenes except those in the dining room. Simon's mother, Deborah, appears in a cameo role when she confronts Con Melody and lectures Sara, recounting the Harford family propensity for evil ambition and equating Sara's grasping personality with that of the Harford sisters. This long speech is central to the cycle as a whole and serves as an important link between *Poet* and *More Stately Mansions;* the second play continues the rivalry between Deborah and Sara, now Simon's wife. Sara represents those traits in the Harfords that O'Neill outlined in an interview with journalist Elizabeth Shepley Sergeant: "The family are people with guts. When they feel negative, they burn the building. They are the kind of people who go after success and succeed and fail but never stay fallen."[1]

Much of the fictional material in the plays was grounded in historical fact. O'Neill read widely in American, European, and Irish history and, when designing his sets, made sure they were faithful to their respective periods. He was drawn to a character from Irish history—one who would become Con Melody in *Poet,* an officer in the Duke of Wellington's army. Intrigued by Con and his family, O'Neill decided to write a play about them and then merge the two families—Harford and Melody—in *Mansions.* As time went on, he was determined to recount the entire history of America and depict its corruption by materialism and greed. The strong peasant roots of the Melody family, integrated with the gentility and education of the Harfords, reflected similar family mergers in American history. Honey, one of the Harford sons, is named after Rose Kennedy's father, John Francis Fitzgerald ("Honey Fitz"), mayor of Boston (1906–7). The mansion in the second play was modeled after houses built by famous Boston architects Charles Bulfinch and Samuel McIntire, and it also resembles Tao House, O'Neill's magnificent home in Danville, California.

In both plays, characters refer to current affairs, and O'Neill's strong interest in the American Transcendentalist and the Romantic periods is reflected in myriad references to Emerson, Whitman, and Thoreau. In fact, in notes to the plays entitled "Thoreau in Simon," O'Neill recorded excerpts from the journals of Thoreau and Emerson. Simon's cabin, described at the beginning of act 1, scene 2, of *Mansions,* is a replica of Thoreau's hut on Walden Pond.[2]

The other cycle plays survive only in fragments and scenarios at the Yale Beinecke Library, but enough was salvaged to give us a sense of their plots, characters, and themes. Although it may seem tragic that the other cycle manuscripts were destroyed, the loss was not in vain. O'Neill was rehearsing in the composition of the cycle for his late great plays, *A Long Day's Journey into Night, A Moon for the Misbegotten,* and *The Iceman Cometh*—all written concurrently with the cycle plays. Woven into the fabric of the cycle is O'Neill's own experience. Central to the action is the tension between peasant and patrician—the same tension that dogged the O'Neill family in New London, the Tyrones in *Long Day's Journey,* and the Hogans in *A Moon for the Misbegotten.* In *A Touch of the Poet,* Con Melody bears a strong resemblance to Eugene's father, James O'Neill. The conflicts between Sara and Con are more than coincident with the ones between O'Neill and his own daughter, Oona. *Work Diary* entries recorded at a time when the tension between O'Neill and Oona was most intense coincide with the dates of revision notes that involve Con and Sara.[3]

Connections between the two extant cycle plays and O'Neill's life abound. Sara Melody bears more than a coincidental likeness to O'Neill's wife, Carlotta. Both women were a "blend of aristocratic and peasant characteristics." According to Louis Sheaffer, Carlotta, like Sara, "looked patrician from the waist up, but she had strong hands, short sturdy legs, and a peasant like capacity for hard work."[4] The marriage between Simon and Sara resembles that of the O'Neills when Sara tells Deborah Harford in *Mansions* that Simon "has nothing left but me. . . . I'm mother, wife and mistress in one." It is commonly known that Carlotta fulfilled these three roles for O'Neill. Simon also possesses the requisites of the frail poetic O'Neill figure. Deborah Harford finds her model in

O'Neill's mother, Ella O'Neill. Although described in slightly different words, the women are unequivocal look-alikes—youthful, pretty, white haired, and full lipped, with high foreheads, deep-set eyes, long fingers, and nervous gestures.

It is essential that any published version of *Mansions* be in its most complete form. The version edited by Donald Gallup, published in 1964, consists of less than half the play.[5] It alters O'Neill's intentions and tampers with significant elements of plot, character, and theme as well as *Mansions'* index to the subsequent plays of the cycle. Its excisions—act 1, scene 1, the beginning of act 3, scene 2, and the epilogue—are restored in this unexpurgated edition. In addition, numerous words, lines, and phrases elsewhere in the original play have been restored to retain O'Neill's poetic diction and his intended dramatic impact, pointing up nuances of character and scene.

Act 1, scene 1, supplies transitional information that links *A Touch of the Poet* to *More Stately Mansions* and motivates the three main characters in the remainder of the play. In *Mansions,* as in *Poet,* Maloy and Cregan (Con's drinking cronies) open the play, providing the exposition that closes the four-year gap between the two plays. While Cornelius Melody lies dead in an upstairs room of the Melody Inn, barkeep and barfly rehearse Con's exploits and his career as an officer in Wellington's army—some of the same history that they relate in *Poet.* It was important to O'Neill that this background be repeated, not only because it joins the earlier play with the later one, but also because it allows audiences to read and view the two plays separately.

No less important are restored scenes with Sara and Cregan and with Sara and Nora (her mother). In a dialogue with Cregan, Sara describes and comments on Con's retreat from life and his amassed debts. In her scene with Nora, we learn that Sara and Simon are going to buy out their partner's share of the mill business and that, if not rich, they are happy—a fact that intensifies the conflict that ensues after they move in with Deborah. In the same scene Sara, the mother of three sons and pregnant with a fourth, reaffirms her determination to "rise to the top." Another key element evident in the restored version is the renewal of the mother-daughter bond between Sara and Nora, which is placed in sharp contrast to Sara and

Deborah's intense rivalry. In this edition, act 3 of *Mansions* has been expanded per the original typescript from nineteen to twenty-two pages. Simon recites a monologue that is equal in impact to Hickey's long sermons in *The Iceman Cometh,* again reflecting a blending of truth and insanity. Sixty-one lines formerly deleted from this speech have been restored. Although laden with the repetition typical of O'Neill, Simon's monologue depicts graphically and sensationally the full range of his complex and contradictory personality. When he says of Sara that "it has been a long time since I have slept with her—but at home her body has become repugnant, her beauty ugly," and expresses his desire to take revenge for the wounds inflicted by both wife and mother, his ambivalent sexuality is fused with O'Neill's own. The second scene of act 3, in which the Harford sons appear in the garden with their grandmother, Deborah, has been restored by two-thirds. The ubiquitous and monochromatic green of the sculpted garden reflects the monotony of the Harfords' lives and hides the murky underside of this faux Eden. Yet Deborah, interacting with her grandsons, reveals her human side, which adds to the complexity of her character. In addition, the introduction of the young Harford sons connects *Mansions* with subsequent cycle plays in which each son was to play a role in politics, railroads, banking, and shipping.

In act 4, scene 1, this edition restores many lines that give definition to Sara's bizarre role as Simon's mistress; here she is reduced to an object of his sexual desire. She wears clothes that are "designed with the purpose of accentuating her large breasts, her slender waist, her heavy rounded thighs and buttocks, and revealing them as nakedly as the fashion will permit." Sara's monologue, increased by fifty-one lines, exposes the extent to which she believes she has whored herself. Her sexual overtures toward Joel (Simon's brother) are given more play in this complete version, and when she repeats her yearning for wealth and power we have reverberations of a theme that echoes throughout the cycle: the relentless pursuit of material gain.

O'Neill revised the play so that the conflict between Sara and Deborah would be more powerful, thus casting the women as mighty opposites. Simon's role, though central, becomes more passive, more malleable. The restoration of several speeches in the shocking confrontation in act 4, scene 2, shows how far each woman is willing to go in the battle over Simon. One crucial speech elucidates Deborah's extreme "unscrupulousness," her sick mind at work, when she tells Sara that Simon hinted that "I might find some subtle way . . . to poison you!" Then she explodes with "I could watch you lashed to death, with the blood running down your gross white back, and never raise a finger to save you!"

The epilogue (left out of the shortened version) is carefully designed to recapitulate for the audience the action of the past year. Jonathan and Honey (sons of Sara and Simon) replace Cregan and Maloy as harbingers of exposition. Rather than end the play in act 4 with Deborah's rejection of Simon and her retreat into the never-never land of the "summerhouse," and with Simon in a state of nervous collapse, O'Neill adds an epilogue in which Sara, Simon, and their sons have been "dispossessed" of the previous generations' materialistic trappings; more important, they are ready to begin life anew without the curse of the Harford money. After a year in a mental institution, Simon is cured of his obsession with his mother. They have returned to the Melody farm—Sara to her peasant roots, and Simon to be a writer and dreamer with "a touch of the poet." Yet Sara cannot tame her desire for a profitable future for her sons and predicts that Ethan will "own his fleet of ships! And Wolfe will have his banks! And Johnny his railroads! And Honey be in the White House before he stops, maybe! And each of them will have wealth and power and a grand estate."

All of the performances of *More Stately Mansions* have been based on Donald Gallup's shortened version, which was originally cut and produced in 1962 by Karl Ragnar Gierow, the Swedish director, with Carlotta O'Neill's blessing. Carlotta encouraged Gallup, then curator of the American Collection at the Beinecke Library at Yale, to create a "reading" version of *Mansions* based on Gierow's script. In 1967 Jose Quintero directed a production of *Mansions,* amending the script according to what he thought O'Neill would have intended. The play was mounted on Broadway with Ingrid Bergman, Colleen Dewherst, and Arthur Hill but was not well received, even with this stellar cast.[6]

In October 1997 Ivo van Hove directed another production of *Mansions,* based on the Geirow/Gallup script. It was performed at the New York Theater Workshop. Again, van Hove played fast and loose with the script and among other innovations presented Deborah and Sara naked on stage—a liberty that Carlotta and Eugene O'Neill would surely have considered a profanity.

There is no doubt that *A Touch of the Poet* is a complete play, as it was published during O'Neill's lifetime, in 1946. *More Stately Mansions,* however, remains the subject of controversy, mainly because O'Neill slipped a note into the script donated to Yale by Carlotta O'Neill that said, "Unfinished work. This script is to be destroyed in case of my death!" Having studied all versions of the play and all the notes and revisions, I do not see this play as an "unfinished work," but as one that O'Neill edited with a sense of artistry and logic. The fact that he destroyed a third handwritten draft but continued, until November 1942, to make deletions and additions to the 1938 typescript (coincidental with changes made on the typescript of *Poet*) confirms my judgment. Doubtless, O'Neill might have continued to tinker with the play during its staging and production, as he did with all his plays. But with the exception of one missing page, absent when Carlotta sent the typescript to Yale, the play is whole and complete. In fact, the typescript is a hefty 290 pages. Thus, if it is to be published or performed at all, it should be as it is presented in this edition. Surely O'Neill would rather have had it this way. As Donald Gallup said in a *New York Times* interview about the van Hove production, "When a work by a distinguished dramatist survives, you have to do something with it. You can't let it sit, and you certainly can't destroy it" (October 5, 1997).[7] If O'Neill has been "howling with fury" in his grave,[8] it is because his play has been read and performed as a drastically truncated piece, and he should now rest assured that the most complete version is now accessible and affordable.

I think O'Neill would applaud the decision to publish *More Stately Mansions* in tandem with *A Touch of the Poet.* Through this theatrical ensemble, and O'Neill's tragic vision, we witness America's propensity for violence in and outside the domestic sphere, its obsession with sex, and its self-destructive appetite for material acquisition. It is a vision that bares O'Neill's soul and reveals a somber truth about ourselves. Although the revelation is dark, it is penetrated by the occasional light of American resilience and the spirit of those who "succeed and fail but never stay fallen."

NOTES

1. Donald Gallup showed me this interview, which he said took place in August 1945.
2. In notes to early versions of *Mansions* and *Poet* now housed at the Beinecke Library at Yale, O'Neill made several notations on the Transcendental period and described Thoreau's hut in detail (ZA O'Neill III). He also used Van Wyck Brooks' *The Flowering of New England* to a large extent. Harold Bloom misspeaks when he asserts, in his introduction to *Long Day's Journey into Night* (New Haven: Yale University Press, 2002), that "O'Neill would appear to be the most non-Emersonian author of any eminence in our literature" (vi).
3. O'Neill's *Work Diary* was transcribed and edited by Donald Gallup (New Haven: Yale University Press, 1981). It consists of a daily record of composition data and brief entries describing what O'Neill did each day during his productive years. Volume 1 covers the years 1924–33 and volume 2 covers 1934–43. There is a separate 1925 "Scribbling Diary."
4. Louis Sheaffer, *O'Neill: Son and Artist* (Boston: Little, Brown, 1973), 482.
5. In his prefatory note to this edition (New Haven: Yale University Press, 1964), Gallup admits that his version "represents less than half of O'Neill's typed script."
6. *Mansions,* as directed by Quintero, opened in Los Angeles on September 11, 1967, and in New York on November 11. He retained the first scene of act 1 and the epilogue but shortened the original script by three hours.
7. As I said in that same interview, I agree with Gallup's statement but disagree with van Hove's mounting of the abridged version.
8. Barbara and Arthur Gelb oppose any performance or publication of *More Stately Mansions.* They felt that O'Neill's ghost was howling "with fury" when the van Hove production was mounted (*New York Times,* October 5, 1997). In that case, it probably was.

A Touch of the Poet

Scenes

ACT 1
*Dining room of Melody's Tavern
morning of July 27, 1828.*

ACT 2
The same, later that morning.

ACT 3
The same, that evening.

ACT 4
The same, that night.

Characters

MICKEY MALOY

JAMIE CREGAN

SARA MELODY

NORA MELODY

CORNELIUS MELODY

DEBORAH *(Mrs. Henry Harford)*

DAN ROCHE

PADDY O'DOWD

PATCH RILEY

NICHOLAS GADSBY

Act One

The dining room of Melody's Tavern, in a village a few miles from Boston. The tavern is over a hundred years old. It had once been prosperous, a breakfast stop for the stagecoach, but the stage line had been discontinued and for some years now the tavern has fallen upon neglected days.

The dining room and barroom were once a single spacious room, low-ceilinged, with heavy oak beams and paneled walls—the taproom of the tavern in its prosperous days, now divided into two rooms by a flimsy partition, the barroom being off left. The partition is painted to imitate the old paneled walls but this only makes it more of an eyesore.

At left front, two steps lead up to a closed door opening on a flight of stairs to the floor above. Farther back is the door to the bar. Between these doors hangs a large mirror. Beyond the bar door a small cabinet is fastened to the wall. At rear are four windows. Between the middle two is the street door. At right front is another door, open, giving on a hallway and the main stairway to the second floor, and leading to the kitchen. Farther front at right, there is a high schoolmaster's desk with a stool.

In the foreground are two tables. One, with four chairs, at left center; a larger one, seating six, at right center. At left and right, rear, are two more tables, identical with the ones at right center. All these tables are set with white tablecloths, etc., except the small ones in the foreground at left.

It is around nine in the morning of July 27, 1828. Sunlight shines in through the windows at rear.

MICKEY MALOY *sits at the table at left front, facing right. He is glancing through a newspaper. Maloy is twenty-six, with a sturdy physique and an amiable, cunning face, his mouth usually set in a half-leering grin.*

JAMIE CREGAN *peers around the half-open door to the bar. Seeing Maloy, he comes in. As obviously Irish as Maloy, he is middle-aged, tall, with a lantern-jawed face. There is a scar of a saber cut over one cheekbone. He is dressed neatly but in old, worn clothes. His eyes are bloodshot, his manner sickly, but he grins as he greets Maloy sardonically.*

CREGAN
God bless all here—even the barkeep.

MALOY
With an answering grin.
Top o' the mornin'.

CREGAN
Top o' me head.
He puts his hand to his head and groans.
Be the saints, there's a blacksmith at work on it!

MALOY
Small wonder. You'd the divil's own load when you left at two this mornin'.

CREGAN
I must have. I don't remember leaving.
He sits at right of table.
Faix, you're takin' it aisy.

MALOY
There's no trade this time o' day.

CREGAN
It was a great temptation, when I saw no one in the bar, to make off with a bottle. A hair av the dog is what I need, but I've divil a penny in my pantaloons.

MALOY

Have one on the house.

He goes to the cupboard and takes out a decanter of whiskey and a glass.

CREGAN

Thank you kindly. Sure, the good Samaritan was a crool haythen beside you.

MALOY

Putting the decanter and glass before him.

It's the same you was drinking last night—his private dew. He keeps it here for emergencies when he don't want to go in the bar.

CREGAN

Pours out a big drink.

Lave it to Con never to be caught dry.

Raising his glass.

Your health and inclinations—if they're virtuous!

He drinks and sighs with relief.

God bless you, Whiskey, it's you can rouse the dead! Con hasn't been down yet for his morning's morning?

MALOY

No. He won't be till later.

CREGAN

It's like a miracle, me meeting him again. I came to these parts looking for work. It's only by accident I heard talk of a Con Melody and come here to see was it him. Until last night, I'd not seen hide nor hair of him since the war with the French in Spain—after the battle of Salamanca in '12. I was a corporal in the Seventh Dragoons and he was major.

Proudly.

I got this cut from a saber at Talavera, bad luck to it! — serving under him. He was a captain then.

MALOY

So you told me last night.

CREGAN
With a quick glance at him.
Did I now? I must have said more than my prayers, with the lashings of whiskey in me.

MALOY
With a grin.
More than your prayers is the truth.
Cregan glances at him uneasily. Maloy pushes the decanter toward him.
Take another taste.

CREGAN
I don't like sponging. Sure, my credit ought to be good in this she-been! Ain't I his cousin?

MALOY
You're forgettin' what himself told you last night as he went up to bed. You could have all the whiskey you could pour down you, but not a penny's worth of credit. This house, he axed you to remember, only gives credit to gentlemen.

CREGAN
Divil mend him!

MALOY
With a chuckle.
You kept thinking about his insults after he'd gone out, getting madder and madder.

CREGAN
God pity him, that's like him. He hasn't changed much.
He pours out a drink and gulps it down—with a cautious look at Maloy.
If I was mad at Con, and me blind drunk, I must have told you a power of lies.

MALOY
Winks slyly.
Maybe they wasn't lies.

CREGAN
If I said any wrong of Con Melody—

MALOY

Arrah, are you afraid I'll gab what you said to him? I won't, you can take my oath.

CREGAN

His face clearing.

Tell me what I said and I'll tell you if it was lies.

MALOY

You said his father wasn't of the quality of Galway like he makes out, but a thievin' shebeen keeper who got rich by moneylendin' and squeezin' tenants and every manner of trick. And when he'd enough he married, and bought an estate with a pack of hounds and set up as one of the gentry. He'd hardly got settled when his wife died givin' birth to Con.

CREGAN

There's no lie there.

MALOY

You said none of the gentry would speak to auld Melody, but he had a tough hide and didn't heed them. He made up his mind he'd bring Con up a true gentleman, so he packed him off to Dublin to school, and after that to the College with sloos of money to prove himself the equal of any gentleman's son. But Con found, while there was plenty to drink on him and borrow money, there was few didn't sneer behind his back at his pretensions.

CREGAN

That's the truth, too. But Con wiped the sneer off their mugs when he called one av thim out and put a bullet in his hip. That was his first duel. It gave his pride the taste for revenge and after that he was always lookin' for an excuse to challenge someone.

MALOY

He's done a power av boastin' about his duels, but I thought he was lyin'.

CREGAN

There's no lie in it. It was that brought disgrace on him in the end, right after he'd been promoted to major. He got caught by a Spanish noble making love to his wife, just after the battle of Salamanca, and there was a duel and Con killed him. The scandal was hushed up but Con had to resign from the army. If it wasn't for his fine record for bravery in battle, they'd have court-martialed him.

Then guiltily.

But I'm sayin' more than my prayers again.

MALOY

It's no news about his women. You'd think, to hear him when he's drunk, there wasn't one could resist him in Portugal and Spain.

CREGAN

If you'd seen him then, you wouldn't wonder. He was as strong as an ox, and on a thoroughbred horse, in his uniform, there wasn't a handsomer man in the army. And he had the chance he wanted in Portugal and Spain where a British officer was welcome in the gentry's houses. At home, the only women he'd known was whores.

He adds hastily.

Except Nora, I mean.

Lowering his voice.

Tell me, has he done any rampagin' wid women here?

MALOY

He hasn't. The damned Yankee gentry won't let him come near them, and he considers the few Irish around here to be scum beneath his notice. But once in a while there'll be some Yankee stops overnight wid his wife or daughter and then you'd laugh to see Con, if he thinks she's gentry, sidlin' up to her, playin' the great gentleman and makin' compliments, and then boasting afterward he could have them in bed if he'd had a chance at it, for all their modern Yankee airs.

CREGAN

And maybe he could. If you'd known him in the auld days, you'd nivir doubt any boast he makes about fightin' and women, and gamblin' or any kind av craziness. There nivir was a madder divil.

MALOY

Lowering his voice.

Speakin' av Nora, you nivir mentioned her last night, but I know all about it without you telling me. I used to have my room here, and there's nights he's madder drunk than most when he throws it in her face he had to marry her because— Mind you, I'm not saying anything against poor Nora. A sweeter woman never lived. And I know you know all about it.

CREGAN

Reluctantly.

I do. Wasn't I raised on his estate?

MALOY

He tells her it was the priests tricked him into marrying her. He hates priests.

CREGAN

He's a liar, then. He may like to blame it on them but it's little Con Melody cared what they said. Nothing ever made him do anything, except himself. He married her because he'd fallen in love with her, but he was ashamed of her in his pride at the same time because her folks were only ignorant peasants on his estate, as poor as poor. Nora was as pretty a girl as you'd find in a year's travel, and he'd come to be bitter lonely, with no woman's company but the whores was helpin' him ruin the estate.

He shrugs his shoulders.

Well, anyways, he married her and then went off to the war, and left her alone in the castle to have her child, and nivir saw her again till he was sent home from Spain. Then he raised what money he still was able, and took her and Sara here to America where no one would know him.

MALOY

Thinking this over for a moment.

It's hard for me to believe he ever loved her. I've seen the way he treats her now. Well, thank you for telling me, and I take my oath I'll nivir breathe a word of it—for Nora's sake, not his.

CREGAN
Grimly.
You'd better kape quiet for fear of him, too. If he's one-half the man he was, he could bate the lights out of the two av us.

MALOY
He's strong as a bull still for all the whiskey he's drunk.
He pushes the bottle toward Cregan.
Have another taste.
Cregan pours out a drink.
Drink hearty.

CREGAN
Long life.
He drinks. Maloy puts the decanter and glass back on the cupboard. A girl's voice is heard from the hall at right. Cregan jumps up—hastily.
That's Sara, isn't it? I'll get out. She'll likely blame me for Con getting so drunk last night. I'll be back after Con is down.
He goes out. Maloy starts to go in the bar, as if he too wanted to avoid Sara. Then he sits down defiantly.

MALOY
Be damned if I'll run from her.
He takes up the paper as SARA MELODY *comes in from the hall at right.*

Sara is twenty, an exceedingly pretty girl with a mass of black hair, fair skin with rosy cheeks, and beautiful, deep-blue eyes. There is a curious blending in her of what are commonly considered aristocratic and peasant characteristics. She has a fine forehead. Her nose is thin and straight. She has small ears set close to her well-shaped head, and a slender neck. Her mouth, on the other hand, has a touch of coarseness and sensuality and her jaw is too heavy. Her figure is strong and graceful, with full, firm breasts and hips, and a slender waist. But she has large feet and broad, ugly hands with stubby fingers. Her voice is soft and musical, but her speech has at times a self-conscious, stilted quality about it, due to her restraining a tendency to lapse into brogue. Her everyday working dress is of cheap material, but she wears it in a way that gives a pleasing effect of beauty unadorned.

SARA

With a glance at Maloy, sarcastically.

I'm sorry to interrupt you when you're so busy, but have you your bar book ready for me to look over?

MALOY

Surlily.

I have. I put it on your desk.

SARA

Thank you.

She turns her back on him, sits at the desk, takes a small account book from it, and begins checking figures.

MALOY

Watches her over his paper.

If it's profits you're looking for, you won't find them—not with all the drinks himself's been treating to.

She ignores this. He becomes resentful.

You've got your airs of a grand lady this morning, I see. There's no talkin' to you since you've been playin' nurse to the young Yankee upstairs.

She makes herself ignore this, too.

Well, you've had your cap set for him ever since he came to live by the lake, and now's your chance, when he's here sick and too weak to defend himself.

SARA

Turns on him—with quiet anger.

I warn you to mind your own business, Mickey, or I'll tell my father of your impudence. He'll teach you to keep your place, and God help you.

MALOY

Doesn't believe this threat but is frightened by the possibility.

Arrah, don't try to scare me. I know you'd never carry tales to him. *Placatingly.*

Can't you take a bit of teasing, Sara?

SARA
Turns back to her figuring.
Leave Simon out of your teasing.

MALOY
Oho, he's Simon to you now, is he? Well, well.
He gives her a cunning glance.
Maybe, if you'd come down from your high horse, I could tell you
some news.

SARA
You're worse than an old woman for gossip. I don't want to hear it.

MALOY
When you was upstairs at the back taking him his breakfast, there
was a grand carriage with a nigger coachman stopped at the corner
and a Yankee lady got out and came in here. I was sweeping and Nora
was scrubbing the kitchen.
Sara has turned to him, all attention now.
She asked me what road would take her near the lake—

SARA
Starts.
Ah.

MALOY
So I told her, but she didn't go. She kept looking around, and said
she'd like a cup of tea, and where was the waitress. I knew she must
be connected someway with Harford or why would she want to go
to the lake, where no one's ever lived but him. She didn't want tea
at all, but only an excuse to stay.

SARA
Resentfully.
So she asked for the waitress, did she? I hope you told her I'm the
owner's daughter, too.

MALOY
I did. I don't like Yankee airs any more than you. I was short with

her. I said you was out for a walk, and the tavern wasn't open yet, anyway. So she went out and drove off.

SARA
Worriedly now.
I hope you didn't insult her with your bad manners. What did she look like, Mickey?

MALOY
Pretty, if you like that kind. A pale, delicate wisp of a thing with big eyes.

SARA
That fits what he's said of his mother. How old was she?

MALOY
It's hard to tell, but she's too young for his mother, I'd swear. Around thirty, I'd say. Maybe it's his sister.

SARA
He hasn't a sister.

MALOY
Grinning.
Then maybe she's an old sweetheart looking for you to scratch your eyes out.

SARA
He's never had a sweetheart.

MALOY
Mockingly.
Is that what he tells you, and you believe him? Faix, you must be in love!

SARA
Angrily.
Will you mind your own business? I'm not such a fool!
Worried again.
Maybe you ought to have told her he's here sick to save her the drive in the hot sun and the walk through the woods for nothing.

MALOY

Why would I tell her, when she never mentioned him?

SARA

Yes, it's her own fault. But— Well, there's no use thinking of it now—or bothering my head about her, anyway, whoever she was. *She begins checking figures again. Her mother appears in the doorway at right.*

NORA MELODY *is forty, but years of overwork and worry have made her look much older. She must have been as pretty as a girl as Sara is now. She still has the beautiful eyes her daughter has inherited. But she has become too worn out to take care of her appearance. Her black hair, streaked with gray, straggles in untidy wisps about her face. Her body is dumpy, with sagging breasts, and her old clothes are like a bag covering it, tied around the middle. Her red hands are knotted by rheumatism. Cracked working shoes, run down at the heel, are on her bare feet. Yet in spite of her slovenly appearance there is a spirit which shines through and makes her lovable, a simple sweetness and charm, something gentle and sad and, somehow, dauntless.*

MALOY

Jumps to his feet, his face lighting up with affection.

God bless you, Nora, you're the one I was waitin' to see. Will you keep an eye on the bar while I run to the store for a bit av 'baccy?

SARA

Sharply.

Don't do it, Mother.

NORA

Smiles—her voice is soft, with a rich brogue.

Why wouldn't I? "Don't do it, Mother."

MALOY

Thank you, Nora.

He goes to the door at rear and opens it, burning for a parting shot at Sara.

And the back o' my hand to you, your Ladyship!

He goes out, closing the door.

SARA

You shouldn't encourage his laziness. He's always looking for excuses to shirk.

NORA

Ah, nivir mind, he's a good lad.
She lowers herself painfully on the nearest chair at the rear of the table at center front.
Bad cess to the rheumatism. It has me destroyed this mornin'.

SARA

Still checking figures in the book—gives her mother an impatient but at the same time worried glance. Her habitual manner toward her is one of mingled love and pity and exasperation.
I've told you a hundred times to see the doctor.

NORA

We've no money for doctors. They're bad luck, anyway. They bring death with them.
A pause. Nora sighs.
Your father will be down soon. I've some fine fresh eggs for his breakfast.

SARA

Her face becomes hard and bitter.
He won't want them.

NORA

Defensively.
You mean he'd a drop too much taken last night? Well, small blame to him, he hasn't seen Jamie since—

SARA

Last night? What night hasn't he?

NORA

Ah, don't be hard on him.
A pause—worriedly.
Neilan sent round a note to me about his bill. He says we'll have to settle by the end of the week or we'll get no more groceries.

With a sigh.

I can't blame him. How we'll manage, I dunno. There's the intrist on the mortgage due the first. But that I've saved, God be thanked.

SARA

Exasperatedly.

If you'd only let me take charge of the money.

NORA

With a flare of spirit.

I won't. It'd mean you and himself would be at each other's throats from dawn to dark. It's bad enough between you as it is.

SARA

Why didn't you pay Neilan the end of last week.? You told me you had the money put aside.

NORA

So I did. But Dickinson was tormentin' your father with his feed bill for the mare.

SARA

Angrily.

I might have known! The mare comes first, if she takes the bread out of our mouths! The grand gentleman must have his thoroughbred to ride out in state!

NORA

Defensively.

Where's the harm? She's his greatest pride. He'd be heartbroken if he had to sell her.

SARA

Oh yes, I know well he cares more for a horse than for us!

NORA

Don't be saying that. He has great love for you, even if you do be provokin' him all the time.

SARA

Great love for me! Arrah, God pity you, Mother!

NORA

Sharply.

Don't put on the brogue, now. You know how he hates to hear you. And I do, too. There's no excuse not to cure yourself. Didn't he send you to school so you could talk like a gentleman's daughter?

SARA

Resentfully, but more careful of her speech.

If he did, I wasn't there long.

NORA

It was you insisted on leavin'.

SARA

Because if he hadn't the pride or love for you not to live on your slaving your heart out, I had that pride and love!

NORA

Tenderly.

I know, Acushla. I know.

SARA

With bitter scorn.

We can't afford a waitress, but he can afford to keep a thoroughbred mare to prance around on and show himself off! And he can afford a barkeep when, if he had any decency, he'd do his part and tend the bar himself.

NORA

Indignantly.

Him, a gentleman, tend bar!

SARA

A gentleman! Och, Mother, it's all right for the two of us, out of our own pride, to pretend to the world we believe that lie, but it's crazy for you to pretend to me.

NORA

Stubbornly.

It's no lie. He *is* a gentleman. Wasn't he born rich in a castle on a

grand estate and educated in college, and wasn't he an officer in the
Duke of Wellington's army—

SARA

All right, Mother. You can humor his craziness, but he'll never make
me pretend to him I don't know the truth.

NORA

Don't talk as if you hated him. You ought to be shamed—

SARA

I do hate him for the way he treats you. I heard him again last night,
raking up the past, and blaming his ruin on his having to marry you.

NORA
Protests miserably.
It was the drink talkin', not him.

SARA
Exasperated.
It's you ought to be ashamed, for not having more pride! You bear
all his insults as meek as a lamb! You keep on slaving for him when
it's that has made you old before your time!
Angrily.
You can't much longer, I tell you! He's getting worse. You'll have to
leave him.

NORA
Aroused.
I'll never! Howld your prate!

SARA

You'd leave him today, if you had any pride!

NORA

I've pride in my love for him! I've loved him since the day I set eyes
on him, and I'll love him till the day I die!
With a strange superior scorn.
It's little you know of love, and you never will, for there's the same
divil of pride in you that's in him, and it'll kape you from ivir givin'
all of yourself, and that's what love is.

SARA

I could give all of myself if I wanted to, but—

NORA

If! Wanted to! Faix, it proves how little of love you know when you prate about if's and want-to's. It's when you don't give a thought for all the if's and want-to's in the world! It's when, if all the fires of hell was between you, you'd walk in them gladly to be with him, and sing with joy at your own burnin', if only his kiss was on your mouth! That's love, and I'm proud I've known the great sorrow and joy of it!

SARA

Cannot help being impressed—looks at her mother with wondering respect.
You're a strange woman, Mother.
She kisses her impulsively.
And a grand woman!
Defiant again, with an arrogant toss of her head.
I'll love—but I'll love where it'll gain me freedom and not put me in slavery for life.

NORA

There's no slavery in it when you love!
Suddenly her exultant expression crumbles and she breaks down.
For the love of God, don't take the pride of my love from me, Sara, for without it what am I at all but an ugly, fat woman gettin' old and sick!

SARA

Puts her arm around her—soothingly.
Hush, Mother. Don't mind me.
Briskly, to distract her mother's mind.
I've got to finish the bar book. Mickey can't put two and two together without making five.
She goes to the desk and begins checking figures again.

NORA

Dries her eyes—after a pause she sighs worriedly.
I'm worried about your father. Father Flynn stopped me on the road

yesterday and told me I'd better warn him not to sneer at the Irish around here and call thim scum, or he'll get in trouble. Most of thim is in a rage at him because he's come out against Jackson and the Democrats and says he'll vote with the Yankees for Quincy Adams.

SARA

Contemptuously.

Faith, they can't see a joke, then, for it's a great joke to hear him shout against mob rule, like one of the Yankee gentry, when you know what he came from. And after the way the Yanks swindled him when he came here, getting him to buy this inn by telling him a new coach line was going to stop here.

She laughs with bitter scorn.

Oh, he's the easiest fool ever came to America! It's that I hold against him as much as anything, that when he came here the chance was before him to make himself all his lies pretended to be. He had education above most Yanks, and he had money enough to start him, and this is a country where you can rise as high as you like, and no one but the fools who envy you care what you rose from, once you've the money and the power goes with it.

Passionately.

Oh, if I was a man with the chance he had, there wouldn't be a dream I'd not make come true!

She looks at her mother, who is staring at the floor dejectedly and hasn't been listening. She is exasperated for a second—then she smiles pityingly.

You're a fine one to talk to, Mother. Wake up. What's worrying you now?

NORA

Father Flynn tould me again I'd be damned in hell for lettin' your father make a haythen of me and bring you up a haythen, too.

SARA

With an arrogant toss of her head.

Let Father Flynn mind his own business, and not frighten you with fairy tales about hell.

NORA

It's true, just the same.

SARA

True, me foot! You ought to tell the good Father we aren't the ignorant shanty scum he's used to dealing with.

She changes the subject abruptly—closing Mickey's bar book.

There. That's done.

She puts the book in the desk.

I'll take a walk to the store and have a talk with Neilan.

Maybe I can blarney him to let the bill go another month.

NORA

Gratefully.

Oh, you can. Sure, you can charm a bird out of a tree when you want
to. But I don't like you beggin' to a Yankee. It's all right for me but
I know how you hate it.

SARA

Puts her arms around her mother—tenderly.

I don't mind at all, if I can save you a bit of the worry that's killing
you.

She kisses her.

I'll change to my Sunday dress so I can make a good impression.

NORA

With a teasing smile.

I'm thinkin' it isn't on Neilan alone you want to make an impression.
You've changed to your Sunday best a lot lately.

SARA

Coquettishly.

Aren't you the sly one! Well, maybe you're right.

NORA

How was he when you took him his breakfast?

SARA

Hungry, and that's a good sign. He had no fever last night. Oh, he's
on the road to recovery now, and it won't be long before he'll be back
in his cabin by the lake.

NORA
I'll never get it clear in my head what he's been doing there the past year, living like a tramp or a tinker, and him a rich gentleman's son.

SARA
With a tender smile.
Oh, he isn't like his kind, or like anyone else at all. He's a born dreamer with a raft of great dreams, and he's very serious about them. I've told you before he wanted to get away from his father's business, where he worked for a year after he graduated from Harvard College, because he didn't like being in trade, even if it is a great company that trades with the whole world in its own ships.

NORA
Approvingly.
That's the way a true gentleman would feel—

SARA
He wanted to prove his independence by living alone in the wilds, and build his own cabin, and do all the work, and support himself simply, and feel one with Nature, and think great thoughts about what life means, and write a book about how the world can be changed so people won't be greedy to own money and land and get the best of each other but will be content with little and live in peace and freedom together, and it will be like heaven on earth.
She laughs fondly—and a bit derisively.
I can't remember all of it. It seems crazy to me, when I think of what people are like. He hasn't written any of it yet, anyway—only the notes for it.
She smiles coquettishly.
All he's written the last few months are love poems.

NORA
That's since you began to take long walks by the lake.
She smiles.
It's you are the sly one.

SARA
Laughing.

Well, why shouldn't I take walks on our own property?
Her tone changes to a sneer.
The land our great gentleman was swindled into buying when he
came here with grand ideas of owning an American estate! —a bit of
farm land no one would work any more, and the rest all wilderness!
You couldn't give it away.

NORA
Soothingly.
Hush, now.
Changing the subject.
Well, it's easy to tell young Master Harford has a touch av the poet
in him—
She adds before she thinks.
the same as your father.

SARA
Scornfully.
God help you, Mother! Do you think Father's a poet because he
shows off reciting Lord Byron?

NORA
With an uneasy glance at the door at left front.
Whist, now. Himself will be down any moment.
Changing the subject.
I can see the Harford lad is falling in love with you.

SARA
Her face lights up triumphantly.
Falling? He's fallen head over heels. He's so timid, he hasn't told me
yet, but I'll get him to soon.

NORA
I know you're in love with him.

SARA
Simply.
I am, Mother.
She adds quickly.
But not too much. I'll not let love make me any man's slave. I want

to love him just enough so I can marry him without cheating him, or myself.
Determinedly.
For I'm going to marry him, Mother. It's my chance to rise in the world and nothing will keep me from it.

NORA
Admiringly.
Musha, but you've boastful talk! What about his fine Yankee family? His father'll likely cut him off widout a penny if he marries a girl who's poor and Irish.

SARA
He may at first, but when I've proved what a good wife I'll be— He can't keep Simon from marrying me. I know that. Simon doesn't care what his father thinks. It's only his mother I'm afraid of. I can tell she's had great influence over him. She must be a queer creature, from all he's told me. She's very strange in her ways. She never goes out at all but stays home in their mansion, reading books, or in her garden.
She pauses.
Did you notice a carriage stop here this morning, Mother?

NORA
Preoccupied—uneasily.
Don't count your chickens before they're hatched. Young Harford seems a dacent lad. But maybe it's not marriage he's after.

SARA
Angrily.
I won't have you wronging him, Mother. He has no thought—
Bitterly.
I suppose you're bound to suspect—
She bites her words back, ashamed.
Forgive me, Mother. But it's wrong of you to think badly of Simon.
She smiles.
You don't know him. Faith, if it came to seducing, it'd be me that'd have to do it. He's that respectful you'd think I was a holy image. It's only in his poems, and in the diary he keeps— I had a peek in it

one day I went to tidy up the cabin for him. He's terribly ashamed of his sinful inclinations and the insult they are to my purity.
She laughs tenderly.

NORA
Smiling, but a bit shocked.
Don't talk so bould. I don't know if it's right, you to be in his room so much, even if he is sick. There's a power av talk about the two av you already.

SARA
Let there be, for all I care! Or all Simon cares, either. When it comes to not letting others rule him, he's got a will of his own behind his gentleness. Just as behind his poetry and dreams I feel he has it in him to do anything he wants. So even if his father cuts him off, with me to help him we'll get on in the world. For I'm no fool, either.

NORA
Glory be to God, you have the fine opinion av yourself!

SARA
Laughing.
Haven't I, though!
Then bitterly.
I've had need to have, to hold my head up, slaving as a waitress and chambermaid so my father can get drunk every night like a gentleman!

The door at left front is slowly opened and CORNELIUS MELODY *appears in the doorway above the two steps. He and Sara stare at each other. She stiffens into hostility and her mouth sets in scorn. For a second his eyes waver and he looks guilty. Then his face becomes expressionless. He descends the steps and bows—pleasantly.*

MELODY
Good morning, Sara.

SARA
Curtly.
Good morning.

Then, ignoring him.
I'm going up and change my dress, Mother.
She goes out right.

Cornelius Melody is forty-five, tall, broad-shouldered, deep-chested, and powerful, with long muscular arms, big feet, and large hairy hands. His heavy-boned body is still firm, erect, and soldierly. Beyond shaky nerves, it shows no effects of hard drinking. It has a bull-like, impervious strength, a tough peasant vitality. It is his face that reveals the ravages of dissipation—a ruined face, which was once extraordinarily handsome in a reckless, arrogant fashion. It is still handsome—the face of an embittered Byronic hero, with a finely chiseled nose over a domineering, sensual mouth set in disdain, pale, hollow-cheeked, framed by thick, curly iron-gray hair. There is a look of wrecked distinction about it, of brooding, humiliated pride. His bloodshot gray eyes have an insulting cold stare which anticipates insult. His manner is that of a polished gentleman. Too much so. He overdoes it and one soon feels that he is overplaying a role which has become more real than his real self to him. But in spite of this, there is something formidable and impressive about him. He is dressed with foppish elegance in old, expensive, finely tailored clothes of the style worn by English aristocracy in Peninsular War days.

MELODY
Advancing into the room—bows formally to his wife.
Good morning, Nora.
His tone condescends. It addresses a person of inferior station.

NORA
Stumbles to her feet—timidly.
Good mornin', Con. I'll get your breakfast.

MELODY
No. Thank you. I want nothing now.

NORA
Coming toward him.
You look pale. Are you sick, Con, darlin'?

MELODY
No.

NORA

Puts a timid hand on his arm.

Come and sit down.

He moves his arm away with instinctive revulsion and goes to the table at center front, and sits in the chair she had occupied. Nora hovers round him.

I'll wet a cloth in cold water to put round your head.

MELODY

No! I desire nothing—except a little peace in which to read the news.

He picks up the paper and holds it so it hides his face from her.

NORA

Meekly.

I'll lave you in peace.

She starts to go to the door at right but turns to stare at him worriedly again. Keeping the paper before his face with his left hand, he reaches out with his right and pours a glass of water from the carafe on the table. Although he cannot see his wife, he is nervously conscious of her. His hand trembles so violently that when he attempts to raise the glass to his lips the water sloshes over his hand and he sets the glass back on the table with a bang. He lowers the paper and explodes nervously.

MELODY

For God's sake, stop your staring!

NORA

I— I was only thinkin' you'd feel better if you'd a bit av food in you.

MELODY

I told you once— !

Controlling his temper.

I am not hungry, Nora.

He raises the paper again. She sighs, her hands fiddling with her apron. A pause.

NORA

Dully.

Maybe it's a hair av the dog you're needin'.

MELODY

As if this were something he had been waiting to hear, his expression loses some of its nervous strain. But he replies virtuously.

No, damn the liquor. Upon my conscience, I've about made up my mind I'll have no more of it. Besides, it's a bit early in the day.

NORA

If it'll give you an appetite—

MELODY

To tell the truth, my stomach is out of sorts.

He licks his lips.

Perhaps a drop wouldn't come amiss.

Nora gets the decanter and glass from the cupboard and sets them before him. She stands gazing at him with a resigned sadness. Melody, his eyes on the paper, is again acutely conscious of her. His nerves cannot stand it. He throws his paper down and bursts out in bitter anger.

Well? I know what you're thinking! Why haven't you the courage to say it for once? By God, I'd have more respect for you! I hate the damned meek of this earth! By the rock of Cashel, I sometimes believe you have always deliberately encouraged me to— It's the one point of superiority you can lay claim to, isn't it?

NORA

Bewilderedly—on the verge of tears.

I don't— It's only your comfort— I can't bear to see you—

MELODY

His expression changes and a look of real affection comes into his eyes. He reaches out a shaking hand to pat her shoulder with an odd, guilty tenderness. He says quietly and with genuine contrition.

Forgive me, Nora. That was unpardonable.

Her face lights up. Abruptly he is ashamed of being ashamed. He looks away and grabs the decanter. Despite his trembling hand he manages to pour a drink and get it to his mouth and drain it. Then he sinks back in his chair and stares at the table, waiting for the liquor to take effect. After a pause he sighs with relief

I confess I needed that as medicine. I begin to feel more myself.

He pours out another big drink and this time his hand is steadier, and he downs it without much difficulty. He smacks his lips.

By the Immortal, I may have sunk to keeping an inn but at least I've a conscience in my trade. I keep liquor a gentleman can drink.

He starts looking over the paper again—scowls at something—disdainfully, emphasizing his misquote of the line from Byron.

"There shall he rot—Ambition's *dis*honored fool!" The paper is full of the latest swindling lies of that idol of the riffraff, Andrew Jackson. Contemptible, drunken scoundrel! But he will be the next President, I predict, for all we others can do to prevent. There is a cursed destiny in these decadent times. Everywhere the scum rises to the top.

His eyes fasten on the date and suddenly he strikes the table with his fist.

Today is the 27th! By God, and I would have forgotten!

NORA

Forgot what?

MELODY

The anniversary of Talavera!

NORA

Hastily.

Oh, ain't I stupid not to remember.

MELODY

Bitterly.

I had forgotten myself and no wonder. It's a far cry from this dung-hill on which I rot to that glorious day when the Duke of Wellington—Lord Wellesley, then—did me the honor before all the army to commend my bravery.

He glances around the room with loathing.

A far cry, indeed! It would be better to forget!

NORA

Rallying him.

No, no, you mustn't. You've never missed celebratin' it and you won't today. I'll have a special dinner for you like I've always had.

MELODY

With a quick change of manner—eagerly.

Good, Nora. I'll invite Jamie Cregan. It's a stroke of fortune he is here. He served under me at Talavera, as you know. A brave soldier, if he isn't a gentleman. You can place him on my right hand. And we'll have Patch Riley to make music, and O'Dowd and Roche. If they are rabble, they're full of droll humor at times. But put them over there.

He points to the table at left front.

I may tolerate their presence out of charity, but I'll not sink to dining at the same table.

NORA

I'll get your uniform from the trunk, and you'll wear it for dinner like you've done each year.

MELODY

Yes, I must confess I still welcome an excuse to wear it. It makes me feel at least the ghost of the man I was then.

NORA

You're so handsome in it still, no woman could take her eyes off you.

MELODY

With a pleased smile.

I'm afraid you've blarney on your tongue this morning, Nora.

Then boastfully.

But it's true, in those days in Portugal and Spain—

He stops a little shamefacedly, but Nora gives no sign of offense. He takes her hand and pats it gently—avoiding her eyes.

You have the kindest heart in the world, Nora. And I—

His voice breaks.

NORA

Instantly on the verge of grateful tears.

Ah, who wouldn't, Con darlin', when you—

She brushes a hand across her eyes—hastily.

I'll go to the store and get something tasty.

Her face drops as she remembers.

But, God help us, where's the money?

MELODY
Stiffens—haughtily.
Money? Since when has my credit not been good?

NORA
Hurriedly.
Don't fret, now. I'll manage.
He returns to his newspaper, disdaining further interest in money matters.

MELODY
Ha. I see work on the railroad at Baltimore is progressing.
Lowering his paper.
By the Eternal, if I had not been a credulous gull and let the thieving Yankees swindle me of all I had when we came here, that's how I would invest my funds now. And I'd become rich. This country, with its immense territory cannot depend solely on creeping canal boats, as shortsighted fools would have us believe. We must have railroads. Then you will see how quickly America will become rich and great!
His expression changes to one of bitter hatred.
Great enough to crush England in the next war between them, which I know is inevitable! Would I could live to celebrate that victory! If I have one regret for the past—and there are few things in it that do not call for bitter regret—it is that I shed my blood for a country that thanked me with disgrace. But I will be avenged. This country—my country, now—will drive the English from the face of the earth their shameless perfidy has dishonored!

NORA
Glory be to God for that! And we'll free Ireland!

MELODY
Contemptuously.
Ireland? What benefit would freedom be to her unless she could be freed from the Irish?
Then irritably.
But why do I discuss such things with you?

NORA
Humbly.
I know. I'm ignorant.

MELODY
Yet I tried my best to educate you, after we came to America—until I saw it was hopeless.

NORA
You did, surely. And I tried, too, but—

MELODY
You won't even cure yourself of that damned peasant's brogue. And your daughter is becoming as bad.

NORA
She only puts on the brogue to tease you. She can speak as fine as any lady in the land if she wants.

MELODY
Is not listening—sunk in bitter brooding.
But, in God's name, who am I to reproach anyone with anything? Why don't you tell me to examine my own conduct?

NORA
You know I'd never.

MELODY
Stares at her—again he is moved—quietly.
No. I know you would not, Nora.
He looks away—after a pause.
I owe you an apology for what happened last night.

NORA
Don't think of it.

MELODY
With assumed casualness.
Faith, I'd a drink too many, talking over old times with Jamie Cregan.

NORA
I know.

MELODY
I am afraid I may have— The thought of old times— I become bitter. But you understand, it was the liquor talking, if I said anything to wound you.

NORA
I know it.

MELODY
Deeply moved, puts his arm around her.
You're a sweet, kind woman, Nora—too kind.
He kisses her.

NORA
With blissful happiness.
Ah, Con darlin', what do I care what you say when the black thoughts are on you? Sure, don't you know I love you?

MELODY
A sudden revulsion of feeling convulses his face. He bursts out with disgust, pushing her away from him.
For God's sake, why don't you wash your hair? It turns my stomach with its stink of onions and stew!
He reaches for the decanter and shakingly pours a drink. Nora looks as if he had struck her.

NORA
Dully.
I do be washin' it often to plaze you. But when you're standin' over the stove all day, you can't help—

MELODY
Forgive me, Nora. Forget I said that. My nerves are on edge. You'd better leave me alone.

NORA
Her face brightening a little.
Will you ate your breakfast now? I've fine fresh eggs—

Grasping at this chance to get rid of her—impatiently.

Yes! In a while. Fifteen minutes, say. But leave me alone now.

She goes out right. Melody drains his drink. Then he gets up and paces back and forth, his hands clasped behind him. The third drink begins to work and his face becomes arrogantly self-assured. He catches his reflection in the mirror on the wall at left and stops before it. He brushes a sleeve fastidiously, adjusts the set of his coat, and surveys himself.

Thank God, I still bear the unmistakable stamp of an officer and a gentleman. And so I will remain to the end, in spite of all fate can do to crush my spirit!

He squares his shoulders defiantly. He stares into his eyes in the glass and recites from Byron's "Childe Harold," as if it were an incantation by which he summons pride to justify his life to himself.

"I have not loved the World, nor the World me;
  I have not flattered its rank breath, nor bowed
  To its idolatries a patient knee,
  Nor coined my cheek to smiles,—nor cried aloud
  In worship of an echo: in the crowd
  They could not deem me one of such—I stood
  Among them, but not of them . . ."

He pauses, then repeats:

"Among them, but not of them." By the Eternal, that expresses it! Thank God for you, Lord Byron—poet and nobleman who made of his disdain immortal music!

Sara appears in the doorway at right. She has changed to her Sunday dress, a becoming blue that brings out the color of her eyes. She draws back for a moment—then stands watching him contemptuously. Melody senses her presence. He starts and turns quickly away from the mirror. For a second his expression is guilty and confused, but he immediately assumes an air of gentlemanly urbanity and bows to her.

Ah, it's you, my dear. Are you going for a morning stroll? You've a beautiful day for it. It will bring fresh roses to your cheeks.

SARA

I don't know about roses, but it will bring a blush of shame to my cheeks. I have to beg Neilan to give us another month's credit, because you made Mother pay the feed bill for your fine thoroughbred mare!

He gives no sign he hears this. She adds scathingly.

I hope you saw something in the mirror you could admire!

MELODY

In a light tone.

Faith, I suppose I must have looked a vain peacock, preening himself, but you can blame the bad light in my room. One cannot make a decent toilet in that dingy hole in the wall.

SARA

You have the best room in the house, that we ought to rent to guests.

MELODY

Oh, I've no complaints. I was merely explaining my seeming vanity.

SARA

Seeming!

MELODY

Keeping his tone light.

Faith, Sara, you must have risen the wrong side of the bed this morning, but it takes two to make a quarrel and I don't feel quarrelsome. Quite the contrary. I was about to tell you how exceedingly charming and pretty you look, my dear.

SARA

With a mocking, awkward, servant's curtsy—in broad brogue.

Oh, thank ye, yer Honor.

MELODY

Every day you resemble your mother more, as she looked when I first knew her.

SARA

Musha, but it's you have the blarneyin' tongue, God forgive you!

MELODY

In spite of himself, this gets under his skin—angrily.

Be quiet! How dare you talk to me like a common, ignorant—You're my daughter, damn you.

He controls himself and forces a laugh.

A fair hit! You're a great tease, Sara. I shouldn't let you score so easily. Your mother warned me you only did it to provoke me.

Unconsciously he reaches out for the decanter on the table—then pulls his hand back.

SARA

Contemptuously—without brogue now.

Go on and drink. Surely you're not ashamed before me, after all these years.

MELODY

Haughtily.

Ashamed? I don't understand you. A gentleman drinks as he pleases —provided he can hold his liquor as he should.

SARA

A gentleman!

MELODY

Pleasantly again.

I hesitated because I had made a good resolve to be abstemious to-day. But if you insist—

He pours a drink—a small one—his hand quite steady now.

To your happiness, my dear.

She stares at him scornfully. He goes on graciously.

Will you do me the favor to sit down? I have wanted a quiet chat with you for some time.

He holds out a chair for her at rear of the table at center.

SARA

Eyes him suspiciously—then sits down.

What is it you want?

MELODY

With a playfully paternal manner.

Your happiness, my dear, and what I wish to discuss means happi-

ness to you, unless I have grown blind. How is our patient, young
Simon Harford, this morning?

SARA
Curtly.
He's better.

MELODY
I am delighted to hear it.
Gallantly.
How could he help but be with such a charming nurse?
She stares at him coldly. He goes on.
Let us be frank. Young Simon is in love with you. I can see that with
half an eye—and, of course, you know it. And you return his love,
I surmise.

SARA
Surmise whatever you please.

MELODY
Meaning you do love him? I am glad, Sara.
He becomes sentimentally romantic.
Requited love is the greatest blessing life can bestow on us poor mor-
tals; and first love is the most blessed of all. As Lord Byron has it:
He recites.
  "But sweeter still than this, than these, than all,
    Is first and passionate Love—it stands alone,
    Like Adam's recollection of his fall . . ."

SARA
Interrupts him rudely.
Was it to listen to you recite Byron— ?

MELODY
Concealing discomfiture and resentment—pleasantly.
No. What I was leading up to is that you have my blessing, if that
means anything to you. Young Harford is, I am convinced, an estimable youth. I have enjoyed my talks with him. It has been a privilege
to be able to converse with a cultured gentleman again. True, he is a

bit on the sober side for one so young, but by way of compensation, there is a romantic touch of the poet behind his Yankee phlegm.

SARA
It's fine you approve of him!

MELODY
In your interest I have had some enquiries made about his family.

SARA
Angered—with taunting brogue.
Have you, indade? Musha, that's cute av you! Was it auld Patch Riley, the Piper, made them? Or was it Dan Roche or Paddy O'Dowd, or some other drunken sponge—

MELODY
As if he hadn't heard—condescendingly.
I find his people will pass muster.

SARA
Oh, do you? That's nice!

MELODY
Apparently, his father is a gentleman—that is, by Yankee standards, insofar as one in trade can lay claim to the title. But as I've become an American citizen myself, I suppose it would be downright snobbery to hold to old-world standards.

SARA
Yes, wouldn't it be!

MELODY
Though it is difficult at times for my pride to remember I am no longer the master of Melody Castle and an estate of three thousand acres of as fine pasture and woodlands as you'd find in the whole United Kingdom, with my stable of hunters, and—

SARA
Bitterly.
Well, you've a beautiful thoroughbred mare now, at least—to prove you're still a gentleman!

MELODY

Stung into defiant anger.

Yes, I've the mare! And by God, I'll keep her if I have to starve myself so she may eat.

SARA

You mean, make Mother slave to keep her for you, even if she has to starve!

MELODY

Controls his anger—and ignores this.

But what was I saying? Oh, yes, young Simon's family. His father will pass muster, but it's through his mother, I believe, he comes by his really good blood. My information is, she springs from generations of well-bred gentlefolk.

SARA

It would be a great pride to her, I'm sure, to know you found her suitable!

MELODY

I suppose I may expect the young man to request an interview with me as soon as he is up and about again?

SARA

To declare his honorable intentions and ask you for my hand, is that what you mean?

MELODY

Naturally. He is a man of honor. And there are certain financial arrangements Simon's father or his legal representative will wish to discuss with me. The amount of your settlement has to be agreed upon.

SARA

Stares at him as if she could not believe her ears.

My settlement! Simon's father! God pity you— !

MELODY

Firmly.

Your settlement, certainly. You did not think, I hope, that I would give you away without a penny to your name as if you were some poverty-stricken peasant's daughter? Please remember I have my own position to maintain. Of course, it is a bit difficult at present. I am temporarily hard pressed. But perhaps a mortgage on the inn—

SARA

It's mortgaged to the hilt already, as you very well know.

MELODY

If nothing else, I can always give my note at hand for whatever amount—

SARA

You can give it, sure enough! But who'll take it?

MELODY

Between gentlemen, these matters can always be arranged.

SARA

God help you, it must be a wonderful thing to live in a fairy tale where only dreams are real to you.
Then sharply.
But you needn't waste your dreams worrying about my affairs. I'll thank you not to interfere. Attend to your drinking and leave me alone.
He gives no indication that he has heard a word she has said. She stares at him and a look almost of fear comes into her eyes. She bursts out with a bitter exasperation in which there is a strong undercurrent of entreaty.
Father! Will you never let yourself wake up—not even now when you're sober, or nearly? Is it stark mad you've gone, so you can't tell any more what's dead and a lie, and what's the living truth?

MELODY

His face is convulsed by a spasm of pain as if something vital had been stabbed in him—with a cry of tortured appeal.
Sara!
But instantly his pain is transformed into rage. He half rises from his chair threateningly.
Be quiet, damn you! How dare you— !
She shrinks away and rises to her feet. He forces control on himself and sinks back in his chair, his hands gripping the arms.

The street door at rear is flung open and DAN ROCHE, PADDY O'DOWD, *and* PATCH RILEY *attempt to pile in together and get jammed for a moment in the doorway. They all have hangovers, and Roche is talking boisterously. Dan Roche is middle-aged, squat, bowlegged, with a potbelly and short arms lumpy with muscle. His face is flat with a big mouth, protruding ears, and red-rimmed little pig's eyes. He is dressed in dirty, patched clothes. Paddy O'Dowd is thin, roundshouldered, flat-chested, with a pimply complexion, bulgy eyes, and a droopy mouth. His manner is oily and fawning, that of a born sponger and parasite. His clothes are those of a cheap sport. Patch Riley is an old man with a thatch of dirty white hair. His washed-out blue eyes have a wandering, half-witted expression. His skinny body is clothed in rags and there is nothing under his tattered coat but his bare skin. His mouth is sunken in, toothless. He carries an Irish bagpipe under his arm.*

ROCHE
His back is half turned as he harangues O'Dowd and Riley, and he does not see Melody and Sara.
And I says, it's Andy Jackson will put you in your place, and all the slave-drivin' Yankee skinflints like you! Take your damned job, I says, and—

O'DOWD
Warningly, his eyes on Melody.
Whist! Whist! Hold your prate!
Roche whirls around to face Melody, and his aggressiveness oozes from him, changing to a hangdog apprehension. For Melody has sprung to his feet, his eyes blazing with an anger which is increased by the glance of contempt Sara casts from him to the three men. O'Dowd avoids Melody's eyes, busies himself in closing the door. Patch Riley stands gazing at Sara with a dreamy, admiring look, lost in a world of his own fancy, oblivious to what is going on.

ROCHE
Placatingly.
Good mornin' to ye, Major.

O'DOWD
Fawning.

Good mornin', yer Honor.

MELODY
How dare you come tramping in here in that manner! Have you mistaken this inn for the sort of dirty shebeen you were used to in the old country where the pigs ran in and out the door?

O'DOWD
We ask pardon, yer Honor.

MELODY
To Roche—an impressive menace in his tone.
You, Paddy. Didn't I forbid you ever to mention that scoundrel Jackson's name in my house or I'd horsewhip the hide off your back?
He takes a threatening step toward him.
Perhaps you think I cannot carry out that threat.

ROCHE
Backs away frightenedly.
No, no, Major. I forgot—Good mornin' to ye, Miss.

O'DOWD
Good mornin', Miss Sara.
She ignores them. Patch Riley is still gazing at her with dreamy admiration, having heard nothing, his hat still on his head. O'Dowd officiously snatches it off for him—rebukingly.
Where's your wits, Patch? Didn't ye hear his Honor?

RILEY
Unheeding—addresses Sara.
Sure it's you, God bless you, looks like a fairy princess as beautiful as a rose in the mornin' dew. I'll raise a tune for you.
He starts to arrange his pipes.

SARA
Curtly.
I want none of your tunes.
Then, seeing the look of wondering hurt in the old man's eyes, she adds kindly.

That's sweet of you, Patch. I know you'd raise a beautiful tune, but I have to go out.

Consoled, the old man smiles at her gratefully.

MELODY

Into the bar, all of you, where you belong! I told you not to use this entrance!

With disdainful tolerance.

I suppose it's a free drink you're after. Well, no one can say of me that I turned away anyone I knew thirsty from my door.

O'DOWD

Thank ye, yer Honor. Come along, Dan.

He takes Riley's arm.

Come on, Patch.

The three go into the bar and O'Dowd closes the door behind them.

SARA

In derisive brogue.

Sure, it's well trained you've got the poor retainers on your American estate to respect the master!

Then as he ignores her and casts a furtive glance at the door to the bar, running his tongue over his dry lips, she says acidly, with no trace of brogue.

Don't let me keep you from joining the gentlemen!

She turns her back on him and goes out the street door at rear.

MELODY

His face is again convulsed by a spasm of pain—pleadingly.

Sara!

Nora enters from the hall at right, carrying a tray with toast, eggs, bacon, and tea. She arranges his breakfast on the table at front center, bustling garrulously.

NORA

Have I kept you waitin'? The divil was in the toast. One lot burned black as a naygur when my back was turned. But the bacon is crisp, and the eggs not too soft, the way you like them. Come and sit down now.

Melody does not seem to hear her. She looks at him worriedly.
What's up with you, Con? Don't you hear me?

O'DOWD
Pokes his head in the door from the bar.
Mickey won't believe you said we could have a drink, yer Honor,
unless ye tell him.

MELODY
Licking his lips.
I'm coming.
He goes to the bar door.

NORA
Con! Have this in your stomach first! It'll all get cauld.

MELODY
Without turning to her—in his condescendingly polite tone.
I find I am not the least hungry, Nora. I regret your having gone to
so much trouble.
*He goes into the bar, closing the door behind him. Nora slumps on a
chair at the rear of the table and stares at the breakfast with a pitiful
helplessness. She begins to sob quietly.*

CURTAIN

Act Two

Same as Act One. About half an hour has elapsed. The barroom door opens and Melody comes in. He has had two more drinks and still no breakfast, but this has had no outward effect except that his face is paler and his manner more disdainful. He turns to give orders to the spongers in the bar.

MELODY

Remember what I say. None of your loud brawling. And you, Riley, keep your bagpipe silent, or out you go. I wish to be alone in quiet for a while with my memories. When Corporal Cregan returns, Mickey, send him in to me. He, at least, knows Talavera is not the name of a new brand of whiskey.

He shuts the door contemptuously on Mickey's "Yes, Major" and the obedient murmur of the others. He sits at rear of the table at left front. At first, he poses to himself, striking an attitude—a Byronic hero, noble, embittered, disdainful, defying his tragic fate, brooding over past glories. But he has no audience and he cannot keep it up. His shoulders sag and he stares at the table top, hopelessness and defeat bringing a trace of real tragedy to his ruined, handsome face.

The street door is opened and Sara enters. He does not hear the click of the latch, or notice her as she comes forward. Fresh from the humiliation of cajoling the storekeeper to extend more credit, her eyes are bitter. At sight of her father they become more so. She moves toward the door at right, determined to ignore him, but something unusual in his attitude strikes her and she stops to regard him searchingly. She starts to say something bitter—stops—finally, in spite of herself, she asks with a trace of genuine pity in her voice.

SARA

What's wrong with you, Father? Are you really sick or is it just—
He starts guiltily, ashamed of being caught in such a weak mood.

MELODY
Gets to his feet politely and bows.
I beg your pardon, my dear. I did not hear you come in.
With a deprecating smile.
Faith, I was far away in spirit, lost in memories of a glorious battle
in Spain, nineteen years ago today.

SARA
Her face hardens.
Oh. It's the anniversary of Talavera, is it? Well, I know what that
means—a great day for the spongers and a bad day for this inn!

MELODY
Coldly.
I don't understand you. Of course I shall honor the occasion.

SARA
You needn't tell me. I remember the other celebrations—and this
year, now Jamie Cregan has appeared, you've an excuse to make it
worse.

MELODY
Naturally, an old comrade in arms will be doubly welcome—

SARA
Well, I'll say this much. From the little I've seen of him, I'd rather
have free whiskey go down his gullet than the others'. He's a relation,
too.

MELODY
Stiffly.
Merely a distant cousin. That has no bearing. It's because Corporal
Cregan fought by my side—

SARA
I suppose you've given orders to poor Mother to cook a grand feast
for you, as usual, and you'll wear your beautiful uniform, and I'll

have the honor of waiting on table. Well, I'll do it just this once more for Mother's sake, or she'd have to, but it'll be the last time.

She turns her back on him and goes to the door at right.

You'll be pleased to learn your daughter had almost to beg on her knees to Neilan before he'd let us have another month's credit. He made it plain it was to Mother he gave it because he pities her for the husband she's got. But what do you care about that, as long as you and your fine thoroughbred mare can live in style!

Melody is shaken for a second. He glances toward the the bar as if he longed to return there to escape her. Then he gets hold of himself. His face becomes expressionless. He sits in the same chair and picks up the paper, ignoring her. She starts to go out just as her mother appears in the doorway. Nora is carrying a glass of milk.

NORA

Here's the milk the doctor ordered for the young gentleman. It's time for it, and I knew you'd be going upstairs.

SARA

Takes the milk.

Thank you, Mother.

She nods scornfully toward her father.

I've just been telling him I begged another month's credit from Neilan, so he needn't worry.

NORA

Ah, thank God for that. Neilan's a kind man.

MELODY

Explodes.

Damn his kindness! By the Eternal, if he'd refused, I'd have— !

He controls himself, meeting Sara's contemptuous eyes. He goes on quietly, a bitter, sneering antagonism underneath.

Don't let me detain you, my dear. Take his milk to our Yankee guest, as your mother suggests. Don't miss any chance to play the ministering angel.

Vindictively.

Faith, the poor young devil hasn't a chance to escape with you two scheming peasants laying snares to trap him!

SARA

That's a lie! And leave Mother out of your insults!

MELODY

And if all other tricks fail, there's always one last trick to get him through his honor!

SARA

Tensely.

What trick do you mean?

Nora grabs her arm.

NORA

Hould your prate, now! Why can't you leave him be? It's your fault, for provoking him.

SARA

Quietly.

All right, Mother. I'll leave him to look in the mirror, like he loves to, and remember what he said, and be proud of himself.

Melody winces. Sara goes out right.

MELODY

After a pause—shakenly.

I— She mistook my meaning— It's as you said. She goads me into losing my temper, and I say things—

NORA

Sadly.

I know what made you say it. You think maybe she's like I was, and you can't help remembering my sin with you.

MELODY

Guiltily vehement.

No! No! I tell you she mistook my meaning, and now you—

Then exasperatedly.

Damn your priests' prating about your sin!

With a strange, scornful vanity.

To hear you tell it, you'd think it was you who seduced me! That's likely, isn't it? —remembering the man I was then!

NORA

I remember well. Sure, you was that handsome, no woman could resist you. And you are still.

MELODY

Pleased.

None of your blarney, Nora.

With Byronic gloom.

I am but a ghost haunting a ruin.

Then gallantly but without looking at her.

And how about you in those days? Weren't you the prettiest girl in all Ireland?

Scornfully.

And be damned to your lying, pious shame! You had no shame then, I remember. It was love and joy and glory in you and you were proud!

NORA

Her eyes shining.

I'm still proud and will be to the day I die!

MELODY

Gives her an approving look which turns to distaste at her appearance—looks away irritably.

Why do you bring up the past? I do not wish to discuss it.

NORA

After a pause—timidly.

All the same, you shouldn't talk to Sara as if you thought she'd be up to anything to catch young Harford.

MELODY

I did not think that! She is my daughter—

NORA

She is surely. And he's a dacent lad.

She smiles a bit scornfully.

Sure, from all she's told me, he's that shy he's never dared even to kiss her hand!

MELODY

With more than a little contempt.

I can well believe it. When it comes to making love the Yankees are clumsy, fish-blooded louts. They lack savoir-faire. They have no romantic fire! They know nothing of women.

He snorts disdainfully.

By the Eternal, when I was his age—

Then quickly.

Not that I don't approve of young Harford, mind you. He is a gentleman. When he asks me for Sara's hand I will gladly give my consent, provided his father and I can agree on the amount of her settlement.

NORA

Hastily.

Ah, there's no need to think of that yet.

Then lapsing into her own dream.

Yes, she'll be happy because she loves him dearly, a lot more than she admits. And it'll give her a chance to rise in the world. We'll see the day when she'll live in a grand mansion, dressed in silks and satins, and riding in a carriage with coachman and footman.

MELODY

I desire that as much as you do, Nora. I'm done finished—no future but the past. But my daughter has the looks, the brains—ambition, youth—She can go far.

Then sneeringly.

That is, if she can remember she's a gentlewoman and stop acting like a bogtrotting peasant wench!

He hears Sara returning downstairs.

She's coming back.

He gets up—bitterly.

As the sight of me seems to irritate her, I'll go in the bar a while. I've had my fill of her insults for one morning.

He opens the bar door. There is a chorus of eager, thirsty welcome from inside. He goes in, closing the door. Sara enters from right. Her face is flushed and her eyes full of dreamy happiness.

NORA

Rebukingly.

Himself went in the bar to be out of reach of your tongue. A fine thing! Aren't you ashamed you haven't enough feeling not to torment him, when you know it's the anniversary—

SARA

All right, Mother. Let him take what joy he can out of the day. I'll even help you get his uniform out of the trunk in the attic and brush and clean it for you.

NORA

Ah, God bless you, that's the way—

Then, astonished at this unexpected docility.

Glory be, but you've changed all of a sudden. What's happened to you?

SARA

I'm so happy now—I can't feel bitter against anyone.

She hesitates—then shyly.

Simon kissed me.

Having said this, she goes on triumphantly.

He got his courage up at last, but it was me made him. I was freshening up his pillows and leaning over him, and he couldn't help it, if he was human.

She laughs tenderly.

And then you'd have laughed to see him. He near sank through the bed with shame at his boldness. He began apologizing as if he was afraid I'd be so insulted I'd never speak to him again.

NORA

Teasingly.

And what did you do? I'll wager you wasn't as brazen as you pretend.

SARA

Ruefully.

It's true, Mother. He made me as bashful as he was. I felt a great fool.

NORA

And was that all? Sure, kissing is easy. Didn't he ask you if you'd
marry—?

SARA

No.
Quickly.
But it was my fault he didn't. He was trying to be brave enough. All
he needed was a word of encouragement. But I stood there, dumb as
a calf, and when I did speak it was to say I had to come and help you,
and the end was I ran from the room, blushing as red as a beet—
*She comes to her mother. Nora puts her arms around her. Sara hides her
face on her shoulder, on the verge of tears.*
Oh, Mother, ain't it crazy to be such a fool?

NORA

Well, when you're in love—

SARA

Breaking away from her—angrily.
That's just it! I'm too much in love and I don't want to be! I won't
let my heart rule my head and make a slave of me!
Suddenly she smiles confidently.
Ah well, he loves me as much, and more, I know that, and the next
time I'll keep my wits.
She laughs happily.
You can consider it as good as done, Mother. I'm Mrs. Simon Har-
ford, at your pleasure.
She makes a sweeping bow.

NORA

Smiling.
Arrah, none of your airs and graces with me! Help me, now, like you
promised, and we'll get your father's uniform out of the trunk. It
won't break your back in the attic, like it does me.

SARA

Gaily puts her arm around her mother's waist.
Come along then.

NORA

As they go out right.

I disremember which trunk—and you'll have to help me find the key.

There is a pause. Then the bar door is opened and Melody enters again in the same manner as he did at the beginning of the act. There is the same sound of voices from the bar but this time Melody gives no parting orders but simply shuts the door behind him. He scowls with disgust.

MELODY

Cursed ignorant cattle.

Then with a real, lonely yearning.

I wish Jamie Cregan would come.

Bitterly.

Driven from pillar to post in my own home! Everywhere ignorance —or the scorn of my own daughter!

Then defiantly.

But by the Eternal God, no power on earth, nor in hell itself, can break me!

His eyes are drawn irresistibly to the mirror. He moves in front of it, seeking the satisfying reassurance of his reflection there. What follows is an exact repetition of his scene before the mirror in Act One. There is the same squaring of his shoulders, arrogant lifting of his head, and then the favorite quote from Byron, recited aloud to his own image.

"I have not loved the World, nor the World me;
    I have not flattered its rank breath, nor bowed
    To its idolatries a patient knee,
    Nor coined my cheek to smiles,—nor cried aloud
    In worship of an echo: in the crowd
    They could not deem me one of such—I stood
    Among them, but not of them . . ."

He stands staring in the mirror and does not hear the latch of the street door click. The door opens and DEBORAH (Mrs. Henry Harford), Simon's mother, enters, closing the door quietly behind her. Melody continues to be too absorbed to notice anything. For a moment, blinded by the sudden change from the bright glare of the street, she does not see him.

When she does, she stares incredulously. Then she smiles with an amused and mocking relish.

Deborah is forty-one, but looks to be no more than thirty. She is small, a little over five feet tall, with a fragile, youthful figure. One would never suspect that she is the middle-aged mother of two grown sons. Her face is beautiful—that is, it is beautiful from the standpoint of the artist with an eye for bone structure and unusual character. It is small, with high cheekbones, wedge-shaped, narrowing from a broad forehead to a square chin, framed by thick, wavy, red-brown hair. The nose is delicate and thin, a trifle aquiline. The mouth, with full lips and even, white teeth, is too large for her face. So are the long-lashed, green-flecked brown eyes, under heavy, angular brows. These would appear large in any face, but in hers they seem enormous and are made more startling by the pallor of her complexion. She has tiny, high-arched feet and thin, tapering hands. Her slender, fragile body is dressed in white with calculated simplicity. About her whole personality is a curious atmosphere of deliberate detachment, the studied aloofness of an ironically amused spectator. Something perversely assertive about it too, as if she consciously carried her originality to the point of whimsical eccentricity.

DEBORAH
I beg your pardon.
Melody jumps and whirls around. For a moment his face has an absurdly startled, stupid look. He is shamed and humiliated and furious at being caught for the second time in one morning before the mirror. His revenge is to draw himself up haughtily and survey her insolently from head to toe. But at once, seeing she is attractive and a lady, his manner changes. Opportunity beckons and he is confident of himself, put upon his mettle. He bows, a gracious, gallant gentleman. There is seductive charm in his welcoming smile and in his voice.

MELODY
Good morning, Mademoiselle. It is an honor to welcome you to this unworthy inn.
He draws out a chair at rear of the larger table in the foreground—bowing again.

If I may presume. You will find it comfortable here, away from the glare of the street.

DEBORAH
Regards him for a second puzzledly. She is impressed in spite of herself by his bearing and distinguished, handsome face.
Thank you.
She comes forward. Melody makes a gallant show of holding her chair and helping her be seated. He takes in all her points with sensual appreciation. It is the same sort of pleasure a lover of horseflesh would have in the appearance of a thoroughbred horse. Meanwhile he speaks with caressing courtesy.

MELODY
Mademoiselle—
He sees her wedding ring.
Pray forgive me, I see it is Madame— Permit me to say again, how great an honor I will esteem it to be of any service.
He manages, as he turns away, as if by accident to brush his hand against her shoulder. She is startled and caught off guard. She shrinks and looks up at him. Their eyes meet and at the nakedly physical appraisement she sees in his, a fascinated fear suddenly seizes her. But at once she is reassured as he shifts his gaze, satisfied by her reactions to his first attack, and hastens to apologize.
I beg your pardon, Madame. I am afraid my manners have grown clumsy with disuse. It is not often a lady comes here now. This inn, like myself, has fallen upon unlucky days.

DEBORAH
Curtly ignoring this.
I presume you are the innkeeper, Melody?

MELODY
A flash of anger in his eyes—arrogantly.
I am *Major* Cornelius Melody, one time of His Majesty's Seventh Dragoons, at your service.
He bows with chill formality.

DEBORAH

Is now an amused spectator again—apologetically.

Oh. Then it is I who owe you an apology, Major Melody.

MELODY

Encouraged—gallantly.

No, no, dear lady, the fault is mine. I should not have taken offense.
With the air of one frankly admitting a praiseworthy weakness.

Faith, I may as well confess my besetting weakness is that of all
gentlemen who have known better days. I have a pride unduly sensitive to any fancied slight.

DEBORAH

Playing up to him now.

I assure you, sir, there was no intention on my part to slight you.

MELODY

*His eyes again catch hers and hold them—his tone insinuatingly caress-
ing.*

You are as gracious as you are beautiful, Madame.

*Deborah's amusement is gone. She is again confused and, in spite of her-
self, frightened and fascinated. Melody proceeds with his attack, full of
confidence now, the successful seducer of old. His voice takes on a calculated melancholy cadence. He becomes a romantic, tragic figure, appeal-
ing for a woman's understanding and loving compassion.*

I am a poor fool, Madame. I would be both wiser and happier if I
could reconcile myself to being the proprietor of a tawdry tavern, if
I could abjure pride and forget the past. Today of all days it is hard
to forget, for it is the anniversary of the battle of Talavera. The most
memorable day of my life, Madame. It was on that glorious field I
had the honor to be commended for my bravery by the great Duke of
Wellington, himself—Sir Arthur Wellesley, then. So I am sure you
can find it in your heart to forgive—

His tone more caressing.

One so beautiful must understand the hearts of men full well, since
so many must have given their hearts to you.

A coarse passion comes into his voice.

Yes, I'll wager my all against a penny that even among the fish-blooded Yankees there's not a man whose heart doesn't catch flame from your beauty!

He puts his hand over one of her hands on the table and stares into her eyes ardently.

As mine does now!

DEBORAH

Feeling herself borne down weakly by the sheer force of his physical strength, struggles to release her hand. She stammers, with an attempt at lightness.

Is this—what the Irish call blarney, sir?

MELODY

With a fierce, lustful sincerity.

No! I take my oath by the living God, I would charge a square of Napoleon's Old Guard singlehanded for one kiss of your lips.

He bends lower, while his eyes hold hers. For a second it seems he will kiss her and she cannot help herself. Then abruptly the smell of whiskey on his breath brings her to herself, shaken with disgust and coldly angry. She snatches her hand from his and speaks with withering contempt.

DEBORAH

Pah! You reek of whiskey! You are drunk, sir! You are insolent and disgusting! I do not wonder your inn enjoys such meager patronage, if you regale all your guests of my sex with this absurd performance!

Melody straightens up with a jerk, taking a step back as though he had been slapped in the face. Deborah rises to her feet, ignoring him disdainfully. At this moment Sara and her mother enter through the doorway at right. They take in the scene at a glance. Melody and Deborah do not notice their entrance.

NORA

Half under her breath.

Oh, God help us!

SARA

Guesses at once this must be the woman Mickey had told her about. She hurries toward them quickly, trying to hide her apprehension and anger and shame at what she knows must have happened.

What is it, Father? What does the lady wish?

Her arrival is a further blow for Melody, seething now in a fury of humiliated pride. Deborah turns to face Sara.

DEBORAH

Coolly self-possessed—pleasantly.

I came here to see you, Miss Melody, hoping you might know the present whereabouts of my son, Simon.

This is a bombshell for Melody.

MELODY

Blurts out with no apology in his tone but angrily, as if she had intentionally made a fool of him.

You're his mother? In God's name, Madame, why didn't you say so!

DEBORAH

Ignoring him—to Sara.

I've been out to his hermit's cabin, only to find the hermit flown.

SARA

Stammers.

He's here, Mrs. Harford—upstairs in bed. He's been sick—

DEBORAH

Sick? You don't mean seriously?

SARA

Recovering a little from her confusion.

Oh, he's over it now, or almost. It was only a spell of chills and fever he caught from the damp of the lake. I found him there shivering and shaking and made him come here where there's a doctor handy and someone to nurse him.

DEBORAH

Pleasantly.

The someone being you, Miss Melody?

SARA

Yes, me and—my mother and I.

DEBORAH
Graciously.
I am deeply grateful to you and your mother for your kindness.

NORA
Who has remained in the background, now comes forward—with her sweet, friendly smile.
Och, don't be thankin' us, ma'am. Sure, your son is a gentle, fine lad, and we all have great fondness for him. He'd be welcome here if he never paid a penny—
She stops embarrassedly, catching a disapproving glance from Sara. Deborah is repelled by Nora's slovenly appearance, but she feels her simple charm and gentleness, and returns her smile.

SARA
With embarrassed stiffness.
This is my mother, Mrs. Harford.
Deborah inclines her head graciously. Nora instinctively bobs in a peasant's curtsy to one of the gentry. Melody, snubbed and seething, glares at her.

NORA
I'm pleased to make your acquaintance, ma'am.

MELODY
Nora! For the love of God, stop—
Suddenly he is able to become the polished gentleman again—considerately and even a trifle condescendingly.
I am sure Mrs. Harford is waiting to be taken to her son. Am I not right, Madame?
Deborah is so taken aback by his effrontery that for a moment she is speechless. She replies coldly, obviously doing so only because she does not wish to create further embarrassment.

DEBORAH
That is true, sir.
She turns her back on him.
If you will be so kind, Miss Melody. I've wasted so much of the

morning and I have to return to the city. I have only time for a short visit—

SARA

Just come with me, Mrs. Harford.
She goes to the door at right, and steps aside to let Deborah precede her.
What a pleasant surprise this will be for Simon. He'd have written you he was sick, but he didn't want to worry you.
She follows Deborah into the hall.

MELODY

Damned fool of a woman! If I'd known— No, be damned if I regret! Cursed Yankee upstart!
With a sneer.
But she didn't fool me with her insulted airs! I've known too many women—
In a rage.
"Absurd performance," was it? God damn her!

NORA

Timidly.
Don't be cursing her and tormenting yourself. She seems a kind lady. She won't hold it against you, when she stops to think, knowing you didn't know who she is.

MELODY

Tensely.
Be quiet!

NORA

Forget it now, do, for Sara's sake. Sure, you wouldn't want anything to come between her and the lad.
He is silent. She goes on comfortingly.
Go on up to your room now and you'll find something to take your mind off. Sara and I have your uniform brushed and laid out on the bed.

MELODY

Harshly.
Put it back in the trunk! I don't want it to remind me—

With humiliated rage again.

By the Eternal, I'll wager she believed what I told her of Talavera and the Great Duke honoring me was a drunken liar's boast!

NORA

No, she'd never, Con. She couldn't.

MELODY

Seized by an idea.

Well, seeing would be believing, eh, my fine lady? Yes, by God, that will prove to her—

He turns to Nora, his self-confidence partly restored.

Thank you for reminding me of my duty to Sara. You are right. I do owe it to her interests to forget my anger and make a formal apology to Simon's mother for our little misunderstanding.

He smiles condescendingly.

Faith, as a gentleman, I should grant it is a pretty woman's privilege to be always right even when she is wrong.

He goes to the door at extreme left front and opens it.

If the lady should come back, kindly keep her here on some excuse until I return.

This is a command. He disappears, closing the door behind him.

NORA

Sighs.

Ah well, it's all right. He'll be on his best behavior now, and he'll feel proud again in his uniform.

She sits at the end of center table right and relaxes wearily. A moment later Sara enters quickly from right and comes to her.

SARA

Where's Father?

NORA

I got him to go up and put on his uniform. It'll console him.

SARA

Bitterly.

Console *him?* It's me ought to be consoled for having such a great fool for a father!

NORA

Hush now! How could he know who—?

SARA

With a sudden reversal of feeling—almost vindictively.

Yes, it serves her right. I suppose she thinks she's such a great lady anyone in America would pay her respect. Well, she knows better now. And she didn't act as insulted as she might. Maybe she liked it, for all her pretenses.

Again with an abrupt reversal of feeling.

Ah, how can I talk such craziness! Him and his drunken love-making! Well, he got put in his place, and aren't I glad! He won't forget in a hurry how she snubbed him, as if he was no better than dirt under her feet!

NORA

She didn't. She had the sense to see he'd been drinking and not to mind him.

SARA

Dully.

Maybe. But isn't that bad enough? What woman would want her son to marry the daughter of a man like—

She breaks down.

Oh, Mother, I was feeling so happy and sure of Simon, and now— Why did she have to come today? If she'd waited till tomorrow, even, I'd have got him to ask me to marry him, and once he'd done that no power on earth could change him.

NORA

If he loves you no power can change him, anyway.

Proudly.

Don't I know!

Reassuringly.

She's his mother, and she loves him and she'll want him to be happy, and she'll see he loves you. What makes you think she'll try to change him?

SARA
Because she hates me, Mother—for one reason.

NORA
She doesn't. She couldn't.

SARA
She does. Oh, she acted as nice as nice, but she didn't fool me. She's the kind would be polite to the hangman, and her on the scaffold.
She lowers her voice.
It isn't just to pay Simon a visit she came. It's because Simon's father got a letter telling him about us, and he showed it to her.

NORA
Who did a dirty trick like that?

SARA
It wasn't signed, she said. I suppose someone around here that hates Father—and who doesn't?

NORA
Bad luck to the blackguard, whoever it was!

SARA
She said she'd come to warn Simon his father is wild with anger and he's gone to see his lawyer— But that doesn't worry me. It's only her influence I'm afraid of.

NORA
How do you know about the letter?

SARA
Avoiding her eyes.
I sneaked back to listen outside the door.

NORA
Shame on you! You should have more pride!

SARA
I was ashamed, Mother, after a moment or two, and I came away.
Then defiantly.
No, I'm not ashamed. I wanted to learn what tricks she might be

up to, so I'll be able to fight them. I'm not ashamed at all. I'll do anything to keep him.

Lowering her voice.

She started talking the second she got in the door. She had only a few minutes because she has to be home before dinner so her husband won't suspect she came here. He's forbidden her to see Simon ever since Simon came out here to live.

NORA

Well, doesn't her coming against her husband's orders show she's on Simon's side?

SARA

Yes, but it doesn't show she wants him to marry me.

Impatiently.

Don't be so simple, Mother. Wouldn't she tell Simon that anyway, even if the truth was her husband sent her to do all she could to get him away from me?

NORA

Don't look for trouble before it comes. Wait and see, now. Maybe you'll find—

SARA

I'll find what I said, Mother—that she hates me.

Bitterly.

Even if she came here with good intentions, she wouldn't have them now, after our great gentleman has insulted her. Thank God, if he's putting on his uniform, he'll be hours before the mirror, and she'll be gone before he can make a fool of himself again.

Nora starts to tell her the truth—then thinks better of it. Sara goes on, changing her tone.

But I'd like her to see him in his uniform, at that, if he was sober. She'd find she couldn't look down on him—

Exasperatedly.

Och! I'm as crazy as he is. As if she hadn't the brains to see through him.

NORA

Wearily.

Leave him be, for the love of God.

SARA

After a pause—defiantly.

Let her try whatever game she likes. I have brains too, she'll discover.
Then uneasily.
Only, like Simon's told me, I feel she's strange and queer behind her
lady's airs, and it'll be hard to tell what she's really up to.
They both hear a sound from upstairs.
That's her, now. She didn't waste much time. Well, I'm ready for her.
Go in the kitchen, will you, Mother? I want to give her the chance
to have it out with me alone.
*Nora gets up—then, remembering Melody's orders, glances toward the
door at left front uneasily and hesitates. Sara says urgently.*
Don't you hear me? Hurry, Mother!
*Nora sighs and goes out quickly, right. Sara sits at rear of the center table
and waits, drawing herself up in an unconscious imitation of her father's
grand manner. Deborah appears in the doorway at right. There is nothing in her expression to betray any emotion resulting from her interview
with her son. She smiles pleasantly at Sara, who rises graciously from her
chair.*

DEBORAH

Coming to her.

I am glad to find you here, Miss Melody. It gives me another opportunity to express my gratitude for your kindness to my son during
his illness.

SARA

Thank you, Mrs. Harford. My mother and I have been only too
happy to do all we could.
She adds defiantly.
We are very fond of Simon.

DEBORAH

A glint of secret amusement in her eyes.

Yes, I feel you are. And he has told me how fond he is of you.

Her manner becomes reflective. She speaks rapidly in a remote, detached way, lowering her voice unconsciously as if she were thinking aloud to herself.

This is the first time I have seen Simon since he left home to seek self-emancipation at the breast of Nature. I find him not so greatly changed as I had been led to expect from his letters. Of course, it is some time since he has written. I had thought his implacably honest discovery that the poetry he hoped the pure freedom of Nature would inspire him to write is, after all, but a crude imitation of Lord Byron's would have more bitterly depressed his spirit.

She smiles.

But evidently he has found a new romantic dream by way of recompense. As I might have known he would. Simon is an inveterate dreamer—a weakness he inherited from me, I'm afraid, although I must admit the Harfords have been great dreamers, too, in their way. Even my husband has a dream—a conservative, material dream, naturally. I have just been reminding Simon that his father is rigidly unforgiving when his dream is flouted, and very practical in his methods of defending it.

She smiles again.

My warning was the mechanical gesture of a mother's duty, merely. I realized it would have no effect. He did not listen to what I said. For that matter, neither did I.

She laughs a little detached laugh, as if she were secretly amused.

SARA

Stares at her, unable to decide what is behind all this and how she should react—with an undercurrent of resentment.

I don't think Simon imitates Lord Byron. I hate Lord Byron's poetry. And I know there's a true poet in Simon.

DEBORAH

Vaguely surprised—speaks rapidly again.

Oh, in feeling, of course. It is natural you should admire that in him—now. But I warn you it is a quality difficult for a woman to keep on admiring in a Harford, judging from what I know of the family history. Simon's great-grandfather, Jonathan Harford, had it. He was killed at Bunker Hill, but I suspect the War for Independence was merely a symbolic opportunity for him. His was a personal war, I am sure—for pure freedom. Simon's grandfather, Evan Harford, had the quality too. A fanatic in the cause of pure freedom, he became scornful of our Revolution. It made too many compromises with the ideal to free him. He went to France and became a rabid Jacobin, a worshiper of Robespierre. He would have liked to have gone to the guillotine with his incorruptible Redeemer, but he was too unimportant. They simply forgot to kill him. He came home and lived in a little temple of Liberty he had built in a corner of what is now my garden. It is still there. I remember him well. A dry, gentle, cruel, indomitable, futile old idealist who used frequently to wear his old uniform of the French Republican National Guard. He died wearing it. But the point is, you can have no idea what revengeful hate the Harford pursuit of freedom imposed upon the women who shared their lives. The three daughters-in-law of Jonathan, Evan's half-sisters, had to make a large, greedy fortune out of privateering and the Northwest trade, and finally were even driven to embrace the profits of the slave trade—as a triumphant climax, you understand, of their long battle to escape the enslavement of freedom by enslaving it. Evan's wife, of course, was drawn into this conflict, and became their tool and accomplice. They even attempted to own me, but I managed to escape because there was so little of me in the flesh that aged, greedy fingers could clutch. I am sorry they are dead and cannot know you. They would approve of you, I think. They would see that you are strong and ambitious and determined to take what you want. They would have smiled like senile, hungry serpents and welcomed you into their coils.

She laughs.

Evil old witches! Detestable, but I could not help admiring them—pitying them, too—in the end. We had a bond in common. They idolized Napoleon. They used to say he was the only man they would ever have married. And I used to dream I was Josephine—even after my marriage, I'm afraid. The Sisters, as everyone called them, and all of the family accompanied my husband and me on our honeymoon—to Paris to witness the Emperor's coronation.

She pauses, smiling at her memories.

SARA

Against her will, has become a bit hypnotized by Deborah's rapid, low, musical flow of words, as she strains to grasp the implication for her. She speaks in a low, confidential tone herself, smiling naturally.

I've always admired him too. It's one of the things I've held against my father, that he fought against him and not for him.

DEBORAH

Starts, as if awakening—with a pleasant smile.

Well, Miss Melody, this is tiresome of me to stand here giving you a discourse on Harford family history. I don't know what you must think of me—but doubtless Simon has told you I am a bit eccentric at times.

She glances at Sara's face—amusedly.

Ah, I can see he has. Then I am sure you will make allowances. I really do not know what inspired me—except perhaps, that I wish to be fair and warn you, too.

SARA

Stiffens.

Warn me about what, Mrs. Harford?

DEBORAH

Why, that the Harfords never part with their dreams even when they deny them. They cannot. That is the family curse. For example, this book Simon plans to write to denounce the evil of greed and posses-sive ambition, and uphold the virtue of freeing oneself from the lust for power and saving our souls by being content with little. I cannot imagine you taking that seriously.

She again flashes a glance at Sara.

I see you do not. Neither do I. I do not even believe Simon will ever write this book on paper. But I warn you it is already written on his conscience and—

She stops with a little disdaining laugh.

I begin to resemble Cassandra with all my warnings. And I continue to stand here boring you with words.

She holds out her hand graciously.

Goodbye, Miss Melody.

SARA
Takes her hand mechanically.
Goodbye, Mrs. Harford.
*Deborah starts for the door at rear. Sara follows her, her expression con-
fused, suspicious, and at the same time hopeful. Suddenly she blurts out
impulsively.*
Mrs. Harford, I—

DEBORAH
Turns on her, pleasantly.
Yes, Miss Melody?
*But her eyes have become blank and expressionless and discourage any
attempt at further contact.*

SARA
Silenced—with stiff politeness.
Isn't there some sort of cooling drink I could get you before you go?
You must be parched after walking from the road to Simon's cabin
and back on this hot day.

DEBORAH
Nothing, thank you.
Then talking rapidly again in her strange detached way.
Yes, I did find my walk alone in the woods a strangely overpowering
experience. Frightening—but intoxicating, too. Such a wild feeling
of release and fresh enslavement. I have not ventured from my garden in many years. There, nature is tamed, constrained to obey and
adorn. I had forgotten how compelling the brutal power of primi-
tive, possessive nature can be—when suddenly one is attacked by it.
She smiles.
It has been a most confusing morning for a tired, middle-aged ma-
tron, but I flatter myself I have preserved a philosophic poise, or
should I say, pose, as well as may be. Nevertheless, it will be a relief to return to my garden and books and meditations and listen
indifferently again while the footsteps of life pass and recede along
the street beyond the high wall. I shall never venture forth again to
do my duty. It is a noble occupation, no doubt, for those who can
presume they know what their duty to others is; but I—

She laughs.

Mercy, here I am chattering on again.

She turns to the door.

Cato will be provoked at me for keeping him waiting. I've already caused his beloved horses to be half-devoured by flies. Cato is our black coachman. He also is fond of Simon, although since Simon became emancipated he has embarrassed Cato acutely by shaking his hand whenever they meet. Cato was always a self-possessed free man even when he was a slave. It astonishes him that Simon has to prove that he—I mean Simon—is free.

She smiles.

Goodbye again, Miss Melody. This time I really am going.

Sara opens the door for her. She walks past Sara into the street, turns left, and, passing before the two windows, disappears. Sara closes the door and comes back slowly to the head of the table at center. She stands thinking, her expression puzzled, apprehensive, and resentful. Nora appears in the doorway at right.

NORA

God forgive you, Sara, why did you let her go? Your father told me—

SARA

I can't make her out, Mother. You'd think she didn't care, but she does care. And she hates me. I could feel it. But you can't tell— She's crazy, I think. She talked on and on as if she couldn't stop— queer blather about Simon's ancestors, and herself, and Napoleon, and Nature, and her garden and freedom, and God knows what— but letting me know all the time she had a meaning behind it, and was warning and threatening me. Oh, she may be daft in some ways, but she's no fool. I know she didn't let Simon guess she'd rather have him dead than married to me. Oh, no, I'm sure she told him if he was sure he loved me and I meant his happiness—But then she'd say he ought to wait and prove he's sure—anything to give her time. She'd make him promise to wait. Yes, I'll wager that's what she's done!

NORA

Who has been watching the door at left front, preoccupied by her own worry—frightenedly.

Your father'll be down any second. I'm going out in the garden.
She grabs Sara's arm.
Come along with me, and give him time to get over his rage.

SARA

Shakes off her hand—exasperatedly.
Leave me be, Mother. I've enough to worry me without bothering about him. I've got to plan the best way to act when I see Simon. I've got to be as big a liar as she was. I'll have to pretend I liked her and I'd respect whatever advice she gave him. I mustn't let him see—But I won't go to him again today, Mother. You can take up his meals and his milk, if you will. Tell him I'm too busy. I want to get him anxious and afraid maybe I'm mad at him for something, that maybe his mother said something. If he once has the idea maybe he's lost me—that ought to help, don't you think, Mother?

NORA

Sees the door at left front begin to open—in a whisper.
Oh, God help me!
She turns in panicky flight and disappears through the doorway, right.

The door at left front slowly opens—slowly because Melody, hearing voices in the room and hoping Deborah is there, is deliberately making a dramatic entrance. And in spite of its obviousnesss, it is effective. Wearing the brilliant scarlet full-dress uniform of a major in one of Wellington's dragoon regiments, he looks extraordinarily handsome and distinguished—a startling, colorful, romantic figure, possessing now a genuine quality he has not had before, the quality of the formidably strong, disdainfully fearless cavalry officer he really had been. The uniform has been preserved with the greatest care. Each button is shining and the cloth is spotless. Being in it has notably restored his self-confident arrogance. Also, he has done everything he can to freshen up his face and hide any effect of his morning's drinks. When he discovers Deborah is not in the room, he is mildly disappointed and, as always when he first confronts Sara alone, he seems to shrink back guiltily within himself. Sara's face hardens and she gives no sign of knowing he is there. He comes slowly around the table at left front, until he stands at the end of the center table facing her. She still refuses to notice him and he is forced to speak.

He does so with the air of one who condescends to be amused by his own foibles.

MELODY

I happened to go to my room and found you and your mother had laid out my uniform so invitingly that I could not resist the temptation to put it on at once instead of waiting until evening.

SARA

Turns on him. In spite of herself she is so struck by his appearance that the contempt is forced back and she can only stammer a bit foolishly.
Yes, I—I see you did.
There is a moment's pause. She stares at him fascinatedly—then blurts out with impulsive admiration.
You look grand and handsome, Father.

MELODY

As pleased as a child.
Why, it is most kind of you to say that, my dear Sara.
Preening himself.
I flatter myself I do not look too unworthy of the man I was when I wore this uniform with honor.

SARA

An appeal forced out of her that is both pleading and a bitter reproach.
Oh, Father, why can't you ever be the thing you can seem to be?
A sad scorn comes into her voice.
The man you were. I'm sorry I never knew that soldier. I think he was the only man who wasn't just a dream.

MELODY

His face becomes a blank disguise—coldly.
I don't understand you.
A pause. He begins to talk in an arrogantly amused tone.
I suspect you are still holding against me my unfortunate blunder with your future mother-in-law. I would not blame you if you did.
He smiles.
Faith, I did put my foot in it.
He chuckles.

The devil of it is, I can never get used to these Yankee ladies. I do them the honor of complimenting them with a bit of harmless flattery and, lo and behold, suddenly my lady acts as if I had insulted her. It must be their damned narrow Puritan background. They can't help seeing sin hiding under every bush, but this one need not have been alarmed. I never had an eye for skinny, pale snips of women—

Hastily.

But what I want to tell you is I am sorry it happened, Sara, and I will do my best, for the sake of your interests, to make honorable amends. I shall do the lady the honor of tendering her my humble apologies when she comes downstairs.

With arrogant vanity.

I flatter myself she will be graciously pleased to make peace. She was not as outraged by half as her conscience made her pretend, if I am any judge of feminine frailty.

SARA

Who has been staring at him with scorn until he says this last—impulsively, with a sneer of agreement.

I'll wager she wasn't for all her airs.

Then furious at herself and him.

Ah, will you stop telling me your mad dreams!

Controlling herself—coldly.

You'll have no chance to make bad worse by trying to fascinate her with your beautiful uniform. She's gone.

MELODY

Stunned.

Gone?

Furiously.

You're lying, damn you!

SARA

I'm not. She left ten minutes ago, or more.

MELODY

Before he thinks.

But I told your mother to keep her here until—

He stops abruptly.

SARA

So that's why Mother is so frightened. Well, it was me let her go, so don't take out your rage on poor Mother.

MELODY

Rage? My dear Sara, all I feel is relief. Surely you can't believe I could have looked forward to humbling my pride, even though it would have furthered your interests.

SARA

Furthered my interests by giving her another reason to laugh up her sleeve at your pretenses?
With angry scorn, lapsing into broad brogue.
Arrah, God pity you!
She turns her back on him and goes off, right. Melody stands gripping the back of the chair at the foot of the table in his big, powerful hands in an effort to control himself. There is a crack as the chair back snaps in half. He stares at the fragments in his hands with stupid surprise. The door to the bar is shoved open and Mickey calls in.

MALOY

Here's Cregan back to see you, Major.

MELODY

Startled, repeats stupidly.
Cregan?
Then his face suddenly lights up with pathetic eagerness and his voice is full of welcoming warmth as he calls.
Jamie! My old comrade in arms!
As Cregan enters, he grips his hand.
By the Powers, I'm glad you're here, Jamie.
Cregan is surprised and pleased by the warmth of his welcome. Melody draws him into the room.
Come. Sit down. You'll join me in a drink, I know.
He gets Cregan a glass from the cupboard. The decanter and Melody's glass are already on the table.

CREGAN

Admiringly.

Be God, it's the old uniform, no less, and you look as fine a figure in it as ever you did in Spain.

He sits at right of table at left front as Melody sits at rear.

MELODY

Immensely pleased—deprecatingly.

Hardly, Jamie—but not a total ruin yet, I hope. I put it on in honor of the day. I see you've forgotten. For shame, you dog, not to remember Talavera.

CREGAN

Excitedly.

Talavera, is it? Where I got my saber cut. Be the mortal, I remember it, and you've a right to celebrate. You was worth any ten men in the army that day!

Melody has shoved the decanter toward him. He pours a drink.

MELODY

This compliment completely restores him to his arrogant self.

Yes, I think I may say I did acquit myself with honor.

Patronizingly.

So, for that matter, did you.

He pours a drink and raises his glass.

To the day and your good health, Corporal Cregan.

CREGAN

Enthusiastically.

To the day and yourself, God bless you, Con!

He tries to touch brims with Melody's glass, but Melody holds his glass away and draws himself up haughtily.

MELODY

With cold rebuke.

I said, to the day and your good health, *Corporal Cregan.*

CREGAN

For a second is angry—then he grins and mutters admiringly.

Be God, it's you can bate the world and never let it change you!

Correcting his toast with emphasis.

To the day and yourself, *Major Melody.*

MELODY
Touches his glass to Cregan's—graciously condescending.
Drink hearty, Corporal.
They drink.

CURTAIN

Act Three

The same. The door to the bar is closed. It is around eight that evening and there are candles on the center table. Melody sits at the head of this table. In his brilliant uniform he presents more than ever an impressively colorful figure in the room, which appears smaller and dingier in the candlelight. Cregan is in the chair on his right. The other chairs at this table are unoccupied. Riley, O'Dowd, and Roche sit at the table at left front. Riley is at front, but his chair is turned sideways so he faces right. O'Dowd has the chair against the wall, facing right, with Roche across the table from him, his back to Melody. All five are drunk, Melody more so than any of them, but except for the glazed glitter in his eyes and his deathly pallor, his appearance does not betray him. He is holding his liquor like a gentleman.

Cregan is the least drunk. O'Dowd and Roche are boisterous. The effect of the drink on Riley is merely to sink him deeper in dreams. He seems oblivious to his surroundings.

An empty and a half-empty bottle of port are on the table before Melody and Cregan, and their glasses are full. The three at the table have a decanter of whiskey.

Sara, wearing her working dress and an apron, is removing dishes and the remains of the dinner. Her face is set. She is determined to ignore them, but there is angry disgust in her eyes. Melody is arranging forks, knives, spoons, saltcellar, etc., in a plan of battle on the table before him. Cregan watches him. Patch Riley gives a few tuning-up quavers on his pipes.

MELODY

Here's the river Tagus. And here, Talavera. This would be the French position on a rise of ground with the plain between our lines and theirs. Here is our redoubt with the Fourth Division and the Guards. And here's our cavalry brigade in a valley toward our left, if you'll remember, Corporal Cregan.

CREGAN

Excitedly.

Remember? Sure I see it as clear as yesterday!

RILEY

Bursts into a rollicking song, accompanying himself on the pipes, his voice the quavering ghost of a tenor but still true—to the tune of "Baltiorum."
   "She'd a pig and boneens,
   She'd a bed and a dresser,
   And a nate little room
   For the father confessor;
   With a cupboard and curtains, and something, I'm
      towld,
   That his riv'rance liked when the weather was cowld.
   And it's hurroo, hurroo! Biddy O'Rafferty!"
Roche and O'Dowd roar after him, beating time on the table with their glasses—"Hurroo, hurroo! Biddy O'Rafferty!"—*and laugh drunkenly. Cregan, too, joins in this chorus. Melody frowns angrily at the interruption, but at the end he smiles with lordly condescension, pleased by the irreverence of the song.*

O'DOWD

After a cunning glance at Melody's face to see what his reaction is—derisively.

Och, lave it to the priests, divil mend thim! Ain't it so, Major?

MELODY

Ay, damn them all! A song in the right spirit, Piper. Faith, I'll have you repeat it for my wife's benefit when she joins us. She still has a secret fondness for priests. And now, less noise, you blackguards. Corporal Cregan and I cannot hear each other with your brawling.

O'DOWD
Smirkingly obedient.
Quiet it is, yer Honor. Be quiet, Patch.
He gives the old man, who is lost in dreams, a shove that almost knocks him off his chair. Riley stares at him bewilderedly. O'Dowd and Roche guffaw.

MELODY
Scowls at them, then turns to Cregan.
Where was I, Corporal? Oh, yes, we were waiting in the valley. We heard a trumpet from the French lines and saw them forming for the attack. An aide-de-camp galloped down the hill to us—

SARA
Who has been watching him disdainfully, reaches out to take his plate— rudely in mocking brogue.
I'll have your plate, av ye plaze, Major, before your gallant dragoons charge over it and break it.

MELODY
Holds his plate on the table with one hand so she cannot take it, and raises his glass of wine with the other—ignoring her.
Wet your lips, Corporal. Talavera was a devilish thirsty day, if you'll remember.
He drinks.

CREGAN
Glances uneasily at Sara.
It was that.
He drinks.

MELODY
Smacking his lips.
Good wine, Corporal. Thank God, I still have wine in my cellar fit for a gentleman.

SARA
Angrily.
Are you going to let me take your plate?

MELODY

Ignoring her.

No, I have no need to apologize for the wine. Nor for the dinner, for that matter. Nora is a good cook when she forgets her infernal parsimony and buys food that one can eat without disgust. But I do owe you an apology for the quality of the service. I have tried to teach the waitress not to snatch plates from the table as if she were feeding dogs in a kennel but she cannot learn.

He takes his hand from the plate—to Sara.

There. Now let me see you take it properly.

She stares at him for a moment, speechless with anger—then snatches the plate from in front of him.

CREGAN

Hastily recalls Melody to the battlefield.

You were where the aide-de-camp galloped up to us, Major. It was then the French artillery opened on us.

Sara goes out right, carrying a tray laden with plates.

MELODY

We charged the columns on our left—here—

He marks the tablecloth.

that were pushing back the Guards. I'll never forget the blast of death from the French squares. And then their chasseurs and lancers were on us! By God, it's a miracle any of us came through!

CREGAN

You wasn't touched except you'd a bullet through your coat, but I had this token on my cheek to remember a French saber by.

MELODY

Brave days, those! By the Eternal, then one lived! Then one forgot!

He stops—when he speaks again it is bitterly.

Little did I dream then the disgrace that was to be my reward later on.

CREGAN

Consolingly.

Ah well, that's the bad luck of things. You'd have been made a colonel soon, if you'd left the Spanish woman alone and not fought that duel.

MELODY
Arrogantly threatening.
Are you presuming to question my conduct in that affair, Corporal Cregan?

CREGAN
Hastily.
Sorra a bit! Don't mind me, now.

MELODY
Stiffly.
I accept your apology.
He drinks the rest of his wine, pours another glass, then stares moodily before him. Cregan drains his glass and refills it.

O'DOWD
Peering past Roche to watch Melody, leans across to Roche—in a sneering whisper.
Ain't he the lunatic, sittin' like a play-actor in his red coat, lyin' about his battles with the French!

ROCHE
Sullenly—but careful to keep his voice low.
He'd ought to be shamed he ivir wore the bloody red av England, God's curse on him!

O'DOWD
Don't be wishin' him harm, for it's thirsty we'd be without him. Drink long life to him, and may he always be as big a fool as he is this night!
He sloshes whiskey from the decanter into both their glasses.

ROCHE
With a drunken leer.
Thrue for you! I'll toast him on that.
He twists round to face Melody, holds up his glass and bawls.

To the grandest gintleman ivir come from the shores av Ireland!
Long life to you, Major!

O'DOWD
Hurroo! Long life, yer Honor!

RILEY
Awakened from his dream, mechanically raises his glass.
And to all that belong to ye.

MELODY
Startled from his thoughts, becomes at once the condescending squire—
smiling tolerantly.
I said, less noise, you dogs. All the same, I thank you for your toast.
They drink. A pause. Abruptly Melody begins to recite from Byron. He
reads the verse well, quietly, with a bitter eloquence.
　　"But midst the crowd, the hum, the shock of men,
　　　To hear, to see, to feel, and to possess,
　　　And roam along, the World's tired denizen,
　　　With none who bless us, none whom we can bless;
　　　Minions of Splendour shrinking from distress!
　　　None that, with kindred consciousness endued,
　　　If we were not, would seem to smile the less,
　　　Of all that flattered—followed—sought, and sued;
　　　This is to be alone—This, this is Solitude!"
He stops and glances from one face to another. Their expressions are all
blank. He remarks with insulting derisiveness.
What? You do not understand, my lads? Well, all the better for you.
So may you go on fooling yourselves that I am fooled in you.
Then with a quick change of mood, heartily.
Give us a hunting song, Patch. You've not forgotten "Modideroo,"
I'll be bound.

RILEY
Roused to interest immediately.
Does a duck forget wather? I'll show ye!
He begins the preliminary quavers on his pipes.

O'DOWD
Modideroo!

ROCHE
Hurroo!

RILEY
Accompanying himself, sings with wailing melancholy the first verse that comes to his mind of an old hunting song.
   "And the fox set him down and looked about,
   And many were feared to follow;
   'Maybe I'm wrong,' says he, 'but I doubt
   That you'll be as gay tomorrow.
   For loud as you cry, and high as you ride,
   And little you feel my sorrow,
   I'll be free on the mountainside
   While you'll lie low tomorrow.'
   Oh, Modideroo, aroo, aroo!"
Melody, excited now, beats time on the table with his glass along with Cregan, Roche, and O'Dowd, and all bellow the refrain, "Oh, Modideroo, aroo, aroo!"

MELODY
His eyes alight, forgetting himself, a strong lilt of brogue coming into his voice.
Ah, that brings it back clear as life! Melody Castle in the days that's gone! A wind from the south, and a sky gray with clouds—good weather for the hounds. A true Irish hunter under me that knows and loves me and would raise to a jump over hell if I gave the word! To hell with men, I say!—and women, too!—with their cowardly hearts rotten and stinking with lies and greed and treachery! Give me a horse to love and I'll cry quits to men! And then away, with the hounds in full cry, and after them! Off with divil a care for your neck, over ditches and streams and stone walls and fences, the fox doubling up the mountainside through the furze and the heather— !
Sara has entered from right as he begins this longing invocation of old hunting days. She stands behind his chair, listening contemptuously. He suddenly feels her presence and turns his head. When he catches the sneer

in her eyes, it is as if cold water were dashed in his face. He addresses her as if she were a servant.

Well? What is it? What are you waiting for now?

SARA

Roughly, with coarse brogue.

What would I be waitin' for but for you to get through with your blather about lovin' horses, and give me a chance to finish my work? Can't you—and the other gintlemen—finish gettin' drunk in the bar and lave me clear the tables?

O'Dowd conceals a grin behind his hand; Roche stifles a malicious guffaw.

CREGAN

With an apprehensive glance at Melody, shakes his head at her admonishingly.

Now, Sara, be aisy.

But Melody suppresses any angry reaction. He rises to his feet, a bit stiffly and carefully, and bows.

MELODY

Coldly.

I beg your pardon if we have interfered with your duties.

To O'Dowd and his companions.

Into the bar, you louts!

O'DOWD

The bar it is, sorr. Come, Dan. Wake up, Patch.

He pokes the piper. He and Roche go into the bar, and Riley stumbles vaguely after them. Cregan waits for Melody.

MELODY

Go along, Corporal. I'll join you presently. I wish to speak to my daughter.

CREGAN

All right, Major.

He again shakes his head at Sara, as if to say, don't provoke him. She ignores him. He goes into the bar, closing the door behind him. She stares at her father with angry disgust.

SARA

You're drunk. If you think I'm going to stay here and listen to—

MELODY

His face expressionless, draws out his chair at the head of the center table for her—politely.
Sit down, my dear.

SARA

I won't. I have no time. Poor Mother is half dead on her feet. I have to help her. There's a pile of dishes to wash after your grand anniversary feast!
With bitter anger.
Thank God it's over, and it's the last time you'll ever take satisfaction in having me wait on table for drunken scum like O'Dowd and—

MELODY

Quietly.
A daughter who takes satisfaction in letting even the scum see that she hates and despises her father!
He shrugs his shoulders.
But no matter.
Indicating the chair again.
Won't you sit down, my dear?

SARA

If you ever dared face the truth, you'd hate and despise yourself!
Passionately.
All I pray to God is that someday when you're admiring yourself in the mirror something will make you see at last what you really are! That will be revenge in full for all you've done to Mother and me!
She waits defiantly, as if expecting him to lose his temper and curse her. But Melody acts as if he had not heard her.

MELODY

His face expressionless, his manner insistently bland and polite.
Sit down, my dear. I will not detain you long, and I think you will find what I have to tell you of great interest.
She searches his face, uneasy now, feeling a threat hidden behind his cold,

*quiet, gentlemanly tone. She sits down and he sits at rear of table, with
an empty chair separating them.*

SARA

You'd better think well before you speak, Father. I know the devil
that's in you when you're quiet like this with your brain mad with
drink.

MELODY

I don't understand you. All I wish is to relate something which happened this afternoon.

SARA

Giving way to bitterness at her humiliation again—sneeringly.
When you went riding on your beautiful thoroughbred mare while
Mother and I were sweating and suffocating in the heat of the
kitchen to prepare your Lordship's banquet? Sure, I hope you didn't
show off and jump your beauty over a fence into somebody's garden,
like you've done before, and then have to pay damages to keep out
of jail!

MELODY

Roused by mention of his pet—disdainfully.
The damned Yankee yokels should feel flattered that she deigns to
set her dainty hooves in their paltry gardens! She's a truer-born, well-
bred lady than any of their women—than the one who paid us a visit
this morning, for example.

SARA

Mrs. Harford was enough of a lady to put you in your place and
make a fool of you.

MELODY

Seemingly unmoved by this taunt—calmly.
You are very simple-minded, my dear, to let yourself be taken in by
such an obvious bit of clever acting. Naturally, the lady was a bit dis-
composed when she heard you and your mother coming, after she
had just allowed me to kiss her. She had to pretend—

SARA

Eagerly.

She let you kiss her?

Then disgustedly.

It's a lie, but I don't doubt you've made yourself think it's the truth by now.

Angrily.

I'm going. I don't want to listen to the whiskey in you boasting of what never happened—as usual!

She puts her hands on the table and starts to rise.

MELODY

With a quick movement pins hers down with one of his.

Wait!

A look of vindictive cruelty comes into his eyes—quietly.

Why are you so jealous of the mare, I wonder? Is it because she has such slender ankles and dainty feet?

He takes his hand away and stares at her hands—with disgust, commandingly.

Keep your thick wrists and ugly, peasant paws off the table in my presence, if you please! They turn my stomach! I advise you never to let Simon get a good look at them—

SARA

Instinctively jerks her hands back under the table guiltily. She stammers.

You—you cruel devil! I knew you'd—

MELODY

For a second is ashamed and really contrite.

Forgive me, Sara. I didn't mean—the whiskey talking—as you said.

He adds in a forced tone, a trace of mockery in it.

An absurd taunt, when you really have such pretty hands and feet, my dear.

She jumps to her feet, so hurt and full of hatred her lips tremble and she cannot speak. He speaks quietly.

Are you going? I was about to tell you of the talk I had this afternoon with young Harford.

She stares at him in dismay. He goes on easily.

It was after I returned from my ride. I cantered the mare by the river and she pulled up lame. So I dismounted and led her back to the barn. No one noticed my return and when I went upstairs it occurred to me I would not find again such an opportunity to have a frank chat with Harford—free from interruptions.

He pauses, as if he expects her to be furious, but she remains tensely silent, determined not to let him know her reaction.

I did not beat about the bush. I told him he must appreciate, as a gentleman, it was my duty as your father to demand he lay his cards on the table. I said he must realize that even before you began nursing him here and going alone to his bedroom, there was a deal of gossip about your visits to his cabin, and your walks in the woods with him. I put it to him that such an intimacy could not continue without gravely compromising your reputation.

SARA
Stunned—weakly.
God forgive you! And what did he say?

MELODY
What could he say? He is a man of honor. He looked damn embarrassed and guilty for a moment, but when he found his tongue, he agreed with me most heartily. He said his mother had told him the same thing.

SARA
Oh, she did, did she? I suppose she did it to find out by watching him how far—

MELODY
Coldly.
Well, why not? Naturally, it was her duty as his mother to discover all she could about you. She is a woman of the world. She would be bound to suspect that you might be his mistress.

SARA
Tensely.
Oh, would she!

MELODY

But that's beside the point. The point is, my bashful young gentleman finally blurted out that he wanted to marry you.

SARA

Forgetting her anger—eagerly.
He told you that?

MELODY

Yes, and he said he had told his mother, and she had said all she
wanted was his happiness but she felt in fairness to you and to himself—and I presume she also meant to both families concerned—
he should test his love and yours by letting a decent interval of time
elapse before your marriage. She mentioned a year, I believe.

SARA

Angrily.
Ah! Didn't I guess that would be her trick!

MELODY

Lifting his eyebrows—coldly.
Trick? In my opinion, the lady displayed more common sense and
knowledge of the world than I thought she possessed. The reasons
she gave him are sound and show a consideration for your good
name which ought to inspire gratitude in you and not suspicion.

SARA

Arrah, don't tell me she's made a fool of you again! A lot of consideration she has for me!

MELODY

She pointed out to him that if you were the daughter of some family
in their own little Yankee clique, there would be no question of a
hasty marriage, and so he owed it to you—

SARA

I see. She's the clever one!

MELODY

Another reason was—and here your Simon stammered so embarrassedly I had trouble making him out—she warned him a sudden

wedding would look damnably suspicious and start a lot of evil-minded gossip.

SARA
Tensely.
Oh, she's clever, all right! But I'll beat her.

MELODY
I told him I agreed with his mother. It is obvious that were there a sudden wedding without a suitable period of betrothal, everyone would believe—

SARA
I don't care what they believe! Tell me this! Did she get him to promise her he'd wait?
Before he can answer—bitterly.
But of course she did! She'd never have left till she got that out of him!

MELODY
Ignores this.
I told him I appreciated the honor he did me in asking for your hand, but he must understand that I could not commit myself until I had talked to his father and was assured the necessary financial arrangements could be concluded to our mutual satisfaction. There was the amount of settlement to be agreed upon, for instance.

SARA
That dream, again! God pity you!
She laughs helplessly and a bit hysterically.
And God help Simon. He must have thought you'd gone out of your mind! What did he say?

MELODY
He said nothing, naturally. He is well bred and he knows this is a matter he must leave to his father to discuss. There is also the equally important matter of how generous an allowance Henry Harford is willing to settle on his son. I did not mention this to Simon, of course, not wishing to embarrass him further with talk of money.

SARA
Thank God for that, at least!
She giggles hysterically.

MELODY
Quietly.
May I ask what you find so ridiculous in an old established custom?
Simon is an elder son, the heir to his father's estate. No matter what
their differences in the past may have been, now that Simon has decided to marry and settle down his father will wish to do the fair
thing by him. He will realize, too, that although there is no more
honorable calling than that of poet and philosopher, which his son
has chosen to pursue, there is no decent living to be gained by its
practice. So naturally he will settle an allowance on Simon, and I
shall insist it be a generous one, befitting your position as my daughter. I will tolerate no niggardly trader's haggling on his part.

SARA
Stares at him fascinatedly, on the edge of helpless, hysterical laughter.
I suppose it would never occur to you that old Harford might not
think it an honor to have his son marry your daughter.

MELODY
Calmly.
No, it would never occur to me—and if it should occur to him, I
would damned soon disabuse his mind. Who is he but a money-
grubbing trader? I would remind him that I was born in a castle and
there was a time when I possessed wealth and position, and an estate
compared to which any Yankee upstart's home in this country is but
a hovel stuck in a cabbage patch. I would remind him that you, my
daughter, were born in a castle!

SARA
Impulsively, with a proud toss of her head.
Well, that's no more than the truth.
Then furious with herself and him.
Och, what crazy blather!
She springs to her feet.
I've had enough of your mad dreams!

MELODY

Wait! I haven't finished yet.

He speaks quietly, but as he goes on there is an increasing vindictiveness in his tone.

There was another reason why I told young Harford I could not make a final decision. I wished time to reflect on a further aspect of this proposed marriage. Well, I have been reflecting, watching you and examining your conduct, without prejudice, trying to be fair to you and make every possible allowance—

He pauses.

Well, to be brutally frank, my dear, all I can see in you is a common, greedy, scheming, cunning peasant girl, whose only thought is money and who has shamelessly thrown herself at a young man's head because his family happens to possess a little wealth and position.

SARA

Trying to control herself.

I see your game, Father. I told you when you were drunk like this— But this time, I won't give you the satisfaction—

Then she bursts out angrily.

It's a lie! I love Simon, or I'd never—

MELODY

As if she hadn't spoken.

So, I have about made up my mind to decline for you Simon Harford's request for your hand in marriage.

SARA

Jeers angrily now.

Oh, you have, have you? As if I cared a damn what you— !

MELODY

As a gentleman, I feel I have a duty, in honor, to Simon. Such a marriage would be a tragic misalliance for him—and God knows I know the sordid tragedy of such a union.

SARA

It's Mother has had the tragedy!

MELODY

I hold young Harford in too high esteem. I cannot stand by and let him commit himself irrevocably to what could only bring him disgust and bitterness, and ruin to all his dreams.

SARA

So I'm not good enough for him, you've decided now?

MELODY

That is apparent from your every act. No one, no matter how charitably inclined, could mistake you for a lady. I have tried to make you one. It was an impossible task. God Himself cannot transform a sow's ear into a silk purse!

SARA

Furiously.
Father!

MELODY

Young Harford needs to be saved from himself. I can understand his physical infatuation. You are pretty. So was your mother pretty once. But marriage is another matter. The man who would be the ideal husband for you, from a standpoint of conduct and character, is Mickey Maloy, my bartender, and I will be happy to give him my parental blessing—

SARA

Let you stop now, Father!

MELODY

You and he would be congenial. You can match tongues together. He's a healthy animal. He can give you a raft of peasant brats to squeal and fight with the pigs on the mud floor of your hovel.

SARA

It's the dirty hut in which your father was born and raised you're remembering, isn't it?

MELODY

Stung to fury, glares at her with hatred. His voice quivers but is deadly quiet.

Of course, if you trick Harford into getting you with child, I could not refuse my consent.

Letting go, he bangs his fist on the table.

No, by God, even then, when I remember my own experience, I'll be damned if I could with a good conscience advise him to marry you!

SARA

Glaring back at him with hatred.

You drunken devil!

She makes a threatening move toward him, raising her hand as if she were going to slap his face—then she controls herself and speaks with quiet, biting sarcasm.

Consent or not, I want to thank you for your kind fatherly advice on how to trick Simon. I don't think I'll need it but if the worst comes to the worst I promise you I'll remember—

MELODY

Coldly, his face expressionless.

I believe I have said all I wished to say to you.

He gets up and bows stiffly.

If you will excuse me, I shall join Corporal Cregan.

He goes to the bar door. Sara turns and goes quietly out right, forgetting to clear the few remaining dishes on the center table. His back turned, he does not see her go. With his hand on the knob of the bar door, he hesitates. For a second he breaks—torturedly.

Sara!

Then quietly.

There are things I said which I regret—even now. I— I trust you will overlook— As your mother knows, it's the liquor talking, not— I must admit that, due to my celebrating the anniversary, my brain is a bit addled by whiskey—as you said.

He waits, hoping for a word of forgiveness. Finally, he glances over his shoulder. As he discovers she is not there and has not heard him, for a second he crumbles, his soldierly erectness sags and his face falls. He looks sad and hopeless and bitter and old, his eyes wandering dully. But, as in the two preceding acts, the mirror attracts him, and as he moves from the bar door to stand before it he assumes his arrogant, Byronic pose again.

He repeats in each detail his pantomime before the mirror. He speaks proudly.

Myself to the bitter end! No weakening, so help me God!

There is a knock on the street door but he does not hear it. He starts his familiar incantation quotes from Byron.

"I have not loved the World, nor the World me;

I have not flattered its rank breath, nor bowed

To its idolatries a patient knee . . ."

The knock on the door is repeated more loudly. Melody starts guiltily and steps quickly away from the mirror. His embarrassment is transformed into resentful anger. He calls.

Come in, damn you! Do you expect a lackey to open the door for you?

The door opens and NICHOLAS GADSBY *comes in. Gadsby is in his late forties, short, stout, with a big, bald head, round, florid face, and small, blue eyes. A rigidly conservative, best-family attorney, he is stiffly correct in dress and manner, dryly portentous in speech, and extremely conscious of his professional authority and dignity. Now, however, he is venturing on unfamiliar ground and is by no means as sure of himself as his manner indicates. The unexpected vision of Melody in his uniform startles him and for a second he stands, as close to gaping as he can be, impressed by Melody's handsome distinction. Melody, in his turn, is surprised. He had not thought the intruder would be a gentleman. He unbends, although his tone is still a bit curt. He bows a bit stiffly, and Gadsby finds himself returning the bow.*

Your pardon, sir. When I called, I thought it was one of the damned riffraff mistaking the barroom door. Pray be seated, sir.

Gadsby comes forward and takes the chair at the head of the center table, glancing at the few dirty dishes on it with distaste. Melody says.

Your pardon again, sir. We have been feasting late, which accounts for the disarray. I will summon a servant to inquire your pleasure.

GADSBY

Beginning to recover his aplomb—shortly.

Thank you, but I want nothing, sir. I came here to seek a private interview with the proprietor of this tavern, by name, Melody.

He adds a bit hesitantly.

Are you, by any chance, he?

MELODY
Stiffens arrogantly.
I am not, sir. But if you wish to see Major Cornelius Melody, one
time of His Majesty's Seventh Dragoons, who served with honor
under the Duke of Wellington in Spain, I am he.

GADSBY
Dryly.
Very well, sir. Major Melody, then.

MELODY
Does not like his tone—insolently sarcastic.
And whom have I the *honor* of addressing?
*As Gadsby is about to reply, Sara enters from right, having remembered
the dishes. Melody ignores her as he would a servant. Gadsby examines
her carefully as she gathers up the dishes. She notices him staring at her
and gives him a resentful, suspicious glance. She carries the dishes out,
right, to the kitchen, but a moment later she can be seen just inside the
hall at right, listening. Meanwhile, as soon as he thinks she has gone,
Gadsby speaks.*

GADSBY
With affected casualness.
A pretty young woman. Is she your daughter, sir? I seemed to detect
a resemblance—

MELODY
Angrily.
No! Do I look to you, sir, like a man who would permit his daughter
to work as a waitress? Resemblance to me? You must be blind, sir.
Coldly.
I am still waiting for you to inform me who you are and why you
should wish to see me.

GADSBY
Hands him a card—extremely nettled by Melody's manner—curtly.
My card, sir.

MELODY

Glances at the card.

Nicholas Gadsby.

He flips it aside disdainfully.

Attorney, eh? The devil take all your tribe, say I. I have small liking for your profession, sir, and I cannot imagine what business you can have with me. The damned thieves of the law did their worst to me many years ago in Ireland. I have little left to tempt you. So I do not see—

Suddenly an idea comes to him. He stares at Gadsby, then goes on in a more friendly tone.

That is, unless— Do you happen by any chance to represent the father of young Simon Harford?

GADSBY

Indignant at Melody's insults to his profession—with a thinly veiled sneer.

Ah, then you were expecting— That makes things easier. We need not beat about the bush. I do represent Mr. Henry Harford, sir.

MELODY

Thawing out, in his total misunderstanding of the situation.

Then accept my apologies, sir, for my animadversions against your profession. I am afraid I may be prejudiced. In the army, we used to say we suffered more casualties from your attacks at home than the French ever inflicted.

He sits down on the chair on Gadsby's left, at rear of table—remarking with careless pride.

A word of explanation as to why you find me in uniform. It is the anniversary of the battle of Talavera, sir, and—

GADSBY

Interrupts dryly.

Indeed, sir? But I must tell you my time is short. With your permission, we will proceed at once to the matter in hand.

MELODY

Controlling his angry discomfiture—coldly.

I think I can hazard a guess as to what that matter is. You have come about the settlement?

GADSBY

Misunderstanding him, replies in a tone almost openly contemptuous.
Exactly, sir. Mr. Harford was of the opinion, and I agreed with him, that a settlement would be foremost in your mind.

MELODY

Scowls at his tone but, as he completely misunderstands Gadsby's meaning, he forces himself to bow politely.
It does me honor, sir, that Mr. Harford appreciates he is dealing with a gentleman and has the breeding to know how these matters are properly arranged.
Gadsby stares at him, absolutely flabbergasted by what he considers a piece of the most shameless effrontery. Melody leans toward him confidentially.
I will be frank with you, sir. The devil of it is, this comes at a difficult time for me. Temporary, of course, but I cannot deny I am pinched at the moment—devilishly pinched. But no matter. Where my only child's happiness is at stake, I am prepared to make every possible effort. I will sign a note of hand, no matter how ruinous the interest demanded by the scoundrelly moneylenders. By the way, what amount does Mr. Harford think proper? Anything in reason—

GADSBY

Listening in utter confusion, finally gets the idea Melody is making him the butt of a joke—fuming.
I do not know what you are talking about, sir, unless you think to make a fool of me! If this is what is known as Irish wit—

MELODY

Bewildered for a second—then in a threatening tone.
Take care, sir, and watch your words or I warn you you will repent them, no matter whom you represent! No damned pettifogging dog can insult me with impunity!
As Gadsby draws back apprehensively, he adds with insulting disdain.
As for making a fool of you, sir, I would be the fool if I attempted to improve on God's handiwork!

GADSBY

Ignoring the insults, forces a placating tone.

I wish no quarrel with you, sir. I cannot for the life of me see— I fear we are dealing at cross-purposes. Will you tell me plainly what you mean by your talk of settlement?

MELODY

Obviously, I mean the settlement I am prepared to make on my daughter.

As Gadsby only looks more dumfounded, he continues sharply.

Is not your purpose in coming here to arrange, on Mr. Harford's behalf, for the marriage of his son with my daughter?

GADSBY

Marriage? Good God, no! Nothing of the kind!

MELODY

Dumfounded.

Then what have you come for?

GADSBY

Feeling he has now the upper hand—sharply.

To inform you that Mr. Henry Harford is unalterably opposed to any further relationship between his son and your daughter, whatever the nature of that relationship in the past.

MELODY

Leans forward threateningly.

By the Immortal, sir, if you dare insinuate— !

GADSBY

Draws back again, but he is no coward and is determined to carry out his instructions.

I insinuate nothing, sir. I am here on Mr. Harford's behalf, to make you an offer. That is what I thought you were expecting when you mentioned a settlement. Mr. Harford is prepared to pay you the sum of three thousand dollars—provided, mark you, that you and your daughter sign an agreement I have drawn up which specifies that you relinquish all claims, of whatever nature. And also provided you agree to leave this part of the country at once with your family.

Mr. Harford suggests it would be advisable that you go West—to Ohio, say.

MELODY

So overcome by a rising tide of savage, humiliated fury, he can only stammer hoarsely.
So Henry Harford does me the honor—to suggest that, does he?

GADSBY

Watching him uneasily, attempts a reasonable, persuasive tone.
Surely you could not have spoken seriously when you talked of marriage. There is such a difference in station. The idea is preposterous. If you knew Mr. Harford, you would realize he would never countenance—

MELODY

His pent-up rage bursts out—smashing his fist on the table.
Know him? By the Immortal God, I'll know him soon! And he'll know me!
He springs to his feet.
But first, you Yankee scum, I'll deal with you!
He draws back his fist to smash Gadsby in the face, but Sara has run from the door at right and she grabs his arm. She is almost as furious as he is and there are tears of humiliated pride in her eyes.

SARA

Father! Don't! He's only a paid lackey. Where is your pride that you'd dirty your hands on the like of him?
While she is talking the door from the bar opens and Roche, O'Dowd, and Cregan crowd into the room. Mickey stands in the doorway. Nora follows Sara in from right.

ROCHE

With drunken enthusiasm.
It's a fight! For the love of God, clout the damned Yankee, Major!

MELODY

Controls himself—his voice shaking.
You are right, Sara. It would be beneath me to touch such a vile lickspittle. But he won't get off scot-free.

Sharply, a commander ordering his soldiers.
Here you, Roche and O'Dowd! Get hold of him!
They do so with enthusiasm and yank Gadsby from his chair.

GADSBY
You drunken ruffians! Take your hands off me!

MELODY
Addressing him—in his quiet, threatening tone now.
You may tell the swindling trader, Harford, who employs you that
he'll hear from me!
To Roche and O'Dowd.
Throw this thing out! Kick it down to the crossroads!

ROCHE
Hurroo!
*He and O'Dowd run Gadsby to the door at rear. Cregan jumps ahead,
grinning, and opens the door for them.*

GADSBY
Struggling futilely as they rush him through the door.
You scoundrels! Take your hands off me! Take—
*Melody looks after them. The two women watch him, Nora frightened,
Sara with a strange look of satisfied pride.*

CREGAN
In the doorway, looking out—laughing.
Oh, it'd do your heart good, Con, to see the way they're kicking his
butt down the street!
He comes in and shuts the door.

MELODY
*His rage welling again, as his mind dwells on his humiliation—starting
to pace up and down.*
It's with his master I have to deal, and, by the Powers, I'll deal with
him! You'll come with me, Jamie. I'll want you for a witness. He'll
apologize to me—more than that, he'll come back here this very
night and apologize publicly to my daughter, or else he meets me in
the morning! By God, I'll face him at ten paces or across a handkerchief! I'll put a bullet through him, so help me, Christ!

NORA

Breaks into a dirgelike wail.

God forgive you, Con, is it a duel again—murtherin' or gettin' murthered?

MELODY

Be quiet, woman! Go back to your kitchen! Go, do you hear me!
Nora turns obediently toward the door at right, beginning to cry.

SARA

Puts an arm around her mother. She is staring at Melody apprehensively now.

There, Mother, don't worry. Father knows that's all foolishness. He's only talking. Go on now in the kitchen and sit down and rest, Mother.
Nora goes out right. Sara closes the door after her and comes back.

MELODY

Turns on her with bitter anger.

Only talking, am I? It's the first time in my life I ever heard anyone say Con Melody was a coward! It remains for my own daughter— !

SARA

Placatingly.

I didn't say that, Father. But can't you see—you're not in Ireland in the old days now. The days of duels are long past and dead, in this part of America anyway. Harford will never fight you. He—

MELODY

He won't, won't he? By God, I'll make him! I'll take a whip. I'll drag him out of his house and lash him down the street for all his neighbors to see! He'll apologize, or he'll fight, or I'll brand him a craven before the world!

SARA

Frightened now.

But you'll never be let see him! His servants will keep you out! He'll have the police arrest you, and it'll be in the papers about another drunken Mick raising a crazy row!
She appeals to Cregan.

Tell him I'm telling the truth, Jamie. You've still got some sober sense in you. Maybe he'll listen to you.

CREGAN
Glances at Melody uneasily.
Maybe Sara's right, Major.

MELODY
When I want your opinion, I'll ask for it!
Sneeringly.
Of course, if you've become such a coward you're afraid to go with me—

CREGAN
Stung.
Coward, is ut? I'll go, and be damned to you!

SARA
Jamie, you fool! Oh, it's like talking to crazy men!
She grabs her father's arm—pleadingly.
Don't do it, Father, for the love of God! Have I ever asked you anything? Well, I ask you to heed me now! I'll beg you on my knees, if you like! Isn't it me you'd fight about, and haven't I a right to decide? You punished that lawyer for the insult. You had him thrown out of here like a tramp. Isn't that your answer to old Harford that insults him? It's for him to challenge you, if he dares, isn't it? Why can't you leave it at that and wait—

MELODY
Shaking off her hand—angrily.
You talk like a scheming peasant! It's a question of my honor!

SARA
No! It's a question of my happiness, and I won't have your mad interfering— !
Desperately forcing herself to reason with him again.
Listen, Father! If you'll keep out of it, I'll show you how I'll make a fool of old Harford! Simon won't let anything his father does keep him from marrying me. His mother is the only one who might have the influence over him to come between us. She's only watching for

a good excuse to turn Simon against marrying me, and if you go raising a drunken row at their house, and make a public scandal, shouting you want to murder his father, can't you see what a chance that will give her?

MELODY
Raging.
That damned, insolent Yankee bitch! She's all the more reason. Marry, did you say? You dare to think there can be any question now of your marrying the son of a man who has insulted my honor— and yours?

SARA
Defiantly.
Yes, I dare to think it! I love Simon and I'm going to marry him!

MELODY
And I say you're not! If he wasn't sick, I'd— But I'll get him out of here tomorrow! I forbid you ever to see him again! If you dare disobey me I'll— !
Beginning to lose all control of himself.
If you dare defy me—for the sake of the dirty money you think you can beg from his family, if you're his wife— !

SARA
Fiercely.
You lie!
Then with quiet intensity.
Yes. I defy you or anyone who tries to come between us!

MELODY
You'd sell your pride as my daughter— !
His face convulsed by fury.
You filthy peasant slut! You whore! I'll see you dead first— ! By the living God, I'd kill you myself!
He makes a threatening move toward her.

SARA
Shrinks back frightenedly.
Father!

Then she stands and faces him defiantly.

CREGAN
Steps between them.
Con! In the name of God!
Melody's fit of insane fury leaves him. He stands panting for breath, shuddering with the effort to regain some sort of poise. Cregan speaks, his only thought to get him away from Sara.
If we're going after old Harford, Major, we'd better go. That thief of a lawyer will warn him—

MELODY
Seizing on this—hoarsely.
Yes, let's go. Let's go, Jamie. Come along, Corporal. A stirrup cup, and we'll be off. If the mare wasn't lame, I'd ride alone—but we can get a rig at the livery stable. Don't let me forget to stop at the barn for my whip.
By the time he finishes speaking, he has himself in hand again and his ungovernable fury has gone. There is a look of cool, menacing vengeful-ness in his face. He turns toward the bar door.

SARA
Helplessly.
Father!
Desperately, as a last, frantic threat.
You'll force me to go to Simon—and do what you said!
If he hears this, he gives no sign of it. He strides into the bar. Cregan follows him, closing the door. Sara stares before her, the look of defi-ant desperation hardening on her face. The steeet door is flung open and O'Dowd and Roche pile in, laughing uproariously.

ROCHE
Hurroo!

O'DOWD
The army is back, Major, with the foe flying in retreat.
He sees Melody is not there—to Sara.
Where's himself?
Sara appears not to see or hear him.

ROCHE

After a quick glance at her.
Lave her be. He'll be in the bar. Come on.
He goes to the bar.

O'DOWD

Following him, speaks over his shoulder to Sara.
You should have seen the Yank! His coachman had to help him in
his rig at the corner—and Roche gave the coachman a clout too, for
good measure!
*He disappears, laughing, slamming the door behind him. Nora opens the
door at right and looks in cautiously. Seeing Sara alone, she comes in.*

NORA

Sara.
She comes over to her.
Sara.
She takes hold of her arm—whispers uneasily.
Where's himself?

SARA

Dully.
I couldn't stop him.

NORA

I could have told you you was wastin' breath.
With a queer pride.
The divil himself couldn't kape Con Melody from a duel!
Then mournfully.
It's like the auld times come again, and the same worry and sorrow.
Even in the days before ivir I'd spoke a word to him, or done more
than make him a bow when he'd ride past on his hunter, I used to lie
awake and pray for him when I'd hear he was fightin' a duel in the
mornin'.
She smiles a shy, gentle smile.
I was in love with him even then.
*Sara starts to say something bitter but what she sees in her mother's face
stops her. Nora goes on, with a feeble attempt at boastful confidence.*
But I'll not worry this time, and let you not, either. There wasn't a

man in Galway was his equal with a pistol, and what chance will this auld stick av a Yankee have against him?

There is a noise of boisterous farewells from the bar and the noise of an outer door shutting. Nora starts.

That's him leavin'!

Her mouth pulls down pitiably. She starts for the bar with a sob.

Ah, Con darlin', don't— !

She stops, shaking her head helplessly.

But what's the good?

She sinks on a chair with a weary sigh.

SARA

Bitterly, aloud to herself more than to her mother.

No good. Let him go his way—and I'll go mine.

Tensely.

I won't let him destroy my life with his madness, after all the plans I've made and the dreams I've dreamed. I'll show him I can play at the game of gentleman's honor too!

Nora has not listened. She is sunk in memories of old fears and her present worry about the duel. Sara hesitates—then, keeping her face turned away from her mother, touches her shoulder.

I'm going upstairs to bed, Mother.

NORA

Starts—then indignantly.

To bed, is it? You can think of sleepin' when he's—

SARA

I didn't say sleep, but I can lie down and try to rest.

Still avoiding looking at her mother.

I'm dead tired, Mother.

NORA

Tenderly solicitous now, puts an arm around her.

You must be, darlin'. It's been the divil's own day for you, with all—
With sudden remorse.

God forgive me, darlin'. I was forgettin' about you and the Harford lad.

Miserably.

Oh, God help us!
Suddenly with a flash of her strange, fierce pride in the power of love.
Never mind! If there's true love between you, you'll not let a duel or
anything in the world kape you from each other, whatever the cost!
Don't I know!

SARA
Kisses her impulsively, then looks away again.
You're going to sit up and wait down here?

NORA
I am. I'd be destroyed with fear lying down in the dark. Here, the
noise of them in the bar kapes up my spirits, in a way.

SARA
Yes, you'd better stay here. Good night, Mother.

NORA
Good night, darlin'.
Sara goes out at right, closing the door behind her.

CURTAIN

Act Four

The same. It is around midnight. The room is in darkness except for one candle on the table, center. From the bar comes the sound of Patch Riley's pipes playing a reel and the stamp of dancing feet.

Nora sits at the foot of the table at center. She is hunched up in an old shawl, her arms crossed over her breast, hugging herself as if she were cold. She looks on the verge of collapse from physical fatigue and hours of worry. She starts as the door from the bar is opened. It is Mickey. He closes the door behind him, shutting out an uproar of music and drunken voices. He has a decanter of whiskey and a glass in his hand. He has been drinking, but is not drunk.

NORA
Eagerly.
There's news of himself?

MALOY
Putting the decanter and glass on the table.
Sorra a bit. Don't be worryin' now. Sure, it's not so late yet.

NORA
Dully.
It's aisy for you to say—

MALOY
I came in to see how you was, and bring you a taste to put heart in you.
As she shakes her head.
Oh, I know you don't indulge, but I've known you once in a while, and you need it this night.

As she again shakes her head—with kindly bullying.
Come now, don't be stubborn. I'm the doctor and I highly recommend a drop to drive out black thoughts and rheumatism.

NORA
Well—maybe—a taste, only.

MALOY
That's the talkin'.
He pours a small drink and hands it to her.
Drink hearty, now.

NORA
Takes a sip, then puts the glass on the table and pushes it away listlessly.
I've no taste for anything. But I thank you for the thought. You're a kind lad, Mickey.

MALOY
Here's news to cheer you. The word has got round among the boys, and they've all come in to wait for Cregan and himself.
With enthusiasm.
There'll be more money taken over the bar than any night since this shebeen started!

NORA
That's good.

MALOY
If they do hate Con Melody, he's Irish, and they hate the Yanks worse. They're all hopin' he's bate the livin' lights out of Harford.

NORA
With belligerent spirit.
And so he has, I know that!

MALOY
Grins.
That's the talk. I'm glad to see you roused from your worryin'.
Turning away.
I'd better get back. I left O'Dowd to tend bar and I'll wager he has three drinks stolen already.

He hesitates.
Sara's not been down?

NORA
No.

MALOY
Resentfully.
It's a wonder she wouldn't have more thought for you than to lave you sit up alone.

NORA
Stiffens defensively.
I made her go to bed. She was droppin' with tiredness and destroyed with worry. She must have fallen asleep, like the young can. None of your talk against Sara, now!

MALOY
Starts an exasperated retort.
The divil take—
He stops and grins at her with affection.
There's no batin' you, Nora. Sure, it'd be the joy av me life to have a mother like you to fight for me—or, better still, a wife like you.

NORA
A sweet smile of pleased coquetry lights up her drawn face.
Arrah, save your blarney for the young girls!

MALOY
The divil take young girls. You're worth a hundred av thim.

NORA
With a toss of her head.
Get along with you!
Mickey grins with satisfaction at having cheered her up and goes in the bar, closing the door. As soon as he is gone, she sinks back into apprehensive brooding.

Sara appears silently in the doorway at right. She wears a faded old wrapper over her nightgown, slippers on her bare feet. Her hair is clown over her shoulders, reaching to her waist. There is a change in her. All the bitterness and defiance have disappeared from her face. It looks gentle and calm and at the same time dreamily happy and exultant. She is much prettier than she has ever been before. She stands looking at her mother, and suddenly she becomes shy and uncertain—as if, now that she'd come this far, she had half a mind to retreat before her mother discovered her. But Nora senses her presence and looks up.

NORA
Dully.
Ah, it's you, darlin'!
Then gratefully.
Praise be, you've come at last! I'm sick with worry and I've got to the place where I can't bear waitin' alone, listenin' to drunks dancin' and celebratin'.
Sara comes to her. Nora breaks. Tears well from her eyes.
It's cruel, it is! There's no heart or thought for himself in divil a one av thim.
She starts to sob. Sara hugs her and kisses her cheek gently. But she doesn't speak. It is as if she were afraid her voice would give her away. Nora stops sobbing. Her mood changes to resentment and she speaks as if Sara had spoken.
Don't tell me not to worry. You're as bad as Mickey. The Yankee didn't apologize or your father'd been back here long since. It's a duel, that's certain, and he must have taken a room in the city so he'll be near the ground. I hope he'll sleep, but I'm feared he'll stay up drinkin', and at the dawn he'll have had too much to shoot his best and maybe—
Then defiantly self-reassuringly.
Arrah, I'm the fool! It's himself can keep his head clear and his eyes sharp, no matter what he's taken!
Pushing Sara away—with nervous peevishness.
Let go of me. You've hardened not to care. I'd rather stay alone.
She grabs Sara's hand.
No. Don't heed me. Sit down, darlin'.
Sara sits down on her left at rear of table. She pats her mother's hand,

but remains silent, her expression dreamily happy, as if she heard Nora's words but they had no meaning for her. Nora goes on worriedly again.

But if he's staying in the city, why hasn't he sent Jamie Cregan back for his duelin' pistols? I know he'd nivir fight with any others.

Resentful now at Melody.

Or you'd think he'd send Jamie or someone back with a word for me. He knows well how tormented I'd be waiting.

Bitterly.

Arrah, don't talk like a loon! Has he ever cared for anyone except himself and his pride? Sure, he'd never stoop to think of me, the grand gentleman in his red livery av bloody England! His pride, in-dade! What is it but a lie? What's in his veins, God pity him, but the blood of thievin' auld Ned Melody who kept a dirty shebeen?

Then is horrified at herself as if she had blasphemed.

No! I won't say it! I've nivir! It would break his heart if he heard me! I'm the only one in the world he knows nivir sneers at his dreams!

Working herself to rebellion again.

All the same, I won't stay here the rist of the night worryin' my heart out for a man who—it isn't only fear over the duel. It's because I'm afraid it's God's punishment, all the sorrow and trouble that's come on us, and I have the black tormint in my mind that it's the fault of the mortal sin I did with him unmarried, and the promise he made me make to leave the Church that's kept me from ever confessin' to a priest.

She pauses—dully.

Go to a doctor, you say, to cure the rheumatism. Sure, what's rheu-matism but a pain in your body? I could bear ten of it. It's the pain of guilt in my soul. Can a doctor's medicine cure that? No, only a priest of Almighty God—

With a roused rebellion again.

It would serve Con right if I took the chance now and broke my promise and woke up the priest to hear my confession and give me God's forgiveness that'd bring my soul peace and comfort so I wouldn't feel the three of us were damned.

Yearningly.

Oh, if I only had the courage!

She rises suddenly from her chair—with brave defiance.
I'll do it, so I will! I'm going to the priest's, Sara.
She starts for the street door—gets halfway to it and stops.

SARA
A strange, tenderly amused smile on her lips—teasingly.
Well, why don't you go, Mother?

NORA
Defiantly.
Ain't I goin'?
She takes a few more steps toward the door—stops again—she mutters beatenly.
God forgive me, I can't. What's the use pretendin'?

SARA
As before.
No use at all, Mother. I've found that out.

NORA
As if she hadn't heard, comes back slowly.
He'd feel I'd betrayed him and my word and my love for him—and for all his scorn, he knows my love is all he has in the world to comfort him.
Then spiritedly, with a proud toss of her head.
And it's my honor, too! It's not for his sake at all! Divil mend him, he always prates as if he had all the honor there is, but I've mine, too, as proud as his.
She sits down in the same chair.

SARA
Softly.
Yes, the honor of her love to a woman. I've learned about that too, Mother.

NORA
As if this were the first time she was really conscious of Sara speaking, and even now had not heard what she said—irritably.
So you've found your tongue, have you? Thank God. You're cold comfort, sitting silent like a statue, and me making talk to myself.

Regarding her as if she hadn't really seen her before—resentfully.
Musha but it's pleased and pretty you look, as if there wasn't a care in the world, while your poor father—

SARA
Dreamily amused, as if this no longer had any importance or connection with her.
I know it's no use telling you there won't be any duel, Mother, and it's crazy to give it a thought. You're living in Ireland long ago, like Father. But maybe you'll take Simon's word for it, if you won't mine. He said his father would be paralyzed with indignation just at the thought he'd ever fight a duel. It's against the law.

NORA
Scornfully.
Och, who cares for the law? He must be a coward.
She looks relieved.
Well, if the young lad said that, maybe it's true.

SARA
Of course it's true, Mother.

NORA
Your father'd be satisfied with Harford's apology and that'd end it.

SARA
Helplessly.
Oh, Mother!
Then quickly.
Yes, I'm sure it ended hours ago.

NORA
Intent on her hope.
And you think what's keeping him out is he and Jamie would take a power av drinks to celebrate.

SARA
They'd drink, that's sure, whatever happened.
She adds dreamily.
But that doesn't matter now at all.

NORA

Stares at her—wonderingly.

You've a queer way of talking, as if you'd been asleep and was still half in a dream.

SARA

In a dream right enough, Mother, and it isn't half of me that's in it but all of me, body and soul. And it's a dream that's true, and always will be to the end of life, and I'll never wake from it.

NORA

Sure, what's come over you at all?

SARA

Gets up impulsively and comes around in back of her mother's chair and slips to her knees and puts her arms about her—giving her a hug.

Joy. That's what's come over me. I'm happy, Mother. I'm happy because I know now Simon is mine, and no one can ever take him from me.

NORA

At first her only reaction is pleased satisfaction.

God be thanked! It was a great sorrow tormentin' me that the duel would come between you.

Defiantly.

Honor or not, why should the children have their lives and their love destroyed!

SARA

I was a great fool to fear his mother could turn him against me, no matter what happened.

NORA

You've had a talk with the lad?

SARA

I have. That's where I've been.

NORA

You've been in his room ever since you went up?

SARA

Almost. After I'd got upstairs it took me a while to get up my courage.

NORA

Rebukingly.
All this time—in the dead of the night!

SARA

Teasingly.
I'm his nurse, aren't I? I've a right.

NORA

That's no excuse!

SARA

Her face hardening.
Excuse? I had the best in the world. Would you have me do nothing to save my happiness and my chance in life, when I thought there was danger they'd be ruined forever? Don't you want me to have love and be happy, Mother?

NORA

Melting.
I do, darlin'. I'd give my life—
Then rebuking again.
Were you the way you are, in only a nightgown and wrapper?

SARA

Gaily.
I was—and Simon liked my costume, if you don't, although he turned red as a beet when I came in.

NORA

Small wonder he did! Shame on you!

SARA

He was trying to read a book of poetry, but he couldn't he was that worried hoping I'd come to say goodnight, and being frightened I wouldn't.
She laughs tenderly.

Oh, it was the cutest thing I've ever done, Mother, not to see him at all since his mother left. He kept waiting for me and when I didn't come, he got scared to death that his kissing me this morning had made me angry. So he was wild with joy to see me—

NORA

In your bare legs with only your nightgown and wrapper to cover your nakedness! Where's your modesty?

SARA

Gaily teasing.

I had it with me, Mother, though I'd tried hard to leave it behind. I got as red as he was.

She laughs.

Oh, Mother, it's a great joke on me. Here I'd gone to his room with my mind made up to be as bold as any street woman and tempt him because I knew his honor would make him marry me right away if—

She laughs.

And then all I could do was stand and gape at him and blush!

NORA

Oh.

Rebukingly.

I'm glad you had the dacency to blush.

SARA

It was Simon spoke first, and once he started, all he'd been holding back came out. The waiting for me, and the fear he'd had made him forget all his shyness, and he said he loved me and asked me to marry him the first day we could. Without knowing how it happened, there I was with his arms around me and mine around him and his lips on my lips and it was heaven, Mother.

NORA

Moved by the shining happiness in Sara's face.

God bless the two av you.

SARA

Then I was crying and telling him how afraid I'd been his mother hated me, Father's madness about the duel would give her a good chance to come between us; Simon said no one could ever come between us and his mother would never try to, now she knew he loved me, which was what she came over to find out. He said all she wanted was for him to be free to do as he pleased, and she only suggested he wait a year, she didn't make him promise. And Simon said I was foolish to think she would take the duel craziness serious. She'd only be amused at the joke it would be on his father, after he'd been so sure he could buy us off, if he had to call the police to save him.

NORA

Aroused at the mention of police.

Call the police, is it? The coward!

SARA

Goes on, unheedingly.

Simon was terribly angry at his father for that. And at Father too when I told how he threatened he'd kill me. But we didn't talk of it much. We had better things to discuss.

She smiles tenderly.

NORA

Belligerently.

A lot Con Melody cares for police, and him in a rage! Not the whole dirty force av thim will dare interfere with him!

SARA

Goes on as if she hadn't heard.

And then Simon told me how scared he'd been I didn't love him and wouldn't marry him. I was so beautiful, he said, and he wasn't handsome at all. So I kissed him and told him he was the handsomest in the world, and he is. And he said he wasn't worthy because he had so little to offer, and was a failure at what he'd hoped he could be, a poet. So I kissed him and told him he was too a poet, and always would be, and it was what I loved most about him.

NORA

The police! Let one av thim lay his dirty hand on Con Melody, and he'll knock him senseless with one blow.

Then Simon said how poor he was, and he'd never accept a penny from his father, even if he offered it. And I told him never mind, that if we had to live in a hut, or sleep in the grass of a field without a roof to our heads, and work our hands to the bone, or starve itself, I'd be in heaven and sing with the joy of our love!

She looks up at her mother.

And I meant it, Mother! I meant every word of it from the bottom of my heart!

NORA

Answers vaguely from her preoccupation with the police — patting Sara's hair mechanically.

Av course you did, darlin'.

SARA

But he kissed me and said it wouldn't be as bad as that, he'd been thinking and he'd had an offer from an old college friend who'd inherited a cotton mill and who wants Simon to be equal partners if he'll take complete charge of it. It's only a small mill and that's what tempts Simon. He said maybe I couldn't believe it but he knows from his experience working for his father he has the ability for trade, though he hates it, and he could easily make a living for us from this mill — just enough to be comfortable, and he'd have time over to write his book, and keep his wisdom, and never let himself become a slave to the greed for more than enough that is the curse of mankind. Then he said he was afraid maybe I'd think it was weakness in him, not wisdom, and could I be happy with enough and no more. So I kissed him and said all I wanted in life was his love, and whatever meant happiness to him would be my only ambition.

She looks up at her mother again — exultantly.

And I meant it, Mother! With all my heart and soul!

NORA

As before, patting her hair.

I know, darlin'.

SARA

Isn't that a joke on me, with all my crazy dreams of riches and a grand estate and me a haughty lady riding around in a carriage with coachman and footman!

She laughs at herself.

Wasn't I the fool to think that had any meaning at all when you're in love? You were right, Mother. I knew nothing of love, or the pride a woman can take in giving everything—the pride in her own love! I was only an ignorant, silly girl boasting, but I'm a woman now, Mother, and I know.

NORA

As before, mechanically.

I'm sure you do, darlin'.

She mutters fumingly to herself.

Let the police try it! He'll whip them back to their kennels, the dirty curs!

SARA

Lost in her happiness.

And then we put out the light and talked about how soon we'd get married, and how happy we'd be the rest of our lives together, and we'd have children—and he forgot whatever shyness was left in the dark and said he meant all the bold things he'd written in the poems I'd seen. And I confessed that I was up to every scheme to get him, because I loved him so much there wasn't anything I wouldn't do to make sure he was mine. And all the time we were kissing each other, wild with happiness. And—

She stops abruptly and looks down guiltily.

NORA

As before.

Yes, darlin', I know.

SARA

Guiltily, keeping her eyes down.

You—know, Mother?

NORA

Abruptly comes out of her preoccupation, startled and uneasy.

I know what? What are you sayin'? Look up at me!

She pulls Sara's head back so she can look down in her face—falteringly.
I can see— You let him! You wicked, sinful girl!

SARA
Defiantly and proudly.
There was no letting about it, only love making the two of us!

NORA
Helplessly resigned already but feeling it her duty to rebuke.
Ain't you ashamed to boast— ?

SARA
No! There was no shame in it!
Proudly.
Ashamed? You know I'm not! Haven't you told me of the pride in your love? Were you ashamed?

NORA
Weakly.
I was. I was dead with shame.

SARA
You were not! You were proud like me!

NORA
But it's a mortal sin. God will punish you—

SARA
Let Him! If He'd say to me, for every time you kiss Simon you'll have a thousand years in hell, I wouldn't care, I'd wear out my lips kissing him!

NORA
Frightenedly.
Whist, now! He might hear you.

SARA
Wouldn't you have said the same—?

NORA
Distractedly.

Will you stop! Don't torment me with your sinful questions! I won't answer you!

SARA

Hugging her.

All right. Forgive me, Mother.

A pause—smilingly.

It was Simon who felt guilty and repentant. If he'd had his way, he'd be out of bed now, and the two of us would be walking around in the night, trying to wake up someone who could marry us. But I was so drunk with love, I'd lost all thought or care about marriage. I'd got to the place where all you know or care is that you belong to love, and you can't call your soul your own any more, let alone your body, and you're proud you've given them to love.

She pauses—then teasing lovingly.

Sure, I've always known you're the sweetest woman in the world, Mother, but I never suspected you were a wise woman too, until I knew tonight the truth of what you said this morning, that a woman can forgive whatever the man she loves could do and still love him, because it was through him she found the love in herself; that, in one way, he doesn't count at all, because it's love, your own love, you love in him, and to keep that your pride will do anything.

She smiles with a self-mocking happiness.

It's love's slaves we are, Mother, not men's—and wouldn't it shame their boasting and vanity if we ever let them know our secret?

She laughs—then suddenly looks guilty.

But I'm talking great nonsense. I'm glad Simon can't hear me.

She pauses. Nora is worrying and hasn't listened. Sara goes on.

Yes, I can even understand now—a little anyway—how you can still love Father and be proud of it, in spite of what he is.

NORA

At the mention of Melody, comes out of her brooding.

Hush, now!

Miserably.

God help us, Sara, why doesn't he come, what's happened to him?

SARA
Gets to her feet exasperatedly.
Don't be a fool, Mother.
Bitterly.
Nothing's happened except he's made a public disgrace of himself, for Simon's mother to sneer at. If she wanted revenge on him, I'm sure she's had her fill of it. Well, I don't care. He deserves it. I warned him and I begged him, and got called a peasant slut and a whore for my pains. All I hope now is that whatever happened wakes him from his lies and mad dreams so he'll have to face the truth of himself in that mirror.
Sneeringly.
But there's devil a chance he'll ever let that happen. Instead, he'll come home as drunk as two lords, boasting of his glorious victory over old Harford, whatever the truth is!
But Nora isn't listening. She has heard the click of the latch on the street door at rear.

NORA
Excitedly.
Look, Sara!
The door is opened slowly and Jamie Cregan sticks his head in cautiously to peer around the room. His face is battered, nose red and swollen, lips cut and puffed, and one eye so blackened it is almost closed. Nora's first reaction is a cry of relief.
Praise be to the Saints, you're back, Jamie!

CREGAN
Puts a finger to his lips—cautioningly.
Whist!

NORA
Frightenedly.
Jamie! Where's himself?

CREGAN
Sharply.
Whist, I'm telling you!

In a whisper.
I've got him in a rig outside, but I had to make sure no one was here. Lock the bar door, Sara, and I'll bring him in.
She goes and turns the key in the door, her expression contemptuous. Cregan then disappears, leaving the street door half open.

NORA

Did you see Jamie's face? They've been fightin' terrible. Oh, I'm afraid, Sara.

SARA

Afraid of what? It's only what I told you to expect. A crazy row—and now he's paralyzed drunk.
Cregan appears in the doorway at rear. He is half leading, half supporting Melody. The latter moves haltingly and woodenly. But his movements do not seem those of drunkenness. It is more as if a sudden shock or stroke had shattered his coordination and left him in a stupor. His scarlet uniform is filthy and torn and pulled awry. The pallor of his face is ghastly. He has a cut over his left eye, a blue swelling on his left cheekbone, and his lips are cut and bloody. From a big raw bruise on his forehead, near the temple, trickles of dried blood run down to his jaw. Both his hands are swollen, with skinned knuckles, as are Cregan's. His eyes are empty and lifeless. He stares at his wife and daughter as if he did not recognize them.

NORA

Rushes and puts her arm around him.
Con, darlin'! Are you hurted bad?
He pushes her away without looking at her. He walks dazedly to his chair at the head of the center table. Nora follows him, breaking into lamentation.
Con, don't you know me? Oh, God help us, look at his head!

SARA

Be quiet, Mother. Do you want them in the bar to know he's come home—the way he is.
She gives her father a look of disgust.

CREGAN

Ay, that's it, Sara. We've got to rouse him first. His pride'd nivir forgive us if we let thim see him dead bate like this.

There is a pause. They stare at him and he stares sightlessly at the table top. Nora stands close by his side, behind the table, on his right, Sara behind her on her right, Cregan at right of Sara.

SARA

He's drunk, isn't that all it is, Jamie?

CREGAN

Sharply.

He's not. He's not taken a drop since we left here. It's the clouts on the head he got, that's what ails him. A taste of whiskey would bring him back, if he'd only take it, but he won't.

SARA

Gives her father a puzzled, uneasy glance.

He won't?

NORA

Gets the decanter and a glass and hands them to Cregan.

Here. Try and make him.

CREGAN

Pours out a big drink and puts it before Melody—coaxingly.

Drink this now, Major, and you'll be right as rain!

Melody does not seem to notice. His expression remains blank and dead. Cregan scratches his head puzzledly.

He won't. That's the way he's been all the way back when I tried to persuade him.

Then irritably.

Well, if he won't, I will, be your leave. I'm needin' it bad.

He downs the whiskey, and pours out another—to Nora and Sara.

It's the divil's own rampage we've had.

SARA

Quietly contemptuous, but still with the look of puzzled uneasiness at her father.

From your looks it must have been.

CREGAN

Indignantly.

You're takin' it cool enough, and you seein' the marks av the batin' we got!

He downs his second drink—boastfully.

But if we're marked, there's others is marked worse and some av thim is police!

NORA

God be praised! The dirty cowards!

SARA

Be quiet, Mother. Tell us what happened, Jamie.

CREGAN

Faix, what didn't happen? Be the rock av Cashel, I've nivir engaged in a livelier shindy! We had no trouble findin' where Harford lived. It's a grand mansion, with a big walled garden behind it, and we wint to the front door. A flunky in livery answered wid two others behind. A big black naygur one was. That pig av a lawyer must have warned Harford to expect us. Con spoke wid the airs av a lord. "Kindly inform your master," he says, "that Major Cornelius Melody, late of His Majesty's Seventh Dragoons, respectfully requests a word with him." Well, the flunky put an insolent sneer on him. "Mr. Harford won't see you," he says. I could see Con's rage risin' but he kept polite. "Tell him," he says, "if he knows what's good for him he'll see me. For if he don't, I'll come in and see him." "Ye will, will ye?" says the flunky, "I'll have you know Mr. Harford don't allow drunken Micks to come here disturbing him. The police have been informed," he says, "and you'll be arrested if you make trouble." Then he started to shut the door. "Anyway, you've come to the wrong door," he says, "the place for the loiks av you is the servants' entrance."

NORA

Angrily.

Och, the impident divil!

SARA

In spite of herself her temper has been rising. She looks at Melody with angry scorn.

You let Harford's servants insult you!

Then quickly.

But it serves you right! I knew what would happen! I warned you!

CREGAN

Let thim be damned! Kape your mouth shut, and lave me tell it, and you'll see if we let them! When he'd said that, the flunky tried to slam the door in our faces, but Con was too quick. He pushed it back on him and lept in the hall, roarin' mad, and hit the flunky a cut with his whip across his ugly mug that set him screaming like a stuck pig!

NORA

Enthusiastically.

Good for you, Con darlin'!

SARA

Humiliatedly.

Mother! Don't!

To Melody with biting scorn.

The famous duelist—in a drunken brawl with butlers and coach-men!

But he is staring sightlessly at the table top as if he didn't see her or know her.

CREGAN

Angrily, pouring himself another drink.

Shut your mouth, Sara, and don't be trying to plague him. You're wastin' breath anyway, the way he is. He doesn't know you or hear you. And don't put on lady's airs about fighting when you're the whole cause of it.

SARA

Angrily.

It's a lie! You know I tried to stop—

CREGAN

Gulps down his drink, ignoring this, and turns to Nora—enthusiastically.

Wait till you hear, Nora!

He plunges into the midst of battle again.

The naygur hit me a clout that had my head dizzy. He'd have had me down only Con broke the butt av the whip over his black skull and knocked him to his knees. Then the third man punched Con and I gave him a kick where it'd do him least good, and he rolled on the floor, grabbin' his guts. The naygur was in again and grabbed me, but Con came at him and knocked him down. Be the mortal, we had the three av thim licked, and we'd have dragged auld Harford from his burrow and tanned his Yankee hide if the police hadn't come!

NORA

Furiously.

Arrah, the dirthy cowards! Always takin' sides with the rich Yanks against the poor Irish!

SARA

More and more humiliated and angry and torn by conflicting emotions —pleadingly.

Mother! Can't you keep still?

CREGAN

Four av thim wid clubs came behind us. They grabbed us before we knew it and dragged us into the street. Con broke away and hit the one that held him, and I gave one a knee in his belly. And then, glory be, there was a fight! Oh, it'd done your heart good to see himself! He was worth two men, lettin' out right and left, roarin' wid rage and cursin' like a trooper—

MELODY

Without looking up or any change in his dazed expression, suddenly speaks in a jeering mumble to himself.

Bravely done, Major Melody! The Commander of the Forces honors your exceptional gallantry! Like the glorious field of Talavera! Like the charge on the French square! Cursing like a drunken, foul-mouthed son of a thieving shebeen keeper who sprang from the filth of a peasant hovel, with pigs on the floor—with that pale Yankee bitch watching from a window, sneering with disgust!

NORA
Frightenedly.
God preserve us, it's crazed he is!

SARA
Stares at him startled and wondering. For a second there is angry pity in her eyes. She makes an impulsive move toward him.
Father!
Then her face hardening.
He isn't crazed, Mother. He's come to his senses for once in his life!
To Melody.
So she was sneering, was she? I don't blame her! I'm glad you've been taught a lesson!
Then vindictively.
But I've taught her one, too. She'll soon sneer from the wrong side of her mouth!

CREGAN
Angrily.
Will you shut your gab, Sara! Lave him be and don't heed him. It's the same crazy blather he's talked every once in a while since they brought him to—about the Harford woman—and speakin' av the pigs and his father one minute, and his pride and honor and his mare the next.
He takes up the story again.
Well, anyways, they was too much for us, the four av thim wid clubs. The last thing I saw before I was knocked senseless was three av thim dubbing Con. But, be the Powers, we wint down fightin' to the last for the glory av auld Ireland!

MELODY
In a jeering mutter to himself.
Like a rum-soaked trooper, brawling before a brothel on a Saturday night, puking in the gutter!

SARA
Strickenly.
Don't, Father!

CREGAN
Indignantly to Melody.
We wasn't in condition. If we had been—but they knocked us senseless and rode us to the station and locked us up. And we'd be there
yet if Harford hadn't made thim turn us loose, for he's rich and has
influence. Small thanks to him! He was afraid the row would get in
the paper and put shame on him.
*Melody laughs crazily and springs to his feet. He sways dizzily, clutching
his head—then goes toward the door at left front.*

NORA
Con! Where are you goin'?
*She starts after him and grabs his arm. He shakes her hand off roughly
as if he did not recognize her.*

CREGAN
He don't know you. Don't cross him now, Nora. Sure, he's only goin'
upstairs to bed.
Wheedlingly.
You know what's best for you, don't you, Major?
*Melody feels his way gropingly through the door and disappears, leaving
it open.*

SARA
Uneasy, but consoling her mother.
Jamie's right, Mother. If he'll fall asleep, that's the best thing—
Abruptly she is terrified.
Oh God, maybe he'll take revenge on Simon—
She rushes to the door and stands listening—with relief.
No, he's gone to his room.
She comes back—a bit ashamed.
I'm a fool. He'd never harm a sick man, no matter—
She takes her mother's arm—gently.
Don't stand there, Mother. Sit down. You're tired enough—

NORA
Frightenedly.
I've never heard him talk like that in all the years—with that crazy dead look in his eyes. Oh, I'm afeered, Sara. Lave go of me. I've got to make sure he's gone to bed.
She goes quickly to the door and disappears. Sara makes a move to follow her.

CREGAN
Roughly.
Stay here, unless you're a fool, Sara. He might come to all av a sudden and give you a hell av a thrashin'. Troth, you deserve one. You're to blame for what's happened. Wasn't he fightin' to revenge the insults to you?
He sprawls on a chair at rear of the table at center.

SARA
Sitting down at rear of the small table at left front—angrily.
I'll thank you to mind your own business, Jamie Cregan. Just because you're a relation—

CREGAN
Harshly.
Och, to hell with your airs!
He pours out a drink and downs it. He is becoming drunk again.

SARA
I can revenge my own insults, and I have! I've beaten the Harfords— and he's only made a fool of himself for her to sneer at. But I've beaten her and I'll sneer last!
She pauses, a hard, triumphant smile on her lips. It fades. She gives a little bewildered laugh.
God forgive me, what a way to think of—I must be crazy, too.

CREGAN
Drunkenly.
Ah, don't be talkin'! Didn't the two of us lick them all! And Con's all right. He's all right, I'm sayin'! It's only the club on the head makes him quare a while. I've seen it often before. Ay, and felt it meself. I

remember at a fair in the auld country I was clouted with the butt av a whip and I didn't remember a thing for hours, but they told me after I never stopped gabbin' but went around tellin' every stranger all my secrets.

He pauses. Sara hasn't listened. He goes on uneasily.

All the same, it's no fun listening to his mad blather about the pale bitch, as he calls her, like she was a ghost, haunting and scorning him. And his gab about his beautiful thoroughbred mare is madder still, raving what a grand, beautiful lady she is, with her slender ankles and dainty feet, sobbin' and beggin' her forgiveness and talkin' of dishonor and death—

He shrinks superstitiously—then angrily, reaching for the decanter.

Och, be damned to this night!

Before he can pour a drink, Nora comes hurrying in from the door at left front.

NORA

Breathless and frightened.

He's come down! He pushed me away like he didn't see me. He's gone out to the barn. Go after him, Jamie.

CREGAN

Drunkenly.

I won't. He's all right. Lave him alone.

SARA

Jeeringly.

Sure, he's only gone to pay a call on his sweetheart, the mare, Mother, and hasn't he slept in her stall many a time when he was dead drunk, and she never even kicked him?

NORA

Distractedly.

Will you shut up, the two av you! I heard him openin' the closet in his room where he keeps his auld set of duelin' pistols, and he was carryin' the box when he came down—

CREGAN

Scrambles hastily to his feet.

Oh, the lunatic!

NORA

He'll ride the mare back to Harford's! He'll murther someone! For the love av God, stop him, Jamie!

CREGAN

Drunkenly belligerent.
Be Christ, I'll stop him for you, Nora, pistols or no pistols!
He walks a bit unsteadily out the door at left front.

SARA

Stands tensely—bursts out with a strange triumphant pride.
Then he's not beaten!
Suddenly she is overcome by a bitter, tortured revulsion of feeling.
Merciful God, what am I thinking? As if he hadn't done enough to destroy—
Distractedly.
Oh, the mad fool! I wish he was—
From the yard, off left front, there is the muffled crack of a pistol shot hardly perceptible above the noise in the barroom. But Sara and Nora both hear it and stand frozen with horror. Sara babbles hysterically.
I didn't mean it, Mother! I didn't!

NORA

Numb with fright—mumbles stupidly.
A shot!

SARA

You know I didn't mean it, Mother!

NORA

A shot! God help us, he's kilt Jamie!

SARA

Stammers.
No—not Jamie—
Wildly.
Oh, I can't bear waiting! I've got to know—
She rushes to the door at left front—then stops frightenedly.

I'm afraid to know! I'm afraid—

NORA

Mutters stupidly.

Not Jamie? Then who else?

She begins to tremble—in a horrified whisper.

Sara! You think— Oh, God have mercy!

SARA

Will you hush, Mother! I'm trying to hear—

She retreats quickly into the room and backs around the table at left front until she is beside her mother.

Someone's at the yard door. It'll be Jamie coming to tell us—

NORA

It's a lie! He'd nivir. He'd nivir!

They stand paralyzed by terror, clinging to each other, staring at the open door. There is a moment's pause in which the sound of drunken roistering in the bar seems louder. Then Melody appears in the doorway with Cregan behind him. Cregan has him by the shoulder and pushes him roughly into the room, like a bouncer handling a drunk. Cregan is shaken by the experience he has just been through and his reaction is to make him drunkenly angry at Melody. In his free hand is a dueling pistol. Melody's face is like gray wax. His body is limp, his feet drag, his eyes seem to have no sight. He appears completely possessed by a paralyzing stupor.

SARA

Impulsively.

Father! Oh, thank God!

She takes one step toward him—then her expression begins to harden.

NORA

Sobs with relief.

Oh, praise God you're alive! Sara and me was dead with fear—

She goes toward them.

Con! Con, darlin'!

CREGAN

Dumps Melody down on the nearest chair at left of the small table—roughly, his voice trembling.

Let you sit still now, Con Melody, and behave like a gintleman!

To Nora.

Here he is for ye, Nora, and you're welcome, bad luck to him!

He moves back as Nora comes and puts her arms around Melody and hugs him tenderly.

NORA

Oh, Con, Con, I was so afeered for you!

He does not seem to hear or see her, but she goes on crooning to him comfortingly as if he were a sick child.

CREGAN

He was in the stable. He'd this pistol in his hand, with the mate to it on the floor beside the mare.

He shudders and puts the pistol on the table shakenly.

It's mad he's grown entirely! Let you take care av him now, his wife and daughter! I've had enough. I'm no damned keeper av lunatics!

He turns toward the barroom.

SARA

Wait, Jamie. We heard a shot. What was it?

CREGAN

Angrily.

Ask him, not me!

Then with bewildered horror.

He kilt the poor mare, the mad fool!

Sara stares at him in stunned amazement.

I found him on the floor with her head in his lap, and her dead. He was sobbing like a soul in hell—

He shudders.

Let me get away from the sight of him where there's men in their right senses laughing and singing!

He unlocks the barroom door.

And don't be afraid, Sara, that I'll tell the boys a word av this. I'll talk of our fight in the city only, because it's all I want to remember.

He jerks open the door and goes in the bar, slamming the door quickly behind him. A roar of welcome is heard as the crowd greets his arrival. Sara locks the door again. She comes back to the center table, staring at Melody, an hysterical, sneering grin making her lips quiver and twitch.

SARA

What a fool I was to be afraid! I might know you'd never do it as long as a drink of whiskey was left in the world! So it was the mare you shot?
She bursts into uncontrollable, hysterical laughter. It penetrates Melody's stupor and he stiffens rigidly on his chair, but his eyes remain fixed on the table top.

NORA

Sara! Stop! For the love av God, how can you laugh—!

SARA

I can't—help it, Mother. Didn't you hear—Jamie? It was the mare he shot!
She gives way to laughter again.

NORA

Distractedly.
Stop it, I'm sayin'!
Sara puts her hand over her mouth to shut off the sound of her laughing, but her shoulders still shake. Nora sinks on the chair at rear of the table. She mutters dazedly.
Kilt his beautiful mare? He must be mad entirely.

MELODY

Suddenly speaks, without looking up, in the broadest brogue, his voice coarse and harsh.
Lave Sara laugh. Sure, who could blame her? I'm roarin' meself inside me. It's the damnedest joke a man ivir played on himself since time began.
They stare at him. Sara's laughter stops. She is startled and repelled by his brogue. Then she stares at him suspiciously, her face hardening.

SARA

What joke? Do you think murdering the poor mare a good joke?

Melody stiffens for a second, but that is all. He doesn't look up or reply.

NORA
Frightened.
Look at the dead face on him, Sara. He's like a corpse.
She reaches out and touches one of his hands on the table top with a furtive tenderness—pleadingly.
Con, darlin'. Don't!

MELODY
Looks up at her. His expression changes so that his face loses all its remaining distinction and appears vulgar and common, with a loose, leering grin on his swollen lips.
Let you not worry, Allanah. Sure, I'm no corpse, and with a few drinks in me, I'll soon be lively enough to suit you.

NORA
Miserably confused.
Will you listen to him, Sara—puttin' on the brogue to torment us.

SARA
Growing more uneasy but sneering.
Pay no heed to him, Mother. He's play-acting to amuse himself. If he's that cruel and shameless after what he's done—

NORA
Defensively.
No, it's the blow on the head he got fightin' the police.

MELODY
Vulgarly.
The blow, me foot! That's Jamie Cregan's blather. Sure, it'd take more than a few clubs on the head to darken my wits long. Me brains, if I have any, is clear as a bell. And I'm not puttin' on brogue to tormint you, me darlint. Nor play-actin', Sara. That was the Major's game. It's quare, surely, for the two av ye to object when I talk in me natural tongue, and yours, and don't put on airs loike the late lamented auld liar and lunatic, Major Cornelius Melody, av His Majesty's Seventh Dragoons, used to do.

NORA

God save us, Sara, will you listen!

MELODY

But he's dead now, and his last bit av lyin' pride is murthered and stinkin'.

He pats Nora's hand with what seems to be genuine comforting affection.
So let you be aisy, darlint. He'll nivir again hurt you with his sneers, and his pretindin' he's a gintleman, blatherin' about pride and honor, and his boastin' av duels in the days that's gone, and his showin' off before the Yankees, and thim laughin' at him, prancing around drunk on his beautiful thoroughbred mare—

He gulps as if he were choking back a sob.
For she's dead, too, poor baste.

SARA

This is becoming unbearable for her—tensely.
Why—why did you kill her?

MELODY

Why did the Major, you mean! Be Christ, you're stupider than I thought you, if you can't see that. Wasn't she the livin' reminder, so to spake, av all his lyin' boasts and dreams? He meant to kill her first wid one pistol, and then himself wid the other. But faix, he saw the shot that killed her had finished him, too. There wasn't much pride left in the auld lunatic, anyway, and seeing her die made an end av him. So he didn't bother shooting himself, because it'd be a mad thing to waste a good bullet on a corpse!

He laughs coarsely.

SARA

Tensely.
Father! Stop it!

MELODY

Didn't I tell you there was a great joke in it? Well, that's the joke.
He begins to laugh again but he chokes on a stifled sob. Suddenly his face loses the coarse, leering, brutal expression and is full of anguished grief. He speaks without brogue, not to them but aloud to himself.

Blessed Christ, the look in her eyes by the lantern light with life ebbing out of them—wondering and sad, but still trustful, not reproaching me—with no fear in them—proud, understanding pride —loving me—she saw I was dying with her. She understood! She forgave me!

He starts to sob but wrenches himself out of it and speaks in broad, jeering brogue.

Begorra, if that wasn't the mad Major's ghost speakin'! But be damned to him, he won't haunt me long, if I know it! I intind to live at my ease from now on and not let the dead bother me, but enjoy life in my proper station as auld Nick Melody's son. I'll bury his Major's damned red livery av bloody England deep in the ground and he can haunt its grave if he likes, and boast to the lonely night av Talavera and the ladies of Spain and fightin' the French!

With a leer.

Troth, I think the boys is right when they say he stole the uniform and he nivir fought under Wellington at all. He was a terrible liar, as I remember him.

NORA

Con, darlin', don't be grievin' about the mare. Sure, you can get another. I'll manage—

SARA

Mother! Hush!

To Melody, furiously.

Father, will you stop this mad game you're playing—?

MELODY

Roughly.

Game, is it? You'll find it's no game. It was the Major played a game all his life, the crazy auld loon, and cheated only himself. But I'll be content to stay meself in the proper station I was born to, from this day on.

With a cunning leer at Sara.

And it's meself feels it me duty to give you a bit av fatherly advice, Sara darlint, while my mind is on it. I know you've great ambition, so remember it's to hell wid honor if ye want to rise in this world.

Remember the blood in your veins and be your grandfather's true descendent. There was an able man for you! Be Jaysus, he nivir felt anything beneath him that could gain him something, and for lyin' tricks to swindle the bloody fools of gintry, there wasn't his match in Ireland, and he ended up wid a grand estate, and a castle, and a pile av gold in the bank.

SARA
Distractedly.
Oh, I hate you!

NORA
Sara!

MELODY
Goes on as if he hadn't heard.
I know he'd advise that to give you a first step up, darlint, you must make the young Yankee gintleman have you in his bed, and afther he's had you, weep great tears and appeal to his honor to marry you and save yours. Be God, he'll nivir resist that, if I know him, for he's a young fool, full av dacency and dreams, and looney, too, wid a touch av the poet in him. Oh, it'll be aisy for you—

SARA
Goaded beyond bearing.
I'll make you stop your dirty brogue and your play-acting!
She leans toward him and speaks with taunting vindictiveness, in broad brogue herself.
Thank you kindly but I've already taken your wise advice, Father. I made him have me in his bed, while you was out drunk fightin' the police!

NORA
Frightenedly.
Sara! Hault your brazen tongue!

MELODY
His body stiffens on his chair and the coarse leer vanishes from his face. It becomes his old face. His eyes fix on her in a threatening stare. He speaks slowly, with difficulty keeping his words in brogue.

Did you now, God bless you! I might have known you'd not take any chance that the auld loon av a Major, going out to revenge an insult to you, would spoil your schemes.

He forces a horrible grin.

Be the living God, it's me should be proud this night that one av the Yankee gintry has stooped to be seduced by my slut av a daughter! *Still keeping his eyes fixed on hers, he begins to rise from his chair, his right hand groping along the table top until it clutches the dueling pistol. He aims it at Sara's heart, like an automaton, his eyes as cold, deadly, and merciless as they must have been in his duels of long ago. Sara is terrified but she stands unflinchingly.*

NORA

Horror-stricken, lunges from her chair and grabs his arm.

Con! For the love av God! Would you be murthering Sara?

A dazed look comes over his face. He grows limp and sinks back on his chair and lets the pistol slide from his fingers on the table. He draws a shuddering breath—then laughs hoarsely.

MELODY

With a coarse leer.

Murtherin' Sara, is it? Are ye daft, Nora? Sure, all I want is to congratulate her!

SARA

Hopelessly.

Oh!

She sinks down on her chair at rear of the center table and covers her face with her hands.

NORA

With pitifully well-meant reassurance.

It's all right, Con. The young lad wants to marry her as soon as can be, she told me, and he did before.

MELODY

Musha, but that's kind of him! Be God, we ought to be proud av our daughter, Nora. Lave it to her to get what she wants by hook or crook. And won't we be proud watchin' her rise in the world till she's a grand lady!

NORA
Simply.
We will, surely.

SARA
Mother!

MELODY
She'll have some trouble, rootin' out his dreams. He's set in his proud, noble ways, but she'll find the right trick! I'd lay a pound, if I had one, to a shilling she'll see the day when she'll wear fine silks and drive in a carriage wid a naygur coachman behind spankin' thoroughbreds, her nose in the air; and she'll live in a Yankee mansion, as big as a castle, on a grand estate av stately woodland and soft green meadows and a lake.
With a leering chuckle.
Be the Saints, I'll start her on her way by making her a wedding present av the Major's place where he let her young gintleman build his cabin—the land the Yankees swindled him into buyin' for his American estate, the mad fool!
He glances at the dueling pistol—jeeringly.
Speakin' av the departed, may his soul roast in hell, what am I doin' wid his pistol? Be God, I don't need pistols. Me fists, or a club if it's handy, is enough. Didn't me and Jamie lick a whole regiment av police this night?

NORA
Stoutly.
You did, and if there wasn't so many av thim—

MELODY
Turns to her—grinningly.
That's the talk, darlint! Sure, there's divil a more loyal wife in the whole world—
He pauses, staring at her—then suddenly kisses her on the lips, roughly but with a strange real tenderness.

and I love you.

NORA
With amazed, unthinking joy.
Oh, Con!

MELODY
Grinning again.
I've meant to tell you often, only the Major, damn him, had me
under his proud thumb.
He pulls her over and kisses her hair.

NORA
Is it kissin' my hair— !

MELODY
I am. Why wouldn't I? You have beautiful hair, God bless you! And
don't remember what the Major used to tell you. The gintleman's
sneers he put on is buried with him. I'll be a real husband to you, and
help ye run this shebeen, instead of being a sponge. I'll fire Mickey
and tend the bar myself, like my father's son ought to.

NORA
You'll not! I'll nivir let you!

MELODY
Leering cunningly.
Well, I offered, remember. It's you refused. Sure, I'm not in love with
work, I'll confess, and maybe you're right not to trust me too near
the whiskey.
He licks his lips.
Be Jaysus, that reminds me. I've not had a taste for hours. I'm dyin'
av thirst.

NORA
Starts to rise.
I'll get you—

MELODY
Pushes her back on her chair.
Ye'll not. I want company and singin' and dancin' and great laugh-

ter. I'll join the boys in the bar and help Cousin Jamie celebrate our wonderful shindy wid the police.

He gets up. His old soldierly bearing is gone. He slouches and his movements are shambling and clumsy, his big hairy hands dangling at his sides. In his torn, disheveled, dirt-stained uniform, he looks like a loutish, grinning clown.

NORA

You ought to go to bed, Con darlin', with your head hurted.

MELODY

Me head? Faix, it was nivir so clear while the Major lived to tormint me, makin' me tell mad lies to excuse his divilments.
He grins.
And I ain't tired a bit. I'm fresh as a man new born. So I'll say goodnight to you, darlint.
He bends and kisses her. Sara has lifted her tear-stained face from her hands and is staring at him with a strange, anguished look of desperation. He leers at her.
And you go to bed, too, Sara. Troth, you deserve a long, dreamless slape after all you've accomplished this day.

SARA

Please! Oh, Father, I can't bear— Won't you be yourself again?

MELODY

Threatening her good-humoredly.
Let you kape your mouth closed, ye slut, and not talk like you was ashamed of me, your father. I'm not the Major who was too much of a gintleman to lay hand on you. Faix, I'll give you a box on the ear that'll teach you respect, if ye kape on trying to raise the dead!
She stares at him, sick and desperate. He starts toward the bar door.

SARA

Springs to her feet.
Father! Don't go in with those drunken scum! Don't let them hear and see you! You can drink all you like here. Jamie will come and keep you company. He'll laugh and sing and help you celebrate Talavera—

MELODY
Roughly.
To hell wid Talavera!
His eyes are fastened on the mirror. He leers into it.
Be Jaysus, if it ain't the mirror the auld loon was always admirin' his
mug in while he spouted Byron to pretend himself was a lord wid a
touch av the poet—
*He strikes a pose which is a vulgar burlesque of his old before-the-mirror
one and recites in mocking brogue.*
  "I have not loved the World, nor the World me;
    I have not flatthered uts rank breath, nor bowed
    To uts idolatries a pashunt knee,
    Nor coined me cheek to smiles,—nor cried aloud
    In worship av an echo: in the crowd
    They couldn't deem me one av such—I stood
    Among thim, but not av thim . . ."
He guffaws contemptuously.
Be Christ, if he wasn't the joke av the world, the Major. He should
have been a clown in a circus. God rest his soul in the flames av tor-
mint!
Roughly.
But to hell wid the dead.
*The noise in the bar rises to an uproar of laughter as if Jamie had just
made some climactic point in his story. Melody looks away from the mir-
ror to the bar door.*
Be God, *I'm* alive and in the crowd they *can* deem me one av such!
I'll be among thim and av thim, too—and make up for the lonely
dog's life the Major led me.
He goes to thc bar door.

SARA
Starts toward him—beseechingly.
Father! Don't put this final shame on yourself. You're not drunk now.
There's no excuse you can give yourself. You'll be as dead to yourself
after, as if you'd shot yourself along with the mare!

MELODY
Leering—with a wink at Nora.

Listen to her, Nora, reproachin' me because I'm not drunk. Troth, that's a condition soon mended.
He puts his hand on the knob of the door.

SARA
Father!

NORA
Has given way to such complete physical exhaustion, she hardly hears, much less comprehends what is said—dully.
Lave him alone, Sara. It's best.

MELODY
As another roar is heard from the bar.
I'm missin' a lot av fun. Be God, I've a bit of news to tell the boys that'll make them roar the house down. The Major's passin' to his eternal rest has set me free to jine the Democrats, and I'll vote for Andy Jackson, the friend av the common men like me, God bless him!
He grins with anticipation.
Wait till the boys hear that!
He starts to turn the knob.

SARA
Rushes to him and grabs his arm.
No! I won't let you! It's my pride, too!
She stammers.
Listen! Forgive me, Father! I know it's my fault—always sneering and insulting you—but I only meant the lies in it. The truth—Talavera—the Duke praising your bravery—an officer in his army—even the ladies in Spain—deep down that's been my pride, too—that I was your daughter. So don't— I'll do anything you ask— I'll even tell Simon—that after his father's insult to you—I'm too proud to marry a Yankee coward's son!

MELODY
Has been visibly crumbling as he listens until he appears to have no character left in which to hide and defend himself. He cries wildly and despairingly, as if he saw his last hope of escape suddenly cut off.

Sara! For the love of God, stop—let me go—!

NORA

Dully.

Lave your poor father be. It's best.

In a flash Melody recovers and is the leering peasant again.

SARA

With bitter hopelessness.

Oh, Mother! Why couldn't you be still!

MELODY

Roughly.

Why can't you, ye mean. I warned ye what ye'd get if ye kept on interferin' and tryin' to raise the dead.

He cuffs her on the side of the head. It is more of a playful push than a blow, but it knocks her off balance back to the end of the table at center.

NORA

Aroused—bewilderedly.

God forgive you, Con!

Angrily.

Don't you be hittin' Sara now. I've put up with a lot but I won't—

MELODY

With rough good nature.

Shut up, darlint. I won't have to again.

He grins leeringly at Sara.

That'll teach you, me proud Sara! I know you won't try raisin' the dead any more. And let me hear no more gab out of you about not marryin' the young lad upstairs. Be Jaysus, haven't ye any honor? Ye seduced him and ye'll make an honest gentleman av him if I have to march ye both by the scruff av the neck to the nearest church.

He chuckles—then leeringly.

And now with your permission, ladies both, I'll join me good friends in the bar.

He opens the door and passes into the bar, closing the door behind him. There is a roar of welcoming drunken shouts, pounding of glasses on bar and tables, then quiet as if he had raised a hand for silence, followed by his voice greeting them and ordering drinks, and other roars of acclaim mingled with the music of Riley's pipes. Sara remains standing by the side of the center table, her shoulders bowed, her head hanging, staring at the floor.

NORA

Overcome by physical exhaustion again, sighs.
Don't mind his giving you a slap. He's still quare in his head. But he'll sing and laugh and drink a power av whiskey and slape sound after, and tomorrow he'll be himself again—maybe.

SARA

Dully—aloud to herself rather than to her mother.
No. He'll never be. He's beaten at last and he wants to stay beaten. Well, I did my best. Though why I did, I don't know. I must have his crazy pride in me.
She lifts her head, her face hardening—bitterly.
I mean, the late Major Melody's pride. I mean, I did have it. Now it's dead—thank God—and I'll make a better wife for Simon.
There is a sudden lull in the noise from the bar, as if someone had called for silence—then Melody's voice is plainly heard in the silence as he shouts a toast: "Here's to our next President, Andy Jackson! Hurroo for Auld Hickory, God bless him!" *There is a drunken chorus of answering* "hurroos" *that shakes the walls.*

NORA

Glory be to God, cheerin' for Andy Jackson! Did you hear him, Sara?

SARA

Her face hard.
I heard someone. But it wasn't anyone I ever knew or want to know.

NORA

As if she hadn't heard.
Ah well, that's good. They won't all be hatin' him now.
She pauses—her tired, worn face becomes suddenly shy and tender.
Did you hear him tellin' me he loved me, Sara? Did you see him kiss me on the mouth—and then kiss my hair?
She gives a little, soft laugh.

Sure, he must have gone mad altogether!

SARA

Stares at her mother. Her face softens.

No, Mother, I know he meant it. He'll keep on meaning it, too, Mother. He'll be free to, now.

She smiles strangely.

Maybe I deserved the slap for interfering.

NORA

Preoccupied with her own thoughts.

And if he wants to kape on makin' game of everyone, puttin' on the brogue and actin' like one av thim in there—

She nods toward the bar.

Well, why shouldn't he if it brings him peace and company in his loneliness? God pity him, he's had to live all his life alone in the hell av pride.

Proudly.

And I'll play any game he likes and give him love in it. Haven't I always?

She smiles.

Sure, I have no pride at all—except that.

SARA

Stares at her—moved.

You're a strange, noble woman, Mother. I'll try and be like you.

She comes over and hugs her—then she smiles tenderly.

I'll wager Simon never heard the shot or anything. He was sleeping like a baby when I left him. A cannon wouldn't wake him.

In the bar, Riley starts playing a reel on his pipes and there is the stamp of dancing feet. For a moment Sara's face becomes hard and bitter again. She tries to be mocking.

Faith, Patch Riley don't know it but he's playing a requiem for the dead.

Her voice trembles.

May the hero of Talavera rest in peace!

She breaks down and sobs, hiding her face on her mother's shoulder— bewilderedly.

But why should I cry, Mother? Why do I mourn for him?

NORA

At once forgetting her own exhaustion, is all tender, loving help and comfort.

Don't, darlin', don't. You're destroyed with tiredness, that's all. Come on to bed, now, and I'll help you undress and tuck you in.

Trying to rouse her—in a teasing tone.

Shame on you to cry when you have love. What would the young lad think of you?

CURTAIN

More Stately Mansions

Scenes

ACT 1, SCENE 1

Dining room of Melody's Tavern, an Inn in a Massachusetts village near a city—night in October 1832

ACT 1, SCENE 2

A cabin on the shore of a small lake near the village—the following afternoon

ACT 2, SCENE 1

Deborah's garden, Henry Harford's home in the city—a night in summer 1836

ACT 2, SCENE 2

Sitting-room of Sara Harford's home in a neighboring textile mill town—the following night

ACT 3, SCENE 1

Simon Harford's office at Simon Harford, Inc. in the city—a morning in Fall of 1840

ACT 3, SCENE 2

Deborah's garden, the Harford home in the city—afternoon of the same day

ACT 3, SCENE 3

The parlor of the Harford home—night of the same day

ACT 4, SCENE 1
Simon Harford's office again—morning in summer 1841

ACT 4, SCENE 2
Deborah's garden—evening of the same night

EPILOGUE
*Same as Act One, Scene Two, the cabin on the lake—
afternoon in Spring, 1842*

Characters

JAMIE CREGAN

MICKEY MALOY

NORA MELODY

SARA *(Mrs. Simon Harford), her daughter*

SIMON HARFORD, *Sara's husband*

JOEL HARFORD, *his brother*

DEBORAH *(Mrs. Henry Harford), mother of Simon and Joel*

ETHAN

WOLFE

JONATHAN

OWEN *(Honey)*

} *children of Simon and Sara Harford*

NICHOLAS GADSBY, *an attorney*

CATO, *the Harfords' coachman*

Act One, Scene One

The dining room of Melody's Tavern, an Inn in a Massachusetts village near a city. The Tavern is over a hundred years old. It had once been a prosperous haven for travellers, a breakfast stop for the stagecoach, but the stage line had been discontinued years ago and the Inn fallen upon lean, unprosperous days.

The dining room, and what is now the barroom, had once been a single spacious room, low-ceilinged, with heavy oak beams and panelled walls. It is now divided into two rooms by a pine partition, the barroom being the section off left. The partition is painted in a poor imitation of the panelled walls, which only makes it stand out more as an eyesore.

The appearance of the dining room gives evidence of a poverty-stricken neglect. Nothing in it has been repaired or freshened in years. The table-cloths are dirty and stained. On the partition at left, front, is a cracked mirror, hanging askew. Farther back, near the door leading to the Bar, a cupboard is fixed to the partition. In the rear wall, center, is the door leading to the street with two windows on either side of it. In the right wall, toward front, is a door to a little hallway off the kitchen, where the stairs to the upper floor are. At extreme front, right, is a high school-master's desk with a stool.

Four tables are placed around the room, one at left, front, one at rear, to the left of the street entrance, one at right in back of the door to the hall, and the fourth at center, front. The two which are at left, front, and at right are square with four chairs. The other two are larger with three chairs to each long side and a chair at each end. It is night of a day in Fall, 1832. The room is lighted by three cheap lamps in brackets, one to each wall, and a candle on the table at center, front.

Jamie Cregan is discovered sitting in the chair at front of the table at left front. He is fifty-two but drunkenness has aged him and he looks in his sixties. An obviously Irish peasant type, he is tall and emaciated. His face is long, hollow-cheeked and lantern-jawed with small dark eyes, a wide, loose-lipped mouth, a twisted broken pug nose. There is the scar of a saber-slash over one cheekbone. His ragged hair is a dirty white. He is dressed in old black clothes that are worn threadbare. A drunkard, there yet remains in him something likable, a fundamental decency, the dim flicker of an old soldier's courage and devil-may-care spirit. He sits slumped forward in his chair, sober now, in a stupor of melancholy, staring before him. A decanter of whiskey, three-quarters full, and several empty glasses are on the table in front of him.

For a moment after the rise of the curtain, there is silence. Then from the floor above comes the sound of voices and the rising and falling wail of an Irish keen for the dead. Cregan stirs and mutters to himself resentfully.

CREGAN
Ah, keen with your mouths and pretend, but there's divil a one in the world but miself and Nora cares in their hearts he's gone.
He slumps into brooding dejection again. The door from the Bar is opened and Mickey Maloy, the barkeep, comes in. Mickey is as typically the Irish peasant as Cregan. He is thirty-four with a sturdy physique beginning to run into fat. He has a healthy, honest, common, fresh-complected face with curly dark hair and small blue eyes, twinkling with an amiable cunning. His mouth is set in the half-leering grin of a bartender's would-be, worldly-wise cynicism. He glances at Cregan with a look of mingled liking and contempt for his weakness.

MALOY
Automatically appraising the decanter—grinning.
Glory be, it's three-quarters full yet! Are ye sick, Jamie?
Cregan gives no sign of having heard the jibe. Mickey sits in the chair opposite it.

I've been takin' stock of what liquor's left. There's enough for Nora to kape on. With me to help her—

Grudgingly.

and you too, if you'd stay sober—she'll have a livin' from this place.

He pauses, then goes on resentfully.

We'd have no cause to worry for Nora if it wasn't for the debts himself run up in the days he was playin' the grand gentleman.

CREGAN

Starts from his stupor and pounds his fist on the table angrily.

Let you close your big mouth—and him dead upstairs! I'll not hear a word against him!

MALOY

Unimpressed—contemptuously.

To hell wid you.

Cregan relapses into dejection again. Maloy glances at him with a grudging sympathy.

But I know how ye feel, Jamie, and I'm glad for him there's one to mourn him widout lyin'!

From upstairs there comes again the wail of the keen. Maloy glances up.

Well, it's a beautiful wake Nora's givin' him, anyways, and a grand funeral tomorrow.

He gives Cregan a nudge.

Let you rouse yourself, Jamie, and not sit there half dead. Come on, have a taste wid me like Con Melody'd want you to if he was alive here. You know he'd only laugh at you and call you a liar for pretendin' grief at his death.

CREGAN

With a change of mood—resentfully.

He would, damn him! He couldn't believe there was decency in anyone.

He pours out a big drink from the decanter which Mickey has shoved toward him.

MALOY

Pours a small drink for himself.

Because there was none in him.

Raising his glass.
Here's health.
They drink.

CREGAN
Melancholy again.
Poor auld Con. The dew don't taste the same, an' him not here.

MALOY
Sardonically.
He's needin' a drink bad where he is now.

CREGAN
With a shudder.
Don't say it.

MALOY
Smacking his lips judiciously.
The dew tastes right to me. It's his private stock and he knew whiskey, if it did kill him.

CREGAN
Somberly.
It wasn't the dhrink killed him.

MALOY
Grins.
You'll be tellin' me next it was something he ate.

CREGAN
Angrily.
Yerrah, don't make fool's jokes an' Con Melody a corpse. It wasn't whiskey killed him, I'm sayin'. He was strong as a bull an' his guts was made of iron. He could have drunk a keg a day an' lived for twenty years yet if the pride and spirit wasn't killed inside him ivir since the night he tried to challenge that Yankee coward, Harford, to a duel, and him and me got bate by the police and arrested. And then his own daughter turnin' traitor and marryin' Harford's son. That put the final shame on him! He's been a walkin' corpse ivir since, drinkin' to forget an' waitin' for death, while he'd be talkin' in brogue

wid all the bog-trotters came in, tellin' stories an' roarin' songs, an' dancin' jigs, pretendin' he had no edication an' was no bhetter 'an they were.

MALOY
Stubbornly.
He wasn't better. It was in the days before that happened, when he used to lie about bein' a gintelman, an' his father only a Galway shebeen-keeper, that he was pretendin'.

CREGAN
Harshly.
Arrah, don't talk! Didn't he go to the College in Ireland, and hadn't he his own estate till he ruined himself! Wasn't he as fine an Officer as you'd find in Wellington's Army when he was a Major of Dragoons in Spain and I served under him? To hell wid what his fader was! He raised Con to be a gentleman, and Con Melody was a gentleman!
He adds, making the sign of the cross.
May God rest his soul in peace.

MALOY
Crosses himself automatically.
Amen. I'll say no more. It's bad luck to spake ill of the dead, anyways.
He pauses.
Will Sara come for the funeral, d'you think?

CREGAN
Viciously.
God's curse on her if she don't! Nora wrote her when himself was bad took, and she's had plenty of time.

MALOY
I doubt she'll come. She hated him. You know as well as me there's nivir been a word between them in the four years since she married. And, anyways, she was always stuck up and givin' herself airs. I'll wager by this she's so high and mighty she'd feel shame to visit her poor Irish relations even for her father's funeral.

CREGAN
Fiercely.
Poor relations, is it? Her own mother!
The door from the hall at right is opened and Nora Melody appears.

MALOY
Warningly.
Whist!

*Nora walks slowly toward them. She is forty-five, a typical Irish peas-
ant woman with a shapeless, heavy figure. She must have been extremely
pretty as a girl—she still has beautiful eyes—but drudgery has worn her
down, constant weariness of body and spirit has made her too tired to
care about her appearance, so that, even now dressed in her best black
mourning, she appears older and more unattractive than she really is. She
has a round head with thinning grey hair, almost white, arranged with
a half-hearted attempt at neatness. Her face is broad with high cheekbones, the complexion a blotchy pallor. Everything about her body appears swollen—her neck, her nose, her lips, her sagging breasts, her legs,
feet, ankles, and wrists, her hands with fingers knotted by rheumatism.
Yet despite her appearance, there is a spirit in her that shines through her
grief and exhaustion, some will behind the body's wreckage that is not
broken, something kindly and gentle and unselfish, an essential humble
fineness of character, a charm.*

NORA
As she comes to them—complaining but without bitterness.
Faix, it's a great help you are, Mickey, sittin' here takin' your ease.

MALOY
Gets to his feet guiltily.
I've been makin' a list av the stock—

NORA
Wearily.
Arrah, who cares now? Go up to the wake, that's a good lad, and see
people have what they're wantin', an' lave me a chance to rest. My
legs are broken under me.

She sits down exhaustedly in Mickey's place at the table.

MALOY

I'll go, surely. But be damned if I'll ask what they're havin'! They'll drink ye out of house an' home wid any encouragement.

He goes to the door at right and goes out, grumbling to himself. Nora sags in her chair with a weary sigh. Cregan relapses into his mood of depression, staring before him. Nora glances at him.

NORA

You've nivir been up to the wake at all, Jamie.

CREGAN

Dully.

I don't want to look on him dead.

With bitterness.

An' I don't want to see the crowd av thim pretendin' sorrow to his corpse, who hated and mocked him livin.'

NORA

Gently reproachful.

You're bitter.

He doesn't reply. She looks at him with understanding sympathy—gently.

You're missin' himself, Jamie?

CREGAN

I am, Nora.

NORA

Pats his hand consolingly.

He's grateful for your sorrow, I know. You were the one friend he had in the world.

CREGAN

Bitterly.

I'm thinkin' now I was maybe only a drunken sponge who helped him kill himself.

NORA

Don't think it. Sure, you know as well as me, it was the broken heart of his pride murthered him, not dhrink. Think only of what good you did him. It was only wid you he'd forgit once in a while and let himself remember what he used to be. An' wid me.

Her voice breaking.

I'm missin' him, too, Jamie.

She sobs softly.

CREGAN

Pats her shoulder gently.

Don't cry. We'd ought to be glad for his sake. He's where he longed to be now in the peace of death.

Changing the subject abruptly to distract her mind.

Sara'd ought to come soon, don't you think?

NORA

Has stopped crying—dully.

Yes—if she'll come.

CREGAN

Without conviction.

Av course she'll come.

NORA

I don't know. What do I know of her now? It's four years since I've laid eyes on her. I've only her letters, an' what are letters? It's aisy to remember to write to hide you're forgettin'. An' Sara had great pride in her, her father's own pride, and great ambition to raise herself in the world, and maybe she's grown shamed of me.

CREGAN

God curse her, thin!

NORA

Immediately reacting defensively.

Let you not curse my Sara, Jamie Cregan! But it's my fault. I should be shamed to talk wrong of her, an' her so sweet in every letter, beggin' me kindly to visit her, an' her husban', too, God bless him, an' I nivir had the dacency to go, even when her children was born, but always was afeered to lave Con alone. An' she always asked if I needed money.

CREGAN

She nivir sent any.

NORA

If she didn't, it was because she knew I'd send it right back to her.
So don't you be sayin'—

CREGAN

Sullenly.

I'll say divil a word.

A pause.

What'll you do, Nora, now himself is gone?

NORA

Dully.

Kape on here. What else? It'll pay better now himself is gone. I'll
kape on until all his debts is paid.

She sighs wearily.

It'll take a long time.

CREGAN

Arrah, why don't you let them whistle for their money, like he did.

Admiringly.

It's little Con Melody ivir let debts bother him!

Then with a change of tone.

All the same I know, if he didn't, that the men he owed would have
kicked him out in the gutter, if they hadn't liked and trusted you.

NORA

Simply.

I never let Con know that.

Proudly.

True for you. They trusted me. And I'll pay every penny. I've my
pride, too.

CREGAN

Ye have. You're a good woman, Nora, an' the rist av us are dirt under
your feet.

NORA

With a touching, charming, pathetic little smile of pleased coquetry that lights up her face.

It's you have the blarneyin' tongue, Jamie.

CREGAN

With an answering grin.

I have not. I'm a great one for telling the truth, ye mean.

With a change of tone.

Maybe Sara'll pay off his debts for you.

NORA

Defensively.

She'll not, then! Do you think I'd ask her?

CREGAN

Why not? She's his daughter. She's a right—

NORA

Well, I've no right. She has her husband an' three young children to think of, an' another comin.' An' if I would take her money, what she's got is her husband's not hers.

With scornful pride.

Do you think I'd let a Harford pay for Con Melody? Even if I had no pride, I'd be afeered to. Con would rise from his grave to curse me!

CREGAN

With grim appreciation.

Aye, divil a doubt, he would! His rage'd bring him back from the flames of hell!

Then hastily.

I'm jokin'. Don't heed me, Nora.

Someone tries the handle on the bolted street door at rear. Then there is a knock.

NORA

Wearily.

Go tell them it's the side door for the wake.

Cregan goes and unbolts the door—then backs away as Sara with her husband, Simon Harford, behind her, step into the room.

Sara is twenty-five, exceedingly pretty in a typically Irish fashion, with a mass of black hair, a fair skin with rosy cheeks, and her mother's beautiful deep-blue eyes. There is a curious blending in her appearance of what are commonly considered to be aristocratic and peasant characteristics. She has a fine thoughtful forehead. Her eyes are not only beautiful but intelligent. Her nose is straight and finely modeled. She has small ears set close to her head, a well-shaped head on a slender neck. Her mouth, on the other hand, has a touch of coarse sensuality about its thick, tight lips, and her jaw is a little too long and heavy for the rest of her face, with a quality about it of masculine obstinacy and determination. Her body is concealed by the loose dress of mourning black she wears but, in spite of it, her pregnancy, now six months along, is apparent. One gets the impression of a strong body, full breasted, full of health and vitality, and retaining its grace despite her condition. Its bad points are thick ankles, large feet, and big hands, broad and strong with thick, stubby fingers. Her voice is low and musical. She has rid her speech of brogue, except in moments of extreme emotion.

Simon Harford is twenty-six but the poise of his bearing makes him appear much more mature. He is tall and loose-jointed with a wiry strength of limb. A long Yankee face, with Indian resemblances, swarthy-complected, with a big straight nose, a wide sensitive mouth, a fine forehead, large ears, thick brown hair, light brown eyes, set wide apart, their expression sharply observant, and shrewd but in their depths ruminating and contemplative. A personality that impresses one incongruously as both practical and impractical. He speaks quietly, in a deep voice with a slight drawl. He is dressed in black. He is carrying in his arms the youngest of his three sons, Jonathan, just a year old.

At first sight of Sara and Simon as they enter the room, the impression one gets of their relationship, [sic] *one feels that here is as loving and contented a marriage as one could find.*

SARA
As she enters—to Cregan with genuine warmth.
Jamie!
She holds out her hand.

CREGAN
Takes it coldly, bitter resentment in his voice.
Better late than never.

SARA
Hurt and resentful.
I came as soon as—

NORA
Has jumped to her feet—with a happy cry.
Sara, darlin'—

SARA
Rushing to meet her.
Mother!
They meet at left rear of the table at front and embrace and kiss. Meanwhile, Simon Harford stands just inside the door, smiling a bit embarrassedly. He turns to Cregan, who is closing the door, meaning to greet him pleasantly, but Cregan avoids his eye and leaves him standing there while he goes and sits sulkily in the chair at front of the table at left, rear.

NORA
Weeping with joyous relief.
You've come, God bless you!
She cries sobbingly but triumphantly over Sara's shoulder.
Didn't I tell you she'd come, Jamie Cregan!

SARA
Soothingly.
Of course I've come. There now, Mother dear, don't cry. You're making me cry, too.
She breaks away from her mother's embrace, smiling and brushing tears from her eyes.
And here's Simon waiting to greet you, Mother.

SIMON
Comes toward them, smiling at Nora with a genuine affection.
It's good to see you again, Mother.

NORA

Aware of him for the first time is embarrassed and instinctively bobs him an awkward curtsy—respectfully.

Good evening to you, Sor.

Then a smile of humble gratitude and pleasure as she diffidently takes the free hand he holds out to her.

Mother, did you call me? That is kind of you.

Then forgetting everything as her eyes fall on the baby.

Glory be, you've brought the baby.

SARA

I had to, Mother. The other two are old enough to leave with the servant. But he's too little yet.

NORA

Officiously maternal.

Arrah, ain't he as welcome as the flowers in May, the darlin'. Here! Give him to me, Sor.

Rebukingly to Sara.

Did you make your poor husband carry him, you lazy girl?

SARA

Laughingly.

No, Simon just took him outside the door. But he likes to, anyway.

Then solicitously as Nora cuddles the baby in her arms.

Careful, Mother. Don't wake him.

NORA

Teach your grandmother! If I didn't know how to carry babies, where would you be?

Then to Simon, mindful of her duty as hostess.

Take a chair, Sor. Sit down Sara Darlin'.

She sits at right of the small table at left, front. Sara in the chair at left end of the long table at front, center. Simon in the first chair at the same table to right, rear, of Sara. Nora croons over the baby.

Wake you, would I, Acushla? It's little she knows. My, haven't you a fine handsome face! You're the image of your grandfather—

She stops abruptly.

SARA

Sharply resentful.

He's not! There's not the slightest resemblance—

She stops abruptly, too.

NORA

Half to herself, her eyes sad and haunted.

Never mind, never mind. He's gone now.

She forces her attention on the baby and talks hurriedly.

What's your name, Darlin'? Your mother wrote me. Let me see can I remember. The first was Ethan. That's a quare Yankee name you'd not forget. The next was Wolfe Tone. That's a grand Irish hero's name you can't forget nather. And yours is—wait now—another Yankee name—ah!—Jonathan, that's it.

SARA

Maternally tender now.

And the one that's coming, if it's a boy, we're going to call Owen Roe.

NORA

Solicitously.

Ah, I was forgettin' you're—How are you feelin', Darlin'?

SARA

Embarrassed, with a glance at Simon.

As fine as can be, Mother. I'm so healthy it never has bothered me at all.

Changing the subject abruptly.

It was Simon's idea, the Irish names. He likes the sound of them. It's the poet in him.

Simon starts and gives her a strange suspicious glance.

Only he wanted to call them all Irish, but I wouldn't let him, it wasn't fair.

She laughs.

So we agreed to divide, and I'd choose the American ones, and he could—

CREGAN
Breaks in jeeringly.
So it was your husband had to shame you to give Irish names to your children, was it?
They all start, having forgotten his presence.

SARA
Stung.
Mother! I'll not stand Jamie insulting—

SIMON
Quietly admonishing.
Sara.
She glances at him and bites her lip.

NORA
Angrily.
Jamie! Hush your blather!
Cregan subsides sullenly. She turns to Simon apologetically.
Don't mind him, Sor.
From upstairs, at the wake, comes the sound of a wailing keen of sorrow. Sara starts and her face hardens. Nora's face grows dully grief-stricken. She mutters miserably.
We're all forgettin' him.
She looks at Sara appealingly.
Sara. You'll want to come up and see him now.

SARA
Stiffening—coldly.
If you want me to, Mother.

NORA
Sadly reproachful.
If *I* want?

SIMON
Quietly.
Of course, Sara wishes to pay her last respects to her father.

SARA

Again glances at him—then quietly.
Yes, I do, Mother.

NORA

Relieved—quickly, as if afraid Sara may change her mind.
Then come now.
She and Sara rise.
We'll leave the baby in the back room I've fixed for you. He won't
hear the noise there to wake him.
*She goes to the door at right. Sara starts to follow, her face set to face an
ordeal. As she passes Simon he takes her hand and pats it reassuringly.
For a moment she looks down into his eyes. Then her face softens with
love and she bends over and kisses him impulsively.*

NORA

Are you comin', Sara?

SARA

All hostility gone from her voice.
Yes, Mother.
*She goes quickly over and follows her mother off, right. A pause. Simon
stares before him abstractedly. Cregan, from his chair at left, rear, regards him, frowning. He has been watching everything and is having a
struggle with himself. He begins to feel liking and respect for Simon and
he bitterly resents feeling this. Finally he gets up and comes to the table
at left, front, ignoring Simon, and defiantly pours himself a big drink.
Simon gets up and approaches him smilingly with outstretched hand.*

SIMON

How are you, Mr. Cregan? I guess you've forgotten me. I met you
here once with Major Melody.

CREGAN

Placated in spite of himself, takes his hand—a bit stiffly.
I hadn't forgotten but I was thinkin' maybe you had.
Then punctiliously polite.
Will ye sit down and drink wid me, Mr. Harford?

SIMON

With pleasure, Mr. Cregan.

They sit down, Cregan at left—Simon at right of table. Simon pours a small drink and raises his glass.

Your good health, Sir.

CREGAN

Drink hearty.

Suddenly a fierce look of suspicious distrust comes over his face—harshly.

Wait! I've a better toast for you! To Ireland and the Irish and hell roast the soul of any damned Yank that wud kape thim down!

SIMON

Gravely.

Amen to that, Mr. Cregan. And may they gain what they have longed for and fought for so long—liberty!

He touches his glass to Cregan's and drinks. For a moment Cregan stares at him in comical confusion, then he gulps his own drink hastily.

CREGAN

Wiping the back of his hand across his mouth—abashed and respectful.

Thank ye, Sor.

Then in a burst of honest admiration.

You're a man, divil a less, and Sara has a right to be proud she's your wife.

SIMON

Embarrassed in his turn.

Oh no, it's I who should be proud to be her husband.

CREGAN

Flatly.

I don't agree with you.

He hesitates, staring at Simon uncertainly—then impulsively and appealingly, lowering his voice and speaking rapidly.

Listen, Sor. I've somethin' to say to you, before Nora comes. She's a grand woman!

As Simon is about to assent.

Oh, I know you know that or I'd not be talkin'. An' she's had hell's own life wid Con. Nora deserves peace in the days that's left her, if ivir a woman did. An' now he's gone, she's her chance. But there's his debts. It's her honor to pay them, but it'll take years of more slaving—

Again there is a wailing keen from the room above and suddenly his expression changes to a guilty self-contempt and he stares at the ceiling with a haunted, frightened look and mutters to himself.

Did you hear me, Con? It's a black traitor I am to your pride—beggin' from a Harford!

He turns on Simon fiercely threatening.

You'll forget what I've said, d'ye hear? I'm dead drunk; it's the whiskey talkin'!

Then as he hears a sound from the hall—imploringly.

Whist! Here's someone. For the love av God, don't let on to Nora I told ye or she'd nivir spake to me again!

Then quickly changing his tone as Sara enters from the hall at right.

It's a pleasure to drink wid ye, Mr. Harford. Will ye have another taste?

SIMON

Playing up to him.

Not now, thank you, Mr. Cregan.

Sara comes to them. She is white and shaken, her eyes have a stricken look, and her lips are trembling. Simon rises and puts his arm around her protectingly. She clings to him.

SARA

In a trembling voice.

You shouldn't have made me go, Simon. I'd forgotten him—almost. Now he's alive again—lying there in his Major's uniform I remember so well, with the old sneer I hated on his lips!

She shudders. Simon pats her shoulder but can find nothing to say. She goes on.

I couldn't stay. I can't bear the sight of death. It's the first time I've seen it and I hate it! It's life with you I love. I don't want to think it can ever end.

She stares before her strangely.

He was lying there with the old sneer—like death mocking at life!

SIMON
Soothingly.
Don't think of it. It's over now.

SARA
Controlling herself.
Yes, I know, I won't.
Forcing a smile.
You and Jamie seem to have gotten friendly all of a sudden. Don't you think I've got the best husband a woman could have, Jamie?

CREGAN
He's a man—if he is a Harford.
Sara resents this but sees that Simon is smiling and she smiles too. Cregan goes on hesitantly.
Askin' your pardon, Sor—but, av ye plaze, all them above at the wake will be gossipin' you're here, an' they'll take it bad if you don't go up—

SARA
Angrily.
Let them think what they please!

SIMON
Ignoring her—to Cregan.
I'll go right away.
He turns.

SARA
Clings to his arm.
No! I don't want death seeing you. We—we're so happy now. It'll bring bad luck.

SIMON
Smiles teasingly and pats her cheek.
Now, now. Remember what you promised me about your superstitions.

SARA
That I'd forget all but the good luck ones.

She forces a smile.
I'll try again, Simon.
She kisses him.
Go up then—only don't stay long.
Simon goes out right. Sara's eyes follow him. Then she sits in the first chair at left rear of the long table at center, her expression again strained and fearful. Cregan pours another drink and downs it, regarding her frowningly. Then he gets up and takes the chair on her right, at the end of the table.

CREGAN
With thinly veiled hostility.
You've changed, Sara.

SARA
Resenting his tone.
Have I?
Then resolved not to quarrel, forcing a smile.
Well, I hope it's for the better—for Simon's sake.

CREGAN
Sneeringly.
You've made yourself a fine, high-toned, Yankee woman, God pity you! It's great shame you must feel to have to come here an' associate wid us poor Irish.

SARA
Stung.
Jamie! You know that's a lie! You know it was Father I was always ashamed of and he's dead now.

CREGAN
Bitterly.
Thank God, you're saying.

SARA
You know I was ashamed of him just because he was such a crazy snob himself, with all his lies and pretenses of being a gentleman, and his being ashamed of my poor mother.

CREGAN

Grimly.

He had none of his auld lies and pretenses wid him the past years since you married an' broke his heart.

SARA

Are you trying to blame me—?

CREGAN

He pretended to be one av us, instead. He never spoke except in a brogue you could cut with a knife, like an ignorant bog-trotter had just landed—except when he was too drunk to watch himself.

SARA

With a shrinking movement.

I know. Mother wrote me.

Suddenly deeply moved in spite of herself.

Poor Father! God forgive him. He never knew what he was himself. He never lived in life, but only in a bad dream.

Then with an abrupt change to disdainful scorn.

You don't have to tell me, Jamie. Didn't I see him, before I left, own up life had beaten him and lose the last speck of pride?

CREGAN

An' you scorned him for it, and still do, even while you say it was his lyin' pride shamed you! Faix, you're his daughter still, as you always was! You're like him, inside you, as he was at his worst!

SARA

It's a lie!

Controlling her temper—quietly.

You've been drinking or you wouldn't be so unfair to me. I haven't changed, Jamie, not in the way you suspect.

CREGAN

We'll soon see. Tell me this, are you goin' to help your mother now in her troubles?

SARA

What do you think me? Of course, I'll help her! Don't I love her more than anyone in the world, except Simon and the children!

CREGAN
Eagerly.
That's the talk! Then you'll give your word to pay off his debts?

SARA
Stiffening.
His debts?

CREGAN
Misunderstanding.
Faix, ye didn't think he'd ivir paid them, did ye? He didn't change that much, divil a fear. He owed ivry one in creation—two thousand or more, it must come to. But I know how well your husband's bin doin' in his business. It'd be aisy for you to—

SARA

Would it, indeed! Do you think I'd ever ask Simon to give the money we've slaved to save to pay the debts of his drunken squandering? Two thousand! And just when we're planning to buy out Simon's partner—and us with children to bring up and educate! Do you think I'm a fool?

CREGAN
His anger rising.
It's for your mother's sake. They might take the roof from over her head.

SARA

A fine roof! Let them! It'll be a good thing to free her from it. She's been a slave to this drunkard's roost too long. And I'll look after her, never fear, and see she wants for nothing.

CREGAN

Ye think Nora'd take charity from you? It's plain you've forgot the woman your mother is.
Losing his temper.

You've become a Yankee miser wid no honor ye wouldn't sell for gold!

Furiously.

God's curse on your soul, an' your mother's curse—!

SARA

With a cry of superstitious fear.

No! Don't!

Then flying into a rage herself and lapsing unconsciously into peasant brogue.

Hold your gab! Is it the likes of a drunken fool like you, who's sponged on my father for whiskey since the time you came to America, just because you're his cousin—is it you has the impudence to be talkin' to me about honor?

CREGAN

Delighted at having broken her control—bitingly.

Someone has to—seein' you haven't any.

With a grin of vindictive pleasure.

I'm glad to hear ye talk in your natural brogue an' forget the grand lady. Faix, there may be some red blood in ye yet beneath your airs!

SARA

Shut your mouth or I'll—

She rises and seems about to strike him. Cregan chuckles. She controls herself—quietly.

I am sorry I lost my temper, Jamie. I ought to know better than to mind you.

CREGAN

Enraged again.

Arrah, to hell wid your lady's airs! I'd rather have your insults!

He stops abruptly as Nora appears in the doorway at right—getting to his feet, suddenly.

Here's herself. I'll be goin' up to the wake.

He passes Nora as she comes in and goes out right. Nora sits wearily in the first chair at rear of the center table, right.

NORA
Dully.
Was Jamie quarreling wid you? Don't heed him.

SARA
I don't, Mother.
She sits in the chair at her mother's right.

NORA
Sadly.
He's wild wid loneliness, missin' your father.
A pause. Nora's face lights up.
Mr. Harford came up to the wake.

SARA
Annoyed.
Don't say Mr. Harford. You must call him Simon.

NORA
Humbly.
It sounds too familiar, and him such a gentleman.

SARA
Nonsense, Mother! I don't like you to play humble with him—as though you were a servant. *He doesn't like it either.**

. . . . .

NORA
Resentfully.
Why wouldn't I?

SARA
Because it's crazy. To give up life for a living death! I'd rather kill myself!

---

*Beginning with the end of Sara's speech, "He doesn't like it either," there is a page missing from the typescript (p. 16). It is the page where Nora tells Sara that she is going to enter a convent. The next line ("Why wouldn't I?") is apparently in answer to Sara's negative response to Nora's news.

NORA

Don't be sneerin' just because your father, God forgive him, brought
you up a haythen.

Stubbornly.

I would do it—and I will!

SARA

With a mocking smile.

There's no worse thing you could do if you want to make Father turn
over in his grave.

NORA

Triumphantly.

He'll not, then! I've been waitin' to tell you. He came back to the
Faith before he died.

SARA

Startled.

He never did! I don't believe you!

NORA

It's God's truth, Sara! Afther the doctor said he was dyin' I begged
him. He wouldn't answer for a long time, until I said, "Con, if you've
ivir felt one bit av love for me, you'll do this for me now!" an' I cried
my heart out. Then he opened his eyes an' there was a quare smile in
them, an' he spoke, forgettin' to put on the brogue. "Yes," he says,
"I still owe you that last bit of pride to pay for your love, don't I?
An' I'm a gentleman about debts of honor, at least. So call in your
priest." An' I did, an' he died with the rites av the Church. So ye
needn't talk av his turnin' over in his grave.

SARA

Her face hard—with intense bitterness.

No. I needn't. There's not that much pride left in him now. Even his
spirit is dead.

NORA

Resentful and a bit frightened.

Why do you make that bitter talk, God forgive you? Ain't you glad
his soul's found peace, at last?

SARA

Not the peace of death while he was still alive. Oh, I know he died
long ago—the spirit in him. But maybe I hoped, in spite of hating
him, that he'd kept that last pride! Maybe I admired that one thing
in him—his defiance of a God he denied but really believed in!
She gives a bitter little laugh.
Well, I know now why he died with that sneer on his lips. It was at
himself!

NORA

Protesting pitifully.
It's no sneer at all! It's the smile av his soul at peace!
She breaks down and sobs.
Don't take that from me, Sara!

SARA

Moved and ashamed—patting her shoulder.
There Mother, don't. I—forgive me—
Changing the subject.
When will you go in the Convent?

NORA

Sadly.
God knows. Tomorrow if I could. But there's a pile av debts to be
paid first. I want no dishonor on his name, an' I'd feel it was cheatin'
to go in the Convent widout a clear conscience.
Then hastily.
But nivir mind that. You've your own troubles. And it's nothin' at
all.

SARA

Hesitates—then blurts out.
I can ask Simon—

NORA

Stiffening—proudly.
You'll not! You'll be kind enough to mind your own business av you
plaze!

SARA
Relieved and hating herself for being relieved.
But we'd be only too happy—

NORA
Gently.
I know, Darlin'—an' God bless you. But I'd nivir be able to look myself in the face if I held you back when you're just startin' in life.

SARA
But we could afford—

NORA
Roughly.
No, I'm sayin'! To the divil wid me! My life is done. All I ask for myself is a bit av peace before the end. But I'm askin' more for you! I want you to rise in the world, an' own the things your father once owned an' you was born to—wealth an' a grand estate an' you ridin' in your carriage like a Duchess wid coachman an' footman, an' a raft av servants bowin' an' scrapin'.

SARA
Her face lighting up—with a determined confidence.
I'll have all of that, Mother, I take my oath to you.

NORA
Enthusiastically.
So ye will, Darlin'! I know it! An' won't I be proud, watchin' you rise, an' boastin' to the world! Even in the Convent, I'll be prayin' the Blessed Virgin to help you!
Guiltily.
God forgive me, maybe I shouldn't say that.
Reassuring herself.
Ah, I know Almighty God will find it enough if I give up all worldly thoughts for myself an' He'll forgive my pride in you!
Dismissing this eagerly.
Tell me now—how is the business doin'? You haven't written in a long while.

SARA

Eagerly—unconsciously lapsing a little into brogue.

It's doing fine, Mother. We've just finished building an addition to the mill and the cottons we're weaving are as good or better than any foreign ones. By we I mean Matthew, too, but it'll soon be only us, because Simon is buying him out.

NORA

Proudly.

So he's buyin' out his partner, is he? The last you wrote, you didn't know if you could persuade him.

SARA

With a smile.

I had a hard time, he's that stubborn. I had to plead with him it was for my sake and the children's. He's so afraid of getting in too deep. And it's so silly because after I get his mind made up, there's no stopping him.

With a proud toss of her head.

And don't think it's just a wife, blind with love, boastin'. It's common talk of our town he's the ablest young merchant in the trade and has a great future before him.

NORA

Admiringly.

Ah, ain't that grand, now! You'd nivir think it to meet him—I mean, he's so quiet and gentle.

SARA

With a laugh.

Let you be a man meetin' him in business, and tryin' to get the best of him, you'd find him different.

Practically.

Of course, it doesn't do to boast yet. We're only on the first step. It's only a small mill that you wouldn't notice at all compared to the big ones. But business is leapin' up and once we have Matthew out of it—he wants to travel in Europe and he's only too anxious to sell at a bargain—we'll have all the profits for ourselves.

NORA

Teasing admiringly.

Musha, you have grand business talk! To hear you, you'd think it was you was his partner, no less!

SARA

So I am! I'm no fool, Mother. I've got brains for more than just sleepin' with the man I love an' havin' his children an' keepin' his house. Ask Simon. He talks over everything with me. I've made him. At first, he was all for never sayin' a word about business at home, and treatin' me like a stuffed bird in a glass case he had to protect from the world, but I soon got him over that. Now he depends on me, an' I'll say for myself I've never advised him wrong.

She smiles.

The only foolish thing he ever did he did without askin' me. He had someone buy the old farm here for him where he used to live in the cabin by the lake.

NORA

Did he, now? I heard tell it was sold. Ivery one was wonderin' who was the fool—

Hastily.

I mane, they say divil a one has ivir made it pay.

SARA

Frowning.

I know. It was foolish. But he was that shamed when I found out— like a little boy caught stealing jam—that I couldn't scold. And he had all kinds of excuses that it was a wise notion because, if the worst happened, it'd be easy to fix up the old farmhouse on it, and you could at least raise a living from it, and we'd always have it to fall back on. Then when I laughed at him and said that was no fear it'd ever come to that, he owned up he'd really bought it for sentiment because it was there we first loved each other.

NORA

Guiltily embarrassed.

Arrah, don't think av that now. Wasn't you married right after? God forgave you the sin.

SARA

Proudly defensive.

I've never asked His forgiveness. I'm proud of it.

Changing the subject abruptly.

So, of course, when he told me that, I forgave him. And maybe it'll come in useful in the end. There's over two hundred acres, and he bought it for a song, and the little lake on it is beautiful, and there's grand woods that would make a fine park. With a mansion built on the hill by the lake, where his old cabin was, you couldn't find a better gentleman's estate.

NORA

With admiring teasing.

Glory be, but you're sure av havin' your way!

SARA

Determinedly.

I am, Mother, for this is America not poverty-stricken Ireland where you're a slave! Here you're free to take what you want, if you've the power in yourself.

A pause—her expression suddenly becomes uneasily thoughtful.

I think Simon had other reasons for buying the farm he didn't tell me—maybe that he didn't tell even himself. He has queer lonely spells at times when I feel he's in a dream world far away from me.

NORA

Yes, he's a touch av the poet, God pity him—like your father.

A wailing keen comes from the floor above. Nora's face becomes sorrow-ridden. She shivers, and makes the sign of the cross.

SARA

Her thoughts made more uneasy by this disturbance—irritably.

Why do you let them keen, Mother? It's old ignorant superstition. It belongs back in Ireland, not here!

Then, as her mother doesn't hear her, she goes on uneasily.

Sometimes I feel he's thinking that if it wasn't for me and the children he'd be living alone back in his cabin by the lake writing poetry like he used to, or else writing the book he was planning, to show people how to change the Government and all the laws so there'd be no more poor people, nor anyone getting the best of the next one, and there'd be no rich but everyone would have enough.

She finishes scornfully.

He doesn't talk about that anymore, thank God! I've laughed it out of him! I've told him you can make new laws but you can't make new men and women to fit them, so what's the use of dreaming? I've said, even if he could make it come true, it would be a coward's heaven he'd have, for where is the glory of life if it's not a battle where you prove your strength to rise to the top and let nothing stop you!

She says this last with exultance. Then she smiles fondly.

But I'm a fool to take his dreams seriously. Sure, when he's himself, there's no one takes more joy in getting ahead. If you'd see his pride sometimes when he comes home to tell me of some scheme he's accomplished.

She laughs.

Oh, he's a queer mixture.

Then intensely.

And I love him, every bit of him! I love him more than ever any woman loved a man, I think. I'd give my last drop of blood to make him happy! And he is happy!

Again there is the wailing keen from the wake above. Nora gets to her feet, wearily.

NORA

Dully.

I'd better go up to the wake. They'll think it wrong I'm staying away from him so long.

She hesitates—feeling she must make some comment on what Sara has said, which she has only half heard.

I wouldn't worry over Simon bein' happy. Sure, you've only to see the love in his face when he looks at you.

Then inconsequently.

Does he ever hear from his people?

SARA

Resentfully.

From his father? No fear. He won't ever let Simon's name be spo-

ken in their home. But Simon's mother writes him letters. Not often, though. I'll say this for her, she's never tried to interfere.
Then cynically.
Maybe it's because Simon's father never gives her the chance.
Then honestly.
No, that's not fair. I ought to feel grateful to her. It was the two thousand dollars she sent Simon after we were married gave us our start.
Resentfully.
Not but what we didn't pay her back every penny as soon as we'd saved it. I made Simon do that, for all his saying she wanted it to be a gift and we'd hurt her feelings.
With a toss of her head.
I have my feelings, too. I'm accepting no gifts from her.

NORA
Has not been listening to this at all—dully.
I'll go up to him now.
She starts for the door at right as Simon enters it. He smiles at her and she forces a smile in return and goes out. He comes over and sits beside Sara, giving her a pat on the cheek as she smiles up at him.

SARA
How's the baby?

SIMON
Sound asleep.
He hesitates—then making up his mind—uncomfortably.
Listen, Sara. There's one thing we ought to talk over and decide right away—for your mother's sake.

SARA
Stiffens, glancing at him suspiciously.
What's that?

SIMON
Quietly.
About your father's debts.

SARA
Angrily.

How do you know? Was Jimmie Cregan begging to you?

SIMON
Placatingly.
Now don't blame him.

SARA
Angrily.
Ah, if that drunken fool would only mind his own business!

SIMON
Quietly.
It's your business, isn't it? And we're partners, aren't we? So it's my business, too. Please don't feel bitter toward Cregan. He may have his faults. Who hasn't?
Smiling.
Perhaps even you and I have some.
She glances at him with quick guilty suspicion.
But he is a good friend to your mother.

SARA
Sneeringly.
As long as she has free whiskey for him to sponge!

SIMON
Frowns—a bit sharply.
Sara! That's not—
He controls himself and pats her hand—gently.
I hate to hear you sneering and full of bitterness. That isn't you, you know.

SARA
Clasps his hand—humbly.
No. It isn't the me who loves you. I know that, Simon.
Resentfully.
It's coming here does it to me. It brings back the past. It makes Father live again. Ah, why can't he be dead, and not have his ghost walk in my heart with the sneer on his lips!

SIMON
Repelled.
Sara!
Then more gently—slowly.
One must forgive the dead, for their sakes, but even more for our own.

SARA
Squeezing his hand.
Oh, I know!

SIMON
Persuasively.
Try and forget him. It's of your mother we must think now. She has had a hard life. How hard you know better than anyone.

SARA
Sadly.
I do. Poor Mother! Not an hour of joy or peace did he give her since the day she married him, but only slavery.
Then hurriedly—and guiltily.
But the debts come to two thousand dollars. That's a pile of money, Simon. No matter how much we wanted to, we couldn't afford right now—

SIMON
Easily.
Oh, I think we can. You're forgetting what we've put aside to buy out Matthew. We can use part of that.

SARA
Tensely.
And not buy him out, after all our plans?
Angrily.
No! I won't have it!

SIMON
Sharply.
Sara!

SARA
Hastily.
I mean it means so much to your future that you'd never forgive
yourself!

SIMON
Quietly.
What about your mother's future? Could we forgive ourselves if we
deliberately ignored that?

SARA
Hurriedly.
And anyway, it's no use talking, because I've already talked to her. I
said I'd ask you to pay his debts for her.

SIMON
His face lighting up.
Ah, I knew you—

SARA
An undercurrent of triumph in her voice.
And she told me to mind my business for my pains! She was mad
and insulted. So you might as well put it from your mind.
With incongruous pride.
My mother may be an ignorant, simple woman but she's a proud
woman, too. If you think she'd ever let a Harford pay Father's debts,
you're badly mistaken.

SIMON
Quietly.
I know your mother's pride and I admire her for it.
Then with a smile—calculating.
But I think we can get around her, if we go about it shrewdly. In the
first place, before we let her know, I'll look up all the creditors and
pay them. Then we'll face her with an accomplished fact. She will
resent it, of course, but I've been figuring out a way to put it to her
so that she'll be reconciled—that it's a sin for her to put her duty to
God off just because of pride and that if she waited she might not
live to enter a Convent. I can even see the Priest and persuade him to

talk to her. I'll ask her, too, if it's fair of her to keep on the feud with my father against me, and if it isn't time, now your father's dead, to forgive and forget, for her grandchildren's sake, who have both Melody and Harford blood in them. I'll—

SARA
With a helpless sigh—exasperatedly.
Arrah, you needn't go on!
Her manner changing—with a trembling tender smile.
Don't I know better than any, without your boasting, that you're a sly one to look into a woman's heart and see her weakness and get your own way.
Proudly.
And don't I love you for it, and for being kind and sweet and good, and putting shame on me for a greedy selfish pig.
She raises his hand impulsively and kisses it.

SIMON
Tenderly.
Don't say that! You're the dearest, most precious—
He hugs her to him.

SARA
Stubbornly.
I'm not! I'm a fool always dreaming of wealth and power and pride, even while I know in my heart that doesn't matter at all, that your love is my only wealth—to have you and the children.
Pitifully.
But I can't help dreaming, Darling. I've known what you haven't— poverty—and the lies and dirt and hurt of it that spits on your pride while you try to sneer and hold your head high!

SIMON
Soothingly.
I know, Dear.

SARA
You don't. You couldn't.
Pleadingly.

But please know, Simon Darling, that for all the greed in me, I was only fooling myself. My conscience—and my honor, for I have honor, too—would never have rested easy until we paid the debts for Mother.

She laughs.

So thank you kindly, Sir, for beating me and saving me having to beat myself.

She kisses him.

SIMON
Teasing tenderly.
Maybe I guessed that.
He laughs.
You can't fool me.

SARA
Teasing, with a note of taunting coming in.
No. And you can't fool me. Don't I guess that, besides all your goodness of heart, you're glad of the excuse not to buy out your partner, because you're afraid of the whole weight of the business on your shoulders.

SIMON
Starts—sharply.
What makes you say that! It's not true. I should think I'd already given you ample proof. If I'm afraid it's not for that reason, as you well know.
Bitterly.
But, do you know, I wonder? Will you ever understand—?

SARA
Alarmed now.
Darling, I was only teasing.
Pulling him to her—with rough possessive tenderness.
Come here to me. Don't push away, now! Don't you know I wouldn't hurt you for the world?

SIMON
Giving in—but stiffly.

I don't like that kind of teasing.

She kisses him. He relaxes against her body. His face softens. Finally he forces a laugh.

Forgive me, I'm a fool.

Then almost boastfully.

To show you how wrong you are, I've already figured out how we can pay your father's creditors, and still buy out Matthew's interest.

SARA

Eagerly.

Ah, don't I always tell you you've the brains to beat the world!

SIMON

I'll simply get him to take my note for the difference.

SARA

Uncertainly.

I don't like notes. My father always—

SIMON

Tauntingly.

Who is being afraid, now?

Then eagerly.

But you needn't be. With the profits from the business, as I intend to reorganize it, I can pay him in no time, and then—

SARA

Gloatingly.

Oh, then I know you'll make the money come flying in!

She suddenly looks guilty and forces a laugh.

There I go with my greedy dreaming again. But it's because when we were married it was such a hurt to my pride that I knew your family and their friends thought you'd lowered yourself through me. I swore then I'd help you rise till you were bigger than your father or any of them.

SIMON

His face hardening.

It would be a satisfaction to me, too, to prove to Father, in the only terms he can understand—

SARA
Aggressively.
And to your mother.

SIMON
His expression changing—in a tone that is tinged with self-contempt.
Mother? I hardly think my achievement on that plane could impress
her greatly.

SARA
Why not, I'd like to know?

SIMON
Frowns and shrugs his shoulders.
Well, her point of view is a bit different from yours—ours, I should
say.—
He is interrupted by a knock on the door at rear.

SARA
Irritably.
Someone for the wake, I suppose. I'll go.
*She goes and unbolts the door—then starts back with a surprised gasp
as she sees a tall, black, powerfully-built negro in a coachman's uniform
standing before the door.*
What do you want?

CATO
Removes his hat—with polite dignity.
Mister Simon Harford, Ma'am. Is he heah?

SIMON
Astonished.
Why hello, Cato.
He goes back to meet him.
It's all right, Sara. Let him come in.
*She steps aside and Cato enters. He is about fifty-five with whitening,
crinkly hair. Simon, smiling with genuine pleasure, holds out his hand.
Cato takes it embarrassedly.*
It's good to see you again, Cato.

CATO
Grinning.
Thank you, Mister Simon. I'm happy to see you.
They come forward. Sara follows them, her expression uneasy and suspicious.

SIMON
This is my wife, Cato. She's often heard me speak of you.
Cato bows respectfully. Sara forces a smile.

SARA
Yes, indeed, Cato. He's never forgotten how good you were to him when he was a boy.

SIMON
Oh, Cato and I are old friends, aren't we, Cato?

CATO
Grins embarrassedly.
Thank you, Suh. Thank you, Ma'am. Your mother sent me, Suh. I'se got a letter she tol' me give in your hands and only your hands.
Sara stiffens resentfully. Cato takes a letter from his inside pocket and hands it to Simon.
She say wait til you read it and you tell me de answer and I tell her.

SIMON
Opens the letter. It is only a few lines. As he reads his face lights up.
Tell her my answer is, of course I'll meet her there.

CATO
Yes, Suh. I'll tell her. Now I better git back quick. She tell me sneak out and sneak in so nobody see and tell yo father.
He bows to Sara.
Good night, Ma'am. Good night, Suh.
He hesitates—then blurts out.
Effin you don't mind, I'se wishin' you happiness!

SIMON
Thank you, Cato. Good night.

SARA

Touched, her face softening.

Thank you, Cato. Good night.

Cato makes a hurried sidling-backwards exit through the door at rear, closing it behind him. Sara sits in the chair at right end of the table at center, front, her face again stiff and resentful. Simon stands with the letter in his hands, sunk in a smiling reverie. Then his eyes fall on Sara and he starts as if awakening.

SIMON

Here's Mother's letter, if you'd care to read it.

SARA

Stiffly.

No. It was meant for you alone.

SIMON

Nonsense. I'll read it to you. It's only a note.

He reads.

"I have your letter telling me you are coming up for your father-in-law's funeral and it occurs to me that we might take this opportunity to see each other again, if only for a moment. If you agree, and if Sara will consent to a brief leave-of-absence for you—"

SARA

Why shouldn't I consent? Does she think I'm afraid?

SIMON

Resentful in his turn.

Don't be silly. She's only joking.

He goes on reading.

"—let us meet at your old cabin tomorrow afternoon at three o'clock. I hope you can come. I am most curious to see how much you've changed, and I promise you will discover me to have changed, too, though not by evidence of the ravages of time on my poor face, I trust."

Then he laughs.

Hello. Here's a joke on her. I didn't notice before, but she's signed it "Deborah." She must have been in such a hurry—

SARA

It seems a strange letter to me.

SIMON

Impatiently.

I've always told you you can't judge anything she does by ordinary standards.

He smiles.

She takes a childish pride in being fancifully willful and eccentric. You surely saw that, the one time you met her, even though you only talked with her a moment.

SARA

I saw it, yes. And I guessed beneath it she was a woman with a will of iron to get her own way.

SIMON

Laughs.

Iron and Mother! That's funny, Sara. Quicksilver would describe her better.

SARA

Maybe. But she promises you she's changed.

SIMON

Smiling.

She couldn't change if she tried. From her letters of the past year or so, I'd say she had simply become more herself, if that were possible.

SARA

Maybe.

She hesitates—then slowly.

I wish you wouldn't go, Simon.

SIMON

Astonished.

Not go? When she asks me to? When we haven't seen each other in four years? Surely you wouldn't want me to hurt her like that?

Then shortly.

Anyway, I've already said I would go.

SARA

You could send a note by Jamie. You could lie and make an excuse.

SIMON

Sharply.

Sara!

He stares at her frowningly.

I can't understand—

His face softens and he puts his arm around her.

Here, here. This won't do. What has come over you?

SARA

Doggedly.

Why does she want you to meet her at your old cabin?

SIMON

Cajolingly.

Because it's out of the way and she won't be seen going there. She can't take any chance that Father might find out, you know. And I suppose it naturally suggested itself. I wrote her I had bought the property, so she knows she won't be trespassing.

SARA

Resentfully.

It's mine. You put it in my name. I hope you told her that.

With sudden agitation.

Oh, I know I'm stupid, Simon, but I can't help suspecting she hates me in her heart and would like nothing better than a chance to come between us.

SIMON

Stares at her—then laughs teasingly but with a note of taunting.

Ah, who's the one who is afraid now?

Then with increasing sharpness.

You have absolutely no justification for talking of Mother like that. It's not only absurd, it's ungrateful. She favored our marriage. It was her money that helped us. And now you want me to lie out of seeing her! I don't know what to think of you, Sara, when you act like this!

SARA

Frightened.

Please don't think badly, Simon. I know it's crazy. Maybe it's being pregnant makes me nervous and afraid of everything.

SIMON

Immediately shamefaced.

I, —I'm sorry Dear.

He kisses her with awkward tenderness.

SARA

It's because I love you so much, and I never can believe my good luck in having you. I'm always afraid of something happening.

SIMON

Hushing her—tenderly.

Foolish One! As if anything could—

He kisses her.

SARA

Presses him to her with a fierce possessiveness and kisses him. Then she pushes him back and jumps to her feet with a happy laugh.

There! The craziness is all gone. Of course, you must see your mother. She's been good to us, and I'll never stop being gratefull, and you're to give her my best respect and love.

Then bullying him lovingly.

And now, quick with you, and go to bed. I want you to have a good rest so you'll look healthy and handsome and she'll see how well I take care of you.

She pulls his arm and he gets to his feet smilingly.

Go on. Get along with you.

She urges him toward the door at right.

I'll be in as soon as I've had another word with Mother. But mind you're fast asleep by then!

SIMON

Laughingly.

Oh, I'll mind. Don't I always obey like a devoted slave?

He goes out.

SARA

Looks after him, smiling fondly, then sits down, sighing. She stares before her, deep in thought. Her expression suddenly becomes uneasy, suspicious, and calculating.

She's still got her hold on him. She's up to some trick.

With smouldering anger.

Well, I'll fool her! I'll go there and hide. I can easy get the key from his pocket—

Then guiltily.

What would he think of me? But he won't ever know.

Scornfully.

Ah, the divil take honor! It's something men made up for themselves! As if she'd ever let honor stand in her way!

CURTAIN

Tao House
April 12, 1938
May 11th

Act One, Scene Two

A log cabin by a lake in the woods about two miles from the village. It is just before three in the afternoon of the following day.

The cabin is ten feet by fifteen, made of logs with a roof of warped, hand-hewn shingles. It is placed in a small clearing, overgrown with rank, matted grass. The front of the cabin, with a door at center, and a small window at left of door, faces front, overlooking the lake. Another window is in the wall facing right. At the left side is a stone chimney. Close by the left and rear of the cabin is the wood—oak, pine, birch, and maple trees. The foliage is at the full of brilliant Autumn color, purple and red and gold mingled with the deep green of the conifers.

The cabin gives evidence of having been abandoned for years. The mortar between the stones of the chimney has crumbled and fallen out in spots. The moss stuffing between the logs hangs here and there in straggly strips. The windows have boards nailed across them. A weather-beaten bench stands against the wall at left of the door. It is home-made, heavily constructed, and is still sturdy.

The clearing is partly in sunlight, partly shadowed by the woods.

As the curtain rises Sara appears by the corner of the cabin, right, having come by a short-cut trail from off rear, right, along the shore of the lake. She has evidently hurried for she is breathless and panting. She looks around the clearing furtively. Her expression is a mixture of defiant resentment and guilt. She wears the same mourning of Scene One. She hastily unlocks the door and changes the key to the inside. Leaving the door ajar, she comes stealthily to the edge of the woods at left, front, and

*peers up a path which leads from the clearing into the woods. She starts
and darts back to the door, enters the cabin and closes the door noiselessly behind her and locks herself in. For a moment there is silence. Then
Simon's mother, Deborah Harford, steps into the clearing from the path,
at left, front.*

*Deborah is forty-five but looks much younger. She is small, not over five
feet tall, with the slender, immature figure of a young girl. One cannot believe, looking at her, that she has ever borne children. There is
something about her perversely virginal. Her face is small, heart-shaped,
olive-complected, astonishingly youthful, with only the first tracing of
wrinkles about the eyes and mouth, a foreshadowing of sagging flesh
under the chin, and of scrawniness in the neck. It is framed by a mass
of wavy white hair, which by contrast with the youthfulness of her face,
gives her the appearance of a girl wearing a becoming wig at a costume
ball. Her nose is dainty and delicate above a full-lipped mouth, too large
and strong for her face, showing big, even white teeth when she smiles.
Her forehead is high and a trifle bulging, with sunken temples. Her eyes
are so large they look enormous in her small face. Beautiful eyes, black,
deep-set, beneath pronounced brows that meet above her nose. Her hands
are small with thin, strong, tapering fingers, and she has tiny feet. She
is dressed daintily and expensively, with extreme care and good taste,
entirely in white. Her habitual well-bred manner is one of mercurial
whimsicality—a provocative unconventional frankness of speech. But
one senses that underlying this now is a nervous tension and restlessness,
an insecurity, a brooding discontent and disdain.*

DEBORAH
Looks around the clearing—bitterly.
And I hoped he would be here, eagerly awaiting me!
She forces a self-mocking smile.
What can you expect, Deborah? At your age, a woman must become
resigned to wait upon every man's pleasure, even her son's.
*She picks her way daintily through the long grass toward the bench, an-
swering herself resentfully.*
Age? I am only forty-five. I am still beautiful. You harp on age as
though I were a withered old hag!

Mocking again.

Oh, not yet, Deborah! But now that the great change is upon you, it would be wise, I think, to discipline your mind to accept this fate of inevitable decay with equanimity.

She gives a little shiver of repulsion—determinedly.

No! I will not think of it! I still have years before me.

She breaks a leaf off the branch fastidiously and sits down—sneeringly.

And what will you do with these years, Deborah? Dream them away as you have all the other years since Simon deserted you? Live in the false life of books, in histories of the past? Continue your present silly obsession with scandalous French Eighteenth Century memoirs? Dream yourself back until you live in them an imaginative life more real than reality, until you become not the respectable, if a trifle mad, wife of the well known merchant, but a noble adventuress of Louis's Court, and your little walled garden, the garden of Versailles, your pathetic summerhouse a Temple of Love the King has built as an assignation place where he keeps passionate tryst with you, his mistress, the unscrupulous courtesan, forsooth, greedy for lust and power!

She laughs softly with sneering self-mockery—tauntingly.

Really, Deborah, this latest day dream is the most absurd of all the many ridiculous fantasies in which you have hidden from yourself! I begin to believe that truly you must be more than a little mad! You had better take care! One day you may lose yourself so deeply in that romantic evil, you will not find your way back.

Answering herself with defiant bravado.

Well, let that happen! I would welcome losing myself!

Abruptly—angry.

But you distort and exaggerate, as you always do! You know I do not take it seriously. I am lonely and bored! I am disgusted with watching my revolting body decay. Anything to forget myself. Besides, there is a perfectly rational explanation. I have seriously taken up the study of Eighteenth Century France to occupy my mind. I have always admired the Bourbons—perhaps because Father's stupid adoration of Napoleon prejudiced me against Napoleon, I suppose, and made me want to love his enemies.

Impatiently.

No, no, don't be absurd! That has nothing to do with it. I admire the manners and customs of that period, that is all. I would like to have lived then when life was free and charming and fastidious, not vulgar and ignoble and greedy as it is in this country today.

She stops abruptly—exasperatedly.

But how stupid! These insane interminable dialogues with self!

With a sudden tense desperation.

I must find someone outside myself in whom I can confide, and so escape myself. If I only had a close woman friend, someone strong and healthy and sane, who dares to love and live life greedily instead of reading and dreaming about it! What a mistake it was to warn off friendship from my life like a prying trespasser!

Answering herself mockingly.

Quite true, Deborah, but don't tell me you hope to make Simon into such a friend—a man and your son.

Argumentatively.

Well, that is not so absurd as it appears. He always had a sensitive, feminine streak in him. He used to sense so much intuitively, to understand without my putting into words, and I hope he still—

Then derisively.

You forget he has changed, as you know from his letters. You are thinking of the Simon that was, your Simon, not the contented husband of that vulgar Irish biddy, who evidently has found such a comfortable haven in her arms!

With bitter sadness.

Yes, it is hopeless. What am I doing here? Why did I come? And he keeps me waiting. Perhaps he is not coming. Perhaps she would not permit him—

In a burst of anger.

Am I to sit all afternoon and wait upon his pleasure?

Springing to her feet.

No! I will go!

Controlling herself—in a forced reasonable tone.

Nonsense, he told Cato to tell me he would come. He would never break his word to me, not even for her. I know, from his letters, he still loves me.

She sits down again.

I must stop my ridiculous, suspicious worrying. He is not late. It is I who am early. I have only to be patient—keep my mind off bitter thoughts—stop thinking—wile away the time—with any dream, no matter how absurd, if it serves the purpose of comforting me until he comes—shut my eyes and forget—not open them until he comes—
She relaxes, her head back, her eyes shut. A pause. Then she dreams aloud to herself.
The Palace at Versailles—I wear a gown of crimson satin and gold, embroidered in pearls—Louis gives me his arm, while all the Court watches enviously—the men, old loves that my ambition has used and discarded, or others who desire to be my lovers but dare not hope—the women who hate me for my wit and beauty, who envy me my greater knowledge of love and of men's hearts—my superior talents for unscrupulous intrigue in the struggle for power and possession—I walk with the King in the gardens—the moonlight sobbing in the fountains—he whispers tenderly: "My Throne it is your heart, Beloved, and my fair kingdom your beauty, and so of all Sovereigns of the earth I am most blessed"—he kisses me on the lips—as I lead him into the little Temple of Love he built for me—
There is a sound from up the path at left, through the woods, front. She starts quickly and opens her eyes as Simon comes into the clearing.

SIMON
His face lighting up.
Mother!
He strides toward her.

DEBORAH
Rising—still half in her dream—in a tone of arrogant displeasure.
You have been pleased to keep me waiting, Monsieur.

SIMON
Disconcerted—then decides she is joking and laughs.
Not I, Madame! I'm on the dot. It's you who are early.
He kisses her.
Mother, it's so good to—

DEBORAH
Her arrogance gone—clinging to him, almost hysterically.

Oh, yes! Yes! Dear Simon!
She begins to sob.

SIMON
Moved.
Don't!
Tenderly chiding.
Here, here! You crying! I can't believe it. I don't remember ever see-
ing you cry.

DEBORAH
Stops as suddenly as she had begun—pulling away from him.
No. And it is a poor time to begin. Tears may become a woman while
she's young. When she grows old they are merely disgusting.
She dabs her eyes with her handkerchief.

SIMON
Gives her another puzzled look.
Oh, come now.
Smiling.
You're only fishing for compliments, Mother. You're as young and
pretty as ever.

DEBORAH
Pleased—coquettishly.
You are gallant, Sir. My mirror tells me a crueler story. Do you mean
to say you don't see all the wrinkles? Be truthful, now.

SIMON
I can see a few, just beginning. But for your age it is amazing—

DEBORAH
Flashes him a resentful glance.
It is true, I am well preserved.
Abruptly.
But how foolish of us to waste precious moments discussing an old
woman's vanity.
She puts her hands on his shoulders.
Here. Turn about is fair play. Let me examine you.
She stares into his face critically.

Yes. You have changed. And quite as I had expected. You are getting your father's successful merchant look.

SIMON
Frowns and turns away from her.
I hope not!
Changing the subject.
Sit down, Mother.
She does so. He stands examining the cabin.
I shall have to send someone out here to repair things. I wish I could do it myself.
He passes his hands over the logs lovingly.
What labor it cost me to build this without help. Yet I was never happier.
He tries the door—searches his pocket.
Funny, I could have sworn I had the key. But perhaps it is better. It would only make me melancholy.

DEBORAH
Casts a sharp appraising glance at his face.
Yes, it is always sad to contemplate the corpse of a dream.

SIMON
Answers before he thinks.
Yes.
Then defensively.
Unless you have found a finer dream.

DEBORAH
Oh, I know. Love is worth any sacrifice. I told you that, if you will remember. How is Sara?

SIMON
Well—and happy.

DEBORAH
You are as much in love?

SIMON
More. I cannot imagine a marriage happier than ours.

DEBORAH

I am glad. But, of course, I knew. You have protested in every letter
how happy you were.

He flashes a suspicious look at her. She goes on casually.

And the children? Sara expects another before long, I believe you
wrote.

SIMON

Yes.

DEBORAH

All this child-bearing. It must be a strain. Is she pretty still?

SIMON

More beautiful than ever.

DEBORAH

There speaks the devoted husband! I was wondering if you would
bring her with you today.

SIMON

Surprised.

You said nothing in your note about bringing her. I thought you
wanted to see me alone.

DEBORAH

I did. But perhaps I see now it might have been as well—

Quickly.

I had begun to think perhaps Sara might not permit you to come—

SIMON

Frowning.

Permit me? You talk as though I were a slave.

DEBORAH

Well, one is, isn't one, when one is in love? Or so I have read in the
poets.

SIMON

Smiling.

Oh, to love I am a willing slave. But what made you think Sara—?

DEBORAH

Well, a woman's love is jealously possessive—or so I have read—and she knows how close you and I used to be in the old happy days. You were happy in those days with me, weren't you, before you graduated from Harvard and had to leave me and find your own life in the world?

SIMON

Moved.

Of course I was, Mother—never more happy.

DEBORAH

Tenderly.

I am glad you still remember, Dear.

She pats his hand.

SIMON

And I am grateful for all you did afterwards—your approval of our marriage, your generosity in helping us financially to make a start.

DEBORAH

It was Sara, wasn't it, who insisted on your paying back as a loan what I had meant as a gift?

SIMON

Uncomfortably.

Yes, she didn't understand—She is very sensitive and proud—

Hurriedly.

But she is as grateful to you as I am. She will never forget your kindness.

DEBORAH

With a trace of disdain.

I am grateful for her appreciation.

Changing the subject abruptly.

Tell me, do you ever think now of the book you were so eager to write when you resigned in disgust from your father's business and came out here to live alone—the one inspired by the social philosophy of Jean Jacques Rousseau—your Utopian plan for a new society where there would be no rich nor poor, where all would be content with enough and live in perfect amity without envy or greed. You never mentioned it in your letters. Have you abandoned the idea entirely?

SIMON
Reluctantly.
For the present. I have so little time now.
Defensively.
Oh, I think of it often and some day I'll write it.

DEBORAH
I see.

SIMON
Suspiciously.
What made you ask about that now, Mother?

DEBORAH
Carelessly.
Nothing. This place reminded me, I suppose. And you really should write it. The times are ripe for such a book, in these days when our republic is sinking into a corrupt decline. With four years more of Mr. Jackson in power—and even your father admits he is sure of re-election—the precedent will be irrevocably set. We shall be governed by the ignorant greedy mob for all future time.
She laughs with malicious amusement.
Your poor father! He wishes Massachusetts would secede from the Union. One has but to mention the name of Jackson to give him violent dyspepsia.

SIMON
Grinning.
I can imagine.
Then scornfully.
It's ridiculous snobbery for him to sneer at the common people. He should remember his grandfather was only a Welsh immigrant farmer. Not that I hold any brief for Andrew Jackson. His spoils system is a disgrace to the spirit of true Democracy.
He shrugs his shoulders.
But it is also an inevitable development of our system of govern-

ment. That system was wrong from the beginning. It confused freedom with separation from England, and then mistook the right to vote for Liberty. To be truly free, we must start all over again. In a free society there must be no private property to tempt men's greed into enslaving one another. We must protect man from his stupid possessive instincts until he can be educated to outgrow them spiritually. But at the same time, we must never forget that the least government, the best government. We must renounce the idea of great centralized governments, and divide society into small, self-governing communities where all property is owned in common for the common good. In my book I will prove this can easily be done if only men—

DEBORAH
Cynically.
Ah, yes, if only men—and women—were not men and women!

SIMON
Frowns, then smiles.
Now you're as cynical as Sara.
She stiffens.
That is her objection, too.
Then with embarrassment.
But I'm afraid I'm boring you with my perfect society.

DEBORAH
No. I'm only too happy to discover the old idealistic dreamer still exists in you.

SIMON
Self-consciously.
I haven't spoken of such matters in so long—
He forces a laugh.
Your influence, Mother! You were always such a sympathetic audience.

DEBORAH
Quietly.
I still am. But are you, I wonder?

SIMON

Preoccupied, ignores her question, and goes on doggedly as if he had to finish expressing his ideas.

I still believe with Rousseau, as firmly as ever, that at bottom human nature is good and unselfish. It is what we are pleased to call civilization that has corrupted it. We must return to Nature and simplicity and then we'll find that the People—those whom Father sneers at as the greedy Mob—are as genuinely noble and honorable as the false aristocracy of our present society pretends to be!

DEBORAH

Bitingly.

No doubt. However, I would still be nauseated by their thick ankles, and ugly hands and dirty finger nails, were they ever so noble-hearted!

She suddenly cries with a desperate exasperation.

Good Heavens, did I come here to discuss politics, and the natural rights of man—I, who pray the Second Flood may come and rid the world of this stupid race of men and wash the earth clean!

She gets to her feet—with curt arrogance.

It is getting late, I must go.

SIMON

Go? You've just come!

Pleadingly.

Mother! Please! Forgive me if I've bored you. But it was you who brought it up.

Coaxingly.

Come. Sit down, Mother.

She sits down again.

You haven't told me a word about yourself yet.

DEBORAH

Bitterly.

I am afraid, though you might listen kindly, you could not hear me, Simon.

SIMON

Gently reproachful.

I used to hear, didn't I?

DEBORAH
Bitterly.
Once long ago. In another life. Before we had both changed.

SIMON
I haven't changed—not in my love for you.
Sadly.
It hurts that you can believe that of me, Mother.

DEBORAH
Bitterly.
Oh, I no longer know what to believe about anything or anyone!

SIMON
Not even about me?

DEBORAH
Not even about myself.

SIMON
Regards her worriedly—gently.
What has happened, Mother?
Frowning.
Is it anything Father has done?

DEBORAH
Astonished.
Good Heavens, no!
She bursts into genuinely amused laughter.
My dear boy, what an absurd idea! It is easy to see you have forgotten your old home. Your father is much too worried about what President Jackson will do or say next, and what effect it will have on imports and exports, to bother with me, even if I would permit him to.

SIMON
Is it anything Joel—?

DEBORAH
Worse and worse! If you could see your brother now! He is head of

the bookkeeping department, which is about as high as his ability can ever take him, to your father's disgust.

SIMON
With satisfaction.
I knew Joel had no ability. Father must be disappointed.

DEBORAH
Joel has become a confirmed ledger-worm. I think he tried once to find me listed on the profit side of the ledger. Not finding me there, he concluded he must merely be imagining that I existed.
Simon laughs.
I invited him to visit me in my garden not long ago—

SIMON
With a boyish scowl—jealously.
Why? What could you want with him?

DEBORAH
With a sharp interested look at him.
Anyone for company! You don't know how lonely I have grown since you—Poor Joel! He looked as astounded as if a nun had asked him to her bedroom. And when he came—with the air, I might say, of a correct gentleman who pays a duty call on a woman of whom he disapproves—he determinedly recited impeccable platitudes and stared the flowers out of countenance for half an hour, and then fled! You would have laughed to see him.

SIMON
Resentfully.
Yes, he must have been out of place.

DEBORAH
Smiles with satisfaction at his tone.
He was indeed. So you need not be jealous, Dear. I remembered you and all our old happy days there.
She pauses—then slowly.
No, I have not changed because of anything Joel—Hardly!

SIMON
Gently.
Then what is it, Mother?

DEBORAH
Why, nothing has happened, Dear, except time and change.

SIMON
You seem so lonely.

DEBORAH
Patting his hand.
I am glad you know that. Now I feel less lonely.

SIMON
It's hard to believe that about you. You were always so independent of others, so free and self-sufficient. All you ever needed was the solitude of your garden, or your room—your books and your dreams.

DEBORAH
Bitterly.
Yes, that was my arrogant mistake, presuming myself superior to life. But a time comes when, suddenly, all that security in solitude appears as weakness and cowardice, a craven running away, and hiding from life. You become restless, and discontent gnaws at your heart while you cast longing eyes beyond the garden wall at life which passes by so horribly unaware that you are still alive!

SIMON
How can you say Life has passed you by, Mother? That's foolish. You—

DEBORAH
Unheeding.
While you are still beautiful and life still woos you, it is such a fine gesture of disdainful pride, so satisfying to one's arrogance, to jilt it. But when the change comes and the tables are turned and an indifferent life jilts you—it is a repulsive humiliation to feel yourself a condemned slave to revengeful Time, to cringe while he lashes your

face with wrinkles, or stamps your body into shapelessness, or smears it with tallow-fat with his malicious fingers!

Anticipating his protest.

Oh, I realize I am hardly as bad as that yet. But I will be, for I constantly sense in the seconds and minutes and hours flowing through me, the malignant hatred of life against those who have disdained it! But the body is least important. It is the soul, staring into the mirror of itself, knowing it is too late, that it is rejected and forever alone— seeing the skull of Death leer over its shoulder in the glass like a roué in a brothel ogling some life-sick old trull!

SIMON

Shrinking with repulsion.

Mother! That's—that's too morbid!

DEBORAH

Seeing his shocked face, gives a little mocking laugh.

Poor Simon, I warned you I had changed. Have I shocked you dreadfully? Mothers should never have such thoughts, should they? Not even while dreaming to themselves?

She laughs again.

Forgive me. I am afraid my mind has been corrupted by reading so many French Eighteenth Century memoirs of late. I believe I wrote you that I had started studying history. But perhaps you did not take it seriously. I was always studying something, wasn't I? The time I wasted hiding in my mind!

SIMON

Rebukingly.

Don't tell me you regret—

Abruptly.

You didn't write me it was that kind of history.

DEBORAH

Smiles at him teasingly.

No doubt I was ashamed to confess. But I find the French Eighteenth Century the most instructive and congenial period in modern history for me.

SIMON

Abruptly changing the subject.

What of your old passion for Hindu Philosophy? Don't tell me you have given that up!

DEBORAH

Yes. Long ago. Or, to be exact, a year ago. This past year of change has seemed so long! It happened I awoke one day from my dream of self-renunciation, and indifference to the opposites, to find Life sneaking out my door renouncing me, taking the indifferent opposites along with him. From that moment the Sacred Books became for me merely a rubbish of lifeless words. And Brahma nothing at all but a foreign name for Death.

She smiles bitterly—self-mocking.

As I have said, it is pleasant to your superior disdain to renounce life, but an intolerable insult when life renounces you. As for my excursions into Oriental wisdom, I see it now as the flight of one who, bored at home, blames the surroundings, and sails for far lands, only to find a welcoming figure waiting there to greet one—oneself!

She smiles bitterly.

And straightaway the exotic palms turn into old familiar elms or maples, the houses are the same old houses, the gardens the same gardens, and the natives only one's old neighbors with fewer clothes and a darker sunburn—

Simon chuckles amusedly.

—and one is as bewilderedly at home and not at home as ever!

She pauses—then shrugging her shoulders.

I should have known I could have no enduring faith in any other-life religion. Being a Minister's daughter killed that in me. My father's life and his beyond-life expectations were too absurdly incongruous.

She smiles mischievously.

Poor man, how dreadfully embarrassed he would have been if Christ had ever called on him, especially if he came to the front door, with all the neighbors peering spitefully from behind curtains; hoping this Jacobin tramp would turn out to be a poor relation whose existence Father had concealed from them.

SIMON

Laughs.

Poor Grandfather! You're always so hard on him.

DEBORAH

With gloating malice.

He was so proud of having sprung from an aristocratic old family. And yet he did try so hard to identify himself with Christ. But there was no point of resemblance except his poverty, and he was ashamed of that. And he couldn't help bearing God a grudge because He never kept His promise and let the meek devour the earth. Father's real idol was Napoleon. *He* didn't wait on promises, *he* wasn't meek, *he* took the earth! Father worshipped him. He used even to have the newspaper *Moniteur* sent him from France—his one extravagance— and gloat over each new victory.

She sneers spitefully.

Poor man! If you could imagine anyone less like Napoleon! Except in bodily stature. Poor Father was plump and insignificant.

SIMON

I wish I remembered him. He must have been a strange character.

DEBORAH

Extremely commonplace, you mean. Don't you recognize the symptoms? He was one of the great mob of greedy meek. He was Everyman.

Then with a sudden exasperation.

Great Heavens, why do I recall him? And what a stupid conversation! Politics, first and now, religion and family gossip about the dead! It was silly of me to come!

She makes a move to rise but Simon catches her arm.

SIMON

Soothingly.

Now, Mother! It isn't stupid to me. If you knew how delighted I am to sit and hear you talk again. It's like old times! It brings back all the happiness of the past—the hours together in your garden, as far back as I can remember.

DEBORAH
Moved—pats his hand.
I am happy you have not forgotten, Dear.

SIMON
Smiling musingly.
Are you still as incorrigible a dreamer as ever, Mother?
She stiffens and gives him a suspicious, defensive look.
I can remember times—I must have been very little, then—when you would sink into a dream, your eyes open but no longer seeing me. I would speak to you but you wouldn't hear me. You were off somewhere. Then I'd be frightened—

DEBORAH
Relieved, smiling tenderly.
That was silly, Dear. I was probably dreaming about you, of how, when you grew up, you and I—

SIMON
Again with a musing smile.
Are you still as accomplished an actress as you used to be?

DEBORAH
Starts—forcing a laugh.
Why, what a thing to say, Simon!

SIMON
Oh, I meant it admiringly, Mother. I was remembering—I must have been very little then, too—how you used to act out each part when you'd read me fairy stories. One moment you'd be the good fairy, or the good queen, or the poor abused little Princess—That was wonderful. But the next moment you'd be the evil Queen, or the bad fairy, or the wicked witch, and I'd be all gooseflesh with terror!
He chuckles.

DEBORAH
Gives him a strange glance—almost tauntingly.
You were extremely sensitive and imaginative—as a child.

SIMON

Frowning.

The trouble was, your acting confused my mind about you. Sometimes I got bewildered trying to keep you distinct and separate from the part you played.

DEBORAH

Strangely.

Yes, I have experienced that bewilderment, too—when trying to reconcile my opposites.

SIMON

Suddenly looks at her—smilingly.

What role do you play nowadays, Mother?

DEBORAH

Stiffens, avoiding his eyes and forcing a laugh.

I? What nonsense, Dear. You forget I have no audience now.

SIMON

Teasingly.

Oh, you were always your own audience, too. I felt that. So tell me—

DEBORAH

No, I assure you I've foresworn dream dramas. I'm too painfully conscious of reality these days, and its banality is too grotesquely in contrast—

SIMON

Now, don't tell me you've given up imagination and resigned yourself to the dull humdrum of being merely Mrs. Harford. I won't believe it. You couldn't if you tried. I'm sure you still fly from that deadly boredom into a secret life of your own—or at least, into the life in books—

DEBORAH

Gives him a quick searching glance—with feigned carelessness.

Oh, if that's what you mean, yes. I'll confess there are times now when I become so bored with myself that I do try to escape into Eighteenth Century France. Life was so much more romantic and exciting for a woman then, don't you think? As the Memoirs depict it, anyway, and as I recreate it from them in my imagination.

More decidedly.

Yes, if I had had the choice, I would have chosen to live then. In fact, there are moments when I become so absorbed in the life of that period that I lose all sense of the present and feel that I did live then, that I am living there again.

Forcing a careless smile.

Perhaps my study of Eastern wisdom left me with a desire to believe in reincarnation. Sometimes I feel—

Forcing a careless laugh.

But that is very silly, of course.

SIMON

Why is it silly? Who knows? Anyway, about the life in books, I know I have often felt it more real to me than reality.

He adds with an undercurrent of resentment.

Or I used to in the old days when I had time for books. Especially the poetry you would read aloud to me.

He smiles musingly.

Remember Byron, Mother, and your favorite Childe Harold stanza?

He recites.

> I have not loved the World, nor the World me;
> I have not flattered its rank breath, nor bowed
> To its idolatries a patient knee
> Nor coined my cheek to smiles,—nor cried aloud
> In worship of an echo: in the crowd
> They could not deem me one of such—I stood
> Among them, but not of them—

He breaks off—tenderly.

Do you remember, Mother?

DEBORAH

I do now. I forgot Byron after you had gone. I remember now, too, the stanza that begins: "But quiet to quick bosoms is a hell." And then, in the following one: "—all unquiet things which stir too strongly the soul's secret springs."

She forces a smile.

I fear loneliness is making me into a most unquiet thing.

Then with a laugh.

Your memories of the past encourage me to carry confession further and admit I do still have the childish habit of daydreaming and acting romantic roles in my mind to wile away the time.

SIMON

Grows teasing.

I knew it. I know you.

DEBORAH

Lightly.

You did, but do you? You forget time has changed me.

Still lightly, but with an undercurrent of taunting.

And you. You are a contented husband and father now, a successful merchant, so like your father!

Simon frowns with annoyance.

I greatly fear you would be horribly shocked if I should tell you the nature of the part I play in my Eighteenth Century past!

SIMON

Grins.

I'll chance it, Mother. Remember your old wicked witches led me always to be prepared for the worst!

DEBORAH

Playfully but a growing undercurrent of compulsive, deadly seriousness as she goes on.

Oh, I warn you this is more wicked than any witch. She was a creature of pure fantasy, a fairy tale. But this is real life, even though it be past—and perhaps Time is but another of our illusions, and what was is forever identical with what is, beneath the deceiving, changing masks we wear.

SIMON

A bit impatiently.

Well, out with the terrible secret, Mother. I promise not to be too horrified. Are you an evil Queen of France who never was?

DEBORAH

Suddenly seems to lose herself—arrogantly.

No. I could be if it were my whim, but I prefer to be the secret power behind the Throne—a greedy adventuress who has risen from the gutter to nobility by her wit and charm, by the sale of her beauty, by her talent for marvelous intrigue—who uses love but loves only herself, who is entirely ruthless and lets nothing stand in the way of the final goal of power she has set for herself, to become the favorite of the King and make him, through his passion for her, her slave!

She ends up on a note of strange, passionate exultance.

SIMON

Startled and repelled—sharply rebuking.

Mother!

She starts dazedly. He goes on quickly with a curt resentful contempt.

No, I am not shocked. It is too damned idiotic!

She gives a shrinking, cowering movement as though he had struck her in the face. Suddenly the absurdity strikes his sense of humor and he grins.

No, that's a lie. You really did shock me for a second, Mother. Stunned me, even!

He chuckles.

But now I have a picture in my mind of you sitting in your walled-in garden, dressed all in white, so sedulously protected and aloof from all life's sordidness, so delicate and fastidious and spiritually remote—and yet in your dreams playing make-believe with romantic iniquity out of scandalous French memoirs!

He laughs almost derisively.

DEBORAH

Stung to fury, a flash of bitter hatred in her eyes, drawing herself up with fierce, threatening arrogance.

You dare to laugh at me, Monsieur! Take care—!

Then as he stares at her in petrified amazement, she controls herself and forces an hysterical laugh.

There! You see! I can still be a convincing actress if I wish! Poor Simon, if you could see your horrified face! Don't you see this is all a joke, that I made up that nonsense on the spur of the moment just to tease you?

SIMON
Relieved, grins sheepishly.
You did fool me. For a moment I thought you were serious—

DEBORAH
Serious! My dear boy, I hope you don't think your poor mother has gone quite insane!
Abruptly.
But let's forget my stupid joke and return to common sense in the little time left us. I must go. Tell me, how is your business progressing these days? Judging from your letters, you must be making a great success of it.

SIMON
Reluctantly.
Oh, only in a very modest way as yet, Mother.

DEBORAH
You hope to do even better? I am sure you will—with Sara to inspire you.

SIMON
Yes, it is all for her. Everything I have is in her name.

DEBORAH
Gives him a searching look—smiling curiously.
I see.

SIMON
See what? I owe it to her—

DEBORAH
Of course you do.
She smiles.
But I didn't mean that. My thought was fanciful—that perhaps thus you contrived to hide from yourself.

SIMON
Resentfully.
You are right to call that fanciful.

DEBORAH
Teasingly.
And I think you're playing modest with me about your success. Why, in one of your letters, you boasted that the town considered you the most talented of its young merchants.

SIMON
I wasn't boasting, Mother. Good Heavens, what is there to boast about? It requires no high order of talent to be a successful trades-man—merely a cunning acquisitiveness. I meant my boasting humorously. I thought it would make you laugh.

DEBORAH
Oh, I did laugh then. Now I see there is nothing incongruous about it. After all, you are your father's son. It is natural you should have inherited his ability. You are so like him now, in many ways, it's astonishing.

SIMON
Irritated.
Oh, nonsense, Mother.

DEBORAH
It's true. It struck me the minute I saw you. And do you know, although he never permits himself to speak of you, I am sure he keeps informed of all you do, and is quite proud of you.

SIMON
Coldly.
I can dispense with his approval.

DEBORAH
What a strange boy you are! One would think you were ashamed of your success.

SIMON
Why should I be ashamed?

DEBORAH
Why, indeed? Unless you regret your lost poet's dream of a perfect society.

SIMON

I haven't lost it! And it isn't just a dream. I can prove—

DEBORAH

Carelessly.

Oh, I know. Your book. But you said you had given that up.

SIMON

I said I had had no time lately—

DEBORAH

Four years is a long "lately." But why should you be ashamed of that? You must learn to laugh at your dreams if you hope ever to be happy.

SIMON

Defensively.

I am happy now!

DEBORAH

We all pass through a callow period when our vanity prompts us to believe we may become poets or philosophers or saviours of mankind—when we dream of spiritual beauty and a greedless world. But we soon discover the world we must live in is greedily practical and could bitterly resent being saved from its gross appetite, that we must eat or be eaten, and an ounce of flesh is worth a ton of spirit.

SIMON

Repelled.

I never thought I'd ever hear you—

DEBORAH

I am trying to drive the nonsense from your head, for your own peace of mind, and Sara's. You must forget what you once wanted to be and face yourself as you are, and not be ashamed.

SIMON

I am not ashamed! Why do you keep insisting?—
Then suddenly giving in—moodily.
Well perhaps, now and then, I do feel a little guilty.

DEBORAH

Ah!

SIMON

But I remind myself that what I am doing is merely a means. The end is Sara's happiness. And that justifies any means!

DEBORAH

I've found the means always becomes the end — and the end is always oneself.

SIMON

I propose to retire as soon as we have enough. I'll write my book then.

DEBORAH

You have agreed with Sara how much is enough?

SIMON

Hesitates — then lies.

Yes, of course.

A pause. He frowns and goes on moodily.

I'll admit I do get deathly sick of the daily grind of the counting house — the interminable haggling and figuring and calculation of profits, the scheming to outwit the other man, the fear that he may outwit you — a life where Mammon is God, and money the sole measure of worth! It is not the career I would have chosen. I would have lived here in freedom with nature, and earned just enough to support myself, and kept my dreams, and written my book.

Somberly.

Yes, sometimes I feel spiritually degraded, and a traitor to myself. I would confess that only to you, Mother.

DEBORAH

Ah.

SIMON

Hastily.

But when I come home and see Sara's happiness and hold her in my arms, then my discontent seems mean and selfish and a petty vanity.

DEBORAH
Fights back an expression of repulsion.
Yes. Of course.
Then calculatingly.
The danger is that your discontent will grow and grow with your success until—But, good heavens, I sound like Cassandra! Forgive me! And now I really must go, Simon.
She gets up and they come to the path front at left. Suddenly she says, strangely.
No, you go first.

SIMON
But why don't we walk together as far as the road?

DEBORAH
With strange arrogant petulance.
No! That would be meaningless. Please obey me. It is my whim to send you away.
Then forcing a joking tone.
Goodness, how alarmed you look! You have forgotten me, I think. Can't I be whimsical, as of old, if it please me?

SIMON
Puzzled but smiling.
Of course you can.

DEBORAH
Kissing him.
Goodbye, Dear. Write me frankly of your discontents. There should be no secrets between us. I shall be, as ever, your Mother Confessor.
Then she gives him a little push.
Now go!

SIMON
Hesitates—moved.
I— Goodbye, Mother.
He turns reluctantly.

DEBORAH
Suddenly overcome by contrition and a tender love.

Wait!

She embraces him again.

My dear son! Forgive me for trying to poison your happiness. Forget all I have said! Have no regrets! Love is worth everything! Be happy!

She kisses him—then pushes him away down the path—sharply commanding.

No! Don't speak! Go!

She turns away. Simon stares at her for a moment, deeply moved—then turns and disappears down the path. Deborah turns back to look after him—with a wry smile.

I honestly meant to take back the poison—but I fear it served only to inject it more surely into his soul.

Then self-mockingly.

Bosh, Deborah! You overestimate your powers for intrigue! You confuse life with stupid dreams. He will forget in her arms.

Her face hardening.

Besides, it is ended. I have dismissed that Irish biddy's husband from my life forever. I shall never see him again.

Then she smiles to herself with a perverse pride.

At least I have proven to my own satisfaction, how easy it would be to steal happiness from her, if it were my whim, and I were given the opportunity.

As she says this last the cabin door is silently unlocked and opened and Sara comes out. She stands outside the door for a moment hesitantly. Then, her face set and determined, she advances noiselessly until she stands a few paces from the oblivious Deborah. She takes her in from head to foot with a searching glance, her eyes narrowing. But there is no hatred or anger visible in her expression. If she feels any, she has forced it back beneath the surface, and there is a certain calm dignity and strength of character in her face and whole attitude. Whatever the battle with her passions has been, she has fought it out inside the cabin.

SARA

Speaks quietly in a polite, carefully considered and articulated English.

I beg your pardon, Mrs. Harford.

Deborah gives a frightened gasp, whirling to face her. For a moment the two stare at each other, Sara steady and calm, Deborah recovering from

*her surprise, her face hardening into a haughtily-questioning mask. Sara
makes her a little bow. A hint of a mocking smile on her lips.*

I am happy to meet you again and to know you at last, Mrs. Harford. I feel I do know you now, you see, because I was in the cabin all the while since you came.

DEBORAH
With a flash of arrogant fury.
You dared to listen!

SARA
Quietly.
I did. I came on purpose to listen. I suspected you were up to some trick. I wanted to know what it was so I could guard against it.
A trace of contempt creeping into her voice.
Though after all I've heard, I know now I was a fool to be afraid of you.

DEBORAH
Stammers guiltily.
So you heard—
Then with biting contempt.
You have the effrontery to boast of it! You have so little shame! You are so ignorant of all honor!

SARA
Her face beginning to flush—but still quietly.
I am, yes.

DEBORAH
Well, I expected you to be low and unscrupulous, considering your origin, but I never thought you'd boast of it!

SARA
Stung—her inward anger beginning to show, and with it her brogue, but still keeping her voice quiet.
I have my honor and it's a true woman's honor that you don't know but you'd give your soul to know! To have love and hold it against the world, no matter how! That's my honor!
Gradually losing her control and lapsing more and more into brogue.

As for what you're after saying about my origin—don't put on your fine lady's airs and graces with me! Do you think you'll fool me after what I've heard?

With a savage, jeering scorn, advancing a threatening step.

God pity you for a fool, then!

Deborah in spite of herself, shrinks back. Sara gloats triumphantly.

Ah, you shrink away, don't you? You're afraid! I'm too strong for you! Life is too strong for you! But it's not too strong for me! I'll take what I want from it and make it mine!

Mockingly.

And aren't you envyin' me that strength now in your heart, for all your pretendin'? Aren't you thinkin' that if you could have my strength to love life, and your brains for schemin' and dreamin' of power, you'd make yourself Queen of the world! Oh, I know you now! I know you well! You to put on the airs of a Duchess wid me! You to talk of honor when in your dream what are you but a greedy, contrivin' whore!

Deborah shrinks back cowering still farther. Sara goes on more quietly but with a derisive taunting.

But it's only in a dream! You've the wish for life but you haven't the strength except to run and hide in fear of it, sittin' lonely in your garden, hearin' age creep up on you, and beyond the wall the steps of Life growin' fainter down the street, like the beat of your heart, as he strolls away forgettin' you, whistlin' a love tune to himself, dreaming of another woman!

DEBORAH

Stammers.

That's a lie!

She sways weakly as though she were about to faint—exhaustedly.

I—I feel a little faint—I—

She starts weakly for the bench.

SARA

With an abrupt change to her quiet polite manner, takes her arm.

Let me help you, Mrs. Harford.

She leads Deborah to the bench.

You must rest a while. It's a long walk back to the road.

DEBORAH
Sinks down on it—quietly.
Thank you.

SARA
Stands looking down at her.
I ask your pardon for losing my temper, Mrs. Harford. I'd promised myself I would not. But the things you said—

DEBORAH
Quietly.
I know. Please forgive me.

SARA
I came out of the cabin because there's a lot of things I want to say to you.
Defiantly.
And I'm going to say them.
She pauses but Deborah remains silent. She stares at her and suddenly a look of pity comes over her face. She speaks gently.
But before that I want to tell you how sorry I was when Simon laughed.
Deborah gives a little shrinking shudder.
I was listening. I could feel it coming. I waited, praying he wouldn't. When he did, it was like a knife in me, too.
Deborah raises her eyes for a second to stare at her with an instinctive grateful wonder. Sara goes on.
I want to apologize for him. He didn't know. How can a man know about the truth of the lies in a woman's dreams?

DEBORAH
Lifts her eyes to stare at her wonderingly again—with a faint smile.
I thought you were a fool. I am afraid I am beginning to like you, Sara.

SARA
Embarrassedly—forcing a joking tone.
Oh, don't try to fool me with blarney. You hate me worse than poison, that's the truth. And I hate you.

Then with resentment and now and then a trace of brogue but quietly.

I want to say I'm glad I listened. I've told you I was afraid you were up to some trick. And you were. Oh, I saw through your reminding him about that crazy book of his, although I didn't blame you for trying to get back at him after he'd laughed. You wanted to put doubt and disgust for himself in his mind, and make him blame me for a greedy fool who'd made him a slave and killed his fine poet's dream.

She laughs scornfully.

It's you who are the fool. It's little you know Simon, if you are his mother. Sure, what man doesn't complain of his work, and pretend he's a slave, but if you ever saw him when he comes home to me, so proud and happy because he's beat someone on a sale, laughing and boasting to me, you wouldn't hope you could use his old dream of a book that'll change the world to dissatisfy him. I know what he really likes—the world as it is—and I'm not worried by what he thinks he ought to like.

She pauses. Deborah sits in silence, her eyes on the ground, as though she didn't hear or was completely indifferent. Sara goes on more resentfully.

But what I wanted to say is, you don't know me. I may have a greed in me. I've had good reason to have. There's nothing like hunger to make you greedy. But the thing you don't know is that there's great love in me too, great enough to destroy all the greed in the world. If I thought it meant his happiness, I'd live here in this hut, or in a ditch with him, and steal praties from the farmers to feed him, and beg pennies with my children, on the road, to buy pen and ink and paper for his book, and still I'd laugh with the joy of love!

She pauses again. Deborah remains silent. She goes on.

I heard you, when he said he'd retire to write his book when we had enough, sneer to him that I'd never have enough. It's little you know me, if you think I want him all his life to dirty his hands with trade, when all I'm dreaming of is to make him retire, a landed gentleman the minute we've enough, and to bring my children up as gentlemen. You sneered at my origin. You think in your Yankee pride and ignorance, because my father ruined himself with drink and gambling in Ireland, that the dirty Inn he came down to own here, is all I've known. But I was born on a great estate that was my father's, in a grand mansion like a Castle, with sloos [*sic*] of servants, and stables, and beautiful hunters. My father was a gentleman, and an officer, who served with honor in Spain under the great Duke of Wellington.

Abruptly with exasperated self-scorn.

Arrah, what am I sayin'? Am I boastin' of him?

With a sudden return to her quiet correct manner.

I beg your pardon, Mrs. Harford, for boring you with talk of my father. The truth is, I am not proud I am his daughter. He was a drunken fool, full of lying pretensions—

Hastily, with stubborn defiance.

But what I've said is true all the same!

DEBORAH

Without raising her eyes—smiling strangely.

Did I think you were strong and unscrupulous? But you are also very weak and honorable, I'm afraid.

She laughs softly.

SARA

Stares at her uneasily—then defiantly.

You'd better not think I'm weak, or have any honor but one. I'll tell you something to prove it. You'll remember the night your husband sent his lawyer to buy off my father from any claims I had on Simon, and my father got mad with rage at the insult and went to challenge him to a duel. I was afraid there'd be a row you'd use as an excuse to keep Simon from marrying me, but I knew Simon would feel bound to me in honor if— So I came out here in the night to make him take me.

She smiles tenderly.

I found I didn't need to. He loved me so much, nothing could take him from me. And then I felt guilty and confessed how bad I'd been. And then we— But it was for love only.

Abruptly defiant again.

But I would have done it for the other reason if I'd had to!

DEBORAH

Raises her eyes to stare at her with hate—scornfully.

You need not convince me you are capable of any vileness to get what you want.

Then she drops her eyes—with a strange little mocking laugh.

You are boasting, Sara. Oh, I don't doubt you would have. That's your strength. But afterwards your weak honor would have made you confess to him—perhaps even tell him he need not marry you, anyway.

SARA
Taken aback—blurts out.
Yes, I told him that before—

DEBORAH
Laughs.
I am beginning to know you, Sara.

SARA
Again stares at her uneasily—resentfully threatening.
I don't care what you know. I've only this left to say to you. Stay in your dreams and leave me and mine alone. Simon is mine now.
Then politely.
I must go. Simon will be wondering where I have gone. I promise you I won't confess that. I'll bid you goodbye now, Mrs. Harford.

DEBORAH
Looks up—coldly.
Goodbye. I promise you, in turn, I never intend to see your husband again, or even write to him.
With arrogant disdain.
Do you presume to think I would touch anything of yours?

SARA
Contemptuously.
No. You know I wouldn't let you.
She smiles mockingly and goes off right, rear, to the short cut along the lake.

DEBORAH
Her face full of bitter hatred.

Vulgar, common slut! Boastful fool! If I wished—if I had the opportunity—

Sneeringly.

And now her honor will make her remind him constantly of his book, when he wants to forget—

She laughs spitefully.

I could not have contrived it better!

Abruptly.

No. It is ended. Forgotten. Dead. It is cheap and mean and sordid. Like life. I will not let it touch me.

She frowns as if desperately concentrating her mind. Gradually her tension relaxes and her eyes become dreamy and she stares before her unseeingly. Finally she murmurs happily to herself.

The Palace at Versailles—the King and I walk in the moonlit gardens—"My Throne it is your heart, Beloved, and my fair Kingdom your beauty"—

A faint smile of arrogant satisfaction forms on her lips. Then abruptly she starts awake and springs to her feet, furious at herself.

No! I have done with that insane romantic vaporing! I will never dream again! Never! Not if I have to pluck my idiot brain from my skull! I will face change and loneliness, and Time and Death and make myself resigned!

A bitter ironical smile comes to her lips.

After all, what else can you do now, Deborah? You would always hear his laughter.

CURTAIN

Tao House
May 10th '38

Act Two, Scene One

SCENE

A corner of the garden of Deborah Harford's home in the city on a warm moonlight night in June, 1836.

The corner is formed by a brick enclosing wall, eight feet high, at rear and right. This wall borders a neighboring property at rear, a quiet street lined with elms at right. At center is an octagonal summerhouse, its walls and pointed roof entirely covered by ivy. At left and right of the summerhouse are shrubs with a line of Italian cypresses behind them along the wall. The shrubs, of various sizes, are all clipped into geometrical shapes, cones, cubes, cylinders, spheres, pyramids, etc. They give the place a curious artificial atmosphere. It is like a fantastic toy garden magnified, in which nature is arrogantly restricted and arbitrarily distorted to form an appropriate setting for a perversely whimsical personality.

In the side of the summerhouse facing front is a narrow arched door, painted a Chinese lacquer red. The floor is raised from the ground and three steps lead up to the door. In front of these steps is lawn, with two small stone benches, facing right-front, and left-front, on the edge of a narrow brick-paved walk which surrounds a little oval pool. From this pool two paths lead directly right and left, the left one passing behind a spherical shrub at left-front to the house. The right one leads to an arched door, painted green, in the wall at right, opening on the street. There is a wrought iron lantern hanging from a bracket in the wall above the door, in which a little lamp burns brightly. There is a sound of men's voices from down the path off left, and a moment later Nicholas Gadsby, the Harford lawyer, appears accompanied by Deborah's younger son, Joel. Gadsby is a short, tubby man of fifty-six, with a head almost completely bald, a round red face, and shrewd little grey eyes. Every inch the type of conservative, best-family legal advisor, he is gravely self-important and pretentious in manner and speech, extremely conscious of the respect due his professional dignity. He is dressed with a fastidious propriety in mourning black.

Joel Harford is twenty-nine, tall and thin, with a slight stoop in his carriage. His face is pale and handsome. Judged by its separate features, each of which has an aristocratic distinction, it should possess distinction. But it remains the face of a methodical mediocrity, who within his narrow limits is not without determination, and a rigid integrity, but lacks all self-confidence or ambition beyond these limits. His whole character has something aridly prim and puritanical about it. He has brown hair, cold light blue eyes, a pointed chin, an obstinate mouth. His voice is dry. A voice prematurely old. His mourning suit is well tailored. They stop as they come to the pool. Gadsby stares around him, looking for someone. His manner is shocked and indignant, and at the same time pathetically confused, as though he'd just been confronted by a fact which he knows to be true but which is so outrageous he cannot bring himself to accept it.

GADSBY
Trying to conceal his shattered poise behind a fussy, impatient air.
Well? She isn't here. I didn't think she would be. Under the circumstances. At this time of night. But you insisted—

JOEL
Dryly, indicating the summerhouse.
You will find her hiding in there, I think.

GADSBY
Stares at the summerhouse—with a sort of bewildered offended dismay.
In there? God bless me. I cannot believe—? I know how eccentric your mother— But at such a time, one would think—

JOEL
Dryly.
You have not seen her for some time. She has grown increasingly eccentric. And since the night Father died she has appeared— Well,

to be frank, deliberately deranged is the only way I could truthfully describe—

GADSBY
Appalled.
Deranged?
Rebukingly.
Come, come, Joel. Naturally, the shock—her grief.

JOEL
Coldly.
No. Whatever the cause be, it is not grief.

GADSBY
Shocked.
Come, come. A shocking statement for you to make. I refuse to—
Then bewilderedly.
You said "deliberately."

JOEL
I have felt it was deliberate. You may judge for yourself.

GADSBY
With defensive asperity.
Ridiculous. I have known your mother since before you were born. Eccentric, yes. Deliberately and provokingly unconventional. Childishly self-willed. Irresponsibly whimsical and fanciful. But always a well-bred, distinguished gentlewoman, a charming hostess, witty and gay—and beautiful.

JOEL
Stiffens resentfully.
I have never considered her beautiful. And I think even you will not think her beautiful now.
With thinly concealed relish.
She looks her full age now, and more.
Then guiltily, with abrupt cold reproof.
But you are forgetting the business which brings us here.

GADSBY

Guiltily.

Yes, of course. We must see your mother at once.

Then explosively.

By heaven, I wish I could forget. Joel! I still cannot believe that your father could—

JOEL

Interrupts sharply.

It would be better if you were the one to call her out. I have never been welcome here.

GADSBY

Turns to the summerhouse and calls.

Deborah!

There is no answer. He goes to the foot of the steps—fussily impatient, more sharply.

Deborah! This is Nicholas! I must see you at once. A matter of the gravest importance has come up.

He pauses, then turns to Joel uneasily.

God bless me, Joel, you don't think anything can have happened to her?

But even as he is speaking the door is slowly opened outwards and Deborah appears. Her back is to the door as though she had groped backwards in the darkness, her hand behind her feeling for the knob, keeping her face turned toward something from which she retreats. As the door opens her body, pressed against it, turns as it turns until it faces toward left, front, as the door is two-thirds open. But she keeps her head turned that she is still looking back over her shoulder into the dark interior. Gadsby takes a step back, regarding her bewilderedly. Joel stares at her with a cold emotionlessness. Suddenly a little shudder runs over her; she gives a smothered gasp and wrenches her eyes from the darkness inside and pushes the door back against the house, wide open, and faces front. As he sees her face, Gadsby cannot restrain a startled exclamation of shocked alarm and even backs frightenedly away from her a step or two. For there is a shocking transformation in her appearance. Where she had always before looked astonishingly youthful for her age, she now seems much older than her forty-nine years. Her olive complexion has turned a displeasing swarthy. The dry skin is stretched tightly over the bones and has the lifeless sheen of a shed snakeskin. Her black eyes are sunk in deep hollows beneath their heavy brows and have an unhealthy feverish glitter. They appear more enormous than ever in her small oval face. There are deep lines from her nose and the corners of her mouth, between her eyes and across her forehead. Her lips appear contracted and shrunken over her still perfect set of big, even teeth. There are hollows under her cheekbones and in her slender neck. The skin sags under her chin. There is the quality of a death's head about her face, of a skull beginning to emerge from its mask of flesh. Wherever her figure had been slender it is now thin, but it is still graceful in all its movements, and by contrast with her face, youthful. She is dressed all in white.

DEBORAH
Staring at Gadsby but with eyes that are still fixed inward, frightenedly and fascinatedly, something in her own mind—in a low voice that has lost its old musical quality and become flat and brittle.
I am glad you came, Nicholas, I must never go in there again!
She gives a little shudder.

GADSBY
Trying to recover from his shocked surprise at the change in her.
There is something in there that frightens you, Deborah?

DEBORAH
Strangely, as if talking to herself.
Something? Outside me? No, nothing is there but I. My mind. The past, Dreams. My life, I suppose you might call it, since I have never lived except in mind. A very frightening prison it becomes at last, full of ghosts and corpses. Yes, in the end, and I have reached the end, the longing for a moment's unthinking peace, a second's unquestioning acceptance of oneself, become so terrible that I would do anything, give anything, to escape!
Her voice had become lower and tenser.
That is what frightened me. After you called. Oh, not before. Before, I was so longingly fascinated, I had forgotten fear. The temptation to escape. Open the door. Step boldly across the threshold.

Bitterly.
And, after all, good God, why should I be frightened? What have I
to lose except myself as I am here.

GADSBY
God bless me, Deborah, you cannot mean—

DEBORAH
Death? Oh, no. There is a better way—a way by which we still may
live. As one has always wished to live. As the woman one has always
desired to be. One has only to concentrate one's mind enough, and
one's pride to choose of one's own free will, and one can cheat life,
and death, of oneself. It would be so easy for me! Like pushing open
a door in the mind and then passing through with the freedom of
one's lifelong desire!
Tensely her eyes glowing.
I tell you, before you called, I saw that door, as real as the door I have
just opened, and I was reaching out my hand to—
Then with a frightened shudder.
No, I am glad you called. Because I am not sure that one completely
forgets then. If I were, I would have gone.
*Abruptly shaking off this thought—trying to force a natural tone but still
strangely.*
No, do [not] fear, Nicholas, that I will outrage your sense of propriety by suicide. I assure you Henry's dying completely disillusioned
me with death.

GADSBY
Partly regaining his fussy self-importance—rebukingly.
That is hardly a befitting attitude—
Then solicitously.
It is very bad for you to come out here to brood over Henry's death.

DEBORAH
Strangely.
Brood? No. But I have tried to make it real to myself—to examine it as a fact. I have said to myself: "Why can't you face the new
fact, Deborah? Your husband is dead. He was buried this morn-

ing. These are facts." "Oh, I know. But I can't comprehend them as facts yet." "Why not, Deborah. You surely should be experienced in facing facts by this time." "Yes, God knows I should. I have lived with reality many years now. That afternoon at the cabin with Simon seems a lifetime ago, and he is more dead to me than Henry. I have kept the oath I made to myself then. Have not allowed myself to dream. Have not hidden from my life. Have made myself accept it as it is. Made myself a decently resigned old woman, saying to myself: 'So is so, and you must not hope it could be more.' Made myself each morning and night confront myself in the mirror and bow a well-mannered bow to age and ugliness. Greet them as my life-end guests. As elderly suitors for my body, roués in their bored withered hearts, their smiles insinuating the desire of Death. Not charming company, but a hostess must honor even unwelcome guests." So all day for years I have lived with them. And every night they have lain abed with me.

Smiling strangely with a bitter satisfaction.

Oh, yes, indeed! I have disciplined my will to be possessed by facts— like a whore in a brothel!

GADSBY
Shocked.
Deborah!

DEBORAH
Goes on as if she hadn't heard.
I have deliberately gone out of my way to solicit even the meanest, most sordid facts, to prove how thoroughly I was resigned to reality. Joel will remember one night at supper when I actually asked my husband: "How is trade these days? Tell me. I feel a deep interest. Has President Jackson's feud with the Bank of the United States had an adverse effect on your exports and imports?" A silence that shrank back, stamping on its own toes. In his eyes and Joel's a wondering alarm. Has this alien woman gone completely insane? No, she is merely being fantastical again. Deborah has always been fantastical.

She gives a little mocking laugh.

JOEL
Coldly hostile.
That is what you are being now, Mother. And we have no time to
listen—

GADSBY
*Who has been staring at Deborah fascinatedly, bewilderedly uncompre-
hending but disturbed because he senses her despair, now attempts to regain a brisk, professional air, clearing his throat importantly.*
Humph. Yes, Deborah. We must—

DEBORAH
*Ignoring this—with the same strange inward stare, and the air of talking
aloud to herself.*
And now Henry is dead. Gone from life forever. I am free. Can't you
understand that?
She shakes her head slowly.
No. His death will not live in me. It is meaningless. Perhaps I am too
dead myself—And yet I witnessed his dying. The dutiful wife sat by
his bedside. He seemed not to suffer but to be impatient and exasperated. As though he had an important appointment with God to
discuss terms for the export of his soul, and Life was needlessly de-
laying him. And then came nothing. An expiring into nothing. And
that was death. Is that why it cannot live for me? Did I think death
would be something in itself—a beginning, not just the end of life?
What did I expect? What was I hoping? For Death to open the door
and enter the room, visible to me, the good King of Life come at
last to escort one into his palace of peace, a lover keeping a life-long
promised tryst?
She smiles with a taunting self-mockery.
I regret to see living as a mistress of facts has not entirely killed your
fanciful imagination, Deborah! You and your lover-Kings! Had you,
perchance, personified your own death in your whimsical imagination, and fallen in love with it? Then Henry's extinction should
richly disillusion you! Oh, it has. There was nothing at all but a
meaningless ceasing to breathe, and I suppose that is only logical
and reasonable. If Life had meaning then we might properly expect

its end to have as much significance as—as the period at the close
of a simple sentence, say. But it has no meaning and the sentence,
worn out by futile groping within its own stupid obscurities, stammers haltingly to an unintelligible end—and that is all. Like an aimless improvisation on a far-off, out-of-tune piano that tinkles into
silence. And death is no more than a muddy well into which I and
[a] dead cat are cast aside indifferently!

Suddenly she presses both hands to her temples with an agonized, dis-
tracted gesture—tensely.

Ah, good God, can I never stop this everlasting thinking and questioning, this sneering and jeering and spitting at my own heart—a
helpless slave to a mind that runs on and on like a mad perpetual
motion machine I cannot stop?

Wildly.

Ah, and you wonder I was tempted to open that door and escape! I
tell you I am still tempted—that I will not endure being the tortured
captive of my mind much longer—whatever the cost of release—

GADSBY

Alarmed and bewildered.

Deborah. I beg of you, compose yourself. This—this is most un-
suitable conduct—even when I consider the natural shock of grief.
I cannot condone—such—such lack of decent control—

DEBORAH

Stares at him—a sudden transformation comes over her as she forces her
obsession back and becomes her usual self again. She smiles at him—an
amused, derisive smile.

Your rebuke is well taken, Nicholas. I fear I was boring you as surely
as I was myself.

Dryly.

May I ask to what I owe the honor of your visit, Gentlemen? It is a
rare pleasure indeed to see you in my garden, Joel.

JOEL

Stiffly.

I assure you, Mother, I would never intrude unless circumstances—

GADSBY

Interrupts worriedly, his mind now occupied with the matter at hand.
The circumstances are these, Deborah: In going over Henry's private papers, we made the astounding discovery—
He interrupts himself—indignantly.
Upon my soul, I could not credit the evidence of my own eyes! I knew Henry since we were boys together. I would have sworn he would be the last man on earth to indulge in such outrageous folly!

DEBORAH

Astonished and interested.
Outrageous folly? No, that does not sound like Henry, Nicholas.
Coolly.
I think we could discuss this mystery more calmly if we sat down.
She sits on the step of the summerhouse. Gadsby and Joel on the stone benches by the pool, at left-front and right-front of her, respectively. She notices the look of disapproval Joel gives her white dress.
I see you disapprove of my changing back to my accustomed white, Joel. Please remember, although I detest mourning and think it ridiculous, I did wear it at the funeral before the world. That is all your father would consider my duty. Never that I should play the hypocrite to myself.

GADSBY

Frowns rebukingly.
Now, now. It is no time—
Overcome with indignation again.
I tell you, Deborah, this is incredible!

DEBORAH
What is "this"?

JOEL
Coldly.
We found two letters in Father's strong-box, one addressed to Mr. Gadsby, the other to me. They were written some weeks ago. He had a premonition he might die suddenly. The letters are practically identical. They—

GADSBY
Feels it incumbent on him to take over now—in his best family-lawyer manner.
I must warn you, Deborah, to be prepared for a dreadful surprise.
He pauses. She stares at him calmly. He is thrown off stride by her lack of reaction and becomes even more portentous.
These letters are confessions that Henry had been secretly gambling in Western lands.

DEBORAH
Incredulously.
Gambling? Henry?

GADSBY
Nods solemnly.
Yes, Deborah. Unbelievable!

JOEL
Coldly.
As a result, Mother, the Company stands on the brink of bankruptcy.

GADSBY
It appears he had overreached his resources during the past few years. Sunk too much capital in new ships. Borrowed too freely, and then yielded to the temptation to regain a sound position by making a quick profit in Western lands. He lost, of course. What could an honorable, conservative merchant like Henry know of such wild speculation?
Giving way more and more to indignation and rabid political partisanship.
And what a time he chose to expand the activities of his Company. With his reputation for shrewdness and caution! When the country is in turmoil, with uncertainty the only certainty, thanks to that idol of the scum, that criminal lunatic in the White House! And, even with Jackson's passing, there will be no relief from this damnable demagoguery! It seems tragically probable his jackal, Van Buren, will succeed him!

DEBORAH
Cuttingly but with an amused twinkle in her eye.
An excellent Whig electioneering speech, Nicholas. But wasted on a
poor widow who has no vote. And hardly in the spirit so soon after
a funeral, do you think, although I know Henry would agree with
every word.

GADSBY
Crushed.
I—forgive me. I—er—I am greatly upset—and I blame conditions
for Henry's folly.

DEBORAH
Staring before her strangely.
It would appear I have spent my life with a stranger. If I had guessed
he had folly hidden in his heart and a gambler's daring— Who
knows?
She shrugs her shoulders with a bitter little smile.
Too late, Deborah.

JOEL
Stares at her with chilly disapproval.
I said, Mother, that the Company is faced with ruin. That is what
we came to discuss with you.

DEBORAH
Looks at him with distaste.
Discuss with me? You know I haven't the slightest knowledge of
trade.

JOEL
I know you have never taken the slightest interest. But now you
must.

DEBORAH
Arrogantly.
Must?

GADSBY
Interposing.

What Joel means, Deborah, is that in his letters Henry suggests certain steps should be taken which, if they can be successfully negotiated, may save the firm.

DEBORAH
Indifferently.
Then you have only to take the steps, Nicholas.

GADSBY
They can be taken only with your consent, since Henry's will bequeaths the Company jointly to you and Joel. I may add that Joel has given his consent.

JOEL
Stiffly.
I consider it my duty to Father's memory. What he proposes is the one possible way to preserve the honor of his name. For that I am willing to make any sacrifice of my personal feelings.

DEBORAH
Stares at him exasperatedly.
If you only knew, Joel, how many times I wish to pinch you to discover if you're stuffed!

JOEL
I have long realized I bore you, Mother. You will doubtless find Simon more congenial.

DEBORAH
Stiffens startledly — in a flash her face becomes as hard and cold as Joel's.
Pray, what has your brother to do with this?

GADSBY
If you will permit me to explain, Deborah. Simon has everything to do with it.

DEBORAH
Tensely.
He shall have nothing to do with anything that concerns me. You know his father's attitude regarding him. It was in obedience to what I knew would be my husband's wish that I did not inform Simon

of his death, nor invite him to the funeral. I forbid you to bring his name into this discussion. I have forgotten him.

Joel regards her with a cold surprise. Gadsby is astonished and taken aback.

GADSBY
I did not realize you felt so bitterly toward Simon.

DEBORAH
I do not feel bitter. I feel nothing.

GADSBY
I had thought, and Henry must have thought, or he would never—

DEBORAH
I never let Henry know my thoughts. Simon is dead to me. And I will not have him resurrected. That is final.

GADSBY
With a trace of asperity.
It cannot be final, Deborah. If you will pardon my saying so, it is no time for personal feelings. It is a time to consider what you owe, in honor, to your husband's good name.

DEBORAH
I cannot believe Henry would ever—

GADSBY
With dignity.
I trust you are not doubting my word, Deborah. If you will only let me explain—

DEBORAH
Very well. I will listen. But I warn you—

GADSBY
No, I cannot accept that. You must keep an open mind for the sake of the Company, and—

DEBORAH
I care nothing for the Company!

JOEL

Coldly resentful.

You forget what you owe it, then—your home, the comforts you have enjoyed, the privacy you cherish, the aloofness from life you pride yourself upon! I think you have not yet faced what has happened as it will affect your own future, Mother. You will have to sell this home. You will have nothing. What will you do? Go and beg Simon and his wife to let you live on charity with them?

DEBORAH

Passionately.

I would rather beg in the gutter!

JOEL

Of course, you may always have a home with me. But on a book-keeper's wage—

DEBORAH

Scornfully.

Can you possibly imagine—?

JOEL

Coldly.

No. So I advise you to listen to Mr. Gadsby, as he requests, with an open mind.

GADSBY

Joel is right, Deborah. Your position is—er—precarious, unless—
Plunging into his subject.
What Henry suggests is this:
He hesitates a bit—uncomfortably.
He realized that Joel has not had the requisite executive experience to take control under such difficult circumstances.

JOEL

Emotionlessly.

I am not grateful to you for sparing my feelings, Mr. Gadsby. It is my practice to face the truth about myself. Father knew I have not the ability to be head of the Company under any circumstances. In my narrow sphere, no man could serve the Company more faithfully. But, beyond that, I am worthless to it.

DEBORAH
Stares at him wonderingly—slowly.
There are times when I almost respect you, Joel.
He gives no sign of having heard her.

GADSBY
Clears his throat embarrassedly.
Humm.
Then briskly.
Henry appears to have had complete confidence in Simon's ability, in spite of his disapproval of his personal conduct. He seems to have carefully followed Simon's career.

JOEL
He did. He obtained constant, confidential reports on the condition of my brother's business. I know that because the reports were made through me. Father did not wish to appear in the matter.

DEBORAH
With a sincerely pitying glance.
Poor Joel, your father never had time to spare others' feelings.

JOEL
Seems to become more frozen—icily.
I dislike pity, Mother.

GADSBY
Embarrassedly again.
Henry's suggestion is that you and Joel approach Simon—

DEBORAH
Flaring up again.
I? Go begging to Simon? Never, I tell you! I did that once—
Abruptly stops, as Joel fixes a cold inquisitive stare on her.

GADSBY
Testily.
If you will let me continue, you will see Henry did not suggest you

ask Simon for favors. What he recommended is a straight business deal which involves no personal obligations whatever, which will be equally to Simon's advantage and yours. He knew that Simon's business is still a small local affair. Nothing to compare to the Harford Company, which is known and respected wherever our trade is carried. To be its head is to be a leading figure in commerce—as Simon, who once worked under his father and knows the business, will be the first to appreciate.

DEBORAH
Tensely.
So I am to ask Simon to accept the leadership of the Company, is that it?

GADSBY
Yes. A controlling interest. That is only just if he saves it from ruin. And Henry believed he has the means to save it. According to him, the condition of Simon's business is astonishingly sound from a cash standpoint. He has been shrewd enough to anticipate conditions, and foresee the ruin which is gathering around us. He has been putting all his profit into specie. Of course, from such a small business, it is no tremendous sum, but—

JOEL
It is enough. Specie has become rare and highly prized. A payment in specie here and there will restore confidence.

GADSBY
Henry appreciated, too, that many people here in the city have kept an eye on Simon's success. Because he was Henry Harford's son. The announcement that Simon will assume control will have a very salutary effect. There will be no inclination to grow uneasy and take to prying into conditions—which would be fatal just now. It will be taken for granted the Company is as sound as ever. Henry had learned, too, that Simon had been made a very favorable offer to sell his mill. So there should be no difficulty on that score.
He hesitates—then uncomfortably.
Humm— Of course, Henry foresaw that there might be difficult personal aspects. He knew that Simon still feels a resentment—

DEBORAH

If we are facing facts, let us face them. Simon hated him.

GADSBY

But Henry evidently believed that you and Simon still felt a mutual affection, and that you could persuade—

JOEL
Coldly.
Simon will not wish you to be ruined, Mother.

DEBORAH
Tensely.
So I am cast in the role of chief beggar!
Controlling herself—dryly.
Henry must have lost his shrewdness in more ways than one. He fails to consider the one person who can laugh at his calculations, and who will take great pleasure in doing so—Simon's wife! It is she who controls his affairs. He does nothing without consulting her, and if you think she will ever consent— Oh no, you will find she has never forgiven Henry for humiliating her pride, and this will be a glorious opportunity to revenge herself! And you will discover everything Simon possesses is in her name.

GADSBY

Henry knew that. He—er—evidently relied on your tact and diplomacy, Deborah, to convince her how advantageous for her own future it would be—

DEBORAH

I? She hates me like poison!

GADSBY

I am sure, if you wished, you could easily win her confidence. A woman of her type would be no match for you, with your intelligence and charm.

DEBORAH
Suddenly struck by a thought—with a strange, almost eager, little laugh.
My talent for intrigue? Yes, this could be the opportunity—

Then with a start—violently.
No! That has no meaning now! It is dead and forgotten!

GADSBY
Stares at her puzzledly—then in his lawyer's tone.
One further thing Henry suggested, to make his proposal as equi-
table as possible for Simon and his—er—family. He thought, as they
would have to sell their present home and come to the city, and as
this home, which he bequeaths to you Deborah, is much too large
for you and Joel, that—

DEBORAH
Tensely.
That I should invite that vulgar Irish biddy and her brats to live
with me!
Again suddenly struck by her thought, with almost a gloating smile.
Yes, that would be a greater opportunity than I had ever hoped—
Then resisting more violently than before—furiously.
No! How dare you insult me like this! How dare you make such a
shameless proposal!

JOEL
With cold bitterness.
It is Father who proposes it, Mother. You owe it to him to do all in
your power—

DEBORAH
Stares at him—bitterly.
And I hoped I had at last escaped the dunning of wifely duty!
With a strange desperate anguish.
For the love of God, hasn't his death even that meaning?

JOEL
Coldly relentless.
We are waiting for your consent, Mother.

DEBORAH
Bitterly hostile.
What an implacable bill-collector you would make, Joel!
Violently.

No, I will not have it! What have I to do with the Company? Let it be ruined! Do you think I fear poverty? What have I ever cared for things outside me? And I have experienced poverty before and did not let it touch me—the most degrading form, that of a minister's household, where one must pretend one welcomes it as a mark of kinship with God!

Desperately.

No! He is dead! All my debt to him is paid! I refuse—!

GADSBY

Embarrassed—clears his throat.

Humm! As your attorney, Deborah, I strongly advise you to consent.

DEBORAH

Violently, rising to her feet.

No! I tell you I swore to myself years ago I would never involve myself in such a low intrigue! And I still desired life then. Do you think you can tempt me now when I am an ugly resigned old woman whose life is only in the mind? You are wasting your time, Gentlemen.

She makes a gesture of arrogant dismissal.

You will kindly leave me in peace.

JOEL

With cold condemnation.

How long are you going to keep us waiting here on your perverse whims? I have always disliked this garden.

He stares around him with dislike.

Nothing is natural, not even Nature.

GADSBY

Staring around him in turn—as if fighting against an influence.

Yes, Deborah. The atmosphere is hardly conducive to—common sense, shall I say.

Then strangely and haltingly as if the influence took hold on him, staring at her.

My dear Deborah. Why should you talk of being old? Ridiculous! You, ugly? You are beautiful!

Instinctively her face lights up with an eager grateful smile.

Why, you could be the most wooed widow in the city! I myself would jump at the chance—

Deborah gives a soft, gratified little laugh. He goes on hastily.

Not that there ever was a chance. I know that. Besides, this is hardly the time to speak of— You will forgive me, Joel. Your father always permitted me a little harmless gallantry. He knew your mother could never take a short, fat man seriously. Nor could any other woman. Of course, there was Napoleon. But I admit I am no Napoleon, although at times I have dreamed—

Abruptly wrenching his eyes from her—grumbles irritably to himself.

Humph! What rubbishy thoughts for a man of my years and profession. Her eyes always did make a fool of me.

Reacts to an extreme professional portentousness.

I must protest against your acting so childishly, Deborah. You know there is one honorable course to take. As a woman of breeding and honor, you have no possible choice.

DEBORAH
Staring before her—with an undercurrent of tense eagerness.
Yes, I suppose it is my duty to see it only in that light. And then there is no choice, is there? It is fate!
With a strange urgency.
But you must bear witness, Nicholas, that I fought against this opportunity, that I did not desire it and did all in my power to reject it—that it is destiny—my duty as an honorable woman—and there is no way I could possibly avoid—

JOEL
Coldly impatient.
You consent?

DEBORAH
Slowly—as if forcing the words out in spite of herself.
Yes. I consent.
She suddenly gives a little shiver of dread—strangely.
Ah! I feel tempted to live in life again—and I am afraid!

JOEL
Coldly matter-of-fact now.

It's settled, then. We will go and see Simon tomorrow. I shall arrange for places in the stage the first thing in the morning.

He bows with cold courtesy to his mother.

Good night, Mother. I am going in the house. There is much to do.

To Gadsby.

Are you coming, Sir?

GADSBY

Yes, Joel.

He starts to go with Joel—then stops, after a glance at Deborah.

Go on. I'll follow in a moment.

Joel goes. Deborah is staring before her, oblivious. Gadsby looks at her with a pitying, if uncomprehending, sympathy. He coughs embarrassedly—attempting a joking tone.

Upon my soul, Deborah, I—er—I cannot see what there is to be apprehensive about in your consenting to the one sensible course.

DEBORAH

Strangely.

I am afraid of myself, Nicholas.

GADSBY

Puts on a kindly bullying tone.

Stuff and nonsense! You have done too much brooding alone. It has made you morbid. You should welcome this opportunity to escape—

DEBORAH

I am afraid I do, Nicholas.

GADSBY

It will distract your mind and give you a new, healthy interest in life.

DEBORAH

With a bitter intense yearning.

Ah, if it only could be a new interest, Nicholas, and not an old one risen from my dead. With what joy I would welcome it, then! With what humble gratitude would I give thankfulness to God for the undreamed of miracle!

Passionately.

Oh, if you knew how I have prayed for resurrection from the death in myself!

GADSBY
Worriedly uncertain and pitying.
I—I do not understand you.

DEBORAH
Forcing a smile—contemptuous and at the same time affectionate.
No, that is why I can safely tell you all my secrets, Nicholas.

GADSBY
Offended but determined to finish speaking his mind.
I *do* understand this, Deborah. It is not good to detach oneself as completely from the common life as you have done. But now you have a chance to start anew. It depends entirely on your own attitude whether this shall mean the opportunity for a new life of human warmth and companionship and family affection. I remember how devoted you once were to Simon.

DEBORAH
Stiffening.
I am afraid I could only pretend ever to forgive Simon.

GADSBY
Ignoring this—hurrying on.
You may even find you can like his wife, when you know her. Forgetting prejudice, you must admit she has been an estimable wife and mother. She must have her good points, if you will see them. She is evidently no fool, and it is not fair to blame her for her origin.
Hastily, with an uneasy glance at her.
Oh, I expect you to storm at me for pleading her case, but we must try to be just.

DEBORAH
To his amazement—calmly.
I will not storm. I could find it much easier to forgive her. I understand her feeling toward me. In her place, I would feel the same.
She smiles wryly.
There. You see how just I am.

GADSBY

Astonished—eagerly.

I do, indeed! Why then, there is no obstacle. But I was thinking most of your grandchildren—the opportunity they present to you. You can have no feeling against them, nor blame them in any way for the past. Your blood is in them. They are yours in part. Children in this garden would clear the stifling atmosphere. A little childish laughter and simple joy in being alive. After all, you have given it the aspect of a child's toy garden, made life-size. They would feel at home here. But I am thinking of it from the standpoint of your future happiness, Deborah. Do you see—?

DEBORAH

Slowly with a simple sincerity.

Yes. I do see, Nicholas, like an amazing revelation—a miraculous hope that would never have occurred to me if you hadn't— It could be the chance for a new life—escape from the death within myself, from my mind's torturing treadmill of futility. Resign myself to be a grandmother! That could be a resignation in which I might find a purpose in living and a meaning outside myself.

She stares at Gadsby wonderingly—mockingly but with affection.

You astonish me, Nicholas. I have heard of wisdom from babes, but who could dream of it from a bachelor!

Teasingly.

I really believe you are trying to make a good woman of me, Nicholas!

Then quickly, seeing he is hurt.

No. Forgive my teasing. I am truly grateful.

Intensely.

If you could know how grateful! And I swear to you I will try. It will not be easy. You do not know how bitterly Sara suspects me. Or how well she understands—what I was. It will be difficult to convince her of my good motives and persuade her to trust me with her children. I shall have to show her I no longer want Simon.

Her face hardening.

But that should be easy because I do not. He ceased to be my son four years ago. She is welcome to her husband.

With more and more of vitality in her tone.

In a way it will be a great challenge to my talent for successful intrigue. I shall have to be very cunning. Her weakness is she is sentimentally honorable and proud and full of pity. I must be very meek and humble.

Suddenly, angry at herself.

No! I talk as if I were planning to pretend and play a part! But I *am* meek now! I *am* humble! I am willing to beg her on my knees to give me this chance to be reborn! I can love her for it if she does! Because if she can trust me, I can learn to trust myself again! I can make her love me and her children love me! I can find love again!

She smiles exultantly.

Oh, I may surprise myself, I think, with my undreamed-of talents as a good woman! Already at the mere prospect of escape, I feel a rebirth stirring in me! I feel free!

She laughs with a strange self-conscious embarrassment and shyness.

GADSBY

With an approving, benevolent smile.

Good! Excellent! I am delighted you—

DEBORAH

With an abrupt change to a strange hectic air of bravado.

And to prove my escape—as a symbol— Watch and bear witness, Nicholas!—I will cast out my devil, the old Deborah—drag her from her sneering place in my mind and heart—

She makes a movement with her arms and hands of pulling something out of her head and heart and pushing it from her.

and push her back where she belongs—in there—in perpetual darkness—

She advances up the steps—with a final push.

"Depart from me, ye cursed!"

She grabs the doorknob, shutting the door.

And shut the door! Lock it!

She does so.

There!

Suddenly in a burst of triumphant, vindictive hatred.

Now question, and sneer and laugh at your dreams, and sleep with ugliness, and deny yourself, until at last you fall in love with madness, and you implore it to possess you, and scream in silence, and beat on the walls until you die of starvation. That won't take long, now you no longer have me to devour, Cannibal!

GADSBY
Uneasy.
Come, come, Deborah. This is all most unseemly!

DEBORAH
Turns to him—with the same strange air, but quietly now.
It is done. She is dead to me.
Then her face lighting up—tensely.
Shhhh! Do you hear, Nicholas?

GADSBY
Startled and bewildered.
Hear what?

DEBORAH
The footsteps beyond the wall. They have stopped receding. I think Life remembers he had forgotten me and is turning back.
Suddenly she is conscious of the expression on Gadsby's face and she bursts into natural teasing laughter.
Heavens, Nicholas! What an alarmed face! Did you think it was a burglar I heard?

GADSBY
Relieved—huffily, his dignity ruffled.
God bless me! Who could know what to think? Life, indeed! What fantastic rubbish, Deborah!

CURTAIN

Act Two, Scene Two

Sitting-room of Sara Harford's home in a textile mill town about forty miles from the city. The following night. The room is small, a typical room of the period, furnished without noticeable good or bad taste. The atmosphere is one of comfort and a moderate prosperity.

At front, to the left of center, is a table with a lamp and three chairs grouped around it. In the middle of the left wall is a closed door leading into Simon's study. In the left corner, rear, is a sofa, facing right-front. The doorway to the entrance hall, and the stairs to the second floor, is in the middle of the rear wall. At right of this doorway is a cabinet with a lamp. There are two windows in the right wall, looking out on the front garden and the street. Between the windows is a desk with a chair. At right-front is a big armchair. A rug covers most of the floor.

As the curtain rises, from the hall at rear the sound of small boys' arguing voices is heard coming down the stair well from the floor above. Then Sara's voice trying to quiet them and, for the moment, succeeding. In this pause, the door from the study at left is opened and Simon enters. Physically, he appears to have changed no more than one would normally expect. His spare frame has put on ten pounds or so but it still has the same general effect of loose-jointed, big-boned leanness. His large-featured Yankee face looks his thirty-one years. But there is a noticeable change in the impression his personality projects—a quality of nervous tension, the mental strain of a man who has been working too hard and put unrelieved pressure on himself. As he comes into the room, he is frowning, his eyes preoccupied. He comes to the table and stands staring down at it preoccupiedly. He is startled from his thoughts by a hubbub from the floor above, a chorus of boys' excited voices, the sound of scuf-

fling coming through the ceiling, followed by a resounding thump and a chorus of laughter. Simon's expression changes. His face lights up. He smiles and chuckles to himself. Then Sara's voice is heard in a commanding tone, and the uproar subsides obediently. Simon sits in the chair at left front of table. He picks up two folded newspapers from the table, puts one paper aside, starts to open the other, hesitates, then determinedly opens it. His eyes fix on one story. As he reads it, his face becomes hard and bitter. He hears Sara coming down the stairs in the hall and at once represses his thoughts and looks back toward the doorway at rear smilingly.

Sara enters at rear. She is flushed, her hair disarranged on one side, her eyes laughing and fondly maternal. She exudes an atmosphere of self-confident loving happiness and contentment. She is much better looking than she had been in her pregnancy. Her figure is buxom, but beautifully proportioned with full breasts, still firm and solid in spite of having nursed four children, and a slender waist.

SIMON

Well! What's been going on up there? I thought the ceiling was coming down.

SARA

Comes forward laughingly.

We had a pillow fight. They were so full of high spirits I thought I'd better let them take it out or they'd never settle down to sleep. If you'd seen Honey! He stood on his bed and aimed a great blow at Ethan and missed and came tumbling off to the floor. I was frightened he'd hurt himself, but not a bit. He sat there laughing to kill himself, and we all had to laugh, too.

She laughs—then suddenly shamefaced.

But what a way for me—and you in your study trying to write. Simon, I'm sorry, Darling.

She kisses him impulsively.

SIMON

Gives her a little hug.

Nothing to be sorry about. I couldn't get interested in it tonight, anyway.

He looks away from her. She sits in the chair at right, front, giving him a quick questioning look, trying to read his thoughts.

SARA

Notices the paper in his hand for the first time—too casually.
What paper is it you've been reading?

SIMON

Garrison's *Liberator.*
Teasingly but with a resentment underneath.
I know you don't approve.

SARA

Protestingly.
No, now. I never said that, Simon. I want the poor black niggers set free just as much as you—if they can find a way to do it that won't ruin the country.
As she sees his smile.
Oh, I know. You think I'm thinking only of us. Well, maybe I am. If you don't look after yourself no one else will. And you are a cotton mill owner who depends on the Southern planters. There's many here envy your success and would play you a mean trick if they could, like telling the planters you were Abolition so they'd blacklist you or—

SIMON

Frowning.
I'm not in the habit of advertising my opinions, am I? They're nobody's business but my own.

SARA

With satisfaction.
I know, and that's all I ask you to remember.
She looks at him quizzically and smiles with fond amusement.
It's lucky you don't make speeches about your opinions or you'd have the whole world bewildered. As far as I can make out you're a Massa-

chusetts Whig and a South Carolina Democrat, too. You're for Webster and high tariff—

SIMON
Cynically.
To protect our cotton goods. You approve of that, surely.

SARA
At the same time you were for Calhoun, who hates high tariff, when he wanted Nullification of the Union. I don't approve of that, Simon. I'm all with President Jackson there, that Union must be preserved at any price.

SIMON
Sharply.
I see State rights as a symbol of the individual's right to freedom.
Then quickly.
But why talk of that now. The issue has been settled by a compromise, for the time being.

SARA
I know it's settled.
Then teasingly.
And you're Abolition, too, and that's not Whig nor Democrat.
She laughs.
You're a queer man when it comes to politics. You'd better leave them to me. I'm for the party that protects our interests—as long as it protects them and not one minute longer. That's simple enough, isn't it?
She laughs.

SIMON
I'm quite willing to leave them to you. You know very well I am not really interested, that my one true belief is that the whole system is fundamentally rotten, lock, stock and barrel, and—
He stops abruptly and self-consciously—curtly.
But this argument is ridiculous. I was only teasing you about the *Liberator.* I was reading the newspaper.

SARA
Uneasily.

Oh, I meant to hide it. I didn't want you to see—

SIMON
His face hardening.
Why? I knew Father had died. The report of his funeral means nothing. It seems to have been an eminent occasion. Daniel Webster and every Whig notable in the city were there. That would have pleased Father.

SARA
Resentfully.
I can't understand your mother not inviting you to the funeral.
Bitterly.
Unless she thought I wouldn't let you go without me, and she didn't want her poor Irish relations shaming her before the notables!

SIMON
Mollifyingly.
Now, now. Don't let your mind return to that old bitterness. I think it was simply that she knew Father wouldn't have wished me to come and pretend grief for public opinion's sake. He had his virtues and the foremost was his hatred of hypocrisy in any form.
Then with growing bitterness.
As for her having Joel write me he was dead instead of writing me herself, you know I've never had a letter from her since I saw her that time at my cabin, although I kept writing her until it was all too plain she had no further interest—
He hesitates—then slowly.
I've never told this—it seemed too ridiculous—but I'm afraid I must have done something to offend her, which she's never forgiven, although I can't imagine what. Except one thing, which is too childish— But then, she is childish. She was telling me of some silly flight of her imagination and my sense of humor got the better of my tact, and I couldn't help laughing—

SARA
I know. You shouldn't have laughed, Simon.

SIMON
Staring at her.
You know?

SARA
Quickly.
I know you shouldn't have laughed, whatever it was. There's a time when women have to admit to themselves that age and death are real, and they get touchy about their dreams.
Abruptly.
But I think the reason she hasn't written you is because she's a wise woman and knows it'd do no good for her to interfere—

SIMON
I'd hardly call the letters she once wrote me interfering.

SARA
She was always reminding you about your book.

SIMON
Stares at her—smilingly.
You objected to that? But for the last couple of years, who has been encouraging me to write it?

SARA
I have. But that's different. That was so you'd have anything you wish from life to keep you content. And, anyway, I have a right—
She grasps his hand and presses it—tenderly possessive.
Because I love you, and you're mine, and your happiness is my happiness.

SIMON
Moved.
I know, Dear. And my one happiness is to give you happiness.
A pause. He goes on jokingly but with a resentment underneath.
Why, often I had forgotten all about the darned thing, or I'd want to forget, but you would remind me and send me into my study to work on it like a regular slave-driver!

SARA

Laughingly.

Oh, I'm not as bad as that, Darling. I'd only speak of it when I'd see you had one of your black lonely fits on, and I'd be afraid you were regretting—

SIMON

Frowning.

Regretting what? That's silly, Sara. That's all in your mind. If you'd seen what was really in mine, you'd have discovered it was something to do with the mill that made me preoccupied.

Then jokingly as before.

But I've had a dark suspicion for some time about the secret motive behind your persistence in encouraging me to write the book. I think you calculated very cunningly the best way to convince me it was nonsense was to make me attempt it and then prove to myself—

SARA

Guiltily.

No.

SIMON

You were sure the absurdity of it was bound to strike me finally. There I was at night in my study trying to convince myself of the possibility of a greedless Utopia, while all day in my office I was really getting the greatest satisfaction and sense of self-fulfillment and pride out of beating my competitors in the race for power and wealth and possessions!

He laughs, bitterly amused.

It was too absurd. I couldn't go on forever cheating myself like that, refusing to face myself as I really am. So I made a final decision tonight to forget the book.

Sharply.

Final, do you hear, Sara? Remember that and don't ever mention the damned thing again.

SARA

Unable to keep a certain triumph from her voice.

You're giving it up forever?

SIMON

Yes, to prove that, and wipe the slate clean, I threw all I've done in the fireplace and burned it. Not that there was much beyond notes. I've destroyed so many beginnings at different times. And I can confess to you now that many nights when you thought I was writing, I was simply sitting there with my mind a blank, bored—
He hesitates—then blurts out.
Yes, why not admit it frankly—bored to death with the idea of it!
He suddenly casts a quick glance at her face, as if regretting this admission—in a forced joking tone.
You don't have to look so triumphant, Sara.

SARA

Guiltily.
I'm not. I—
Then bluntly.
No, I won't lie. I am glad you have found it out for yourself. You know I've never believed your dream would work, with men and women what they are.

SIMON

Smiling a bit bitterly.
With us as we are, for example?
Quickly.
But you're quite right. My old romantic obsession with Rousseau's fake conception of the inner nature of man was a stupid mistake. Rousseau, as I see him now, was a weak, moral, sentimentalist—a coward who had neither the courage nor ability to live in a world of facts and accept the obvious truth about man—which is that man is compounded of one-tenth spirit to nine-tenths hog—
Quickly.
No. Rousseau was simply hiding from himself in a superior, idealistic dream.
Sneeringly.
As Mother has always done, in a different way. You were right to blame her, Sara. She did have a weakening influence on me when I was young, encouraging me to live in dreams and take a superior scornful attitude about the world of fact and life as it is. It was really

her influence that made me first conceive the idea of my book. I can see that now—her haughty disdain for Father because he was naturally absorbed in his business.

He laughs scornfully.

And yet all the time she owed everything to his business—the comfort she loved, the protected privacy, her fanciful walled-in garden, the material security which gave her the chance to remain aloof and scornful! It's too idiotic and stupid when you consider it!

Then frowning.

But why think of that now? Except I thank God I freed myself in time, and then met and loved you, who are so simply and courageously and passionately conscious of life as it is, and love it and are healthily eager and happy to be alive and get all you can from it, and don't have to hide from yourself in dreams of what might be in impossible other worlds!

Abruptly.

But I don't know why I'm doing all this talking. All I wanted to tell you was my final decision about the book.

SARA

I'll remember, Darling, and I'll never mention it again. I'm only too happy—

SIMON

Ignoring this—preoccupiedly.

No, all you have to do to see how sentimentally naive Rousseau's conception was, is to study history—or merely read your daily newspaper and see what man is doing with himself. After all, his deeds constitute the true revelation of his nature. What he desires is what he is.

With a bitter enthusiasm.

There's the book that ought to be written—a frank study of the true nature of man as he really is and not as he pretends to himself to be—a courageous facing of the truth about him—and in the end, a daring assertion that what he is, no matter how it shocks our sentimental moral and religious delusions about him, is good because it is true, and should, in a world of facts, become the foundation of a new morality which would destroy all our present hypocritical pretences and virtuous lies about ourselves.

He laughs.

By God, it's a fascinating idea. I've half a mind to try it!

SARA

Who has been listening uneasily—protesting resentfully.

Ah now, don't start thinking of another book and getting one of your lonely fits of discontent! What have you to complain of in life? Haven't you love and me and the children? Isn't that enough?

SIMON

Protests guiltily.

Of course it's enough! I would be an ungrateful fool if—And I'm not discontented or complaining. Don't you see that this new book would show that it was nonsense to complain about oneself or be ashamed of oneself?

Quickly—forcing a laugh.

But you're taking me too seriously, Sara. I was merely amusing myself playing with the idea. I have no intention whatever—

SARA

Relieved, smiling now, maternally amused.

If it isn't just like you to start dreaming a new dream the moment after you've woke up from the old! It's the touch of the poet in you!

SIMON

Resentfully.

Nonsense! Don't be sentimental, Sara. There never was any poet in me. And I'm through with all idiotic ideas of becoming an author. I couldn't spare the time, for one thing, even if I wanted.

With more and more of a business-like air.

It's a difficult period for trade this country is in now. I've got to concentrate all my brains and energy on our business affairs.

Frowning.

Conditions are becoming worse every day.

With a flash of vindictive anger.

That mad fool, Jackson! What does he know of business—an ignorant, mob-rousing, slave-dealing plantation owner! The cowardly tariff compromise he accepted coupled with his insane banking policy are ruining the country!

SARA

Well, he can't ruin us. We've got fifty thousand dollars, the most of it in gold English guineas. The hard times won't touch that.

SIMON

With satisfaction.

No. They will make it more valuable.

SARA

Proudly.

And didn't you have the brains to see the hard times coming before anyone, and guard us against them. I'm so proud of you, Darling!

SIMON

Pleased.

Well, yes, I did, if I do say it myself. Though I deserve no credit except for ordinary horse sense. Any fool should have seen the crash was bound to come. But they didn't. My competitors kept on expanding while I was cutting operations down. And now it's too late. They're caught, poor devils.

He smiles with satisfaction.

Yes, we'll weather the storm, Sara. And when the time comes we will be in a position to take advantage of others' lack of foresight. There will be splendid bargains in bankrupt mill property to be picked up right here in town. That will be our opportunity to expand and profit by the inevitable upturn which must follow the period of stagnation.

Enthusiastically.

And you can bet we will not be blind to our opportunity, will we?

SARA

Proudly.

You won't, I know. It's all your brains.

SIMON

Lovingly, patting her hand.

No, no. There is no you, nor I. There is only we.

Then enthusiastically.

Yes, there are great opportunities ahead of us. It won't take long for us to get the hundred thousand we have set as our goal. Or more.

SARA

No. That's enough. We promised ourselves—

SIMON

Smiling.

But wouldn't two hundred thousand, say, be better than one?

SARA

Smiling.

Maybe, but—

SIMON

It would give you a fine country estate and greater security for the future.

SARA

Give us, you mean. It's for you. I don't want you slaving in trade all your life. I want you to retire a landed gentleman and live at your ease.

Then calculatingly.

Of course, the more you've got to retire on, the safer you'd feel. But I don't want you to take risks and get in too deep.

SIMON

You used to laugh at me for saying that.

He smiles teasingly—with a note of taunting.

Who is being afraid now?

Then earnestly.

You don't realize what extraordinary opportunities there will be, Sara. In shipping, for example, there are many firms, from the rumors I hear, on the verge of bankruptcy already. Later on I know we could buy up one for comparatively nothing.

SARA

Uneasily.

No, stick to your own trade, Simon, whatever you do.

SIMON

But it is one of my trades. Don't forget I had my first business training with my father's Company.

SARA

With a trace of vindictive hope.
You don't think maybe his Company is in trouble?

SIMON

Frowning.
No, of course not. Father was much too cautious and shrewd. He took no chances even in the best times. And I'm sure he had everything arranged for the future, so that in case of his death, all Joel would have to do would be to carry on a traditional ritual of conservative policy—small risks and moderate profits—and be a Harford figurehead, while the real work is done by the competent subordinates Father has trained.
He sneers.
That is about all Joel is good for, as Father knew.
Then impatiently.
But all that is nothing to me. What I was going to say is that we can't dismiss the shipping trade as something that doesn't concern us. Properly considered, it is a part of our business—or it ought to be. Our cotton is brought to us on ships, isn't it? If we owned our own shipping company, managed as economically and efficiently as I know I could manage it, it would be of tremendous advantage to our mills—

SARA

Uneasily.
Oh, I see, Darling. It's only that I have a feeling that railroads are bad luck.
Bitterly scornful, lapsing into brogue.
My father, God pity him, was always prating about the great future for the country there was in them, and how he considered them the proper investment for a patriotic gentleman—and him without a dollar to his name! I can hear him now telling my mother—
Her face suddenly grows sad—scornfully.

Poor Mother! She didn't live long in her Convent to enjoy the rest she'd prayed for. She'd no more than got her wish when she had to die.

She sighs.

Ah well, she died at peace, anyway!

With scorn.

Though it's not the peace of giving up life for a living death I'd ever want for myself.

Then conscience-strickenly to Simon.

But what am I doing, reminding you of death now. Forgive me, Darling.

SIMON

Intent on his own calculating thought, has not been listening—vaguely.

Forgive what?

Then excitedly.

I tell you, Sara, the more I think of it, the more opportunities I foresee. Take banking. Banks are beginning to fail right and left already, and before long I prophesy that some of the strongest and most desirable ones will be so weakened that you could buy control—

SARA

Laughingly.

Stop! You have my head spinning! If you keep on, you'll be dreaming yourself the King of America before you know it!

SIMON

Starts and grins sheepishly.

I was getting a bit beyond myself, wasn't I?

Then with a strange self-compulsive insistence.

Still, if we had that two hundred thousand in specie now, no dream would be too impossible.

SARA

Scolding him as though he were a small boy.

Now, now, you're too greedy. And you mustn't do so much planning and scheming, when it's getting near bed time, or you'll never settle down to sleep. You haven't been sleeping well lately, and I won't have you getting excited and making yourself so tired and nervous.

SIMON
Leans back in his chair, suddenly conscious of weariness.
Yes, I am tired. But I'll sleep soundly again now I've put that damned book out of my mind.
He closes his eyes. Sara looks at him with tender maternal worry. He opens his eyes to stare before him.
What a damned fool a man can make of himself by clinging to the irresponsible, sentimental dreams of his youth long after he has outgrown them and experience has proven how stupidly impractical they are! Keep on deliberately denying what he knows himself to be in fact, and encourage a continual conflict in his mind, so that he lives split into opposites and divided against himself! All in the name of Freedom! As if Freedom could ever exist in Reality! As if at the end of every dream of liberty one did not find the slave, oneself, to whom oneself, the Master, is enslaved!
He chuckles bitterly.

SARA
Uneasily.
Ah now, Darling, don't start that black loneliness—

SIMON
Throws off his mood—with a relieved laugh.
Oh, I'm not. That's finished and done with. I promise not to bewilder you with opposites ever again.
Jokingly.
I'll be all high tariff and Whig and Daniel Webster and pro-Union from now on.
Tenderly.
Above all, pro our union, forever one and indivisible, Sara!

SARA
Moved—pats his hand.
Darling! That's my only politics in life, too!

They are interrupted by the sound of the knocker on the front door, coming from the hall at rear. They look surprised. Sara starts to get up but Simon is before her.

I'll go. Now who the devil—

He goes out, rear, frowning irritably. Sara sits listening. From the hall Simon's voice is heard exclaiming with startled astonishment— "Mother!" *and Deborah's voice* "Simon." *Sara springs to her feet and stands tensely defensive her expression frightened for a second, then hardening into hostility. Deborah's voice again. Then Simon's and Joel's in cold formal greeting to each other. A moment later Deborah and Simon appear in the doorway at rear with Joel behind them. Deborah wears deep mourning. It becomes her, giving her a quality of delicate, fragile sorrow. Outwardly she is all disciplined composure, the gracious wellbred gentlewoman, with just the correct touch of quiet resignation in her bearing which goes with her widow's black. But one senses an inner tense excitement. At sight of her, Sara instantly puts on her most ladylike manner, as if responding in kind to a challenge.*

DEBORAH

Comes forward with a gracious smile, holding out her hand—simply.
I am glad to see you again, Sara. I hope you remember me from our one meeting just before you and Simon were married.

SARA

Takes her hand, smiling in return—a bit stiltedly.
I do. It is a great pleasure, Mrs. Harford.

SIMON

Indicating Joel—coldly.
This is my brother, Joel, Sara.
Joel makes her a formal bow, his face cold and expressionless, but remains silent. Sara, following his lead, acknowledges the introduction in silence, then turns to Deborah.

SARA

Won't you sit down?
She indicates the chair in which she had been sitting. Deborah takes it.
You sit there by your mother, Simon.
She goes to the armchair at right, front. Simon sits in his old place at left, front, of table. Joel takes the chair at rear of table.

SIMON
Confused by this unexpected visit—forcing a smile, his tone almost resentful.
When—? This *is* a surprise, Mother.

DEBORAH
We arrived on the stage about an hour ago and went to the hotel to make ourselves presentable.

SIMON
The hotel? You must stay with us. We have a room for you, if not for Joel—

JOEL
Coldly.
I should stay at the hotel in any case.

DEBORAH
No, no. I would not dream of imposing on Sara's hospitality.

SARA
Smiles cordially.
I insist with Simon, Mrs. Harford.
She goes on in a tone that becomes, in spite of herself, defiantly bragging.
We've a fine room always ready. We've had Southern planters as our guests, and they seemed well pleased, although they're gentlemen who are used to great mansions on their estates—
Abruptly she is ashamed of her bragging and adds lamely.
We should feel very offended if you refused us, Mrs. Harford.

DEBORAH
Why then, since you are kind enough to put it that way, Sara, I accept your hospitality with pleasure. It is the more grateful because it will give me an opportunity of knowing your children. I know when I see them I shall be not only resigned but happy to be an old grandmother.
For a moment she looks into Sara's eyes with a strange, almost pleading earnestness.

SARA
Stares back suspicious and puzzled for a moment—then she softens.
I'm sure you'll like them. No one could help—
She smiles.
But, of course, they're mine and I'd be bound to think that.

JOEL
In his cold emotionless voice.
If you will pardon me, Mother, I think the sooner we make clear the business that brought us here, the better. We must obtain Simon's decision tonight so I can return on the first stage tomorrow.

DEBORAH
Quickly.
And Sara's decision. I suggest Simon take you to his study. You can explain your mission there, and leave me to tell Sara—why I am here. I want her to know that while our reasons for being here have an obvious connection, they are really not the same reasons at all.
She stares at Sara again with the same earnest, almost pleading, look. Sara reacts as before, at first suspiciously, then puzzledly relenting.

SIMON
Frowns—resentfully.
You always take a childish delight in playing the mysterious, Mother.
Turning to his brother—curtly.
My decision on what?

DEBORAH
Certain last wishes of your father's, and a bargain he proposes.
She smiles.
I need not warn you to scrutinize it closely or you may get the worst of it.

JOEL
Coldly rebuking.
Mother!

SIMON
Stares at her and then smiles—dryly.
I naturally would, Mother. But thank you for the warning.

DEBORAH

It was your father's wish that you decide this matter solely on its merits as a business opportunity—as though the party of the other part were a stranger. That is my wish, too. I want that clearly understood because Joel is a sentimentalist and will doubtless urge all sorts of fanciful family obligations. You will kindly disregard any nonsense of that kind.

JOEL
With cold anger.
Mother! I protest!

SIMON
His face hardening.
I flatter myself I do not need to be reminded by Joel or anyone of my just obligation.

JOEL
Coldly.
I shall urge no such obligations on Simon, Mother. I am too well aware he is indifferent to them. Besides, there is no question of obligations.
He turns to Simon.
Father's proposal is immensely to your advantage.

SIMON
Dryly—getting to his feet.
In your opinion. Perhaps not in mine. We shall see.
He starts for the study door at the left, Joel following.

SARA
Uneasy—warningly.
Simon, remember—

SIMON
Turns back reassuringly.
Don't worry. You know I will make no decision without your consent.
He turns and opens the study door and bows curtly to Joel to precede him. They go inside and shut the door. There is a pause of silence in which

Deborah and Sara stare at each other. Deborah again with the strange earnest, almost pleading, look. Sara suspicious, puzzled, yet impressed by the change she senses in Deborah in spite of herself.

DEBORAH
Simply.
It is a long time since our meeting at the cabin. I am sure you notice how greatly I have changed since then.

SARA
Uneasily.
I do. On the outside, I mean. In your looks.
Then with a cruel revengeful satisfaction.
You look an old woman now.
Tauntingly.
But I suppose you still dream you're the King of France's sweetheart, God pity you!

DEBORAH
Winces in spite of herself—then with a quiet smile.
You wish to test me? I cannot blame you for being suspicious. Yes, I look an old woman now, Sara. Well, why not? I am an old woman inside me. And I have not dreamed that dream since that day. Can you believe that, Sara?

SARA
Stares at her—then nods slowly.
I believe you. You couldn't, remembering how he'd laughed.
Then impatiently.
But it's no business of mine. And it isn't telling me why you're here or what you want of me.

DEBORAH
Hesitates—then quietly with a deep pleading sincerity.
I came to beg charity from you, Sara.

SARA
Stares at her, not able to believe her ears.
You! To beg charity from me!
Then with harsh suspicion.

Ah, what trick are you up to now?

DEBORAH

No. Can't you feel how I have changed, Sara? Please do! That old
Deborah you knew and justly suspected is dead. There is no trick
now, Sara. It is the truth that I have come to beg—

SARA

*Staring at her believes—then cannot restrain a burst of gloating triumph
lapsing into broad brogue.*

You, the great lady Harford! Glory be to God, if my father could
have lived to see this day.

DEBORAH

Ignores this—with the same pleading sincerity.

I came to beg you for the chance to live in life again, to begin a new
second life in which I will welcome reality and not fly from it, in
which I will forget as one long dead the old vain selfish greedy fool
and coward you knew who hid from herself in ridiculous romantic
dreams. Forget, too, the self who succeeded her, whom you have not
known, who resigned herself to death-in-life and fell in love with
Death, and even with insanity.

She shudders—then pleadingly again.

There is only one possible chance for me to live again, Sara, and only
you can give it to me.

SARA

Moved.

Ah, you poor woman!

Then hastily wary.

No. I'll see. I'd have to know more. I'm buying no pig in a poke,
thank you!

Then jeering, not unkindly.

Are you sure you could live if you had the chance? You're a timid
dreamy creature and you're not strong like me.

Boastfully.

I'll love life with my last dying groan!

DEBORAH

With your help, I would not be afraid.

Pleadingly again.

I want the chance to be unselfish, to live in others' lives for their sake and not my sake. I want to make myself an unselfish mother and grandmother, to learn how to live for others' happiness, to earn their love by giving and not taking!

She smiles at Sara—a trembling smile pleading for belief.

I want even to become a loving mother-in-law who can rejoice in your happiness as my son's wife and his happiness as your husband.

SARA

Moved—impulsively with a strange, almost servile, humble gratitude.

Ah, that's good and kind of you, Madam.

Then abruptly hostile—contemptuously.

If you're not lying to play me some trick!

DEBORAH

Ignoring this—pleadingly.

I feel now what I felt that day at the cabin, even when I hated you, that you and I are not natural enemies in our hearts—that in a way we complement each other and each has something the other lacks and needs—

SARA

Resentfully.

If you imagine I have any need for your great lady's airs and graces, you're badly mistaken, Mrs. Harford!

DEBORAH

Continuing as if she hadn't heard.

I feel now what I felt then, that if we gave each other the chance, we could be close friends and allies and even grow to love each other.

SARA

Moved.

Are you begging me for—?

Then with a strange derisive satisfaction.

Indeed and you've changed entirely, when you can lower yourself from the high pride of yourself in your dreams to—

She stops abruptly and stares at her warily—grudgingly.

Maybe I could like you. I know I don't hate you anymore. I'm too sure of Simon now. I know nothing you could do—And if I could trust you—

DEBORAH
Earnestly.
You can, I swear to you! Don't you feel you can trust me now?

SARA
Moved but warily.
I do—now. But you'd have to prove—

DEBORAH
All I ask is a chance to prove it, Sara.
Persuasively.
After all, you won't be risking anything. You would know if I tried to deceive you, and you could always make Simon get rid of me again.

SARA
Grimly.
I could. I'm glad you know that. And I would. I hope you know that, too!

DEBORAH
I do know it, and I would be the last to blame you.
Pleadingly.
What I'm begging for above all, Sara, is the chance to find a new life—and unselfish love—through the lives of my grandchildren. I want to become a good, loving grandmother. If you knew how horribly alone I have been for so long, Sara, sitting in my garden with an empty dreamless mind, with only the hope of death for company—a garden where Spring is but the beginning of Winter. It and I need to be reminded that Life is not the long dying of death but the happy greedy laughter of children!
She pauses—then adds quietly.
Will you give me that chance, Sara?

SARA

Moved.

It's true you have nothing in life, poor woman, and how could I be so cruel and hard hearted as to turn you away, when I'm so rich and you so poverty-stricken.

DEBORAH

Then you will! Oh, thank you, Sara. I am more grateful than you can know! It means the difference between life and death to me!

SARA

Uneasy, as if already regretting her consent.

I'm only doing it because it was through the money you loaned us when we were married we got our start, and we owe it to you in honor—I've never liked being in debt to you, but now we'll be square and even.

Then suddenly suspicious.

Wait! What has this got to do with the business his brother is telling Simon? You haven't explained what that business is yet.

DEBORAH

Smilingly evasive.

I'd rather not, Sara, if you don't mind. I know nothing of business, and, anyway, I want you to decide from what Simon tells you about it, purely on its merits as a business opportunity. You will be able to do this without being influenced by your old suspicion of my motives now that you see how I have changed and you know that my only real interest is the chance for a new life, which you can give me whether you and Simon decline his father's offer or not.

SARA

But what is the offer? You can tell me that.

DEBORAH

Carelessly.

Why, all I understand about [it] is that my husband realized that Joel hasn't the ability to be the head of a big company, while Simon has proved he has the ability. So my husband suggested that in case of his death Joel and I should offer Simon a controlling interest if he would assume direction of the Company's affairs.

SARA

Her eyes gleaming triumphantly.

My husband to be head of the Harford Company? Ah, if my father—!

She stops abruptly—then frowning.

But I don't see—If Simon's father wanted that, why didn't he have it in his will?

DEBORAH

With a mocking smile.

No, no, my husband was much too proud a man for that. He could not publicly admit he had been wrong in disinheriting Simon, or that he needed his help. Not even for the sake of the Company which was his one beloved.

Bitterly.

He preferred to bequeath to me the humiliation of begging—

Hastily.

Of course, you understand, Sara, it is a bargain my husband suggested. He was not the man to give anything for nothing. The Company, I believe, is at present in need of cash, and he knew you—

SARA

Her face hardening.

Ah, so that's it! The gold we've slaved to save!

Curtly.

No, thank you, Mrs. Harford. My husband has his own business, and it's enough. We don't want the Harford Company.

DEBORAH

Shrugs her shoulders indifferently.

Well, that's for you and Simon to decide. I appreciate your viewpoint and I won't blame you if you refuse. But please don't make any decision from what I say. Wait until Simon tells you all the facts. He will know if there is any advantage for you in the offer. Oh, there's another thing I was forgetting. My husband proposed that, in fairness to you, since you would necessarily have to make your home in

the city, I make over to you, as part of the bargain, a one-half interest in my house and garden, so that you could live there by right of
ownership and not feel under any obligation—

SARA
Her eyes gleaming again.
The Harford mansion! I know it's one of the finest in the city.

DEBORAH
Yes, it is really a very beautiful and valuable property, Sara. And I
need not tell you how delighted I would be. I will be so horribly lost
living there alone. In fact I want to double my husband's offer, and
deed the whole property over to you so that it will be entirely yours,
and you will have the sole management of it. All I ask in return is
that you allow me to live there with you—and my grandchildren.
She adds laughingly.
Oh, I admit this is shameless bribery on my part, Sara, but I am so
alone, and it would mean so much to me—

SARA
Touched and greedy.
I think it's very generous of you, Mrs. Harford.
Then warily.
But, of course, it depends on what Simon—

DEBORAH
Oh, certainly, but I hope he will find the business part of it advanta-
geous. And now, let us not talk of business anymore. I really know
so little—
Eagerly.
Could I see my grandchildren now? Oh, I know they must be asleep.
All I wish is a peek at them, so I can begin feeling myself an actual,
living, breathing grandmother!
She laughs gaily.

SARA
Smiling—touched.
Indeed you can. Their grandmother has the right.
She runs from her chair and Deborah gets up, too.

Only I better go up alone first and make sure they're asleep. If one of them was awake and saw you he'd be so excited and full of questions—

DEBORAH
Smiling.
Oh, I know. I remember Simon—
She stops abruptly, her expression suddenly bitterly resentful.

SARA
I'll be right back, Mrs. Harford.

DEBORAH
Throws off her mood—smilingly.
I would be grateful if you could call me Deborah from now on.

SARA
With instinctive humility.
No, that's too familiar—
Then hating herself for this—assertively.
All right, I will, Deborah.
She goes out, rear.

DEBORAH
Stares after her—as if in spite of herself, an expression of triumphant gloating forces itself on her face, and she smiles jeeringly.
At least old age has not impaired your talent for acting, Deborah!
Then savagely.
No! You lie! You know you lie! I meant every word sincerely! What if I did misrepresent the business aspect of it? That is nothing to me! That concerns Simon! I only use it! The real issue for me is between Sara and me, and that is decided! And I am grateful to her! I already feel an affection for her! I will make myself love her! She has been kind and generous and understanding! She has given me life again! I feel freed from myself, eager to live! I—
She stops abruptly and sits down again as the door from the study is opened and Simon enters with Joel. Joel's expression is one of cold, bitter humiliation. Simon is repressing a feeling of gloating satisfaction and

excited calculation. He comes and puts a protecting, possessive hand on his mother's shoulder.

SIMON
Gently.
Poor Mother. I'm so sorry.
She gives a quick bitter look up at his face and moves her shoulder away from his hand. He goes on comfortingly.
But never mind. You mustn't worry anymore.
In an almost bragging tone.
I think, without flattering myself, I can promise I'll soon win back for you all his stupid folly has lost.

JOEL
With cold anger.
It is cowardly to insult the dead.

SIMON
Stung—turns on him—bitingly.
Is it an insult to state a fact? He did act like a fool, as Mother will agree—

DEBORAH
Coldly.
I agree with Joel that the dead are, after all, the dead.
Simon stares at her in resentful surprise. She adds curtly.
Am I to understand you accept your father's proposal?

SIMON
Resentfully.
Of course. Did you think I would refuse to save you from being ruined and left a pauper?

DEBORAH
Sharply.
No, no! We will have none of such consideration, if you please. I told you it is my wish, as it was your father's, that there be no hypocritical family sentiment in this bargain.

SIMON
Taken back and hurt.
Hypocritical, Mother?

DEBORAH
Yes, hypocritical. You hated him and you certainly owe him no obligation. As for you and me, we have not even corresponded in years. We have forgotten each other. Our old relationship of mother and son died, from perfectly natural causes, long ago. In the meanwhile, we have both changed completely in character—

SIMON
Bitterly.
Yes, I begin to see how completely you have changed!

DEBORAH
Indifferently.
Good, I am glad you do. And I see as clearly the transformation in you. Well, then? Are we to pretend we are what we were, or are we to be sensible and frankly admit the obvious truth that we are now strangers? Admit it without resentment as the inevitable result of time and circumstance. I believe it is very important for us to do that, Simon—here and now—to free each other from the sentimental duty to remember a past each of us has forgotten. I think it is extremely necessary, now that conditions beyond our control, have brought us together again, that we start our new relationship on a foundation of lasting fact so it may have the chance to develop into a pact between friends who can rejoice in each other's successful freedom.
She pauses—then adds with a little taunting smile.
Anyway, I warn you frankly that, even if I tried, I could never play the role of a slavish loving mother convincingly again.

SIMON
Bitterly.
I am glad you admit it was just a role.

DEBORAH
Ignoring this.

So now you ought to appreciate why I must insist you consider your father's and my proposal purely and simply as a business deal. Accept, if it strikes you as a profitable opportunity. If not, decline it. And no more sentimental maundering about poverty. Why should the Company's ruin necessarily condemn me to rags. I have no doubt you would offer me a home with you. If not, Joel has—

SIMON
Naturally, Mother, I would welcome you—

DEBORAH
Well, then, no need, is there, to have pathetic visions of my begging in the gutter? Besides, I could—or so Nicholas Gadsby assures me— always marry well again.

JOEL
Repelled—coldly.
I consider it grossly improper of you, Mother, with Father scarcely cold in his grave, to—

SIMON
Repelled—coldly.
I agree with you, for once, Joel. It is revolting, Mother!
Then with a sneer.
And I would not take Gadsby's flattery too seriously. It is not so easy to catch a rich husband—even for a young and beautiful woman.

DEBORAH
Smiling.
That jeer might have hurt my vanity once, Simon, but now I am a grandmother, I am long past the desire to possess husbands.
She laughs.
Besides, you'll admit I can always have Nicholas, and he is quite well off.

JOEL
Rebukingly.
Mother! This ill-timed levity is—

DEBORAH

Inconsequential—to you, I know.

She turns to Simon with a return of her cold curtness.

Well, I hope you are thoroughly convinced now that whatever is arranged must be on a strictly business basis so there can be no possibility of any future misunderstanding about sentimental obligations. I refuse to be indebted—to you—for anything.

SIMON

Stares at her—then brusquely.

Very well, Mother.

He sits at the table—Joel behind it—curtly.

As I have told Joel, I will accept Father's proposal only on one condition. If you cannot agree to it, there is no more to be said.

DEBORAH

Coldly.

And what is the condition?

JOEL

With cold anger.

It is preposterous, Mother—an insult to my father's memory!

SIMON

Ignoring him.

There can be no question of my giving up my prosperous business here to take up his bankrupt one. That is absurd. Father, in his blind vanity, grossly overestimated the prestige of his name. I have never needed that prestige. I do not need it now. I have never been his son. I have always been myself. My condition is that I absorb his Company in mine. His Company must cease to exist. There must be only my Company.

JOEL

Angrily.

You see, Mother! Father would rather have faced ruin a thousand times—

DEBORAH

Dryly.

But unfortunately he left me to face it.
She stares at Simon—with a strange smile.
I see, Simon, what an opportunity this is for you to realize a life-long ambition.
Then briskly.
I accept your condition.

JOEL

I protest, Mother! You have let him beat you down like a swindling horse-trader! He sees the tremendous advantage for him in Father's offer. He would accept it unconditionally if you—

DEBORAH

Cuttingly.
Your protest is noted but kindly remember mine is the final decision.
With a smile.
I want your brother to drive the hardest bargain he can, to be unscrupulous and merciless—

SIMON

Dryly.
Naturally you could expect no mercy in a strictly business deal, Mother.
Then matter-of-factly.
Then the matter is settled—provided, of course, Sara consents, and you may take that for granted.

DEBORAH

Yes, I have talked with Sara and I think you will have no trouble convincing her.

SIMON

With resentful curtness.
I know that, Mother. Sara does as I advise in these matters.

JOEL

Gets to his feet—stiffly to Simon.
I bid you good night. I shall go to the city by the morning stage and have the announcement made that you are assuming control of the Company.

SIMON

Curtly giving orders.

Yes, see to that if you please. The sooner it is known the better. You never can tell in these days when creditors may grow uneasy, and suspicious.

JOEL

Stiffly.

Before I go. I wish to protest again, in Father's name, against what I consider the dishonor of your conduct and of my mother's. You will, of course, wish me to resign from my position.

SIMON

Indifferently.

No. You are an excellent head bookkeeper, I know. So why should I? And I shall see that you are given an interest in my Company, commensurate, under the circumstances, with the interest you were left in Father's Company.

JOEL

Stiffly.

I shall engage an attorney to protect that interest.

SIMON

Impatiently.

Attorney or no attorney, I could easily swindle you out of it, if I liked. But you are too helpless a foe.

He nods curtly in dismissal.

Good night.

JOEL

Stiffly.

I will keep my position only because I feel it my duty to Father's memory to do all I can—for I warn you that, whatever you do, the Company will always be my father's Company in my eyes.

SIMON

Irritably.

I do not care a tinker's damn what it is in your eyes.

Joel stares at him, is about to say something more, then bows stiffly to

Simon, ignoring his mother, and stalks out the door at rear. Simon frowns exasperatedly after him—then suddenly chuckles with amusement, with a change of manner towards Deborah of their onetime intimate sharing of a joke.

God, he'll never change, will he, Mother? He isn't a man. He's a stuffed moral attitude!

DEBORAH

Unconsciously falling into the mood of their old affectionate intimacy— laughing maliciously.

Yes, haven't I always said Joel is God's most successful effort in taxidermy!

They laugh amusedly together—then stop abruptly and stare at each other. Deborah defensively, Simon resentfully.

SIMON

I must confess, Mother, after all your explanation, I still do not see why you should suddenly take such an antagonistic attitude toward me as you have.

Hopefully.

Or was that simply for Joel's benefit?

DEBORAH

Lightly.

Good heavens, no! Is Joel important? No, it was for your benefit— and mine.

SIMON

One would think I had in some way deeply offended you. Whereas, if either of us has cause to feel injured, it is I! For some time after we last met, I kept writing you and you never deigned to answer.

DEBORAH

Because at that last meeting I realized that our old relationship was quite dead, and there was no good keeping up a pretense for sentiment's sake. You are wrong to think my present feeling is one of antagonism. I have no reason to feel that. No, my feeling is one of indifference.

Simon looks hurt and startled. She goes on quietly.

I will be quite frank, Simon. If I had heard of your death—Oh, of course, I would have tried to be dutiful and recapture sentimental, fond motherly memories of what used to be between us, but I am afraid I would have been as indifferent to your death as you have changed to be, as I would be to the death of a stranger, which is what you really are to me now.

SIMON
Woundedly.
Mother!

DEBORAH
No, no, please, let us face the truth. You would have felt the same if I had died.

SIMON
No!

DEBORAH
Yes. Why deny it? That is what Time does to us all. We forget and pass on. It is perfectly natural—and necessary. You have your life of a husband to live. You have your children. One can only think of so much. One must forget and eliminate the past. Why not admit that?

SIMON
Coldly—his face hard.
Very well. I do admit it.

DEBORAH
Good! There the past is finally buried, and we can start again and learn to become friends. I want to be the friend of Sara's husband, Simon. I want to be proud of what you are, of what you will do to re-coup the Harford fortune, of the great success in your chosen career I see before you. I am determined to live with a world that exists, Simon, and accept it as good because it is, and all else is not. I have forgotten my old silly presumptuous cowardly disdain for material success. I hope to live to see you become a Napoleon of finance.

SIMON
Stares at her—bursts out with contemptuous disgust.

It is no lie that you have changed—incredibly!

Then abruptly and eagerly.

But what you say is true. Finance is only one medium for ambition in the country today, through which one can conquer the power where possession alone gives you the liberty to be free!

He smiles.

It is a strange coincidence that you should come tonight and say these things. Just before you came I had torn up and burned what I had done on that absurd book—set myself free of the past—

DEBORAH

Quietly.

I congratulate you. You are wise. It was meaningless except as an obstacle in your way—a sentimental memory of a dead self.

Sara enters from the rear. They turn to her. She looks disturbed for a second at finding them close together, then comes forward smilingly.

SARA

I'm sorry to keep you waiting so long, Deborah, but our talking here had wakened Jonathan and I had to get him back to sleep.

Glancing from one to the other—with a trace of suspicion.

What are you talking about? Where's Simon's brother?

DEBORAH

Gaily.

Simon was talking over this business—for the last time, I hope.

SIMON

Joel just left. I'm sending him to the city by the first stage to announce that we are taking over Father's Company and making it a part of our business.

With a gloating grin at her.

Do you understand, Sara? His Company ceases to exist. We absorb it. There will be only one Company.

SARA

Her eyes lighting up with a vindictive triumph.

Ah, leave it to you! If my father had only lived to see—

Then with sudden dismay.

Then you decided it all—without waiting to ask me!

SIMON
Because I was sure of your consent and I knew Mother had talked to you.

SARA
But she didn't—

DEBORAH
No, Simon, you know I haven't the knowledge to explain all the business details.

SARA
She was begging me—

DEBORAH
Yes, I begged Sara to forget all the bitterness in the past, now your father is dead, and allow me to become her friend. And she promised she would try.

SARA
Yes, I did. But—

SIMON
With a strange, resentful air—almost sneeringly.
It is strange to think of you two as friends.

DEBORAH
With a little smile.
He doesn't believe we can be, Sara.

SARA
Defensively.
Why can't we, I'd like to know? I've always felt grateful to her for giving us our start in life.

DEBORAH
Yes, we will prove it to him, won't we? We won't let him discourage us.

SIMON
Frowning—irritably.
Discourage you? What a stupid thing to say, Mother! You know very well nothing would please me more.

DEBORAH
Laughingly.
There, Sara. Now we have your husband's blessing.

SIMON
Changing the subject abruptly—to Sara.
To get back to business: I didn't wait for your consent because I knew you couldn't possibly refuse such a good bargain.
Then almost as if he were showing off his authority before his mother.
And after all, you know from experience you can trust my judgement.

SARA
Uneasily again.
I do know, yes. But—

SIMON
Enthusiastically now.
I tell you, Sara, this is the luckiest kind of coincidence—an extraordinary opportunity for us—exactly the chance for expansion and growth we were hoping for.
With a sly glance at his mother—chuckling complacently.
And a finer bargain than I would have dreamed possible, thanks to Mother. I was going to be merciful and generous, but she insisted I consider it nothing but a business deal, and drive the hardest bargain I could. So I did, and I don't mind confessing in her presence, now the deal is completed, that we will be getting something for practically nothing.

DEBORAH
Laughing.
And so am I. I had nothing and I am getting Sara's friendship and a chance to make a new start in life as a good grandmother.
She turns to Sara—eagerly.

But all this talk of business is meaningless to me. What is important—May I go up and see my grandchildren now, Sara?

SIMON
Frowning—curtly.
No, they're asleep. You'd only wake them.

SARA
Defending her.
All she wants is to peek at them from the door. Isn't it, Deborah?

DEBORAH
Yes. To meet myself as a grandmother by seeing them in the flesh.
And you can trust me not to wake them, Simon.
Smilingly.
You forget I've had experience. Many a time I looked in at you and
never disturbed you.

SARA
Smiling at him maternally—teasingly.
Oh, him. It's hard to get him to sleep but once he drops off you could
fire a cannon and he'd never budge.

DEBORAH
Yes, that's the way he used to be when he was little.
She laughs.
I can see you have made him your eldest son, as well as your husband,
Sara.

SARA
Laughingly.
Oh, he's been that from the day we married.
Teasingly.
Only don't let him hear you, Deborah. I'd offend his dignity.

DEBORAH
Well, I hope you notice I am not one bit jealous of you taking my
place, Sara—now.

SARA
Stares at her.

Yes, I do notice. I feel it.

DEBORAH

I'm so glad you do, Sara, because now there can never be any mis-understanding on that score. And I know you won't be jealous if I can make your children love me. I do want them to love me.

SARA

Ah, don't think that of me. I'm not that selfish and greedy. I'll be only too happy—Don't I know how lonely and lost you must have been all those years without love to live for.

She takes Deborah's arm—gently.

Come along now and see the children.

They start back, ignoring Simon, who has listened frowningly, feeling completely out of it, his face hardening with resentment.

SIMON

Sharply.

Wait!

As they turn back—injuredly.

You might at least wait until I have finished explaining about the bargain I drove, Sara.

SARA

Humoring him.

Of course, Darling.

To Deborah, teasingly.

That's the way he is now. Once he gets his mind set on business the devil himself couldn't stop him.

DEBORAH

Seriously.

Well, I'm sure he owes his great success to that power for concentra-tion, and that it will lead him on to greater and greater achievement. So it's really an admirable quality.

Simon stares at her suspiciously but she appears absolutely sincere.

SARA

Oh, I know, and I'm so proud of him, Deborah.

SIMON

So proud you can't even listen while I tell you—

SARA

Placatingly.

Ah now, don't get angry at me. Darling, can't you take a little teasing without—

Then resentfully herself.

Much good it will do me to listen now after you went ahead and agreed without consulting me at all!

SIMON

Harshly.

You know very well my asking your consent has never been anything but a formality. What do you really know of business? It is I alone who have the right—

SARA

Suddenly frightened and hurt.

Simon! You've never said that before! You—

SIMON

Guiltily.

I'm sorry, Sara. No, and I wouldn't say it now if you'd give me a chance to ask your consent. It isn't too late for you to refuse. Nothing is signed yet. I can still back out, if you wish.

SARA

After you've given your word?

Proudly.

I hope Deborah knows I've too much honor for that!

DEBORAH

Jokingly.

But can't you see, Sara, all he wants is to prove to you how clever he has been for your sake, and have you say you're proud of him.

SARA

Smiling.

Oh, he knows that. I'm all the time telling him how proud I am, and making him vain and spoiling him!
She laughs fondly.
So go on now and tell me, Darling.

SIMON
Made self-conscious and ill at ease—awkwardly.
What I wanted to say is—
Suddenly he stares at his mother—sneeringly.
You a doting old grandmother, Mother? You will forgive me if I cannot picture that transformation! You've never cared about children, except as toys to play with in your garden and beguile your boredom—unless my memory is all wrong!

DEBORAH
Undisturbed—smiling.
Yes, that is true, more's the pity. But that was an old dead me who was afraid of life. I am not that now.
To Sara.
He doesn't want to believe that I have changed, Sara.

SIMON
Sneeringly.
Oh, I'm open to proof. But it will take a lot of proving, Mother.

SARA
Resentful at him—rebukingly.
Ah now, you shouldn't sneer at your mother like that. It's not kind. You ought to help her and take her word. What do you know of women? But I tell you I feel it in her no matter how she's lied to herself in the past, she's not lying to herself now.
She glances at Deborah affectionately—smiling.
I'd still feel that, even if I knew she thought she was lying and wanted to lie.

DEBORAH
Gives her a strange grateful look.
Thank you, Sara. I am absolutely sure now we can become great friends.

SARA

To Simon.

And I'm certain it's going to mean content for her, Simon, if you'll not interfere.

Arrogantly with a touch of brogue.

Sure, do you think I'm that stupid she could fool me? I know the fancy she has for the children already without a sight of them, and once she's seen them she can't help loving them.

Proudly.

Who could? And won't it be a great help for them to grow up fine gentlemen to have a grandmother who's a great lady—

She stops abruptly—guilty and humiliated.

Never mind. What is it you were going to say about the bargain, Simon?

Without waiting for him to answer.

Maybe you don't know or you couldn't act so unfriendly toward her, that your mother, as part of the bargain, is going to deed over her fine mansion and land in the city to us. She'll only live there as our guest and I'll have the whole management and be the mistress.

SIMON

His face hardening.

I will not consent to that.

SARA

Defiantly.

But I have consented, and it's only fair you leave me to decide about our home, which is my business, if you want me to agree with what you've decided about the Company.

SIMON

I told Joel I did not want even the one-half interest in Mother's home that Father suggested she offer me. We will rent a house first, and later buy our own home. We need be under no obligation to Mother—

DEBORAH

Sharply.

I told you there could be no question of obligations. I made the offer to Sara as part of my bargain with her—

Smilingly.

and, to be frank, I think I am getting all the best of it. I will still have all the privileges of my home and none of the responsibilities of actual ownership. And I will have Sara and my grandchildren for company. No, if there is any obligation, I am obliged to Sara.

SARA

Smiling.

No, Deborah, it's a great bargain for us, too.

To Simon, a bit impatiently.

Can't you see, Simon, that we'll be getting a fine mansion for nothing at all, with a beautiful, spacious garden for the children to play in.

DEBORAH

Staring at him with a strange mocking little smile—jokingly.

Really, Sara, your husband's attitude is most unflattering. You would think I was some wicked old witch, the way he dreads the thought, living in the same house with me!

SIMON

Resentfully.

Don't be silly, Mother. I—

DEBORAH

As before.

He seems to feel so antagonistic to me because I didn't answer a few letters. But I know you appreciate my reasons for that, Sara.

SARA

I do, and I'm grateful you had the fairness and good sense not to—

SIMON

Bitterly.

So it is I who am antagonistic, Mother? Well, perhaps I am—now— with good reason—but if I am, whose wish was it—?

Then abruptly with cold curtness, shrugging his shoulders—to Sara.

But, as you said, Sara, our home should be your business, and I am willing to abide by your decision. It is really a matter of indifference to me what house I live in. I shall have to concentrate all my attention on reorganizing my Company and for a long time to come I can see I shall have to do practically all my living at my office.

Becoming more and more enthusiastic—eagerly.

You can't realize what an opportunity this is for me, Sara, and what a tremendous bargain I have got! Father became panic-stricken, the coward, the minute he found himself out of his conservative depth. He greatly exaggerated the danger. It will be easy for me—

DEBORAH

Turning to Sara—gaily.

Let's leave our Napoleon to his ambitious destiny and go up to the children, Sara.

SARA

Teasingly.

Yes, let's. He'll be owning the whole world in his mind before you know it.

They turn towards the door at rear, laughingly.

SIMON

Resentful—coldly.

Wait. Although I have agreed to let you decide where we shall make our home, Sara, I would like to utter a word of warning—in Mother's presence, so that everything may be open and above board.

Sneeringly.

You will forgive me if I do not possess the entire confidence in this sudden friendship between you you both appear to have. Oh, I do not doubt you think you feel it now, but it will be a difficult matter when two such opposites as you are have to live together in the same home day after day, with continual friction and conflict of character developing.

SARA

Resentfully.

You've no right to expect the worst. And if it should happen, we can always change it one way or another, can't we?

DEBORAH

Gaily.

Yes, you can always dispossess me. You will have the legal right to, you know. But I am sure I will never give you just cause. You trust me not to, don't you, Sara?

SARA

Yes, I do.

DEBORAH

Smiling, with a strange undercurrent.

I promise to leave you entirely alone, Simon. So you need not worry. As for you thinking Sara and me as hostile opposites, that, I believe, is something which exists only in your mind, because you persist in remembering the dead me who was your mother. But Sara, at heart, sees how I have changed, and that she and I can have much in common, now.

SARA

Stubbornly.

Yes, I do, Simon.

SIMON

Resentfully.

All right then. I have nothing more to say. But don't forget I warned you. And remember I have the right to expect a peaceful atmosphere in my home. I will have too many important things on my mind to be distracted by domestic dissensions. So please don't come to me—

DEBORAH

Gaily—but with a strange undercurrent.

I hereby take a solemn oath never to come to you.

SARA

Staring at him—puzzled and resentful.

What's come over you, Darling? It is [not] like you to act so grudging and stubborn—I can't see—

DEBORAH

As before.

Yes, one would actually think you resented us becoming friendly, Simon.

To Sara—teasingly.

Men are such vain little boys, Sara. I have an idea he would prefer us to be jealous enemies and fight a duel to the death—

SIMON

Forcing a laugh.

What a fantastic idea, Mother! And you think you have changed!

He comes to them—protesting.

You know very well, and Sara knows, it has always been my dearest hope that circumstances would someday present you and Sara with the opportunity really to know each other. I was sure when that happened, you could not help loving each other, and I am delighted that, at last, my hope has been realized. I made the objection I did only because I wanted to convince myself you were sure of each other's good faith. My experience in business has made me overcautious about contracts entered into in haste, perhaps. But now I admit myself entirely convinced. I congratulate you—and myself on my good fortune. It needed only your reconciliation to complete my happiness and give me absolute confidence in the future.

He kisses them. Sara's face lights up happily. Deborah's remains teasingly mocking.

CURTAIN

Tao House
Oct. 6th '38

Act Three, Scene One

SCENE

Simon's private office in the offices of Simon Harford, Inc. in the city four years later. It is an early morning in the late summer, 1840.

The room is small, well-proportioned, panelled in dark wood. The furniture is old, heavy and conservative. A dark rug is on the floor of polished oak boards. On the walls are pictures of Washington, Hamilton, Daniel Webster, and, incongruously, John C. Calhoun.

In the left wall are two windows looking out on the street. Between the windows is a chair, facing right. Before the chair, a large table with drawers which serves as Simon's desk, with another chair on the other side of it, facing his. In the rear wall right, is a door leading into the hall. At left of this door, a tall cabinet stands against the wall. At right, front, is a door leading into the bookkeeper's office. Farther back against the wall, is a high desk with a tall stool in front of it. At front, right, is another chair facing left.

As the curtain rises, Simon enters at rear and comes to his table. He has changed greatly in the four years and looks older than the thirty-five he is. His body has put on twenty pounds or more of solid flesh, mostly around his chest and shoulders and arms, which gives him a formidably powerful appearance. On the other hand, his face has become thinner, more heavily lined and angular. There are patches of grey over his temples. His expression is that of one habitually tense, with a mind disciplined to function efficiently at a high pitch while suppressing all manifestation of nerves. His manner is curtly dictatorial. He speaks rapidly and incisively. He is dressed conservatively in dark clothes, obviously expensive.

SIMON

Before sitting down, picks up an engagement pad from the table and glances at it.

Nothing of importance—except the railroad directors—that isn't important now—a signing of papers—it is finished—it is mine.

He tosses the pad on the desk and sits down—stares at the table top a moment.

Mustn't forget Sara's engagement—it is time I did something to take her away from Mother's influence—make her my old Sara again—

Then frowning.

Bah!—better leave well enough alone—I really don't want her here interfering in my business—in which she takes no more interest, anyway—as little as Mother—

Then dismissing it.

Well, let's hope she's early before the others begin trooping in—

He picks up the morning mail stacked on his desk and at once becomes concentrated on going through it. The manner in which he does this is characteristic. He goes from one letter to the next with astonishing rapidity, seeming to take in the contents of each at a glance and make an instant decision, setting it on the table at his right, or dropping it in the waste basket.

The door from the bookkeeper's office at right is opened and Joel Har-ford enters, closing the door quietly behind him. He stops to glance at his brother, then comes and stands in front of his desk. Joel looks older. The stoop in his shoulders is more pronounced, with a suggestion of weariness and resignation now beneath the uncompromising rigidity of his habitual poise. He stands waiting, staring at Simon with his customary cold disapproval. Simon deliberately ignores Joel's presence—or attempts to, but it immediately gets on his nerves, and at last he exclaims exasperatedly, stopping his work with a nervous jerk.

SIMON

Well? Don't stare like a frozen codfish! Is this another of your periodical duty-to-the-Company protests against my management? If so, I don't care to listen.

JOEL
Stiffly.
As a stockholder, it is my right—

SIMON
Contemptuously.
Your right has no power, so you have no right. But relieve your conscience, if you must. Only be quick. I have no time—
Tensely explosive again.
Damn you! You have the stupid effrontery to criticize my leadership in the face of all I've accomplished in four years! I have five mills now, all running profitably, instead of one. I have transformed what was Father's bankrupt business into a marine division of my Company which is a model of its kind. I have—

JOEL
Interrupts coldly.
I do not minimize what you have done in that respect. What I object to is your reckless use of credit which continually leaves the Company in a fundamentally unsound position. You pay off debts only in order to borrow more largely. You go on gambling—

SIMON
Don't be a frightened old woman!
Arrogantly.
It is not gambling when I know the dice are loaded in my favor by my ability to turn any possible contingency into a fresh opportunity.

JOEL
You think only of further expansion. That is bad enough when you restrict it to your proper sphere, but when you adventure into new fields—
Stiffly.
I refer now to the deal for the railroad you are to conclude this morning. I am unalterably opposed to this folly. You know nothing of railroading.

SIMON
Neither do most of those engaged in it.

Arrogantly.

But unlike them I *will* know all there is to know. Anything I choose to make mine, I make mine!

JOEL

Finally, I want to warn you again against the growing unscrupulousness of your methods, the ruthlessness with which you take advantage of others' misfortunes. You are making the Company feared and hated.

SIMON

Curtly.

Good! I want it to be feared. As for others, I do to them as they would do to me—if they could! I ask no quarter. Why should they?

Contemptuously.

What a sentimental ass you are, Joel! You would like to apply to business the ethics men and women pretend to observe toward one another in their private lives. That is as stupid as trying to play poker by the rules for chess. The game of Commerce has its own ethics, and they are more frank and honest—and so, more honorable!—truer to the greedy reality of life than our hypocritical personal ones. The only moral law here is that to win is good and to lose is evil. The strong are rewarded, the weak are punished. That is the sole justice which functions in fact. All else is an idealistic lie about things as they are not and never were—and can never be, men—and women—being what they are. A lie that I would be stupid to permit to get in my way, or in my Company's way.

JOEL

Coldly.

I am thinking of my father's Company, not of you. But I realize I am wasting words.

He turns toward the door to right.

I will go back to my work.

SIMON

With nervous exasperation.

Yes, for God's sake! Now your duty to your conscience is done, get out!

Then as Joel goes toward the door, suddenly his whole expression and manner change and he speaks in a strange conciliating tone.

Wait. Sit down a while.

He indicates the chair at right of his desk. As Joel stares in cold surprise without making any move toward the chair, he bursts out angrily.

I said sit down! Either you obey me or you look for another job! Don't think because you happen to be my brother, you can presume—!

Joel's face betrays no emotion. He comes back and sits down stiffly in the chair. Simon's manner abruptly becomes strangely placating.

I'm sorry, Joel. Didn't mean to fly out at you like that. It has been a strain getting this affair of the railroad settled. My nerves are on edge.

He pauses. Joel sits staring at him. He goes on and gradually his eyes drop from Joel to his desk, and more and more it seems he is talking to himself.

It's the usual reaction. I concentrate all my mind and energy to get a thing done. I live with it, think of nothing else, eat with it, take it to bed with me, sleep with it, dream of it—and then suddenly one day it is accomplished—finished, dead!—and I become empty, exhausted, but at the same time restless and aimless and lonely, as if I had lost my meaning to myself—facing the secret that success is its own failure.

With a wry smile.

A vacation would be in order at such times—relaxation, complete change. But where? How? A voyage to France, say. With Sara. A second honeymoon. But Sara would not leave the children, and to take the children along would mean it would be their vacation with their mother, not mine with my wife. It would be no change for me. I have enough of that atmosphere at home.

He pauses—then with a sneer.

Perhaps Sara would even insist on taking Mother with us. She might feel lonely without her. They have grown to be such loving friends, drawn to each other by their devotion to the children!

Forcing a joking tone.

I assure you, I am left entirely out of it now—in the lonely cold, so to speak. Sometimes, I feel a stranger in my own house. That is Mother's doing, of course. She imagines she has been very subtle, that I have not seen—Whereas the truth is, I have had too many important Company affairs on my mind to bother. But I promised myself that as soon as I had time, I would put a stop to her greedy scheming, and now the railroad deal is completed—

He smiles strangely.

That may be the change in activity I need. I have neglected my interests in my home too long, unwisely entrusted them to others to protect—a sure way to be swindled!

He pauses—then strangely.

If you ever fall in love, Joel, take my advice and do not marry. Keep love your mistress with no right of ownership except what she earns day by day, what she can make you pay for possession. Love should be a deal forever incomplete, never finally settled, with each party continually raising the bids but neither ever concluding a final sale.

He laughs mockingly at Joel's coldly disapproving face.

Yes, my advice to you would be to shun marriage and keep a whore instead!

JOEL

With cold disgust.

Such ideas are on a par with your conception of honor in business dealings.

Rebukingly.

I cannot see why you wish to discuss such matters with me.

SIMON

As if surprised at himself.

No, for that matter, neither can I—except that my mind is empty and restless, and I can trust you to listen without hearing much.

Again with a conciliating manner.

I wanted to ask you: Why is it you never come to visit Mother? I am sure she would like—

JOEL

Dryly.

You know she has as little desire to see me as I have to see her.

SIMON

Strangely.

You should come, if only out of curiosity. You would be astounded at the way she has transformed herself
Sneeringly.
into a doting old grandmother. I think you would not know her now, any more than I know her. But the grandmother phase of her transformation is not the strangest. Although difficult to believe of Mother, it is at least understandable as the whim of a lonely old woman. It is her affection for Sara that is most incredible. I never thought that would last a month before they became enemies again. But it has become even more harmonious and intimate—seemingly. I have watched its development with the greatest curiosity. I think they both knew I was watching, and were determined to prove— Mother, at any rate. The strangest thing has been to notice how she has gradually taken what she needed of Sara into herself. Physically she has steadily grown younger and stronger and fleshier. She looks more like the mother of my children now than their grandmother. Or so she appears to me. That is why I would like you to see her. I want an outside observer to verify my perception of her. I know my suspicions cannot be mere fantasies of my mind, and yet I would like to be sure.

JOEL
Stiffly.
If Mother ever requests me to visit her, I will do so, as is my duty as her son. Otherwise, I will not.

SIMON
Ignoring this.
It is as though she had slowly taken possession of Sara in order to make of my wife a second self through which she could live again— to use Sara as a strong sanctuary in which she could hide from her old cowardly self, so terrified by life.
With a strange grim smirk.
Or, in another aspect, trick Sara into being an accessory in the murder of that old self, which was once my mother. And so leave me motherless. Which at the same time by becoming Sara, leave me wifeless, for naturally I could not regard—

He stops abruptly—then goes on with an increasing brooding strangeness.

It has been difficult to see clearly what she was doing, to discern which of many greedy purposes was her main purpose, what the final achievement is she is working and scheming toward. I have been very confused as I have observed the two of them, and yet I have had flashes of revelation, too. Sometimes the two have appeared to lose their separate identities in my mind's eye. Have seemed, through the subtle power of Mother's fantastic will, to merge and become one woman—a woman in Mother's image, but not her as I have ever known her. No, a strange woman, like a figure of woman in the abstract, spirit of Woman made flesh and flesh of her made spirit, mother and wife in one—to whom I was never anything more than a necessary adjunct of a means to motherhood—a son in one case, a husband in the other—but now no longer needed since the mother by becoming the wife has my four sons to substitute for me, and the wife having them, no longer needs a husband to use in begetting—and so I am left alone, an unwanted son, a discarded lover, an outcast without meaning or function in my own home but pleasantly tolerated in memory of old service and as a domestic slave whose greed can be used to bring in money to support Woman!

With a calculating vindictive calculation.

Yes, that is what Mother flatters herself she has accomplished. But she doesn't realize there are fundamental weaknesses in her plan, that the past is never dead as long as we live because all we are is the past. She is going to discover, beginning today, and Sara, too, that whenever I wish, I take back what belongs to me, no matter—

He checks himself with a sudden wary glance at Joel's expressionless face.

But all these fanciful speculations are nonsense, of course, which you mustn't take seriously—the reaction of my mind, left restless and purposeless after the strain of successfully completing the railroad deal.

JOEL

Gets up from his chair—coldly.

I have not listened. I have no interest whatsoever in your private affairs. And I know you were simply using me to talk aloud to yourself. If you have done, may I go back to my work.

SIMON

Explodes with tense exasperation.

Yes. Take your idiotic conscience to hell out of here. I will direct the Company as I choose! And until I ask for your advice, which will be never, kindly keep your mouth shut!

Joel turns and goes into the bookkeeper's office at right, closing the door behind him. Simon looks after him—with angry self-contempt.

By God, when I begin making a spiritual confidant of him, I should begin, also, to doubt my own sanity!

Then he relaxes and falls to brooding again.

But no. Even that dull fool realized I was really addressing myself—because I have no one but myself—because I have been left alone—driven out of all lives but my own—Mother has seen to that—by God, I was right to ask Sara to come here this morning!—it's high time I began to take back what is mine!

He fights down his anger—with brooding bitterness again.

Yes, Mother has been clever and subtle—left me with no life but this one which she always despised—this daily grind of slavery to an unscrupulous greed for power—the ambition to be a Napoleon among traders!—I, who once dreamed—!

Abruptly with self-exasperation.

Rubbish!—no hypocritical pretenses, if you please— You have no right—Your old dream was childish idealism—a stupid boy's misconception of man's true nature—which is that of a hog as your experience with him, and with yourself, has already demonstrated—the possession of power is the only freedom, and your pretended disgust with it is a lie—why, only a week ago you were so completely absorbed in the winning of the railroad you did not give a damn for anything else in the world! You were as passionately enthralled as a lecher gaining a new mistress, as happy as a gambler who risks everything he possesses on the turn of a card—

With a strange satisfied chuckle.

Except, of course, I had stacked the cards beforehand so I could not lose!

Matter-of-factly.

No, you must allow for your present state of mind—the reaction of emptiness after success—you've always felt it—But never so strongly before—there is a finality in this—as if some long patient tension had snapped—as if I'd reached the end of a blind alley in my mind where I no longer have the power to discipline my will to keep myself united—another self rebels—secedes—as if at last I must become two selves from now on—division and confusion—a war—a duel to the death—

He adds with revengeful bitterness.

Well, let those who are responsible for the challenge beware, for I will make it their duel, too! I have learned only too well in my life here the strategy of dividing in order to conquer—of creating strife and rivalry, and waiting until the two opponents are exhausted destroying each other—then I step in and take advantage of their weakness to possess them both.

He smiles with a gloating revengefulness.

Yes, Mother and Sara! Henceforth, I must insist you both sit in this game and take up the two opposing hands you have dealt me and play them with all your greed!—I must demand that each of you henceforth takes upon herself her full responsibility for what I have become, to its last final implication!

Abruptly—impatient.

Bah! What rubbishy fantasies!—As if I really desired two damned possessive women prying and interfering in my private business!— and I talk as though I had conceived some elaborate plan of campaign against their alliance—if I have, it is hidden in my mind— I do not yet see clearly—all I know is that on an impulse I asked Sara to come here—some confused feeling that if I get her alone away from Mother's influence, I would desire her again—it is a long time since I have slept with her—but at home her body has become repugnant, her beauty ugly—and, anyway, she is too preoccupied being the children's mother to have any love to spare—that, also, is part of Mother's scheme to dispossess me—

Irritably.

Rot! For God's sake, forget your idiotic suspicions of her! That silly old woman's senile mind is too occupied with pretending contentment as a doting grandmother, to engage in such elaborate conspiracy—although she is undoubtedly responsible for much of the indifference—but to return to Sara, hadn't I better think out more exactly how I shall attack?—no, wait until you feel her out and see how much of the old greedy Sara still lies behind her present self of contented, satisfied mother—the ambitious Sara who used to long to own an Irish-castle-in-Spain, gentleman's estate!—who was willing to use any means or to pay any price—even her beautiful body— to get what she wanted—as when, that night at the cabin before we were married, she made me take her body so I'd be bound in honor to marry her, and then use me as a first step in her rising in the world!—as unscrupulous and ruthless as a whore selling herself!—if that hadn't happened, I might never have married her—the long engagement Mother advised might have opened my eyes to that common greedy nature hidden behind her beauty—the lust masquerading as love!—if I possessed the insight into woman's true nature I have now I would have swindled her into giving herself by promising marriage—and then having had all I wanted of her, deserted her—it would have served her right to be beaten at her own game— I would have forgotten her and returned to Mother, waiting for me in her garden—

Bitterly.

But she wasn't waiting for you, you fool!—she had driven you out before you knew Sara—she wanted to be rid of you, so she could be free—she was through with you—she no longer wanted or needed your love—she was just as ruthless and unscrupulous about discarding you as Sara was in taking you—your happiness didn't count— yes, again it is a case of Mother being really responsible—I would never have fallen in love with Sara if—and her responsibility began a long time before that, too—I had not felt any really serene happiness in her garden since I was a little boy—she made it plain that I possessed no right to be with her, that I was merely permitted to remain there to amuse her, a toy that her whim tired of and ruthlessly discarded!—that nonsense about her summerhouse—that was her way of showing me—and she took pains to point it out to me by implication that day she deliberately made up the fairy tale about the exiled Prince and the magic door—Yes, I never knew peace or faith in life again from that day—

Angry at himself.

Damnation!—what a sentimental ass, to be digging back in the past to boyhood memories—the pastime of weaklings with no present or future!—

Bitterly.

Nevertheless, it does trace the responsibility—the guilt—to the source—and indicates the line poetic justice should pursue to recompense and punish—In the case of Sara, too—Mother's is the spiritual greed, but the material lust is Sara's—Mother did not drive me to a career in the slave markets of trade where in buying one sells oneself—or sit me at a table in the gambling dive of commerce—she read Byron aloud, and despised business—it was Sara's lust, dreaming of Irish castles in Spain and a landed lady's estate, that has made me a cotton good's Napoleon!—who drove me to make her proud of me at any price—

He pauses—then with an air of bitter satisfaction.

I begin to see in part the plan of the campaign I must start when she comes—she must be forced, gradually, of course, to take over her full responsibility—to share the burden and the cost—to pay back what is mine—all that I still desire from her, at least!

He sits staring before him, frowningly concentrated, his expression becoming coldly ruthless and calculating.

The door from the hall at rear is opened and Sara enters. She has not changed much in appearance in the five years.* Has grown a little more matronly, perhaps, but seems no older. Is still exceedingly pretty, strong and healthy, with the same firm pronouncedly female figure. But she is dressed much better, with discriminating taste and style now, and expensively. In her personality, however, one is at once conscious of a decided change in quality, from her old positive, eagerly-grasping aliveness to a more passive, satisfied contentedness. Her manner has taken on a lot of Deborah's self-assured poise, and her way of speaking copies Deborah, although the rhythm of Irish speech still underlies it. She stands looking at

---

*O'Neill means four, not five, years. It has been four years since the close of act 2 (1836–40). See the synopsis of scenes at the beginning of the play.

Simon but he is oblivious of her presence. Sara smiles assuredly, a smile that has lost its old passionate tenderness and become maternal, complacent in possessiveness—a smile that takes its proprietorship for granted. Smiling with growing amusement, she tip-toes forward until she stands by his table.

SARA

You might ask me to sit down, Simon.
He jumps startledly in his chair.

SIMON

His frayed nerves exploding angrily—as if he did not recognize her.
God damn it, what do you mean by sneaking—!
Then confusedly.
Oh, it's you. I didn't—

SARA

Taken aback but forcing a smile.
Well! That's a nice greeting, I must say, after you begged me to come.

SIMON

I apologize, Sara. For a moment, I didn't recognize who it was.
He springs to his feet—with a forced cordiality, indicating the chair across the table.
Sit down, do.
She sits in it and he sits down again.

SARA

I had no idea you'd gotten so nervous. You haven't seemed to be at home.

SIMON

Affecting carelessness.
Perhaps I control myself better there. Or perhaps, on the other hand, you have been too occupied with family affairs to notice!

SARA

Smiling.
If that isn't like you, to put the blame on me, when it's you who come

home every night with your head so full of business you might as well be on the moon for all the attention you pay your mother or me.

With a trace of bitterness.

Or the children.

Abruptly changing the subject—with a forced interest.

Speaking of business, tell me about the Company. You've been doing wonders with it, I know. You never mention it anymore to us at home, but everyone tells me you're becoming the young Napoleon of trade here in the city.

SIMON

Pleased but at the same time scornful.

The most flattering comparison the mind of woman can imagine! If men and women had ever admired Christ one-tenth as much as they admire that greedy adventurer, what a success Christianity might have been!

He laughs sneeringly—then abruptly with a proud boastful air.

Here's a bit of news about my success you haven't heard yet, Sara. I've got the railroad now. You remember I promised myself I would. Well, it's mine!

SARA

With forced enthusiasm.

Isn't that fine! I congratulate you, Simon.

SIMON

With a preening satisfaction.

I have a final meeting with the directors this morning. Merely a formality. They've already agreed to my terms. Not easy terms for them to accept, I might add! They are left without a vestige of real power. I become absolute master. But they had no choice. They were on the verge of bankruptcy. I did not strike until I knew they were divided among themselves and weakened by dissension and jealousy and conflicting purposes—which I had secretly encouraged, by the way, to hasten the end.

Enthusiastically.

Wait till you see what I do with the road in a couple of years! I have learned from their mistakes. I'll make no mistakes!

SARA
Her enthusiasm more forced.
I'm sure you won't.

SIMON
Noticing her tone—deflated, and for a second boyishly hurt.
You're not very enthusiastic.

SARA
Hastily.
Oh, I am.
Forcing a smile.
Maybe my feelings are a little hurt. You used to say "us" and "ours" and now everything with you is "I" and "mine."

SIMON
Stares at her sharply—as if he saw with satisfaction some calculation verified.
Ah, you feel that?

SARA
Hastily and defensively.
No. It's selfish of me to talk like that. God knows I've more than enough to content me with a beautiful mansion for my home, and as happy a life as a woman could wish with Deborah and my children, without grudging you what is yours.

SIMON
Dryly.
Yes, one should never complain of the price one must pay for what one wants from life—or thinks one wants.

SARA
A bit defiantly.
I know what I want, and I have it.

SIMON
Ignoring this.
For example, I might complain with equal reason that you used to speak of our home and our children, while now—

SARA

In her turn stares at him sharply.
Ah! You feel that, do you?

SIMON

Carelessly.
No, I said I might. But I have too many important affairs on my mind to give much thought to—

SARA

Trying to conceal her disappointment.
I'm glad you're frank about it. After all, it's only natural. You can't give your mind to everything.
Bitterly.
And we've seen for a long time, Deborah and I, that you care more for the Company than anything else in life.

SIMON

Ignoring this last—carelessly but with a taunting undercurrent.
Anyway, I must confess I cannot believe your possessive adjectives are more than a boast. I always have the feeling at home that, although Mother has relinquished all outward show of ownership and authority, she has managed to keep in possession.

SARA

Resentfully.
Well, you're wrong. I have the only say about everything, and she's happy to let me have it.

SIMON

Smiling.
Yes, Mother has always had a subtle talent for contriving it so that others must desire what she desires—and then generously giving them their way!

SARA

She hasn't with me. I'm not such a fool—

SIMON

Not when you're on your guard. But you're so kind and sentimental you never suspect—

SARA

There's nothing to suspect! No woman could be a truer friend than she's been to me! She's more like a sister, or my own mother, than a mother-in-law. And she's been such a good grandmother to the children—even if she does spoil them.

SIMON

Gives her a calculating glance.
Yes, she is spoiling them. There's no doubt about that.

SARA

Defensively.
If she does, it's only because she's still a child in her heart, herself, a great part of her, and like one of them. And there's no harm. I can always correct any bad ways she gets them into.

SIMON

Watching her.
Of course, there's no harm done—if you're sure you haven't let it go too far.

SARA

Angrily.
I haven't! I can take care of my children, thank you, without any advice—
Accusingly.
Is that your reason for inviting me here—to try and make trouble between your mother and me?

SIMON

Curtly.
Don't be ridiculous! I'm delighted at the friendship which has developed between you. The more so, because I never dared hope—

SARA

Almost tauntingly.

We know you didn't. Well, we fooled you!

SIMON

Make trouble? Don't you think I appreciate peace and harmony in my home, if only for selfish reasons.

SARA

You should.

SIMON

Do you imagine I'd prefer to have you at each other's throats?

SARA

No. That'd be crazy.
Then reproachfully.
While we're talking of this, Simon, I want to say something I've meant to for a long time. I know you've kept a secret grudge against her in your heart. But isn't it about time you stopped being so child-ish, and forgave—

SIMON

Sharply.
Don't be stupid. There's nothing to forgive. What makes you say I harbor a grudge? Do we ever quarrel? Am I not always pleasant with her?

SARA

Yes, as you'd be to an acquaintance in the street!

SIMON

Impatiently.
But what's the use of pretending we have anything in common any-more, when we haven't. Just because she happened to bear me into the world! This absurd sentimental sense of obligation between par-ents and children! Obligation for what? Almost any fool of a woman can have a son, and every fool of a man has had a mother! It's no great achievement on either side, and all the hypocritical values we set on the relationship are stupidity.

SARA

Angrily.

That's not true! I've my four sons and I know the love I feel for them, and the love they feel for me!

SIMON
Ignoring this.
And don't tell me Mother minds my indifference. She has learned not to need me.

SARA
With a trace of vindictive satisfaction.
That's true enough. She doesn't miss you now she has the children.

SIMON
Bitterly.
Yes. As you have.

SARA
Stares at him defiantly.
As I have, yes.
Then with a strange eagerness—teasingly.
Don't tell me you're jealous of the children—with me?

SIMON
Curtly resentful.
I have had too many important matters on my mind to bother about your children. That's your business.

SARA
Bitterly.
No. I know you never give them a thought—
Then forcing a smile—placatingly.
But I hope you didn't ask me here—for the first time in Heaven knows how long—just to quarrel with me.
She gets up and comes around the table to him.
I know I didn't come for that.
She puts a hand on his shoulder.

SIMON
Moved.

Forgive me. I'm tired. Worn out and nervy. This railroad deal has been a strain.

SARA
Looks down at him worriedly.
I know, Simon. You haven't looked well for a long time—not like yourself at all.

SIMON
Bitterly.
Then you do notice once in a while.

SARA
Ignoring his tone—smilingly.
Did you think you're the only one can notice anything? Your mother has seen it, too. She pays some attention to you even if you don't to her.

SIMON
Coldly.
Indeed? And what was it you both noticed?

SARA
Pauses—then slowly.
That you've been changing in some queer way inside you. Sometimes at night when you sit in the parlor with us, all of a sudden, it's like a stranger staring at us. It's a frightening feeling, Simon. I think I began to notice it around the time you started sleeping in your own room away from me—

SIMON
Stares at her calculatingly—then with a deliberately provocative coarse sensuality.
Ah, that's it, eh? Your body felt swindled and it made you suspicious, I suppose, that I might have found another woman's body that is more beautiful and desirable to mine than yours? You probably think I must be secretly keeping some beautiful mistress who has stolen your place in bed!
He smiles tauntingly.

SARA

Startled and repelled.

Simon! You know such a nasty thought would never enter my head! It's the last thing I'd ever suspect! And I don't see how it could come to your mind—

She gives him a look of suspicion, all the jealousy of her passionately possessive nature beginning to flare up.

Unless you've had the thought yourself—

SIMON

His face lighting up with satisfaction—provocatively.

No, no. I was only joking.

SARA

Jealously angry—forgetting all ladylike poise.

I don't believe you! You must have had the wish—

With a sudden fierce passion she grabs his head and turns his face up to hers.

Look at me! If I thought you wanted another woman—!

SIMON

Puts his arm around her and hugs her to him, his face triumphantly gratified—teasingly.

Well, what would you do?

SARA

I'll kill her, that's what I'd do! And you, too!

Then miserably frightened.

Simon! You don't deny it! Tell me—!

SIMON

Provocatively unconvincing, hugging her again.

No, no. Of course I would never—

SARA

You don't say that as if you meant it!

Struggling to free herself.

Let me go! I don't want you hugging me—when maybe you're wishing it was another—

Furious at the thought, she grabs his shoulders and shakes him fiercely.

Tell me the truth, I'm saying! Is that the real reason you began sleeping alone—that you'd found someone prettier, and grown tired of me? Is it to confess that you had me come here? Are you going to ask me to set you free to be hers?

Savagely.

If you are, you can hold your prate! I'll see her in hell first! If any woman thinks she can take you, she'll find I'll fight to the death! I'd tear her to pieces, first! And you! And myself! I'd do anything!

She sits down on the arm of his chair and hugs him to her with passionate possessiveness.

You're mine till death, and beyond death, and I'll never let you go, do you hear!

She kisses him passionately on the lips.

SIMON

His face happy now with confident possession and aroused desire.

So you really are jealous?

SARA

Fiercely.

Of course I'm jealous! Am I flesh and blood? Don't I love you more than all the world?

SIMON

Do you? I thought the children—

SARA

Almost contemptuously.

Ah, the children!

Hastily.

Not that I don't love them with all my heart. But they're not my lover and husband! You come first!

SIMON

Do I? I shouldn't say from your actions for a long time—

SARA

My actions! Are you trying to say I'm to blame? Why, there's nights when you stare as if you were wondering who I was and what was my business there. You sit with us deep in your thoughts, as if I was dead. Or you converse with us so pleasant and polite, like a gentle-man guest come in to spend the evening.

SIMON

Perhaps I do feel like a dispossessed intruder. You know I never ap-proved of our living with Mother.

SARA

Impatiently.

Ah, don't blame her. She's as sweet as can be to us.

Then going on.

And behind all your pleasant talk to us, you mean something else, and when you're thinking it isn't about business deals alone you're scheming . . .

Confusedly.

I don't know how to say it, Darling, but it's as though the minute you came home I felt everything begin to change until nothing is what it seems to be, and we all get suspicious of each other.

SIMON

Stares at her fixedly.

What? Even you and Mother?

SARA

Reluctantly.

Yes.

Hastily.

No, I meant it might if we weren't careful. It's like a spell that tries to come between us.

Defiantly.

But we don't let it.

SIMON

Ignoring this last.

Ah. That is strange. I thought you had both entirely forgotten your old jealous animosity, that you lived in a perfect harmonious unity of interests and desires now. Why, sometimes as I watch you I become so intensely conscious of your unity that you appear as one woman to me. I cannot distinguish my wife from — It is a bewildering confusion in which I myself seem to lose my separateness, to dissolve, to have no life except within—

With strange bitter intensity.

Suffocating! Devouring! I have to fight with all my will!

Catching himself and hastily forcing a casual tone.

But that's absurd nonsense, of course—a fanciful flight of imagination. My mind has been under such a strain lately, it's gotten out of control.

SARA

Strangely.

Is that when you stare at us as though you hated us?

Then forcing a smile.

That's a queer crazy notion for you to have, Simon—that you can't tell your own wife from—her.

With strange resentment.

But I think I know the kind of feeling that you mean. I've felt myself at times that she'd like me to have no wish but her wish, and no life that wasn't ruled by her life.

SIMON

Watching her.

Yes, Mother has always been extremely greedy for others' lives. You have to be constantly on guard—

SARA

Defiantly.

But she knows I'm too strong—

Abruptly shamefaced.

Ah, what am I saying! It's mean and wrong of me to suspect her. It's only that she's been so lonely all her life, poor woman. I won't hear a word against her!

Accusingly with rising jealous anger.

And don't think I don't see you've changed the subject to her so you wouldn't have to answer me about having a mistress.

She suddenly breaks—miserably.

Tell me you haven't, Simon! I couldn't bear—

She starts to sob.

SIMON
Springs up and hugs her to him—passionately.
Of course I haven't, Sweetheart! What a mad idea! Here! Look at me!
He lifts her face to his.
I swear on my honor—!

SARA
Relieved—joyously.
Oh, Darling. I know I'm foolish—but I love you so!
She kisses him and he responds, hugging her with a passionate desire. She breaks away, stirred and happy, but modestly embarrassed—with a soft laugh.
We mustn't. Supposing someone came in. It's a long time since you've kissed me—like that—Darling.

SIMON
A long time since you've given me the chance!

SARA
Teasing tenderly.
I like that! When I've been hoping every night! You'll say next it was I that wanted you to sleep alone.
Sadly.
You don't know how you hurt me when you did that, Simon. I tried to believe your excuse that you didn't want to keep me awake when you couldn't sleep because your mind kept making plans for the Company. But I couldn't help fearing the real reason was you didn't want me.

SIMON
Passionately.
You know I want you now, don't you?

SARA
Desirously but embarrassed.
Oh, here—now—yes—But at home—

SIMON
Yes, at home everything changes, as you said.

SARA

You're different there. Here, you're my old Simon. It's like old times.

SIMON

That's why I asked you to come. Because I want to be your old Simon and want you again. Because I want you to want me as you used to. But at home there is always Mother coming between us.

SARA

Frowns.

Yes, it's true you feel her always there, watching—
Simon gives her a sharp calculating glance. She adds hastily, defensive and guilty.

But you mustn't blame her. She doesn't mean to interfere. She can't help being there. And I'm sure she doesn't bother her head about what we do. You only imagine that, Darling, because you think of her as the kind of woman she used to be. The trouble is you've paid so little attention to her for years you haven't noticed the change in her. You don't know the nice, kind contented old grandmother she is now.

SIMON

Sneeringly.

Mother was always an accomplished actress.
Then quickly and calculatingly, pretending to give in.

Well, perhaps you're right. I must admit she seems sincere in her affection for your children.

SARA

Eagerly.

Oh, she is, Simon! She loves them dearly and they love her.

SIMON

From their talk, they must spend a great deal of their time in her garden.

SARA

Resentment shows in her face.

Yes, they do. But now they'll be away at school a lot of the day.
Then defensively.

It's good for them to be with her. She's a great lady and her influence helps train them to grow up gentlemen.

SIMON
Well, of course, if you don't mind—

SARA
Defensively.
Why should I mind?

SIMON
I'd say there can be such a thing as too much of her influence for their good. You see, I remember my experience with her maternal possessiveness. If I hadn't got away from her, before it was too late, she'd have made me entirely dependent upon her for life—a tenth-rate poet—a day-dreaming romantic fool, wasting my days lazily lolling in her garden, without the ambition or courage to be free, contentedly enslaved to her fantastic whims!—
He checks himself—hurriedly.
So you can understand why I am worried about her influence over our children. After all, they are my sons, too, Dear, and although you don't give me credit for it, I do have their futures constantly in mind.

SARA
Gratefully.
I'm so happy to know you think of them. It hurt me to feel you didn't—because they're you and me together—our love—you in me—
She hugs him to her and kisses him—then pushes back from him bashfully.
I ought to be ashamed. I don't know what makes me so brazen.
Hastily.
About her and the children. I'd never mention it if you hadn't, that I don't think it's good her reading poetry at them all the time, especially Byron. I hate him because I remember my father, reciting it to himself before the mirror and putting on the airs of a lord, or a Napoleon, and him sponging on my mother for life, without a dollar to his name!

SIMON

Frowning.

Yes, Mother is very romantic. She used to read Byron to me.

He recites sneeringly.

"This makes the madmen who have made men mad by their contagion—all unquiet things which stir too strongly the soul's secret springs, and are themselves the fools to those they fool."

SARA

Tenderly proud.

Ah, it's different when you recite it! I love it!

She hugs him.

You're a big boy still with the old touch of the poet in you, and I love you for it!

SIMON

Frowns—curtly.

Nonsense. That is dead in me.

Boastfully.

You forget I am the president of a railroad, too, now—or soon will be.

He smiles at her.

The railroad I promised you.

SARA

Happily.

That does sound like my old Simon. I'd like to feel again that what is yours is mine, too.

SIMON

Hugging her.

Then you can begin thinking of yourself as my partner again from this moment on.

With strange boyish enthusiasm.

I have our new partnership all planned, Sara. Wait till you hear.

Then quickly and calculatingly.

But first, let's get this matter of Mother and the children settled. I agree that it's bad to have her muddling their brains with romantic dreams. We want them trained to live with reality so when the time comes they will be capable of serving our Company as we decided long ago they could best serve it—Ethan as manager of our marine division, Wolfe to direct the banking branch which we will own before long, Jonathan as our railroad executive, and Honey our representative in politics.

SARA
Smiling happily.
Ah, you have great dreams for them, haven't you? And I thought you'd forgotten—Forgive me, Darling.

SIMON
Smiling.
No, I have never forgotten our plans for their lives. And I am confident they will have the brains and ability, provided we don't permit Mother to poison their minds with nonsense.

SARA
Resentfully now.
She's always telling them stuff about how they must do what they want, and be free.

SIMON
Sneeringly.
Good God, does she still harp on that stupid dream? As if man born of woman could hope to be free. The freer he is of outside things, the more abject slave he becomes to himself!
Sharply.
It's our duty to the children to put a stop to her interfering before it's too late, Sara.

SARA
Yes.
Hesitantly.
I could ask her not to—
Then guiltily.
No, I'd be ashamed. It would be like breaking my part of a bargain I'd made in honor to trust her.

SIMON
Dryly.
It was no part of the bargain, was it, that she should steal your children and make them her children?

SARA
Defensively.
Ah now, that's going too far. She's never tried—
Resentfully.
Anyway, they know who their mother is and who they love best.

SIMON
Dryly provocative.
Do they? I have the idea they are becoming as confused between you as I.
Quickly.
I mean as I am at home. Here, you yourself, my wife, my partner— my mistress, too, I hope.
He hugs her desirously.

SARA
Responding passionately.
Yes, let me be that above all, Darling! Don't ever dream of having another!

SIMON
Abruptly with a strange, brisk business-like tone.
We've allowed things to get in a confused muddle at home. I've been too preoccupied with the Company's affairs, and you've been too busy housekeeping for Mother and acting as nurse girl while she's left free to play she's their mother to them.

SARA
With a flash of resentful anger.
Ah, I'd like to see her try—! I'm glad you had me come here today. I feel different here with you. I begin to see a lot of things I've been blind to. I begin to remember times when I've made myself not suspect her! Maybe I have been too trusting taking her at her word as I would my own mother that's gone. Maybe I've given in to her too

much, and let her put her thoughts in my mind until I mistook them for my thoughts, and was obeying her without knowing it, and letting her make a slave of me.

Stung at the thought—threateningly.

But she'll not make a fool of me anymore!

SIMON

It's very true that Mother works in peculiar ways to steal what she desires. You must bear in mind that she has never been quite normal. She's always been different from all other women, whimsical and perversely fanciful, not to be judged by normal standards. My father always considered her entirely irresponsible. Even her best friends have put her down as more than a little queer ever since she was a girl. Yes, we might as well be frank, Sara. There is an unbalanced imaginative streak in her that one must continually guard against.

SARA

Uneasily.

You mean she's insane?

Reacting against this.

Ah no, that's crazy, Simon. I won't let you say such wicked things. The poor woman!

SIMON

Sharply.

I didn't say insane. Of course, she's not insane. I meant she has no sense of the right to freedom of others.

Then with a smile.

I don't see why you should be so indignant. I know in the old days you suspected her of being a little crazy.

SARA

Guiltily defensive.

Maybe I did—the way she was. And didn't she tell me herself she'd got to the point where she didn't dare go in that summerhouse of hers for fear she'd never come out again. That's crazy, isn't it?

SIMON

Strangely.

Who knows? It all depends—Do you know if she ever goes in the summerhouse now?

SARA

No. She always keeps it locked. The children used to plague her to open it but she never would.
Uneasily.
Why do you ask?

SIMON

Evasively.
Well, it shows she's not as changed within herself as she pretends, doesn't it?
Again in a brisk, business-like tone.
Then you agree. The children must be forbidden to go to her garden or her rooms in future. She can see quite enough of them, when you and I are present. And you stay away from her garden, too.

SARA

I hardly ever go. I've always had a feeling she didn't want me there.

SIMON

Briskly.
Then you'll give orders to the children.

SARA

Yes.
Then guiltily.
But who will tell her?

SIMON

Why you, of course.

SARA

It'll break her heart. She's been so good—I promised her—When I think of how sweet she's been to me—I hate hurting her.

SIMON

Avoiding her eyes—calculatingly, with feigned reluctance.
Well, I suppose I could tell her, if you want to be spared.

SARA

Relieved—eagerly.

Would you? But promise me you won't be cruel to her, Simon. If you'll put yourself out to be kind, and make up with her, she won't feel so lonely at losing the children.

SIMON

Concealing his satisfaction—matter-of-factly.

Don't be foolish, Dear. You can rely on me to treat Mother considerately, if only for selfish reasons. I want peace in my home. I know her erratic unstable mind, and that a sudden shock to her vanity might have dangerous consequences. So I shall call on my memories of the past and humor her as I would a fanciful child. I'll drop in at her garden on my way home this evening.

With a strange happy satisfied air.

There. That puts Mother in her place—back where she belongs. Let's forget her now and think only of us.

He gives her a loving, possessive hug.

As we did in the old days.

SARA

Happily.

I'm only too glad to, Darling. Tell me the plans you've made for our new partnership.

SIMON

Just what I want to do. I have grown very lonely, Sara. Achievement no longer means what it once did because I have no one to share it. In the old days what made it significant was that it was for you. I knew it was what you desired from me and it was my delight to give you your desire, and prove I had not failed you and that your love could justly be proud of me.

SARA

Protesting a bit guiltily.

And do you think I'm not still proud? But I am, Darling.

SIMON

Here, now, alone with me again, you mean? Yes, I can believe that.

And I want to propose to you that we should start our old life together again.

SARA

I want that as much as you, Darling. If you knew how unhappy and ugly I've felt since you started sleeping alone—and even before that when you'd lie beside me as if I wasn't there.

SIMON

I never felt we were alone—there, in Mother's house. That's why I had you come here. I want to ask you to help me create a new life of opportunity and ambition and boundless desire for our love, distinct and separate from our life as husband and wife at home—a life completely free from the influence of Mother and the children, in which we can be lovers again.
He presses her to him passionately.

SARA

Sensually aroused—kissing his hair.
Darling! You know I'd love nothing better! I'll do whatever you want.

SIMON

Good! I knew Mother couldn't have entirely destroyed in you my old Sara who desired so passionately to take what she wanted from life, no matter what the cost.

SARA

Resentfully.
Destroyed me? She knows better than to try! And don't talk as though I'd ever stopped wanting you. It's you who got so all you wanted was the Company. You even took it to bed with you in your thoughts. It wouldn't let you sleep.

SIMON

Ignoring this, goes on with a smile at her of a strange, perverse, insinuating lechery.
I want the old Sara, whose beautiful body was so greedily hungry for lust and possession, whose will was as devoid of scruple, as ruthlessly determined to devour and live as the spirit of life itself!

He hugs her.

The Sara who came to my cabin on that night long ago, before we were married, with her mind made up to use her beautiful body to keep anyone from taking what she regarded as hers, to make sure of a husband—

SARA

Guiltily.

Ah, don't say—

Reproachfully.

You'd never have known I had that in mind if my honor and my love hadn't confessed it to you! And you were proud I wanted you that much! You loved me for it! So you shouldn't remember it against me.

SIMON

Passionately.

Against you? How can you think that? I tell you I desired her more than anything in life! And now I desire her to come back more than anything in life! She was the inspiration for my career. I owe her all my success. She is the cause of the Company, the spirit of its ambition! Now I need her again to inspire me and it! I want her to come back to me here, as she came to me that night, willing to gamble with the highest possible stake, all she has, to win by any possible means, to sell her dearly.

SARA

Half pleased and flattered and half guiltily defensive.

Ah, don't talk of it that way—as if I was some low street girl who came that night to sell herself. I was bound I'd have you because I loved you so much.

Flusteredly.

But I don't want you to remember it. I never think of it but I'm ashamed I could have been so bold and brazen.

Then proudly.

But, all the same, I'm always proud of it, too.

SIMON

Amorously playful.

Well then, I know you will be willing to become your old true self again for me. It is she I need and want to possess me now, and be as bold and brazen about it as of old—and as beautiful and as desirable! I must confess, Sweetheart, that I have become as bored with the meek, contented, passionless, ambitionless, commonplace, woman, the virtuous good wife and mother that Mother's influence has made you at home, as you must be yourself in your secret heart.

SARA
Impulsively.
Yes. That's true when—

SIMON
Ha! I knew it!
He hugs her.
But [for] the old passionate greedy Sara, I would give all I possess again.

SARA
Teasingly—but with a strange undercurrent of boastfulness.
Well, look out then. I could be her, for I love you just as much now. But, maybe, you'd better let her sleep. She might be bolder than ever and want more!
She kisses him—then suddenly embarrassed and shy, pushes back from him.
But what a way for me to act! Here in your office, of all places!
Then strangely.
But it's strange, I feel in a way it's being here with you makes me feel—there's a queer thing in the air here that makes you—and I'd stayed at home so long I'd forgotten—
Confusedly.
But I don't know what I mean—
She hugs him passionately again.
Except I love you now with all of me and all my strength, and there's no one else in the world, and I'm yours and you're mine, and I don't care how shameless I am!
She kisses him.

SIMON
Sweetheart! That fits in exactly with my plans for our future here. I

hoped you would feel as you do. You ought, because the Company is you. Your nature is its nature. It derived its life from your life. You are its mother. It was born of your—just as my life in it was born of you, and is your life which you must claim for your own again.

SARA

Moved but at the same time puzzled.

Darling! But you're taking it too deep for me and getting me confused. Tell me plainly what your plan is.

SIMON

With a brisk, business-like air now.

This: The children will be away most of the day at school from now on. You'll be free. Well, I want you to work with me here in the Company as my secretary and secret partner.

SARA

Amazed and joyous—her face lighting up eagerly.

Darling! Do you really mean—?

SIMON

Then you'll do it?

SARA

Excitedly.

Will I? It's too good to be true! It's what I always used to want, don't you know that? Even in the old days, before we lived with your mother, I felt shut out from this part of your life, with you away from me in it all day.

She kisses him.

Oh, you make me so happy, Darling, when you prove you want me that much!

SIMON

Teasing with a suggestive lecherous air.

Wait! There's a condition. Nothing for nothing, is the rule here, you know. You'll have to pay for this opportunity.

SARA

Smiling.

Stop teasing now and tell me. I'll do anything you want.

SIMON
Teasing as before.
What! Do you mean to tell me a virtuous wife and mother like you
will agree to become my mistress?

SARA
*Shocked, embarrassed, and at the same time amused and curiously fasci-
nated and delighted.*
So— Then I'm the mistress you were wishing for! Well, God be
thanked, you weren't dreaming of any other!

SIMON
Teasing as before.
No, you are the one. I don't know of anyone else who would be more
desirable. And I can make you a most favorable offer.

SARA
Protestingly, but curiously pleased.
To hear you you'd think I was a wicked fancy woman you were offer-
ing to buy. That's a nice way to talk to a decent wife!
Teasingly.
But let's hear your offer. Maybe it's not enough. I value myself
highly, I'll have you know!

SIMON
Teasingly as before.
I'll agree to pay with all my worldly goods. You can get the whole
Company from me for your own—that is, of course, piece by piece,
as you earn it! I put no limit whatever on the wages you may demand
for your love.

SARA
Greedily.
The whole Company to be mine!
Forcing a joking tone.
Well, I'm flattered you set so high a price on me. It proves I still must
be beautiful to you, for you to want me that much.
She kisses him suddenly with passionate gratitude.

Oh, Darling, and I was so afraid I'd become ugly to you and you were sick of me.

SIMON
Then you will take the place?

SARA
You know I will.
She hides her face on his shoulder shamefacedly—then suddenly lifts it and bursts out.
But don't be talking of wages. Aren't I always yours just for the taking for love of you!

SIMON
Smiling playfully.
No, no! Forget that! I have no rights whatever except what you choose to sell me. This is a new secret life for us, remember, which concerns the Company's life, since it will be lived here in it. So it must be strictly a business partnership, a deal for profit on both our parts. A double life of amorous intrigue for each of us, too, if it pleases our fancy to think of it that way. You will be revenging yourself on your husband who has grown bored with his virtuous wife, by selling yourself to a lover. And I think the husband will be keeping a beautiful mistress to take my wife's place.
He laughs with an undercurrent of taunting.
Come, confess now, doesn't this prospect of a sinful double life with me give something in you a proud feeling of new life and freedom.

SARA
Fascinatedly.
Yes.
Then hugging him, with a little lustful, tender laugh.
Aren't you the big boy, still making up games! But I'll play any game with you you like, as being as you think I'm beautiful and you want me.
She laughs again—this time with a touch of warm boldness.
And it will be fun playing I'm a wicked, lustful, wanton creature and making you a slave to my pleasure and beauty.

With a strange undercurrent of gloating contempt.

All the same, I think you're a fool to let me cheat you into buying what you own already!

Suddenly shocked at herself she stops guiltily and stares at him bewilderedly.

God forgive me, what makes me talk like—Darling, you know I don't mean—

Jokingly but resentfully and suspiciously, too.

I think it's your teasing. You're leading me on to talk before I think—

Confusedly.

No, I don't mean to say that, either.

SIMON

Teasingly.

Well, we needn't go into the meaning of what you mean now, Beautiful Mistress. I am sure that will all become clear to you as you go on. It's enough now to know you've agreed and that's all settled. I am glad it was so simple. I was afraid you might raise objections.

SARA

Tenderly now.

Objections? When you want me and I want you?

SIMON

Well, Mother won't approve of my taking you away, as well as the children.

SARA

Resentfully.

It's none of her business.

SIMON

With a strange gloating air.

Poor Mother. She will be very lonely again. I think she will welcome visits even from me in her garden.

Quickly.

All I'm afraid of now, Sara, is that when you get home with her she will make you change your mind.

SARA

Resentfully.

Make me? I'd like to see her. She knows better. She knows who's the stronger. But don't make me think of her now.

She kisses him.

All I want to think of now is that you want me again.

SIMON

Hugs her — passionately.

I do! I have never wanted you so much! No, not even in the days before we were married! Your body is beautiful, Sweetheart!

SARA

Kisses him passionately.

Darling!

Then she breaks away — with a soft happy laugh.

Aren't we the shameless ones!

Then suddenly staring at him uneasily and sadly.

But I wish — even if you're still joking — you wouldn't talk as if my body was all I meant to you. Love is more than —

SIMON

Ignores this — slowly.

Yes, you will have to learn to be shameless here. That is to say, to free yourself from false shame and be what you are. In your new life and work, in order to be successful, you will have to deal daily with the greedy fact of life as it really lives and devours itself, and forget all the sentimental lies and moral hypocrisies with which its ugliness is hidden. You will have to strip life naked, and face it. And accept it as truth. And strip yourself naked and accept yourself as you are in the greedy mind and flesh. Then you can go on — successfully — with a clear vision — without false scruples — on to demand and take what you want — as I have done!

Then in a more matter-of-fact tone.

But you will discover all this for yourself. You will be successful. You have the natural talent. And I know you will find the game I play here in the Company as fascinating a gamble as I find it.

Strangely now — as if he were talking aloud to himself.

A fascinating game. Resembling love, I think a woman will find. A game of secret cunning stratagems, in which only the fools who are fated to lose reveal their true aims or motives—even to themselves. You have to become a gambler where face is a mask. But one grows lonely and haunted. One finally gets a sense of confusion in the meaning of the game, so that one's winnings have the semblance of losses. The adversary across the table in whose eyes one can read no betraying emotion beyond an identical lust—this familiar stranger to whom with a trustful smile one passes the cards one has marked, or the dice one has loaded, at the moment he accepts them trustfully becomes oneself.

SARA
Protests uneasily.
Now, Darling, please don't be mixing everything up in my mind. I don't know what you mean by that queer talk of marked cards and loaded dice.

SIMON
Smilingly, but with a threat underneath.
Oh, you will someday. I promise you you will.
Then as she stares at him uneasily—abruptly briskly business-like.
Well, I think we've settled everything.
He glances at his watch.
I'll have to ask you to go now. The railroad directors will be here in a few minutes. You will start your work here tomorrow morning.

SARA
Has gotten off the arm of his chair—jokingly bobs him a curtsy.
Yes, Sir. At your service. But you haven't told me my secretary duties yet. Remember I've no experience. You'll have to train me.

SIMON
Curtly now.
I will. By my example. You'll learn quicker that way. At first, all I wish you to do is sit and watch how I deal with everything. As though you were an understudy learning to play my part. As you learn, I will let you act in my stead now and then until finally you will find yourself capable of taking my place—if ever the need arises.

SARA
Excitedly.
Me! Oh Simon, it sounds too grand!

SIMON
In your spare time, when I am away, I want you to draw plans for the country estate with the great mansion you used to dream about where we are going to retire when we have enough.
She looks startled and embarrassed. He smiles strangely.
What's the matter? Is it that the idea of my ever retiring hasn't occurred to you for a long time? I was just to go on and on—while you remained contentedly at home with Mother and your children?

SARA
Guiltily defensive.
I thought that was what you wanted.
Hurriedly and a bit confusedly.
But I never forgot my dream of the estate, never fear! How could I forget I was born on my father's great estate, in a castle, with a great park and stables and—
Hastily.
But I haven't felt I ought to want—I have your mother's house, as beautiful a mansion as there is in the city, and I was content. I mean, I felt I oughtn't to be greedy for more.

SIMON
Well, from now on, remember you cannot want too much! No price is too high for me to pay my mistress for her love, eh?
He pats her cheek playfully.

SARA
Repelled—pulling away.
Darling, I wish you wouldn't talk as if love—

SIMON
Ignoring this.
You shall have your estate. Of course, it wouldn't do to withdraw that much capital from the Company now. There is so much to be accomplished before the Company can be free and independent and

self-sufficient. But as soon as we have enough. Meanwhile, if you get it actually planned to the last detail, then you will have everything all ready when the time comes.

SARA

Excitedly and greedily now.
Yes! Oh, that will be fun! And I've got every bit of it clear in my mind—or I used to have—

SIMON

You can afford to make bigger, more ambitious plans now, in view of the Company's progress since you last dreamed of it.

SARA

Greedily.
Oh, I can always dream bigger dreams, and I'll be only too delighted to make plans—
Then checking herself, guiltily.
Well, I'd better go now, and not be in your way.
She kisses him—tenderly.
Goodbye, my Darling! You've made me so happy. You're the sweetest dearest husband—
Then with shy passion.
No, I'm forgetting. It's love again now, isn't it? And I'm your wicked, evil mistress!
She laughs devilishly.
And don't you forget I'm your mistress now, and start wanting some other woman!
She kisses him again—then breaks from his arms and opens the door.

SIMON

Wait! Mother will be curious about your visit here but don't tell her anything. Leave that to me. I can make the meaning clearer to her I think.

SARA

Pityingly but at same time scornfully.
Ah, poor woman. I'm not anxious to tell her—
Then with a sudden, maliciously gloating smile.

She'll be so suspicious, trying to lead me on to tell, and yet pretending to herself to be too high and mighty a lady to lower her pride to ask me! Well, it'll do her good! She's gotten to think she owns me!
She stops abruptly, guilty and ashamed.
Ah, I ought to be ashamed! What makes me feel like that here?
She looks around the office almost frightenedly — then hastily.
I'll go now.
She goes out and closes the door.

SIMON

Looks after her and smiles strangely — ironically.
Well, that half of my responsibility sharing scheme is launched successfully — Sara is not very clever at bargains — too trustful of promises — not a good judge of real values — or prices — but she will learn by experience — I will see to it she learns — in a year she will not know herself.
He walks back to his desk.
Yes, that part of it will work itself out according to plan.
He suddenly frowns resentfully — impatient.
Plan? — what plan? — you'd think this was some intricate intrigue you were starting, whereas it is very simple — you want Sara — all right, you take her, and that's all there is to it — as for Mother, she has interfered and carried on an intrigue to isolate you — she must be taught to confine her activities to their proper sphere — to remain back where she belongs — very well, put her in her place this afternoon — and that will settle her half of it.
He sits down at his desk — with a strange smile of anticipation.
But it won't be so easy to deceive her — she peers suspiciously behind face values — she knows the real price is always concealed — I shall have to force her mind back into the past where her ambitions belong — where I once belonged with her —
He pauses. His expression becomes relaxed and dreamy. His voice sinks to a low nostalgic musing tone, hardly above a whisper.
It will be pleasant to find myself in her garden again after all these years — it will be a relief to leave this damned slave pen and talk with someone whose mind is not crucified on this insane wheel — whose greed, at least, is of the spirit — I remember it used to be so restful in

her garden—life existed only as a rumor of War beyond a high wall, a distant, drowsy din, a muffled squelching of feet in a trough—far-off, dim, unreal, divorced and separate, with no sense of a confusing union—

He stops. A pause. There is a knock on the door at right. At once Simon becomes the formidable, ruthless head of the Company. He calls curtly.

Come in.

Joel enters.

JOEL

The directors are in the outer office. I thought I should pay them the courtesy of announcing them myself, considering their importance.

SIMON

Acidly.

They have no importance. They had it when they had power. But I took it from them. So now they have none. They are ruined and worthless. They have nothing! And your courtesy is meaningless and a cruel joke which mocks at their plight. If I was one of them, I would knock you down.

Sharply.

Tell them to come in.

Joel stares at him—then goes out.

CURTAIN

Act Three, Scene Two

Same as Scene One of Act Two, the corner of the Harford garden with the octagonal Chinese summerhouse. Late afternoon sunlight from beyond the wall at right, falls on the pointed roof and the upper part of the arched lacquer-red door and ivy covered walls of the summerhouse. The shrubs, clipped as before in arbitrary geometrical designs, and the trees along the brick wall at rear glow in different shades of green. The wall at right casts a long shadow. The lawn is a bright green, setting off the deeper green of shrubbery and trees. The water in the small oval pool before the summerhouse is still another shade of green. The garden has the same appearance as before of everything being meticulously tended and trimmed. This effect is a morbid oppressive one of artificiality, and perverse childish fantasy, of nature distorted and humiliated by a deliberately mocking, petulant arrogance.

Deborah is sitting on the steps leading up to the summerhouse door, dressed all in white. She appears greatly changed from the previous Act. Where she had seemed a prematurely-old, middle-aged woman then, she now has the look of a surprisingly youthful grandmother. Actually, she appears much younger now at fifty-three than she had then at forty-nine. Her body and face have filled out a little. There is something of repose and contentment in her expression, something of an inner security and harmony. But her beautiful dark eyes and her smile still retain their old imaginative, ironical aloofness and detachment.

Her four grandchildren, the sons of Simon and Sara, are grouped about the pool in front of her. Ethan, the eldest, in his twelfth year, is sitting on the stone bench at rear of pool on her right. Wolfe Tone, a year younger, is sprawled on his back on the narrow coping of the pool at front, his folded hands supporting his head, staring up at the sky. Jonathan, a year and a half younger than Wolfe, and Owen Roe ("Honey"), the youngest, who is seven and a half, are sitting sideways, facing each other, on the stone bench on Deborah's left, playing a game of casino with the bench as table.

Ethan is tall and heavily built for his age, broad-shouldered and muscular. His face is strong, broad, good-looking in a rugged, rough-hewn mould. There is a resemblance to Deborah about his forehead and deep-set dark eyes. He has his mother's straight black hair, and obstinate passionate mouth. But his nose and chin and swarthy complexion are his father's. His manner is groping and awkwardly self-conscious, but stubbornly, almost sullenly, determined.

Wolfe is an opposite type, of medium height for his age, slender and wiry. His face is handsome and aristocratic, pale, with light brown hair and hazel eyes. The resemblance to Sara's father, Cornelius Melody, is marked and there is also much that reveals Deborah in his face and expression. Added to this is a cold immobility about the cut of his features as a whole that immediately brings to mind his uncle, Joel Harford. He does not resemble his father or his mother. His manner is politely pleasant and compliant, but it is the distant amiability of indifference.

Jonathan is undersized with a big head too large for his body. He is also thin but one gets no impression of frailty or weakness from him but of an exhaustless energy. The general facial resemblance to his father is so striking one does not notice any other. His hair is brown, his complexion swarthy, his eyes grey-blue. His manner is quick, self-assured, observant and shrewd. "Honey" takes after his mother's side of the family. He is an obvious Irish type with a clear skin, rosy and white complexion, blue eyes and curly black hair. A chubby, roly-poly youngster. He is lazy, laughing and good tempered, full of health and animal spirits, his eyes bright with a sly humor, his smile infectious and charmingly ingratiating.

From all four boys one gets the impression of an underlying natural boyishness—a feeling that each is in one way or another too old for his years.

Deborah is reading aloud from Byron's "Childe Harold." Ethan listens with absorbed interest, his eyes fixed on her face. Wolfe stares at the sky, his expression emotionless. One cannot tell whether he is listening or not. Jonathan's and Honey's attention appears to be wholly concentrated on their game.

DEBORAH

Reads—and one feels that for the moment she has forgotten her audience and is reading aloud to herself.

> But Quiet to quick bosoms is a Hell,
> And there hath been thy bane; there is a fire
> And motion of the Soul which will not dwell
> In its own narrow being, but aspire
> Beyond the fitting medium of desire;
> And, but once kindled, quenchless evermore,
> Preys upon high adventure, nor can tire
> Of aught but rest; a fever at the core,
> Fatal to him who bears, to all who ever bore.
>
> This makes the madmen who have made men mad
> By their contagion; Conquerors and Kings,
> Founders of Sects and Systems, to whom add
> Sophists, Bards, Statesmen, all unquiet things
> Which stir too strongly the soul's secret springs,
> And are themselves the fools to those they fool;
> Envied, yet how unenviable! What stings
> Are theirs! One breast laid open were a school
> Which would unteach Mankind the lust to shine or
>   rule:
> Their breath is agitation, and their life
> A storm whereon they ride, to sink at last,
> And yet so nursed and bigoted to strife,
> That should their days surviving perils past,
> Melt to calm twilight, they feel overcast
> With sorrow and supineness, and so die;
> Even as a flame unfed, which runs to waste

With its own flickering, or a sword laid by,
Which eats into itself, and rusts ingloriously.
She stops and stares before her.

ETHAN
Starts from his concentrated attention—with an affectionate, under-standing smile.
You were reading that to yourself, too, weren't you, Grandmother?

DEBORAH
Starts—then smiles affectionately.
Perhaps, Ethan. There is a lesson in it—a warning for each of us—such as—
With a strange note of self-mockery.
well, to be suitably grateful for a calm twilight, for example. But, of course, that is not the lesson youth should learn from it.

ETHAN
Scowling.
I hate lessons. I don't see any lesson in it.

WOLFE
Speaks up quietly without moving.
I do.

DEBORAH
Stares at him—strangely.
Yes. I'm afraid you may, Wolfe. But perhaps it's the wrong lesson.
Wolfe stirs uneasily but continues staring at the sky.

ETHAN
Jealously.
Oh, him! He sees everything, to hear him tell it!

DEBORAH
Smiling.
I think he does see too much.

ETHAN
He only pretends to, so he can pretend he's too good for anything, and doesn't want what he knows he can't get.

JONATHAN
Without looking up from the cards—grinning.
That's right, Ethan.

DEBORAH
Another country heard from! I didn't know you were listening, Jonathan.

JONATHAN
Self-assuredly.
Oh, I can mind the game and keep track of what's going on at the same time. And win, too.
He plays a card.
There. Big casino. That beats you, Honey.

HONEY
Grins with ungrudging admiration.
You always beat me. But you can't beat Wolfe.

JONATHAN
I would if he wasn't so darned lucky. I play better. It's just his luck.

WOLFE
It is not. It's because I don't care whether I win or not. You only like winning. That's why you make mistakes.

DEBORAH
Smiling.
A profound observation, Wolfe. You will grow up to be a philosopher, I think.

WOLFE
Distrustfully.
What's a philosopher?
Then with a quick indifference.
I don't care what I grow up to be.

JONATHAN
I'm going to own a railroad. Father wants me to.

HONEY

I'm going to be a gentleman and 'lected President of America, like Mother wants me.

DEBORAH
Smiling.
I'm afraid you can't be both nowadays, Honey.

HONEY
For a moment his grin vanishes and he gives her a scornful, defiant look.
Mother says I can.
Smiling again, to Jonathan.
Come on. Let's play 'nother. This time I'll show you.

ETHAN
Jealously.
Aw, don't talk to those crazy kids, Grandmother. Read some poetry.

JONATHAN
Dealing—jeeringly.
We know what Ethan's going to do—to hear him talk big! He won't do what Father and Mother want! Oh, no!

HONEY
Joins in jeeringly.
He won't go to Harvard! He won't be a gentleman!

ETHAN
With sullen doggedness.
Well, I won't. Wait and see.

JONATHAN
He's going to run away to sea and be a sailor!

ETHAN
I will, too.

WOLFE
Indifferently.
Well, why don't you, then? Who cares what you do?

ETHAN
Turns to glance at him.
Shut up, you! Mother and Father care. And Grandmother.

DEBORAH
Gently.
Indeed I do care, Ethan.

WOLFE
Goes on indifferently.
Why anyone with sense would want to be a sailor working like a nigger slave—

JONATHAN
They don't get hardly any pay either. Ethan'll never get rich.

WOLFE
Ignoring this.
On a dirty, smelly ship—

ETHAN
Stung—angrily.
That's a lie! Ships aren't dirty. They're the prettiest things in the world! And I love the sea!
More angrily, stares at his feet threateningly.
You take that back or I'll—

DEBORAH
Now, now. Giving Wolfe a bloody nose wouldn't convince him that ships and the sea are beautiful, would it?

WOLFE
Calmly.
He won't hit me. He knows he can lick me, and Ethan's not a coward.

ETHAN
Abashed.
No. 'Course I won't. Only don't you say—

WOLFE
Indifferently.
All right. Ships are beautiful then. Who cares?

ETHAN
Glances at him again—then sits down, abruptly changing the subject.
Please read some more, Grandmother—that part about the ocean.
That shows how Lord Byron loved the sea.

WOLFE
Who cares about him? Except I'd like to have been born a lord.

DEBORAH
Smiling—assuredly.
Yes, that would entitle you to any amount of disdainful indifference,
wouldn't it?
Then to Ethan.
You must know that part by heart, Ethan.

ETHAN
I do. But it's better when you read it, Mother—
Hastily—embarrassed.
'Scuse me, I mean, Grandmother.

DEBORAH
Gives him a tender look.
You needn't apologize. I like you to call me Mother.

WOLFE
Turns his head to stare at her—enviously.
You like it when I get mixed up, too. Why do you?

DEBORAH
Starts, forcing a smile.
Why, I suppose because I'm so fond of your mother I'd like to be
her. And, of course, because I love you, too.
*He stares, then turns abruptly to gaze up at the sky again. Deborah begins
to read.*
There is a pleasure in the pathless woods,
There is a rapture on the lonely shore,

There is society, where none intrudes,
By the deep Sea, and music in its roar:
I love not Man the less, but Nature more,
From these our interviews, in which I steal
From all I may be, or have been before,
To mingle with the Universe, and feel
What I can ne'er express—yet cannot all conceal.

Roll on, thou deep and dark blue Ocean—roll!
Ten thousand fleets sweep over thee in vain;
Man marks the earth with ruin—his control
Stops with the shore;—upon the watery plain
The wrecks are all thy deed, nor doth remain
A shadow of man's ravage, save his own,
When, for a moment, like a drop of rain,
He sinks into thy depths with bubbling groan—
Without a grave—unknelled, uncoffined, and
    unknown.

JONATHAN
Suddenly speaks without looking up from his game.
Sinks with bubbling groan—no better than a drop of rain—un-
known. That'll be you if you don't watch out, Ethan.
*He adds with a curt, contemptuous, practical finality that recalls his
father.*
And that's foolishness.

HONEY
Echoing him.
Yes, Ethan's a fool.

ETHAN
Who had been listening with dreamy intensity—recoiling.
Shut up, you!
To Deborah—eagerly.
Now skip to the one that begins: "And I have loved thee, Ocean."

WOLFE
Interrupts impatiently.

No! That's enough for Ethan, Grandmother. He's had his share.
Read my part—the one you say you used to like so much, and don't
anymore.
*As she hesitates, strangely reluctant, he turns his head to stare at her—
insistently.*
Go on. Why don't you ever want to read that?

DEBORAH
Starts—evasively.
Why, no particular reason, except that I no longer believe it. And it
hardly strikes the right note of inspiration for a future banker. But
if you insist—
*She recites without looking at the book, a note of personal arrogance
growing more marked in her voice as she goes on, staring straight before
her.*

    I have not loved the World, nor the World me;
    I have not flattered its rank breath, nor bowed
    To its idolatries a patient knee,
    Nor coined my cheek to smiles,—nor cried aloud
    In worship of an echo: in the crowd
    They could not deem me one of such—I stood
    Among them, but not of them—in a shroud
    Of thoughts which were not their thoughts, and still
        could,
    Had I not filed my mind, which thus itself subdued.

    I have not loved the World, nor the World me,—
    But let us part fair foes; I do believe,
    Though I have found them not, that there may be
    Words which are things,—hopes which will not
        deceive,
    And Virtues which are merciful, nor weave
    Snares for the failing: I would also deem
    O'er others' griefs that some sincerely grieve—
    That two, or one, are almost what they seem,—
    That Goodness is no name—and Happiness no
        dream.

WOLFE
Staring at her—strangely.
And you don't agree with that anymore?

DEBORAH
Starts—forcing a smile, carelessly.
No, it is much too bitter and disdainful a dream for a contented grandmother.

WOLFE
Stares at her curiously.
You spoke it then as if you still meant it.

DEBORAH
Forcing a joking manner.
Oh, I'm an accomplished actress, as your father could tell you.
He stares at her—then turns his head to look up at the sky again. Honey gives a sly, laughing chuckle over something in the card game.

WOLFE
Without looking.
Watch out, Jonathan. Honey's cheating. I can tell by his laugh.

JONATHAN
Half turns his head to reply—as he does so Honey transfers cards from his pocket to his hand. Jonathan says laughingly.
Don't I know! He can't help giving himself away. But he's always so tickled with himself he never sees that as soon as he starts cheating I cheat back to show I can win at that game, too.
He turns back to the game—suddenly he grabs Honey's hand.
Hey! That's too much! Look, Wolfe! Look! Ethan! See what he's up to now! He's been putting extra cards in his hand!
He laughs—to Honey.
You ninny! Don't you think I'd notice you have too many cards? How'd you expect—?

HONEY
Choking with merriment.
But that makes it funnier if I did fool you!

He laughs unrestrainedly, a merry entirely shameless and droll guffaw.
Looking at him the others, Deborah included, cannot help joining in.

ETHAN
Disgusted with himself for laughing—scowls.
It's all right to laugh but if Mother knew, wouldn't she take you over her knee! You know she's always telling us about honor.

HONEY
Still chuckling—confidently.
She won't know.

DEBORAH
No, we promised we'd never tell on each other, didn't we?

HONEY
And I did it playing with her the other night, anyway, and she couldn't help laughing.

DEBORAH
Smiles at him.
Well, Honey, all I can say is, if you hope to be President you'll have to learn to be more skillful.
She laughs—then stops suddenly, listening to something beyond the wall at right.
There's your father coming home.

WOLFE
Staring at her wonderingly.
You can always tell his walk from anyone's, can't you?

DEBORAH
Smilingly—with a sneer beneath.
That's easy now, Wolfe. He walks with the proud tread of a conquering Napoleon.
Suddenly, listening, her expression changes to one of alarmed surprise and she stares at the door in the wall with dread—tensely.
He has stopped—
For a moment there is a tense silence in which the boys, conscious of the

change in her, regard her puzzledly. Then there is a sharp rap of the knocker on the door and Deborah quivers frightenedly.

JONATHAN
Starts for the door.
I'll let him in—

DEBORAH
In a panic.
No!
Then she stammers confusedly.
I must be mistaken. It cannot—be your father. He has never dared—I mean, he would never come unless I invited him, and I would never—

WOLFE
Staring at her.
What are you so frightened about, Grandmother?

DEBORAH
Fighting to control herself.
I'm superstitious. I'm afraid—like your mother. I don't like strangers attempting to intrude—
Then with swift urgency.
Run to the house and get your mother, Ethan! Tell her she should come here at once!
But, as he starts to obey, frowning and puzzled, there is a louder knock on the door and Simon's voice calls sharply: "It's I, Mother. Open the door!" Again Deborah's expression changes completely. All fear vanishes from her face; she seems in a flash to become arrogantly self-confident. A little smile of gloating scorn comes to her lips and she murmurs softly.
Well, it is not I who wish—
With abrupt impatience.
Well, Jonathan? Don't you hear your father? Open the door.
He stares at her puzzledly—then goes and opens the door. Simon comes in and Jonathan closes the door after him. Simon approaches his mother, giving a quick glance around, his face set in a coldly pleasant smile.

SIMON

Good evening, Mother.

DEBORAH

Coldly pleasant in her tone.

This is an unexpected pleasure, Simon.

SIMON

Evidently. Such whispering I heard, cooling my heels before the sacred portals. I trust I have not intruded on any secret conspiracy.

DEBORAH

Startled—stares at him.

Conspiracy?

Coldly pleasant again.

Naturally we were surprised. We could not believe our good fortune.

SIMON

Turning to his sons.

You boys go to the house. I have to talk to your grandmother.

DEBORAH

Uneasily.

I would like them to remain in the garden, if you don't mind.

SIMON

Coldly domineering.

As it happens, I do mind, Mother.

For a moment, angered, she stares at him defiantly. Then she shrugs her shoulders with assumed indifference and looks away. He turns to the boys who are standing hesitantly, glancing puzzledly from his face to hers— sharply.

You heard what I said.

They start, reply obediently, "Yes, Father," and hurry off down the path at right. He turns back to Deborah—curtly.

I happen to know their mother is waiting for this chance to see them alone.

She gives him a quick suspicious glance. He bows with dry formality.

If I may sit down, Mother?

DEBORAH
Coldly.
Of course. This is your property. Pray do so.
She sits on the steps again.

SIMON
Sara's property.
He sits on the stone bench on her left.

DEBORAH
With a trace of mockery.
But what is hers is yours. Or so I felt you thought.

SIMON
Pleasantly.
Yes, that is quite true.
He pauses, glancing around the garden. She glances quickly at him again, her expression set in indifference, but her eyes suspicious and curious. He remarks casually.
Sara has probably told you of her visit to my office this morning.

DEBORAH
No.

SIMON
Wondering.
She hasn't?

DEBORAH
No. I am not curious. She told me before she left you had asked her to come there.

SIMON
Feigning surprise.
That I had asked her?
She glances at him sharply. He goes on carelessly.
Well, it is of no importance who asked whom, I suppose. You say she has not mentioned our interview in any way?

DEBORAH
With forced indifference.

No. I imagine it concerned property of yours—her name and papers you wished her to sign. She knows I would not be interested in that.

SIMON

Her purpose in coming had nothing to do with papers. Although, of course, it did concern property.
He adds with a sneering smile.
You know Sara.

DEBORAH

As if caught off guard, starts to sneer herself.
Yes, you may be sure I—
She catches herself and looks at him defensively.

SIMON

As you'll see, Sara suspects—and with good reason, I think—that she is being secretly swindled of what is rightfully hers.

DEBORAH

Startled—with feigned indifference.
I cannot believe Sara imagines that. What is the nature of the plot you claim she suspects, if I may ask?
She sneers.
Not that her husband is defrauding of his love, I trust?

SIMON

Smilingly.
As a matter of fact, that was one of the matters she wished to discuss with me.

DEBORAH

Indeed? It is silly of her to wish to keep what she no longer needs.

SIMON

Ignoring this.
Not that she holds me responsible for her loss. She very shrewdly suspects whose hidden influence is really to blame.

DEBORAH

Stares at him—then coldly scornful.

I am not interested in all this mysterious insinuation. I do not believe
Sara ever—

SIMON
Interrupts as if he hadn't heard.
I was very glad she came. It gave me a chance to talk over with her
a new arrangement at the office I have been contemplating for some
time. I had to obtain her consent—which she was only too willing
to give, as it turned out. I find it advisable, from many standpoints,
to add a private confidential secretary to my employ.

DEBORAH
Scornfully.
And you had to have Sara's consent for that?

SIMON
Smilingly.
You will understand why when I tell you the one person who pos-
sesses the qualifications I desire is a very young and beautiful woman.

DEBORAH
*Starts—her first instinctive reaction one of vindictive satisfaction and
gloating pity.*
Ah! Poor Sara! So this is what your great romantic love comes to in
the end! I always knew—
*Abruptly and guiltily her reaction changes to one of overstressed moral
indignation.*
How dare you mention such filth to your mother! Have you become
so utterly coarse and debased, so lost to all sense of decency, that
you feel no shame but actually boast you are deliberately planning
to dishonor yourself and disgrace your family?
Then with disdain.
But I don't know why I should be surprised. After all, this is an inevitable step in the corruption of your character that I have had to
watch for years, until I could hardly recognize my son in the unscrupulous greedy trader, whose soul was dead, whose one dream was
material gain! Now, after this final degradation, I cannot recognize
my son in you at all! He is dead and you are a repulsive stranger I
will not allow myself to know!

SIMON

Has been watching her with a gloating satisfaction—mockingly.

Yet if I am not mistaken, Mother, you were not altogether displeased to see Sara's husband become so worthy, in your mind, of being her husband.

DEBORAH

It's a lie! That you can have such a vile suspicion proves to what depths your mind—!

SIMON

May I point out that you have been jumping too eagerly to conclusions, Mother. I have not said my secretary was to be anything more intimate than my secretary.

Deborah looks guilty and discomfited. He adds with a mocking smile.

I am afraid the good grandmother you have become has not entirely forgotten the French Eighteenth Century Memoirs in which she once lived, or such an improper suspicion could never enter her mind.

DEBORAH

Stares at him strickenly—pleadingly.

Simon! It is not kind to make me remember—

With dread.

Oh, why did you come here? What—?

SIMON

Ignoring this.

And I don't see how you can think Sara would ever consent—unless you secretly believe her true nature is so greedy that she would sell anything if offered the right price.

DEBORAH

Stares at him fascinatedly—with a strange eagerness.

So that's it! You offered—

With a strange taunting laugh.

Then you have been made a fool of. She has swindled you by selling rights to property she no longer needs or wants!

SIMON

Ah! And you think it was you who brought that about?

DEBORAH

Distractedly.

No! No! How dare you think I could concern myself with your low greeds!

Violently.

And I will not think such ignoble things about Sara's motives! I will not have you put such thoughts in my mind about a woman to whom I owe an eternal debt of gratitude, who is the sweetest, kindest, most generous-hearted—

SIMON

I am sorry to have to disillusion you, Mother, but I think you will discover before our interview is over that Sara has not been as blind as you hoped, nor as unsuspectingly trustful as you imagined.

Deborah starts and stares at him uneasily. He goes on in a pleasant matter-of-fact tone like one disinterestedly stating facts.

You made the mistake of underestimating your adversary. Your vanity made you overconfident in your superior subtlety of mind. It does not do to hold one's enemy in the battle for supremacy in too much contempt—

DEBORAH

I will not have you talk as though Sara and I were engaged in some fantastic duel—as though our home were a battleground! It is insane of you. I bitterly resent your intruding here without my consent and attempting to create suspicion and jealousy between Sara and me. You cannot! We have reached too deep an understanding. We have built up too close a friendship through our mutual love for the children! Through love of them we have learned to love each other! I trust her and I know she trusts me! It would take more than your obviously malicious insinuations to shake my faith in her!

SIMON

Coldly domineering.

We will deal with the facts, if you please, Mother, not with sentimental posing.

DEBORAH

Staring at him with a fascinated dread—stammers.

Simon! Why are you saying such things? What are you trying to do? I feel behind this—I know this is some insane plot to revenge yourself on me!

SIMON

With a cold smile.

Plots and intrigues! You must be still dreaming of eighteenth-century romance, Mother! Revenge on you? That is a mad idea, Mother, coming from you who have seemingly grown so sane. Revenge for what? As far as I remember, there was never a serious quarrel between us—merely a difference in philosophical outlook between you whose true nature is to hide from life in dreams and I whose inner compulsion is to deal solely in reality and the facts of things. I thought even that trifling quarrel of the past had vanished in indifference and been forgotten long ago.

DEBORAH

I have forgotten it. But I know you—

SIMON

As if she hadn't spoken.

I know I have forgotten it.

Suddenly his tone changes to a bitter smouldering resentment.

Revenge for what, I ask you? It was I who long ago, after I graduated from Harvard, decided of my own free will it was high time I began to live in my own life and not in your life! I then freed myself from your influence, which would have kept me always a tenth-rate versifier, scribbling imitations of Byron's romantic doggerel, wasting my mind humoring your fantastic whims and playing roles of childish make-believe here in your garden with you, lost in dreams, while love escaped and life passed down the street beyond the wall, forgetful we were hidden here.

He pauses, staring around the garden. His tone has taken a strange quality of nostalgic yearning. He murmurs as if to himself.

It is so restful here. I had forgotten how restful it was.

Deborah stares at him. Her expression has lost its bitter resentment, has suddenly lighted up with a gloating, triumphant perception.

DEBORAH
With a little smile—carelessly.
So you have never forgotten that old quarrel? As you say, it was childish of us. I remember now I used to be of the opinion it was I who made you leave, who forced you out into your own life. So that I might be free.

SIMON
Curtly.
Yes, you consoled your pride with that lie. But the truth was, if I had wished, I could have remained here with you forever. You are honest enough to confess that now, I hope?

DEBORAH
Still watching him—smilingly.
Yes, if you wish. I appreciate that a Napoleon of affairs must believe implicitly in his own star.
She laughs softly—teasingly.
You are still such a strange greedy boy, do you know it, Dear?

SIMON
Again glancing around the garden—with again the tone of nostalgic yearning.
Yes, I had forgotten the quiet and the peace here. Nothing has changed. The past is the present.
Suddenly he turns on her—harshly accusing.
You are the only jarring discordant note. Because you are not the same. You are a stranger here. This garden of your old self disowns the doting old granny you have made yourself pretend to be.

DEBORAH
Watching him, her eyes gleam with a secret gloating—quietly.
I do not feel alien here. Perhaps it is you whom my garden disowns, in hurt pride, because you long ago disowned it.

SIMON
With sullen boyish boastfulness.

Yes, I did. I'm glad you admit it.
Then justifying himself—placatingly.
Well, it could hardly expect me to stay buried alive forever.

DEBORAH
Quietly, her eyes gleaming.
No, I suppose not.
She pauses, probing under a casual tone.
I am sorry you do not believe in my sincerity as a good grandmother.

SIMON
Sneering resentfully.
Oh, you were always able to play a part so convincingly that you fooled even yourself!

DEBORAH
With a soft teasing laugh.
Don't tell me you are jealous of your children, too!

SIMON
Curtly.
Too? I don't know what you mean. Jealous? Don't be absurd, Mother. Beyond observing your obvious campaign to obtain control of the children, and pitying Sara for what I mistakenly thought was her blind trustfulness, I have regarded the matter as none of my business.

DEBORAH
Starts to protest angrily—checks herself and changes the subject—quietly casual.
Speaking of business, how are the Company's affairs these days? I am sure you must be becoming richer and more powerful all the time.

SIMON
In a boastful tone.
Yes, I am, Mother. I concluded a deal today which adds a railroad to the Company's properties.

DEBORAH
Flatteringly but with underlying sarcasm.

How splendid! My congratulations, Dear.

SIMON
Pleased.
Thank you, Mother.
Then in his brisk, business-like tone.
Oh, it's nothing in itself. But it has significance as another step forward. It's an added link in the chain in which my ships bring cotton to my mills to be made into my cloth and shipped on my railroad.
Frowning impatiently.
But there is a lot to be done before the chain is completed.

DEBORAH
With a little mocking smile.
Yes, I perceive it is not enough.

SIMON
Deadly serious.
Far from it. The next step must be to acquire my own bank. Then I can control and manipulate all the Company's financing.

DEBORAH
I see. And you will want your own stores here in the city to sell your goods.

SIMON
Yes. I have that in mind.

DEBORAH
And at the other end of your chain you should possess plantations in the South and own your own nigger slaves, imported in your own slave ships.

SIMON
Staring before him, tense and concentrated, his expression hard and ruthless—eagerly.
Yes. Of course. I had not considered that but it is obviously the logical final step at that end.
She stares at him and gives a little uneasy shrinking movement. He turns to her with an affectionate teasing smile.

You are wonderfully shrewd and farsighted, Mother, for a beautiful lady who has always affected superior disdain for greedy traders like my father and me.

DEBORAH
Impulsively—with a trace of seductive coquetry.
You find me still a little beautiful? I fear you are merely flattering a poor ugly old woman.

SIMON
Ignores this.
I am glad to find you changed in that one respect, Mother. You now have the courage to face some of the things that have reality. You don't have to cower behind romantic idealisms from every ugliness of truth.
He stares at her strangely.
The ugliness of life you would learn, if you possessed it as long as I have now, can become identical with beauty.

DEBORAH
Uneasily.
I do not understand you.

SIMON
Strangely.
Well, as I admitted to you, I do not understand all the implications of the duel of duality myself—not yet—but I will in the end, I promise you!
She looks away from him, as frightened as if this were a threat. He speaks casually.
Yes, I am glad you appreciate what I am achieving through the Company. I see now that behind your old pose of lofty spiritual contempt, you were proud of Father's ability in trade. I will make you prouder of me than you ever were of him, Mother.

DEBORAH
Her eyes gleaming again—softly.
Ah. But I am already, Dear.

SIMON

Boastfully.

He had scruples. I have none. He disguised his greed with Sabbath potions of God-fearing unction at the First Congregationalist Church. Else he had feared to swallow it. I fear no God but myself! I will conquer every obstacle. I will let nothing stand between me and my goal!

DEBORAH

Uneasily again.

What goal, Simon?

SIMON

Turns to her in surprise.

But I thought you saw that, Mother. My goal is to make the Company entirely self-sufficient. It must not be dependent upon anything outside itself for anything. It must need nothing but what it contains within itself. It must attain the all-embracing security of complete self-possession—the might which is the sole right not to be a slave! Do you see?

DEBORAH

Strangely moved.

I see, Dear—that you have gone very far away from me—and become lost in yourself and very lonely.

SIMON

Vaguely.

Lost? Oh no, don't imagine I have lost. I always win. My destiny is victory at any cost, by any means.

Abruptly boyishly boastful again.

Wait and see, Mother! I'll prove to you I can lead the Company to glorious, final triumph—complete independence and freedom within itself!

He pauses and looks around the garden, then he sighs wearily—strangely.

But sometimes lately, Mother, alone in my office, I have felt so weary of the game—of watching suspiciously each card I led to myself from across the table—even though I had marked them all—watching my winnings pile up and becoming confused with losses—feeling my swindler's victorious gloating die into boredom and discontent—the flame of ambition smoulder into a chill dismay—as though that opponent within had spat an extinguishing poison of disdain—

DEBORAH
Strangely, tenderly sympathetic.
Oh, I know! I know, Dear! I used to know so well!
Tensely.
I tell you I had once reached a point where I had grown so lost, I had not even a dream left I could dream without screaming scornful laughter at myself. I would sit locked in the summerhouse here, so no one could come between and protect me from myself, in the dark, squatting on folded legs in mockery of mystic meditation—sit there for hours in wisdom-ridiculing contemplation of myself, and spit in my mind, and spit in my heart, like a village idiot in a country store spitting at the belly of a stove—cursing the day I was born, the day I indifferently conceived, the day I bore—
With a terrible intensity.
Until I swear to you, I felt I could by just one tiny further wish, one little effort more of will, push open the door to madness where I could at least believe in a dream again! And how I longed for that final escape!
She suddenly turns and stares at him with hatred.
Ah! And you wonder why I hate you!
Abruptly overcome by a panic of dread, starting to her feet.
Simon! What are you trying to do! Leave me alone! Leave the past in its forgotten grave!
Trying to control herself and be indifferent.
But that is foolish. You are simply being childishly morbid and silly. Frankly, I am bored with listening to your nonsense. I will go in the house now. Sara must be wondering what is keeping me, now the sun is setting.
She starts for the path off left. As she does so, Simon, without looking at her begins to speak again in his tone of nostalgic yearning. As he speaks she stops, makes herself go on, stops again, tries to go on, finally stops and turns to stare at him.

SIMON

Then I began to remember lately—and long for this garden—and you, as you used to be and are no longer—and I as I was then before I became a wife's husband and a children's father and a Company's President—that old harmonious union in the spirit of you and me— here in the freedom of a dream—hiding from the slave market of life—in this safe haven, where we could repose our souls in fantasy, in happy masquerades and fairy tales and the sustaining bravadoes of romantic verse—evade, escape, forget, rest in peace!

He sighs wearily.

I regret I have lost that paradise in which you were the good, kind, beloved, beautiful Queen. I have become so weary of what they call life beyond the wall, Mother.

DEBORAH

Moved and fascinated, takes a step toward him—tenderly.

I see you have, my son.

Then diffidently but at the same time putting forth all her charm coquettishly and playfully.

But perhaps—who knows?—your loss is not irrevocable, Dear. We —you and I—in partnership in a new company of the spirit, might reorganize your bankruptcy—if I may put it in terms you understand.

She smiles teasingly.

SIMON

With a passionate eagerness.

Yes!

He grabs her hand.

DEBORAH

As if the touch of his hand alarmed her—shrinks back, turning away from him—guiltily stammers.

No! I swore to her—I would never interfere. I cannot! Unless you offer me more proof I cannot believe she has been guilty of the treachery to me that would set me free to welcome this opportunity—

With sudden fierce passion.

Ah! If she only would be guilty I could be myself! I could be free to dream again!

Horrified at herself.

No! I am content. I have all I desire.

She turns to Simon—resentfully and derisively.

My dear boy, your childish fancies are ridiculous. Do be sensible. We do not really wish such nonsense. And if we did, it would be impossible, we have both changed so much.

Carelessly taunting.

But, if you care to drop in here once in a while on your return from work I know the children would be pleased to see you. You could boast to them of your heroic exploits as the Company's victorious little Napoleon.

SIMON

Stiffens, stares at her with hatred for a second—then coldly, in a curt business-like tone.

I'm glad you mentioned the children. It reminds me of my real purpose in coming here. I must inform you that Sara and I have decided you are having a very bad influence on our children—

DEBORAH

Startled—resentful and uneasy.

That is ridiculous. Why, I have been at pains not to influence them at all! I teach them to rely on themselves, to own their own lives and be what they want to be, to have the courage to preserve their independence and freedom!

SIMON

I remember only too well your ideal of freedom for others, Mother— that they must not be the slave of anyone but you!

DEBORAH

With a strange eagerness.

You say Sara decided—?

Guiltily.

No! I won't believe you!

SIMON

Sara decided that henceforth the children must be forbidden to see you except in the house when either she or I are present to protect them.

DEBORAH

Strickenly—with increasing desperateness.

You mean they are to be taken from me? I am to be left entirely alone again—with no life but the memory of the past— Ah! You can't be so cruel! I have made myself love them! I have created a new life in which I am resigned to age and ugliness and death out of that unselfish devotion to them and to their mother—

Abruptly, her face hardening with an eager hatred.

And you say Sara decided this?

Desperately.

No! I won't believe—

SIMON

Curtly.

I would hardly lie about something you can confirm as soon as you see her.

DEBORAH

Fighting a battle within herself—eagerly.

No, that would be too stupid. It must be true.

SIMON

You'll find she is giving them their orders in the house right now.

DEBORAH

With an almost joyous vindictiveness.

Ah, if she has betrayed me and broken all her pledges! That releases me! I am under no further obligation! I owe her nothing but—

Fighting herself again but more weakly.

No! I still cannot believe! I know her too well! I know she loves and trusts me! She would never suspect me—

SIMON

Curtly.

Nonsense, Mother. You know there is nothing strange about her being jealous of your stealing her children. You used to be jealous of her—

DEBORAH
Arrogantly.
I? Jealous of that common, vulgar biddy?
Then eagerly—with a vindictive satisfaction.
So she is jealous of me? Well, perhaps she has cause to be!

SIMON
Naturally, she is afraid—

DEBORAH
Gratified.
So she is afraid of me?
With a vindictive laugh.
But her fear is too late. I already have Ethan and Wolfe. They can never forget me! The other two still have too much of her in them—
Again fighting herself desperately.
But I know it wasn't Sara who decided this! It was you! But you never think of the children. It must have been she! Yes, yes! You are right! I have been a fool! I should have known! And I *have* known deep down inside me! I have never entirely trusted her! I have always suspected her of hypocrisy! I have resented her interference and possessiveness. I have hated the intolerable debt of daily gratitude!
Then brokenly.
But how could she do this to me! She knows how much the children have meant to me! She knows without them, I shall be lost again!

SIMON
Pleasantly, almost teasingly.
Come now, Mother. Let's have done with posing. You are not really as exercised by the loss of the children as you pretend. I think that you are honestly relieved, and feel liberated from an irksome duty that was becoming a bore.

DEBORAH
Fiercely.
No! I love—

Abruptly with eagerness again.
Well, perhaps you are right, Dear.

SIMON

You were never intended for the job of Sara's unpaid nursemaid. Nor for the role of doting grandmother. You are still too young and beautiful—

DEBORAH
Flattered.
No, I know I am not. But I love your thinking so, Dear.
With a wry, bitter smile.
You are deceived by that false, fleeting Indian summer glow, the mocking presage of impending winter.

SIMON
As if he hadn't heard.
I will confess now, Mother, I have watched with anxiety the corrupting effect of the hypocritical life you have been leading on your character—the gradual loss of your former aristocratic distinction, your old fanciful charm, the quality you once had of being unique and unlike all other women. I have seen you fall completely under Sara's influence and become merely a female, common, vulgar, a greedy home-owner, dreamless and contented!

DEBORAH
Angrily.
You are talking nonsense! I have told you it is I who have influenced her! Deliberately! As part of my scheme!
Hastily.
No! What made me say that? I had no scheme. I simply wished—

SIMON
I have watched her dispossess you from yourself and take possession.
With a resentful intensity.
By God, there have been times when, as I watched you together in the house at night, she would seem to steal all identity from you and absorb you! Until there was but one woman—her!

DEBORAH

With a strange exultant satisfaction.

Ah, you felt that, did you? That we were one, united against—That is what I wished to do!

Gloatingly.

Poor boy, I can appreciate how frightened—

Then angrily.

But you are blind or you would have seen it was I who took possession of her in order to—

She checks herself—hastily.

But, as you say, it is very confusing. One cannot see clearly what or why—

Frightenedly.

And I do not care to see. Why do you put such morbid nonsense in my mind? Besides, it does not matter now that you have shown me clearly, Dear, I do not need her to take back what is mine. I mean, naturally, after the treacherous way she has betrayed my trust in her, there can be no question of any further friendship between us. Although, of course, I shall go on pretending. I will not give her the satisfaction of letting her see how she has hurt—And, anyway, I know I have won and I am already revenged.

SIMON

Staring before him—strangely.

Yes, Mother, I rely on you to help me keep her in her rightful place hereafter.

DEBORAH

Regards him calculatingly—then with a caressingly gentle air.

And my place? What place do you intend me to have now, Dear?

SIMON

With a queer, hesitating embarrassment.

Why, here in your garden, of course, as always in the past.

DEBORAH

Softly insinuating.

Alone? I was not always alone in the past, if you will remember.

She pats his hair with maternal tenderness as if he were a boy—with a teasing laugh.

What? Have you no hope to offer your poor lonely mother?

SIMON

Awkwardly stiff and formal to cover his strange embarrassment.

I do not wish you to be too lonely, Mother. I will be happy to consider any suggestion you—

DEBORAH

With a teasing laugh, ruffling his hair playfully.

Ah! I see! Still Napoleon! Still so proud! It must be I! I must know my new place and beg! Very well. I will play your humble slave, Sire. Will you deign to visit me here and comfort my exile?

SIMON

Stiffly.

I wish you would not speak so fancifully, Mother. Please remember we are dealing with reality now and not with romantic dreams.

Then eagerly under his awkward formality.

In reply to your request, I shall be delighted to drop in and keep you company here for a while each afternoon on my way home.

DEBORAH

Gloatingly tender.

Good! Now that is off your mind, Dear. You have won that victory and can rest on your laurels for a while.

She laughs and kisses him playfully on the forehead, and sits on the steps again. A pause. He looks round the garden and she regards him with an amused motherly smile.

SIMON

Again with the yearning note.

Yes, it is very restful here. A little rest here each day will restore the soul.

He sees the volume of Byron on the steps. He picks it up—with a forced casual air.

What's this? Ah, Byron. Sara bitterly resents your poisoning her children's minds with such romantic rubbish. She wants them to be in-

spired by practical ideals. Her dread is that any of them should resemble her father and shame her pride. I have had to be so careful
never to shame her pride.

He examines the volume—with pleased boyish surprise.

I thought this looked familiar. It is the same, isn't it, Mother—the
one I gave you for your birthday long ago.

Turning over the pages.

Yes, here's the inscription. "To my beloved Mother."

To her, with a boyish, grateful smile.

This makes me happy, Mother. I thought, of course, you must have
burned this—

Abruptly with a taunting, challenging air.

I mean after I decided to leave you and begin my own life.

DEBORAH

Smiles amusedly—softly.

Oh, I agree now it was you who left me and not I who sent you away.
And I did want to burn your gift, I was so furious with you, but I
could not.

SIMON

Satisfied, turning over the pages—eagerly.

Yes, here are the parts I marked, and the parts you marked, and the
parts we marked together.

Again in his tone of yearning nostalgia.

Do you remember, Mother, we would be sitting here just as we are
now, and I'd ask you to read aloud to me—

DEBORAH

Softly.

I remember, Dear, as clearly as if it were yesterday. Or, even, as
though it were now.

SIMON

Intent on the book.

Remember this? We both marked it.

He reads.

> . . . there is a fire
> And motion of the Soul which will not dwell

    In its own narrow being, but aspire
    Beyond the fitting medium of desire;
He stops and stares around the garden — strangely.
It is a long time since I have thought of the soul. Out there in the gutters called streets beyond the wall it appears to be a weak sentimental supposition, a superstitious superfluity — but here in this garden —
He checks himself as he meets her eyes staring at him with a tender gloating fixity. He reads again.
"And, but once kindled, quenchless evermore."
He pauses, giving the pause a tense significance — thoughtfully.
"Evermore." Yes, it is, I think, the most cowardly and convenient of all man's evasions, that he forgets the present is merely the last moment of the past, and the delusion of his hope he calls the future is but the past returning to demand payment of its debt.

DEBORAH
Uneasily, with a little shiver.
I do not like that thought, Dear.

SIMON
Does not seem to hear her — reads again.
    Preys upon high adventure, nor can tire
    Of aught but rest;
He smiles at her — teasingly.
I have observed for some time how tired you were with rest, Mother.
He reads again.
    . . . a fever at the core
    Fatal to him who bears, to all who ever bore
He smiles.
Well, there is no zest in living unless one preys upon high adventure by gambling with danger. I have discovered that as leader of the Company. As for it being fatal, that's a coward's thought, eh, Mother? Remember what Frederick the Great said to his Grenadiers who hesitated to be slaughtered for his greed and glory: "You damned stupid blackguards, do you want to live forever?"
He laughs.

DEBORAH
Forcing a laugh.
Yes, so stupid of them, wasn't it?

SIMON
Turns the pages—with a return to boyish enthusiasm.
Ah! This was our favorite. I don't have to look at the book. I still
know it by heart. I could never forget—I'll bet you can guess what
it is, Mother.

DEBORAH
Smiling fondly—teasingly.
Why, how excited you are, Dear. What a romantic boy you still are
at heart! Yes, I'm sure I can guess—
She recites—with growing arrogance.
 I have not loved the World, nor the World me;
 I have not flattered its rank breath,—

SIMON
Breaks in and takes it up, taking on her tone of arrogant disdain.
 . . . nor bowed
 To its idolatries a patient knee,
 Nor coined my cheek to smiles,—

DEBORAH
With a scornful hauteur.
 . . . nor cried aloud
 In worship of an echo:

SIMON
 . . . in the crowd
 They could not deem me one of such—

DEBORAH
 . . . I stood
 Among them but not of them—
He joins in here and they both finish together.
 . . . in a shroud
 Of thoughts which were not their thoughts,—

They stop abruptly and stare at each other—then they both burst out laughing merrily, and Deborah claps her hands.

SIMON

I remember so well now, Mother!

DEBORAH

Yes, that was just as it used to be, wasn't it?
From the house off left Sara's voice is heard calling in a tone of repressed uneasiness: "Simon, are you in the garden?" *The two both start resentfully. Deborah gives him a hostile contemptuous look.*
She wants her husband. You had better go.

SIMON

Angrily, as if aloud to himself.
God, can I never know a moment's freedom!
He calls curtly, almost insultingly.
I am here with Mother. What do you want now?
Sara's voice answers with an attempt at carelessness, but betraying hurt and anxiety at his tone: "Nothing, Darling. I simply wanted to be sure." *A door is heard closing. Simon says with a chuckle.*
She wants to be sure. I thought she sounded a little uneasy, didn't you, Mother?

DEBORAH

With a malicious smile.
Yes, now you mention it—even a little frightened perhaps.

SIMON

Frowning—with his curt authoritative air.
Never mind, Mother, I will not permit such an intrusion on our privacy to occur again. I have already ordered her never to come here.
Then eagerly insistent.
Now let's forget her existence. We had a moment ago. We were back in the past before she lived in us.

DEBORAH

Tenderly.
I am only too happy, Dear.

She takes his hand—with a seductive playfulness.
Take my hand so you will not get lost.

SIMON
Kisses her hand with a shy boyish impulsiveness.
Oh, don't be afraid, I will never leave you again, Mother.
He pauses—still holding her hand, staring before him with a tender, reminiscent smile.
Do you know what had come into my mind as we laughed together? A memory that goes back long before our Byron days, when I was still at the fairy tale age, and you would read them aloud to me, here. Or, what I liked better, you would make up your own tales. They seemed so much more real than the book ones I couldn't help believing in them.

DEBORAH
Uneasily, forcing a laugh.
Good Heavens, you are going far back! I had forgotten—

SIMON
Insistently.
You can't have forgotten the one I just remembered. It was your favorite. And mine. It comes back so clearly. I can see you sitting there, as you are now, dressed all in white, so beautiful and so unreal, more like a character in your story than a flesh and blood mother, so familiar and yet so strange, so near and yet so far away—
He suddenly stares at her—a bitter accusation in his voice.
You always took such care to preserve your pose of remaining disdainfully aloof from life! One would have thought you were afraid that even your own child was a greedy interloper who was plotting to steal you from your dreams!

DEBORAH
Uneasily and guiltily—forcing a laugh.
Why, what a mean suspicious thought for you to have had about your poor mother, Dear!

SIMON
As if he hadn't heard this last—staring before him into the past again.

You would be sitting there before the summerhouse like a sentry
guarding the door.
Again he turns on her resentfully.
Why did you make that silly rule that no one was ever allowed to go
in the summerhouse but you? You wouldn't even permit me—Why
did you make such a mysterious hocus pocus about it?
He glances at the summerhouse contemptuously.
After all, it's ordinary enough. There are similar ones in many gar-
dens. The way you acted gave the impression it was some secret
temple of which you were high priestess!
He laughs sneeringly.
No one would have cared a damn about going in there, anyway!

DEBORAH
With a strange, taunting smile.
Oh, but you know that isn't true, Dear. You used to plead and beg
by the hour—

SIMON
Only because you made such a mystery of it. Naturally, that made
me curious.

DEBORAH
Yes, you were a dreadfully inquisitive, prying little boy, always asking
questions—You would never learn to mind your own business.

SIMON
Well, when you forbid a boy to go anywhere, without giving him any
sensible reason—

DEBORAH
A bit sharply, as if he were still the boy.
But I did. I explained over and over again that I felt all the rooms in
the house, even my bedroom, were your father's property. And this
garden I shared with you. I naturally desired one place, no matter
how tiny, that would be mine alone, where I could be free to dream
and possess my own soul and mind. It's just that you stubbornly refused to believe that. You were such a vain little boy.
Teasingly.

More Stately Mansions   397

You didn't want to admit I could live, even for a moment, without you, did you, Dear?

Then abruptly.

But you have no cause to complain now. I have not opened the door for years and I will never again set foot in it. As you may guess from what I told you of my last experience alone in there.

She gives a little shudder.

SIMON

Stares at her with a strange fixity.

You mean when you laughed and spat in your heart until you longed to open any door of escape?

DEBORAH

With a shiver—hurriedly.

Yes, yes! Why do you remember that so well? Let us change the subject, if you please.

SIMON

Insistently.

Why haven't you had it torn down, and not let it remain as a constant reminder.

DEBORAH

Defensively.

Because its outside reminds me of nothing. It is part of the garden. It belongs here, that is all. I do not notice it.

Pleadingly.

I asked you to talk of something else, Dear. You were starting to remember a fairy tale.

SIMON

Eagerly.

Yes, I want to tell you, Mother. But the strange part is that there is a connection with the summerhouse.

DEBORAH

Startled.

Ah! Then I do not care to hear—

SIMON

Oh, not in your story. The connection was in my imagination, because of the silly mystery you made of the damned place, I suppose.
He begins to tell the story, staring before him as if he visualized it.
The story was this, Mother. I'll tell it without attempting to repro-
duce the fantastic romanticism with which you delighted to em-
bellish your dreams. There was once upon a time, long ago in the
past, a young King of a happy and peaceful land, who through the
evil magic of a beautiful enchantress had been dispossessed of his
realm, and banished to wander over the world, a homeless, unhappy
outcast. Now the enchantress, it appeared, had in a last moment
of remorse, when he was being sent into exile, revealed to him that
there was a way in which he might regain his lost kingdom. He must
search the world for a certain magic door.

DEBORAH
With a start.
Ah.

SIMON

She told him there was no special characteristic to mark this door
from other doors. It might be any door, but if he wished to find it
with all his heart, he would recognize it when he came to it, and
know that on the other side was his lost kingdom. And so he set
forth and searched for many years, and after enduring bitter trials,
and numberless disappointments, he at last found himself before a
door and the wish in his heart told him his quest was ended. But
just as he was about to open it, confident that he had but to cross
the threshold to re-enter his kingdom, where all had been happiness
and beauty and love and peace, he heard the voice of the enchantress
speaking from the other side, for she was there awaiting his coming.
She called to him mockingly: "Wait. Before you open I must warn
you to remember how evil I can be, and that it is probable I maliciously lied and gave you a false hope. If you dare to open the door
you may discover this is no longer your old happy realm but has been
changed by me into a barren desert, where it is always night, haunted
by terrible ghosts, and ruled over by a hideous old witch, who wishes

to destroy your claim to her realm, and the moment you cross the threshold she will tear you to pieces and devour you."

DEBORAH
With a little shudder—forcing a laugh.
Oh, come now, Dear. I am sure I never—It is you who are adding silly embellishments of fantastic evil. I remember the story as an ironically humorous tale.

SIMON
Goes on as if she had not interrupted.
"So you had better be sure of your courage," the enchantress called warningly, "and remember that as long as you stay where you are you will run no risk of anything worse than your present unhappy exile befalling you." Then he heard her laugh. And that was all. She did not speak again, although he knew she remained there, and would always remain, waiting to see if he would dare open the door.
With a strange bitterness.
But he never did, you said. He could not make up his mind. He felt she was lying to test his courage. Yet, at the same time, he felt she was not lying, and he was afraid. He wanted to turn his back on the door and go far away, but it held him in a spell and he could never leave it. So he remained for the rest of his life standing before the door, and became a beggar, whining for alms from all who passed by, until at last he died.
He turns to stare at her—forcing a smile, resentfully.
That, I suppose, constitutes the humorous irony you remembered?

DEBORAH
Laughingly, a strange gloating in her face and an undercurrent of taunting satisfaction in her voice.
Yes, I remember that ending now, and I must confess I still think it shows an amusing insight into the self-betraying timidities that exist in most of us.
Teasingly.
I remember how resentful you were at the ending. You used to insist I imagine a new ending in which the wicked enchantress had reformed

and become a good fairy and opened the door and welcomed him home and they were both happy ever after.
She laughs.

SIMON

And you would laugh at me.
He stares at her—with a strange challenging look.
I would still like to discover if you could possibly imagine a happy ending to that tale.

DEBORAH

Uneasily, meeting his stare.
Why?
Then hastily turning away and forcing a laugh.
But what silly nonsense, Simon. What a child you are! Fairy tales, indeed! What a preoccupation for a Napoleon of facts!

SIMON

Smiles pleasantly.
Yes, absurd, I admit. It must be the atmosphere of this garden. But the point I was getting at is that I was very impressionable then and your story was very real to me and I connected it with real things. The door of the table became identified in my mind with the door there
He looks at the summerhouse door.
to your forbidden summerhouse. I used to boast to myself that if I were the King I would not be afraid, I would gamble recklessly on the chance—
Suddenly, moved by a strange urgency, he springs to his feet and goes past her up the steps to the door—harshly.
Let's have done with the mystery right now!
He seizes the knob.

DEBORAH

Starts to her feet in a panic of dread and grabs his other arm.
No, Simon! No!
Then her panic is strangely transformed into an outraged, arrogant fury —glaring at him with hatred and repulsion, in a quivering passion, commandingly.

Come away! Obey me this instant! How dare you! Have you lost all decency? Will your vulgar greed leave me nothing I can call my own? Is no solitude sacred to you?

SIMON
Overcome by this outburst, moves back down the steps obediently like a cowed boy.
I'm sorry Mother. I—I didn't think you'd mind now—

DEBORAH
Relieved and a bit guilty.
I can't help minding. Forgive me for losing my temper, Dear. I don't know what I said—or what I meant—The truth is I have become superstitious—remembering the last time I was in there—and I was afraid—and lost.

SIMON
Has recovered his poise as she has weakened—curtly.
That is damned nonsense, Mother. There's nothing there, of course.

DEBORAH
With a little shiver.
You think not? But I remember I am there.

SIMON
Rot! That's insanity, Mother.

DEBORAH
Slowly—with dread.
Yes, I know that is what it is.
Hurriedly.
I suppose it's very ridiculous. There is nothing in there but dark and dust and spider webs—and the silence of dead dreams.

SIMON
Smiling.
Well, anyway, it would not be a happy ending, would it, for me to go in alone? No, someday, I will give you the courage to open the door yourself and we will go together.

He takes her hand, gently—pretending to joke but with an underlying seriousness.

I think I could be absolutely sure then that the beautiful evil enchantress had reformed and become a good fairy and my happy kingdom of peace was here. Surely, you couldn't forbid me that happy dream, Mother?

DEBORAH
Fascinatedly.
No—perhaps, together—I might not be afraid—there may come a time when I might even welcome—now that she is conspiring to take life from me again—
With a strange gloating smile.
Yes, she would have only herself to blame if—
Then with a shiver of dread.
No! I don't know what I mean!
Turning on him with forced scorn.
You are being absurd, Simon. It is grotesque for a grown man to act so childishly. I forbid you ever to mention this subject again. It is only on that condition I can agree to welcome you in my garden, you have the same rights here you had in the past but no more.
Pleadingly.
Surely that is enough for your happiness, Dear.

SIMON
With a mocking gallantry, kissing her hand.
Your wish is my law, Madame. I shall be, as in the past, a slave to your every whim.

DEBORAH
Abruptly changing to a gay, seductive coquetry.
That is as should be, Monsieur.
Laughingly.
I am happy to see that vulgar peasant slut has not made you forget all the old gallantry and gracious manners I taught you, Dear.
From the house off left comes Sara's voice, and now the uneasiness and suspicion in it are obvious behind the casual words. She calls:
"Simon, are you still in the garden?"

SIMON

Starts—calls out angrily.

Yes! Of course, I'm here! Why? What do you want of me now?

A pause. Then Sara's voice comes, hurt and a little forlorn.

"Nothing, Darling. It's getting near supper time, that's all."

Her voice suddenly takes on a resentful commanding tone.

"It's time you came in, do you hear me?"

DEBORAH

Staring at him—with a bitter, jealous derisiveness.

Your slut commands you now, it seems! As the weak slave of her every greedy whim you had better obey!

Then as, stung, he starts to make an angry reply, Deborah anticipates him and calls with an undertone of gloating mockery.

Don't worry, Sara. I'll bring him back to you.

A pause. Then Sara calls, back, uneasily with a forced carelessness.

"Oh, you needn't bother, Deborah. His hunger would drive him here soon, anyway."

A door is heard closing as she goes back in the house. Deborah gives a malicious laugh.

A little forced in its self-confidence, that last, didn't you think, Dear? More than a little frightened!

She gets up. He also rises. She speaks with a cruel eagerness.

Let us go in now, Dear—together. I am eager to see her. I want to see how frightened she is.

She takes his arm—tenderly.

Oh, I am so happy—so very happy, Dear!—to have my son again!

SIMON

Tenderly.

Not half so happy as I am to have my mother again!

They start to go off, left. Abruptly he stops—in a tone of warning advice made more effective by a provocative hint of taunting behind it.

I want to warn you again, Mother, not to underestimate your enemy. It is all very well to be confident of your possessive power, which I would be the last to deny. But remember she is strong, too. She can match your superiority of mind and spirit with her over-powering physical greed for things as they are, your dreams with her facts, your evasions with her eager acceptances. Where you are sickly and over-refined and timidly superstitious, she is healthy and would break down any door that stood between her and ownership. So take care that the moment you see her you do not surrender to her influence again and let her cunning trick you into confusing what is yours with what is hers and identifying your self with her self. You must jealously defend your separate, unique individuality, your right to freedom, or—And I know you do not want her laughing at you up her sleeve anymore, as she has been doing.

DEBORAH

Has been listening with growing anger—blurts out.

Laughing at me! The stupid vulgar fool! If she only knew! And you are equally stupid or you could not say such idiotic things!

Arrogantly boastful.

I tell you it is I who have been laughing in my mind at her! It is I who have made a ridiculous trusting gull of her! Swindled her with lies into feeling affection and friendship so I could steal her children. How simple and blind you are, Simon, despite all your experience in marking cards and loading dice to play successfully the game of dispossession! Who made her feel that she was I, and whose will was it that made her no longer need you but banish you into lonely exile in your separate room? I tell you I have secretly intrigued from the first day you came here, schemed and deceived and hypocritically played the doting grandmother. To what end?

She smiles gloatingly.

Why, you should see that clearly, at least. You are here, are you not? —my son who can never wish again to leave his mother!

She laughs with a coquettish taunting and taps his cheek playfully.

It is singular that such a conquering Napoleon cannot recognize a complete victory and a crushing defeat when he sees them!

SIMON

Stares at her with a curious, objectively appraising look—then with a satisfied objectively approving nod.

Yes, make yourself believe that, Mother, and you can safely defy her. After all, there is a great deal of truth in that aspect of it, as I have suspected. Your truth, of course. Not Sara's. Nor mine. And not even the whole of your truth. But you and I can wait to discover what that is later on.

He smiles with pleasant casualness.

Just now I think we had better go in to supper.

DEBORAH

Pulling away, stares at him with a puzzled frightened dread.

Simon! What—?

Then conquering her fear and suddenly gloating takes his arm again— eagerly.

Yes! Let us go in. I can't wait to tell her you are going to be with me each evening, that you are now my own dear son again!

SIMON

Sharply commanding.

No! Not until I give you permission to speak. I will choose the most effective time.

Coldly and curtly.

You will kindly not forget, Mother, all this reorganization of my home is my affair and must be carried out exactly as I have calculated. You had better not interfere if you expect me ever to keep you company.

Brusquely.

Come. It is getting late.

She is again looking at him with bewildered dread, has shrunk back, taking her hand from his arm. But he ignores this and grasps her arm and makes her walk off beside him up the path to the house.

CURTAIN

Tao House
Nov. 26th '38

Act Three, Scene Three

SCENE

Parlor of the Harford mansion—a high-ceilinged, finely-proportioned room such as one finds in the Massachusetts houses designed by Bulfinch or McIntire and built in the late 1790s. The walls and ceiling are white. A rug covers most of the floor of waxed dark wood. A crystal chandelier hangs from the middle of the ceiling at center, toward front. At extreme left-front a small table against the wall, facing right, then a door leading to the entrance hall, another chair, and farther back, a table. In the middle of the rear wall is the door to Simon's study. On either side of it, a chair facing front. Against the right wall, toward rear, another table. Farther forward, a high window looking out on the street, then a chair, and finally, at right-front, a fireplace. At left, rear of the fireplace, is a long sofa with a small table and reading lamp by its left end. Toward front, at left, is an oval table with another lamp. A chair is by right rear of this table, facing right-front. Another chair is at left-front of this table, facing directly front. It is around nine o'clock at night of the same day.

Sara, Simon, and Deborah are discovered—Sara in the chair at left-front of the table, Simon across the table from her in the chair at rear-right of it, Deborah on the left end of the sofa by the lamp. Sara is pretending to work on a piece of needle-point but she is obviously preoccupied with her thoughts. Deborah has a book in her hands but she stares over it, as preoccupied as Sara. Simon also holds a book and keeps his eyes fixed on it but his eyes do not move and his mind is very evidently elsewhere. All have changed their clothes. The two women wear semi-formal evening gowns, Deborah's all white, Sara's a blue that matches the color of her eyes. Simon is dressed in black.

For a moment after the curtain rises there is an atmosphere of tense quiet in the room, an eavesdropping silence that waits, holding its breath and straining its ears. Then, as though the meaning of the silence were becoming audible, their thoughts are heard.

SARA

Thinking.

Thank God, there's a moment's peace where I can think—ever since they came in, the three of us conversing so pleasant—as if nothing had happened—she's a good one at hiding her feelings—you'd think, taking the children away meant nothing to her—maybe it doesn't—maybe, like he claims, she was only pretending—no, I know she loved them—it's her great-lady pride won't give me the satisfaction to know she's hurt—and there's something more behind it—I thought they'd never come in—I heard them laughing once—and when they came in she looked as gay as you please—something about him, too—sly—like there was a secret between them—I was a fool to let him go to her crazy garden—

Vindictively.

Well, I know he hasn't told her yet I'm going to work with him—I'll tell her the mistress part of it—let her try to smile when she knows that!

Impatiently with a side glance at Simon.

Why doesn't he tell her and get it over—if he doesn't soon, I will!—

DEBORAH

Thinking.

In the garden, at the end, I was so sure of him—but he changed when he saw her—something in his eyes of her old physical power over him—a reflection of her common, vulgar prettiness—a change in her, too—I felt her warm greedy femaleness deliberately exuding lust in a brazen enticement—she was not half as frightened as I hoped—still, she was uneasy—she couldn't hide her suspicion—and when he tells her he is coming to my garden every evening she will realize her crude animalism is of no avail now—that he is my son again—

Impatiently, with a side glance at Simon.

Why does he wait?—does he shrink from hurting her?—well, remembering her base betrayal of my trust, I will not shrink!

SARA

Reassuring herself—thinking.

Ah, I'm a fool to waste a thought on her—hasn't he kept his word about the children?—and don't I remember at the office how much he wanted me—even the part of him that belongs to the Company will be mine now—all of him—and my children, too, will be all mine!—there'll be no more sharing with her—this is my home!—she'll be no better than a strange guest, living on charity—let her keep to her garden where she'll harm no one but herself—let her dream herself into a madhouse, if she likes, as long as she leaves me and mine alone!—it'd serve her right for her lies and meanness, trying to steal my children when I trusted her!—

DEBORAH

Thinking—self-reassuringly and then gloatingly.

She is only pretending to work on her needle-point—thinking—yes, quite as frightened in her thoughts, I think, as Simon and I had hoped—it's merely my imagination that reads desire for her in his eyes—I remember how tender he became in the garden—how loving—how much he needed me—my beloved son!—never to be taken from me again—every evening in the garden I will encourage him to live with me in the past before he knew her—before he ever thought of women—to be my little boy again—I will bind him to me so he can never reject me and escape again—she will become no more than the empty name of wife, a housekeeper, a mother of children, our Irish biddy nurse girl and servant!—

SIMON

Staring at his book—thinks with gloating satisfaction as though his mind guessed their thoughts.

I have good reason to congratulate myself, I think—all goes in accord with my plan—everything moves back into its proper place—they are divided and separate again—they do not sit together on the sofa as has been their wont—I am where I belong between them—there will be no further confusion in my mind—no devouring merging of identities—no more losing myself in their confusion—henceforth all is distinct and clearly defined—two women—opposites—whose only relation derives from the relationship of each to me—whose lives have meaning and purpose only in so far as they live within my living—henceforth this is my home and I own my own mind again!—I am a free slave-owner!

He smiles to himself gloatingly and begins to read. As if their minds had partly sensed the tenor of his thought, the two women turn to stare at him with a stirring of suspicion and resentment. They both look quickly away.

SARA

Thinking.

He isn't reading—just pretending to—smiling to himself—sly—

DEBORAH

Her thoughts in the same key as Sara's.

What is he thinking, I wonder?—of the Company and this secretary-mistress he boasted?—I hate that smug, lustful, greedy trader's smile of his!—

SARA

Thinking resentfully.

I know that smile—when he's managed a foxy deal for the Company and cheated someone—he spoke at the office as though he was driving a bargain for a mistress—I hope he doesn't think he'll cheat me—I was a fool to let him see I wanted him so much!—

DEBORAH

Thinking resentfully.

It was unwise to agree so soon to his pleading—I remember, even when he was little, he realized how his begging made me weak, and he used it to get his own way—well, he will discover again, if he has forgotten, that I have ways of getting my way, too!

SARA

Thinks self-reassuringly and a bit contemptuously.

Ah, I mustn't be uneasy—didn't he show he wanted me as much as I want him?—or maybe more, if I'd tried—so why should I worry

my mind?—I'll attend to my needle-point and not let these foolish thoughts disturb me—
She begins to work determinedly.

DEBORAH
Thinks self-reassuringly.
This is senseless and stupid!—to make myself uneasy and resentful—after he's proved so conclusively—it's unfair to him—I'll be sensible and read my book—
She begins to read determinedly. There is a pause of silence. It is Simon who stops attempting to distract his mind first. His eyes cease reading and stare at the book preoccupiedly.

SIMON
Thinking.
Yes, I think I can foresee every move of my present campaign here— not even Napoleon planning Austerlitz—Good God, what an insane comparison!—Mother's romantic influence!—nevertheless, I can prophesy exactly every possible development in this battle—but will this one victory insure a peace of perpetual conquest?—who knows?—the immediate future is all I can foretell clearly—my plan doesn't go beyond—I don't even know yet what I wish the final outcome to be, or what is the exact nature of the final peace I want to impose—
With forced self-reassurance.
Bah! I will cross those bridges when I come to them—sufficient for the day that I control the game now and can have it played as I wish—make them think that each may win—deal the marked cards to give each in turn the semblance of winning so each may mistake losses for gains—
Frowning again—uneasily.
But it means I must always remain in the game myself—be as careful and watchful now outside the office as in it—never relax my vigilance—there is always the danger of failure—bankruptcy and ruin —alliance of devouring enemies—an unceasing duel to the death with life!—
He makes an unconscious shrinking movement of dread—determinedly self-scornful.

Bah! What nonsense! You would think I saw myself as the victor's spoils—when it is I who will be the victor—

He tries to read again but at once gives up the attempt.

I cannot concentrate on this damned book—I read a paragraph and do not remember the sense or find any meaning—

DEBORAH

Has ceased reading and is staring over her book—thinking resentfully.

I cannot read—my eyes follow words but that is all—I feel a restless dread—I cannot help remembering the past—he has awakened so much I had hoped was dead—it is a dangerous price to pay—

SARA

Has stopped sewing—thinks irritably.

It's no good!—I can't put my mind on sewing—I feel something is staring over my shoulder—watching my thoughts pushing and crowding in my brain like a lot of mad sheep something has frightened, and I'm not able to stop them—it's strange here tonight—it's not the house it's been—not home at all—there's no peace—.

Unconsciously she sighs regretfully.

It's so changed from the contented way we've been here nights for so long—she and I would be sitting together on the sofa laughing and telling each other about the children—he'd sit alone, thinking out schemes for his Company—minding his own business and not bothering us—

DEBORAH

With a little shudder.

Yes, a frightening price to demand of me—to release the forgotten Deborah who was his mother from the tomb of the past—how silly he acted about the summerhouse—a grown man—nothing is sacred or secret to him—how tense the quiet is in this house tonight—as though a bomb were concealed in the room with a fuse slowly sputtering toward—and the silence waits—holding its breath—hands clapped over its ears—a strange haunted house—so changed from what it was last night—and every night for years—she would sit here by my side—we would laugh together, thinking of the children—I had forgotten him sitting alone there—he might have been a million miles away—he was buried in the past—I did not need him—

SIMON
Thinking—uneasily.
Perhaps I should have waited—until I had determined the true nature of the final conquest I desire more clearly—I am more cautious with my campaigns for the Company—I calculate first exactly what I want to win—am sure the game is worth the candle—the unceasing vigilance it will demand of me is going to prove an added strain—it begins already—my home is becoming a battlefield—so different from other nights—there was peace here, of a kind—at least an atmosphere in which I could be indifferent to their existence and concentrate on my ambitions for the Company—a man's work in a man's world of fact and reality—
Irritably.
What made their petty sentimental women's world of lies and trivial greeds assume such a false importance?—why did I have to meddle in their contemptible ambitions and let them involve me in a domestic squabble about the ownership of children?—I, the leader of a great Company, a figure of first importance in the life of a great city, a man men fear and envy—

SARA
Regretfully.
Much as I ought to hate her now for the sneak he showed her to be, I can't help wishing he'd never told me—he's a fool to think she could ever have taken my children—I can keep what's mine from the devil himself—it may be weak of me but I wish I could have kept on thinking she was my friend and trusting her—feeling proud of having helped her—

DEBORAH
Regretfully.
Much as I detest her treachery, I find something in me wishing he had not unmasked her—is there any one of us whose soul, stripped naked, is not ugly with meanness?—life is at best a polite pretending not to see one another—a game in which we tacitly agree to

make believe we are not what we are—a covenant not to watch one's friends too clearly, for the sake of friendship—and I have grown to lean upon her health and strength—as one leans against a tree, deep rooted in the common earth—and what if she had taken the children?—if she had done it herself, I would have understood her jealousy—I have been a loving mother, too—I would have forgiven her, remembering my own greed—

SARA
As though responding to Deborah's thoughts, gives Simon a resentful look.
If only he hadn't interfered—why did he take the sudden notion to start minding our business?—

SIMON
Frowning—thinks self-exasperatedly.
What stupid impulse drove me to start taking a hand in their measly woman's game—now, of all times, when I've just assumed the added responsibility of the railroad!—what the devil possessed me to ask Sara to come to the office?—now I won't have a separate man's life free of woman even there!

SARA
Thinking resentfully.
If I hadn't gone to his office—I had a feeling I shouldn't—that he was up to some scheme—

SIMON
Thinking.
What bosh to tell her I needed a secretary!—she'll only be in my way —and I'll have no privacy—she'll pry greedily into everything—

SARA
Thinking.
As if I hadn't enough to do taking care of my home and my children without his making me slave for his Company!
Scornfully.
Is he that weak he can't even manage his own man's business without my—?

SIMON
Thinking.
My ridiculous proposal to make her my mistress!—if I wanted one I
could buy girls by the dozen—young and pretty—fresh and not yet
possessed—not a body I already own—which possession has made
worthless to me—if she hopes she can ever again make me the greedy
slave to it I once was—
He turns to stare at her with a vindictive hostility.

SARA
Thinking not noticing he is looking at her.
If he thinks his asking me to be his mistress pleased me—treating
his wife as if she was a whore he'd pick up on the street and ask her
price—and he ought to know I was through wanting him—content
he'd left me free to sleep by myself in peace—I was a fool to let him
hug and kiss me like he did at the office and make me remember—
make me like a beast in heat that's a slave to her need and can't help
herself—but I'll show him it will be the other way round this time,
and I'll be the one to keep free!
*She turns to stare at him with revengeful hostility, then as they meet each
other's eyes, each turns away guiltily. Forcing a casual tone—speaks to
him.*
Yes, Simon? You were going to speak to me?

SIMON
In a like casual tone.
I? No. I thought you—

SARA
No.

SIMON
I was preoccupied with my thoughts.

SARA
So was I.

SIMON
A taunt coming into his tone.
I was thinking of Mother, as it happens.

SARA
Casually.
That's strange. So was I.
Neither of them looks at her. A pause.

DEBORAH
Thinking—resentfully.
He lied—he said that to hurt her—much as I ought to hate her, I
pity her when I see him deliberately trying to humiliate—and if he
was thinking of me, it is against my wishes—just as his coming to
my garden this afternoon—forcing his way in—one would think a
man of his birth and breeding would have more delicacy—would
not desire to come where he knows he is unwelcome—

SIMON
Thinking—resentfully.
By that lie I've put Mother back in my mind—what impelled me
to visit her garden again—mysterious summerhouse—all that insane
nonsense—Good God, I'll be playing with toys next, and begging
her to tell me a fairy tale!—so damned weak of me to offer to visit her
each evening—I have no time to waste humoring her senile whims
and pretending to take her crazy dreams of romance seriously—
He stares at her with vindictive hostility.

DEBORAH
Thinking with bitter hostility.
His proposal to visit me each evening—as if he were doing me a
favor, forsooth!—I do not want him intruding on my life—I never
even wanted him to be conceived—I was glad to be rid of him when
he was born—he had made my beauty grotesquely ugly by his presence, bloated and misshapen, disgusting to myself—and then the
compulsion to love him after he was born—like a fate forced on me
from without, in spite of myself, not of my own will, making me
helpless and weak—love like an enslaving curse laid on my heart—
my life made dependent on another's living, my happiness at the
mercy of another's selfish whims—
*She turns to stare at him with vindictive hostility. Then, as each meets
the other's eyes, each turns away guiltily.*

SIMON
Speaks to her forcing a casual tone.
Yes, Mother? You wanted to speak to me?

DEBORAH
Echoing his tone.
No, Simon. I thought you—

SIMON
No.
Then with a taunt in his tone.
I was not thinking of you, but of Sara.

DEBORAH
Carelessly.
That is strange, I was thinking of her, too.
Neither of them look at her. A pause.

SARA
Thinking—resentfully.
He lied to her—it's little thought he ever gives me anymore except when his lust wants something—he said that to hurt her—he's sneering at her—poor woman!—I find it hard to hate her—there's too much pity in my heart—she can't read her book—she's too upset—she's thinking how she'll miss the children—alone all day—I won't be here to keep her company—he'll have me at the office—alone in the past, where she'll have nothing but her old mad dreams to turn to for comfort—he'll have her in an asylum in the end, if he's not careful!—it's a terrible thing he can hate his own mother so!—I didn't even hate my father that much—and if I did hate him, it was on account of my poor mother—the way he sneered at her—Simon sneers at his mother—and Deborah has been like a mother to me—I was proud of having a second mother who's a great lady of a fine Yankee family, who doesn't talk in ignorant brogue like my poor mother did, and is too proud to let love for any man make a fool and a slave of her—who has always kept herself free and independent—
Bewilderedly.
Ah, what makes me remember the past and get the dead mixed up with the living in my mind—like he said he's confused Deborah and

me in his mind—his mind, that's just it—it's he that brings confusion to us!

DEBORAH
Thinking bitterly.
This is all his doing—the malicious plot of a greedy, evil, morbidly jealous child—I know he has lied to me—that he drove her to betray my trust—she would never of her own will—she had begun to look upon me as a second mother—to come to me for advice—to look up to me—and I was happy to regard her as my daughter—because in her affectionate trust I felt safe from myself—because her strength and health and acceptance of life gave me a faith in my own living—a support—and now he dares to take that security away from me!—to offer me in exchange an insane confusion—ghosts from the past to haunt me—with the insolence of one doing a favor or bearing a gift!—

SARA
Thinking.
Why do I let him?—I'm not helpless—I'm not a thought he moves around in his mind to suit his pleasure—I ought to go to her now and talk with her truthfully—get her to be truthful with me—I'll forgive her if she'll forgive me—and between us we can soon put an end to his tricks!—

DEBORAH
Thinking.
What fools we are to allow him to do this to us!—if she'd sit with me here as on other nights, we'd understand and forgive each other—with her strength and health beside me, I can defend myself against his greedy dreams—I have only to call her over—
They both speak to each other simultaneously—"Sara" "Deborah." *They bend forward so they can see each other past him and they smile at each other with a relieved understanding. Deborah speaks with a strange gentleness.*
Yes, Daughter. I ought to have known you guessed my thoughts.

SARA
Getting up—with a gentle smile.

Maybe I did Mother—and I hope you guessed mine. May I come and sit with you?

SARA

DEBORAH

I was going to ask you to. Of course you may, Dear.

Sara goes around the table and passes behind Simon, ignoring him, and goes to the sofa. Deborah pats the sofa on her left, smiling an affectionate welcome.

This is your place, you know, beside me.

SARA

Bends impulsively and gives her a daughterly kiss on the cheek.
I know, Mother.
She sits down, close beside her, so their arms touch.

SIMON

Who has been pretending to read—with contemptuous relief.
Ah, so they have decided to forget and forgive—well, I confess I feel relieved—this hate was becoming a living presence in the room—and in my mind—I felt hopelessly involved in it—through my own fault, too—I was stupid to meddle—but now we will be back where we were on other nights and my mind is free to mind its own business—

A sudden sly malicious look comes to his face.

Meanwhile, keeping an eye on them to make sure this sentimental reunion is not too successful—but each is lying and acting, of course—playing the hypocrite in the hope of gaining some advantage—it will be amusing to watch—

SARA

Turns to Deborah with impulsive frankness.
I want to beg your forgiveness, Mother—about the children. It was mean of me to let myself be made jealous, and not to trust you.

DEBORAH

Takes her hand—gently.
I understand. One cannot help being jealous. It is part of the curse of love.

SARA

With a quick resentful look at Simon.
Yes, you do feel cursed by it when it's too greedy.

DEBORAH

Patting Sara's hand.
Thank goodness, we've understood each other and what might have developed into a stupid quarrel is all forgotten now, isn't it?

SARA

Yes, and I'm happy to be here beside you again, feeling your trust and friendship—

DEBORAH

Presses her hand and keeps it in hers.
And I'm so happy to have you back, Dear. I had begun to feel so weak and at the mercy of the past.

SARA

Gently.
Ah now, don't think of what's past.
With bullying affection.
Shame on you and you with four handsome grandchildren to love, and everything in life to live for.

DEBORAH

Eagerly.
Then I may have the children back?

SARA

Indeed you may! And remember I wasn't really the one who took them away from you.
She casts a resentful look at Simon.

DEBORAH

Deeply moved.
You are so kind and generous, Dear! I hate myself for having permitted my mind to be tempted—
She gives Simon a bitter hostile look.
But that's over. We have beaten him.

A pause. The two women sit with clasped hands, staring defiantly at Simon.

SIMON

Moves restlessly, his eyes fixed on the book—thinking with a forced, uneasy derision.

Is it possible, after all that has happened between us today, that they actually hope to re-establish their selfish, greedy union—which denied me and shut me out and left me alone—

Bitterly vindictive.

Then I'll soon prove to them—Mother forgets I haven't told Sara yet about my plan to visit her every evening from now on—and Sara forgets Mother doesn't know yet she is to be the mistress I—I have hesitated to tell them so far because—because what?—because I know that then the die will be cast irrevocably, and there can be no possible turning back?—because something in me is afraid?—

Forcing a self-scornful tone.

afraid?—nonsense!—it is for them to be afraid—but I wish I could see the exact nature of the final plan I desire more clearly before I—

SARA

As if influenced by his thought, gives him a quick resentful look—slowly.

All the same, Deborah, I know how unhappy you felt, sitting alone here. I was miserable myself over there with him between us.

DEBORAH

Glancing at Simon resentfully—lowering her voice to a whisper.

Yes. That's just it, Sara. We must never again allow him to come between—

SARA

In a whisper.

Ah! It was he who made me believe you were trying to steal my children's love from me.

They bend closer to each other until their heads are about touching, and all during the following scene talk in whispers, their eyes fixed on Simon.

DEBORAH

I am sure he did. Just as he tried to make me believe you had gone to his office with the deliberate purpose of betraying me.

SARA

Stares at Simon with bitter hostility.
So that's what he told you, is it? It's a lie. It was all his scheming. He asked me to come there.

DEBORAH

Yes, I see that clearly now.

SARA

I wonder what mad trick he's up to. Why can't he leave us in peace? What more can he want of us? Haven't we given him all of our time he's any right to?
Bitterly.
But men are the devil's own children! They're never content. They must always grab for more.

DEBORAH

Bitterly.
It's true. You bear them and hope you are free, but it's only the beginning of a new slavery, for they start with their first cry to accuse you and complain of their fate like weaklings and demand your life as if it were their right to possess you!

SARA

It's seeing us content with our children without him. He can't bear the thought—

DEBORAH

Beginning to smile with vindictive satisfaction.
Yes. He was always a greedy jealous boy. That's where we may have him at our mercy, I think, Sara. His jealousy drives him to need us. But we already have four sons—

SARA

Beginning to smile, too.
And so we don't have to need him.

She laughs softly and jeeringly and Deborah laughs with her. Simon stirs uneasily and his eyes cease to follow the lines and stare at the page.

DEBORAH

Yes, the more I consider it, Sara, the more confident I feel that it is really he who is helpless and lonely and lost—who begs for love and is completely at our mercy!

SARA

Threateningly.

Then let him look out how he plays scheming tricks to destroy our peace! We might lose patience with his greediness and he'd find himself driven out in the night without—to sleep in his office with his Company for a mistress!

SIMON

His eyes staring on his book now—thinking with a tense dread.

I still feel hatred like a living presence in this room—stronger—drawing closer—surrounding—threatening—me—

Fighting himself.

But that's absurd—they hate each other now—

Frightenedly.

But it seems to have gotten very cold in this room—nonsense!—you know it is an extremely warm night—but it has become dark in here and the room is unfamiliar—nonsense!—it's the same old parlor in the house where you were born and the lamps burn brightly—but surely it cannot be my imagination that Mother and Sara have vanished—as on so many nights before—Mother took her hand and led her back—as if she opened a door into the past in whose darkness they vanished to reappear as one woman—a woman recalling Mother as I knew her long ago—but not her—a stranger woman —unreal, a ghost inhumanely removed from living, beautiful and coldly remote and arrogant and proud—with eyes deliberately blind —with a smile deliberately amused by its own indifference—because she no longer wants me—has taken all she needed—I have served my purpose—she has ruthlessly got rid of me—she is free—and I am left lost in myself, with nothing!

He has dropped the book in his lap and straightened himself tensely, gripping the arms of his chair, staring before him frightenedly. As his thoughts have progressed, the expressions on the two women's faces have mirrored his description as though, subconsciously, their mood was created by his mind. They become proudly arrogant and coldly indifferent to him. He goes on thinking with increasing dread.

But it is different now—that is what she was on other nights—her nature has changed—not indifferent now—she stares at me with hate—she is revengeful and evil—a cannibal witch whose greed will devour!

Their expressions have changed to revengeful gloating cruelty and they stare at him with hate. He starts forward in his chair as if he were about to fly in horror from the room.

DEBORAH
Smiling gloatingly.
See, Sara, he is not even pretending to read now. He is thinking. He must have heard what we were whispering; he looks so uneasy and defeated.

SARA
Smiling gloatingly.
As scared as if he saw a ghost!

DEBORAH
Her tone becoming contemptuously pitying.
So like a little boy who is lost.

SARA
Contemptuously pitying.
Yes, that's like him. There's so much of that weakness in him. Maybe that's what I've loved most in him.

DEBORAH
Because it makes him need you so terribly! Oh, I know! I know so well! I remember—
Her expression softens to a condescending maternal tenderness.
Perhaps we are being too hard on him. After all, what he has tried to do has been so obviously childish and futile.

SARA

It's because he's jealous, and that proves how much he loves us.

DEBORAH

Yes, I think instead of being angry, we should merely be amused, as we would be at the mischief of a bad sulky boy.

SARA

Smilingly—complacently maternal.
And forgive him if he promises not to do it again.

DEBORAH

Smiling like Sara.
He won't, I know, as soon as he is compelled to realize he can't gain anything by being wicked—except to be severely punished.
She speaks to Simon with an amused, teasing smile.
Wake up, Dear!
He starts and turns to stare at them bewilderedly.
Why do you stare as if we were strangers?

SARA

Teasingly.
It's like he always is lately. His mind is so full of grand schemes for the Company we might as well be in another world!
Laughingly.
You might be more polite to your ladies, Darling.

SIMON

As if suddenly emerging from a spell—with an impulsive grateful relief.
Ah! Thank God, each of you is here again!
He checks himself abruptly and looks away from them hastily and hurries on in a confused, evasive, explanatory tone.
I beg your pardon. I had forgotten you were here. I was thinking of the Company's affairs. I must have dozed off and dreamed—

DEBORAH

Turns to Sara—with gloating amusement.
He must have dreamed we no longer loved him.
She smiles at Simon with a tender, scornful pity.
My poor boy! Do tell us what you dreamed.

He ignores her. She laughs teasingly.

He won't do it, Sara. He was always stubbornly secretive about his dreams, even as a little boy. And so greedily inquisitive about mine. That was the unfair part. He thought I had no right to have any secrets from him.

She calls teasingly.

Simon. Why don't you answer me? What was it you dreamed just now that made you so afraid?

He doesn't seem to hear. She laughs softly.

No, it's no good, Sara. He is pretending to be quite oblivious to our existence again, to be too deeply absorbed in his great schemes of manly ambition, inspired by the career of Napoleon! But we know he is very uneasy now, not sure of himself at all, wondering what we will decide to do about him.

SARA

With a little laugh.

Yes, he has a guilty conscience and he knows he ought to be punished.

SIMON

As if he hadn't heard them, but confusedly apologetic and almost humbly placating and apprehensive, avoiding their eyes.

I—I am afraid I interrupted a private discussion between you. I remember now you were whispering together. Pray continue. I am interested in this book and you need not mind my presence. You can dismiss me from your minds entirely—for the present. I will even regard it as a favor if you do, because, to be truthful, your thinking of me intrudes on my thoughts and confuses me—at a time when it is imperative I concentrate my mind on defining the exact nature of the final goal of my ambition, precisely what peace I desire to impose after—

SARA

Contemptuously.

Ah, he's off at the head of his Company again, Deborah, prancing on a great white thoroughbred Arab stallion around and around his mind, like old Boney himself!

With a strange boastfulness.

But don't forget, Darling, I'm my father's daughter and wasn't he an officer and a gentleman who helped the Duke drive old Boney out of Spain, and took all he'd gained from him!

DEBORAH

Smiling teasingly.

Yes, I agree with you that whatever plans he makes now concern us in making our plans. If he didn't want us to mind him, he shouldn't have minded our business, should he?

She laughs softly, teasing and Sara laughs with her. Simon ignores them, staring at his book, pretending to read but his eyes are motionless. Deborah goes on.

But, of course, if by not mind he means not take too seriously, we agree, don't we? We mustn't mind him. We must make allowances and not judge him too harshly. He has always been a romantic boy in whose backward imagination everything became confused—real life with fairy tales—facts with poetic fancies—common summerhouses with enchanted palaces—and heaven knows what other incredible, presumptuous nonsense! Everyone who ever knew him in the old days considered him a queer, erratic boy, subject to spells in which he was irresponsible and impracticable—a little crazy, to be frank. His own father never thought him strictly dependable. Even I have been afraid at times he has inherited a stupid folly of grandeur hallucination—from my father, who, as I have confessed to you, Sara, was a weak minister who in dreams confused Napoleon with himself and with God.

Her tone has become strange, and bitterly sneering, and she stares before her, smiling with a taunting scorn. Abruptly she checks herself and turns to Sara with a change to a tone of growing, condescending pity.

So we must be fair and not punish his naughtiness too severely, poor boy.

SARA

With condescending pity.

Ah no, we know he loves us and means no harm, poor darling.

DEBORAH

A threat in her tone now.

But we better make it clear to him right now we will not tolerate any more of his malicious meddling in our affairs.

She turns to Simon.

Listen, Simon. When you interrupted us we were discussing your stupid attempt to ruin the peace and harmony of your home and destroy with your morbid jealousy the trust and loving friendship that exists between your wife and mother—

SARA

Bitterly.

Yes, wouldn't it divert him from worrying about the Company to have us fight a duel to the death to see which of us he'd deign to give his love to!

DEBORAH

Coldly.

Unfortunately, Simon, while you may be extremely successful in swindling men at their childish gambling for material possessions, you are far too transparent to cheat us with your obviously marked cards and clumsily loaded dice when you venture to play for the possession of love.

SARA

Yes, we're more than a match for you there. So you'd better stop right now, for your own good.

DEBORAH

Smiles at him now, cajolingly affectionate.

But we have agreed to forgive you, Dear—just because you are such a silly jealous boy.

SARA

Because you've proved, Darling, how dearly you love us.

DEBORAH

And because, now that we know how much you need our love, we cannot blame you for feeling bitter because we let the children take your place so completely. We admit that was very wrong of us. But, you see, Dear, we had misunderstood your seeming preoccupation with the Company's affairs. You should have told us you couldn't be happy without our love. We were completely taken in by your pretending.

To Sara—tenderly mocking.

He appeared to be so free; didn't he, Sara?

SARA

Smiles teasingly.

He did. As independent as you please!

DEBORAH

Teasingly penitent.

We are sorry, Dear. We humbly beg your forgiveness.

SARA

With the same air.

We promise it won't happen again, Darling. We'll never let you out of our love again.

DEBORAH

You will be our first born and best beloved again.

Teasing with a coquettish, enticing air.

So now won't you forget and make up with us, Dear?

Simon continues to stare at the book as if he did not hear them.

SARA

Cajolingly.

Come over here and sit with us now, that's a good lad. You look so lost over there alone.

She moves over and pats the sofa between her and Deborah—enticingly.

Look, you can sit here and have love all around you. What man could ask more of life?

Mockingly.

You'll be between us, as you've been trying to be.

DEBORAH

Laughingly.

Yes, I do not think there is any danger in that now, Sara.

She pats the sofa invitingly.

Come, Dear.

He does not seem to hear. Deborah laughs softly.

What? Still so vain and stubborn?

To Sara.

Well, since the mountain is too proud to come to Mahomet—

She takes Sara's hand and they rise to their feet. Their arms around each other's waists, they advance on Simon with mocking, enticing smiles. They are like two mothers who, confident of their charm, take a possessive gratification in teasing a young, bashful son. But there is something more behind this—the calculating coquetry of two prostitutes trying to entice a man.

We must humor his manly pride, Sara. Anything to keep peace in our home!

She laughs.

SARA

Laughingly.

Yes. Anything to give him his way, as long as it's our way!

They have come to Simon who stares as if he did not notice their approach, and yet instinctively shrinks back in his chair. They group together in back of him, Deborah at left-rear and Sara at right-rear of his chair. They bend over, each with an arm about the other, until their faces touch the side of his head. Their other arms go around him so that their hands touch on his chest.

DEBORAH

Teasing tenderly.

Now don't shrink back into yourself, Dear. Why are you so afraid?

SARA

Teasing tenderly.

We're not going to eat you, Darling, if you are that sweet.

Their arms hug him, tenderly possessive.

SIMON

Tensely, his eyes in a fixed stare on the page of his book, thinking with a mingling of fascinated dread and an anguished yearning.

I cannot keep them separate—they will not remain divided—they unite in spite of me—they are too strong here in their home—the

stronghold of woman, the possessor of children—it is a mistake in strategy to attack them here—they unite against the invader—they hate as one—
More confusedly.
But I must remember they only seem to become one—it is due to the confusion of my thoughts—it exists only in my mind—an hallucination, a dream, not a fact of reality—but I feel her arms around me—they are real—and she is good now, not evil—she loves me—she does not hate me because she loves me, as she always did before—I need not fear her revenge—that she is waiting for an opportunity to get rid of me—no, I can trust her now at last—she is mine and so I can surrender and be hers, as I have always desired—
He relaxes with a dreamy smile of content in their arms and murmurs drowsily in gentle wonder.
Why, I see clearly now that this is the final conquest and peace I must have had in mind when I planned my campaign—and I have won the deciding victory over them already!
He gives a strange chuckle of satisfaction, and closes his eyes.

DEBORAH
Smiles, maternally gloating and tenderly possessive.
You see, Sara. There was no cause for us to be afraid.
With a strange contemptuous arrogance.
I can always, whenever I wish, make him my little boy again.
She kisses him on the cheek.
Can't I, Dear?

SARA
Gives her a quick resentful jealous look.
I wasn't the one who was afraid. Don't I know whenever I want, I can make him my lover again, who'd give anything he has for me!
She kisses his other cheek.
Can't I, Darling?
She and Deborah suddenly turn and stare at each other with defiant, jealous enmity over his head, pulling their hands away so they no longer touch on his chest, but each still holds him. Simon starts and stiffens in his chair.

DEBORAH

Fighting with herself.

Sara—forgive me—I didn't mean—it's what he did in the garden made me forget—

Pleadingly.

But we mustn't let ourselves forget, Sara. We must remember what he has tried to do! We must keep united and defend the peace of our home as one woman or—

SARA

Penitently.

I know—I shouldn't have said—it's what he did to me at the office—but I won't forget again.

Their hands touch around Simon again but now he strains forward against them.

SIMON

Thinking bitterly.

Fool! To allow myself to be swindled by that mad dream again! Your final victory and peace, eh? Are you insane? She loves none but herself, I tell you! She is greedy and evil! Trust her and you will only find yourself again driven out beyond a wall, with nothing, with the door slammed shut forever behind you, and the sound of her mocking arrogant laughter—left alone to marry the first unscrupulous schemer with a beautiful body you meet who wishes to sell herself and fulfill her greedy ambition to own a slave and use him to acquire children and wealth and a nouveau-riche estate!—No!

He jerks forward to his feet from their arms. They each give a frightened pleading cry. He turns to stare from one to the other for a moment in a dazed awakening confusion—stammering.

Ah! You are both there. I thought—I beg your pardon—I must have dozed off again and dreamed—

Then with increasing hostility and derision.

But no, it couldn't have been all a dream, for I remember your coming over to me. I remember watching you with amusement and saying to myself: What damned hypocrites they are! By God, if I didn't know each of them so well I would be swindled into believing in their sincerity! Each has learned tricks of deceit from the other!

Mother has made Sara almost as convincing an actress as she is, while she has stolen from Sara a false appearance of honest frankness which lends a common natural air to her romantic artificiality!
Then curtly and rudely.
Well, now that the little farce is over, if you will permit me to sit down and return where you belong—
The two women's faces grow cold and hostile and defiant. But they are also full of dread.

DEBORAH
Ignoring him, takes Sara's hand.
Come, Sara.
They pass behind him to sit on the sofa side by side, as before, clasping each other's hand. They stare at Simon defiantly and apprehensively. He sits in his chair and stares at his book again, pretending to ignore them.

SIMON
Thinking uneasily.
I feel their hate again—there is no doubt now it is against me—it was a stupid blunder to attack them openly in the woman's home where they have made themselves so strong—my attack has only served to unite them—
Calculatingly.
But one learns by one's mistakes—in future, I shall wait until I have each alone—at the office—the garden—at night here, I shall remain apart—lock myself in my study, if need be, for greater safety— safety?—what nonsense!—what have I to fear?—it is I who deal the cards and control the game—who cannot lose—
Calculating more confidently and gloatingly now.
Yes, if I am not here they must turn upon each other—they cannot keep up this pretense—which is all for my benefit—
He gives them a quick glance—then, as his eyes meet their hostility, he hastily brings them back to his work—uneasily.
How they stare—their hatred for me is obvious now—I shall be glad to be alone in my study—I can think of something more important than this damned, petty domestic war—I almost regret now I ever should have considered it important enough to make its confusion a decisive issue—

He suddenly looks up but avoids their eyes—with a forced angry resentment.

For God's sake, why do you stare like that? Have you no business of your own to mind, or no thought of your own to think?

He snaps his book shut and springs to his feet—angrily to conceal his apprehension.

Can I never have a moment's privacy in my own home in which I can think clearly? I work like a slave all day to stuff your insatiable maws with luxury and wealth and gross security for the rearing of children! Is it too much to ask in return that I be permitted a little peace of mind at night here, and not have my thoughts constantly invaded and distracted?

With an attempt at assertive dictatorial authority that rings hollow.

You force me to remind you of a fact you have chosen to ignore, that I am the man of this household and the master. I will not tolerate any more of your interference! If you persist in it, I will be compelled to force either one or the other of you to leave my home—and my life!—forever! That is my final warning!

He turns toward the door at left, avoiding their eyes. His domineering tone becomes even less convincing.

I'm going to my study. Hereafter, I shall spend my evenings there alone, and you may do as you please. Tear this house apart, destroy it, devour each other in your jealous rage and hatred, if you must, until only one of you survives! After all, that would be one solution of—But leave me alone! I will not let you involve me and attempt to tear me in half between you! It will be useless for you to try to hound me in my study, for I shall lock myself in!

He strides to the study door and opens it—then turns, avoiding their eyes, and murmurs in strange, confused, weakly apologetic tones.

I—I beg your pardon for being rude—I am worn out—have worked too hard on this railroad deal—and now I have it, I seem to have nothing—in victory I feel defeated—the winnings seem like disguised losses—that naturally confuses my mind—

He pauses. Suddenly he has the beaten quality of one begging for pity. But they remain staring as one at him, their eyes hard and unforgiving. He stammers appealingly.

You—you know how much I love each of you—it is only when you unite to dispossess me that you compel me to defend my right to what is mine—all I ask is that each of you keep your proper place in my mind—do not trespass or infringe on the other's property—
Abruptly his tone becomes slyly taunting.
But I am forgetting I arranged all that today. I will leave you now to inform each other of the secret you are each so cunningly concealing. I think, when you have, the issue will be quite clear and free of confusion.
He smiles sneeringly but is afraid to meet their eyes. He turns quickly, goes in his study, and locks the door. They stare at the door. There is a moment's silence.

DEBORAH
Slowly, hardly above a whisper, but with a taunting, threatening scorn in her tone.
He has locked the door.
She smiles faintly.
I have a suspicion, Sara, that our big jealous boy has become very frightened and wishes now he hadn't been so wicked—now, when it's too late.

SARA
Smiling faintly.
I have the same suspicion myself, Deborah.

DEBORAH
Uneasily.
Too late for him, I mean. We have seen through him. We know what he is trying to do. We know what he really is now, in his heart. How vindictive and evil—and mad! I do not recognize him now as the son I gave life to—and once loved. And I am sure you do not recognize in this strange evil man, embittered and hateful—

SARA
Bitterly.
No, he's not the man I loved and gave myself to. I never would have—to this man.

DEBORAH
Urgent and a little desperate.
But we mustn't let him make it too late for us—to continue to be as
we have been to each other. We have proved now that as long as we
constantly remember that this is something his mind is trying to do
to our minds—to make them as evil and vindictive—and mad!—
as his—to poison them with his hatred—we can successfully defend
our home from ruin and remain united in trust and friendship and
love, and keep him outside us where he is powerless, and in the end
force him to surrender and submit rather than have us drive him
from his home! Promise me you will never forget this, Sara. I swear
to you I will not!

SARA
And I swear it to you, Deborah! I know it's all the poison in his mind
trying to make our minds the slave of his, so he can own us body
and soul. Do you think I could ever hate you the way I did when you
came in with him from the garden, if he hadn't poisoned my mind
with the past at his office?

DEBORAH
Slowly.
Yes, he is very clever at poisoning with the past.
She shudders—then urgently.
But we have sworn to each other! We will remember it is he and
not us!

SARA
Yes.

DEBORAH
*Hesitates uneasily—then trying desperately to be confidently matter-of-
fact, and forcing a smile.*
Then I think we can now safely tell each other what the arrangements he spoke of are. As far as I am concerned, I was hiding mine
from you only because he said he wished to tell you and made me
promise I wouldn't.

SARA
He did the same with me.
With a sudden underlying hostility.
I was only too eager to let you know.
Then guiltily.
I mean—

DEBORAH
Stiffening.
Yes, I can imagine you were. But I think not any more eager than I
was—
*She checks herself. In silence, the two women fight together within them-
selves to conquer this hostility. Then Deborah says gently.*
Tell me your secret, Daughter. Whatever it is, I will remember it is
his doing, and I will understand.

SARA
Gratefully.
Thank you, Mother. And I'll understand when you tell me—
She blurts out hastily with an undercurrent of guilty defiance.
It's nothing much. He got me to agree to work with him at his office
from now on. I'm to start tomorrow—

DEBORAH
Her expression startled and unable to conceal an uprush of jealous hate.
Ah! Then you are the woman he boasted he was living with as a—
Instinctively she withdraws her hand from Sara's.

SARA
Bitterly.
You said you'd understand!

DEBORAH
Contritely—grabbing her hand again.
I will! I do!

SARA
Hurriedly and guiltily evasive.
I'm to be his secretary and a secret partner. He seemed so nervous
and tired out and distracted, and he asked me wouldn't I please help

him with his work and share—It's something I always used to want
to do. I used to feel I was shut out of that part of his life.
Appealingly.
You can understand that, Deborah?

DEBORAH
Sneeringly.
I can. I know only too well how greedy—
Fighting this back—guiltily.
I mean, it is your right. Of course I understand, Sara.

SARA
Reacting to the sneer—defensively.
It's my right, surely. I'm glad you admit that.
A gloating boast comes into her tone.
He said he was so lonely. He said he missed me so much and wouldn't
I let him have a life just with me again away from home. He said
I was still so beautiful to him and how much he wanted me, and I
knew he was telling the truth, so I was only too happy to give my
consent.

DEBORAH
Angrily.
Ah!
She again jerks her hand away.

SARA
Guiltily.
I'm sorry. I didn't mean to boast.
She reaches for Deborah's hand again.
But that isn't all of it. Wait till you hear the rest and you won't be
angry. I could feel the change in him as he is now in his office—that
he's grown so greedy and unscrupulous and used to having his own
way as head of the Company, that if I refused him, he'd only buy
another woman to take my place and I'd lose him.
Pleadingly.
So you see he had the power to make me consent. You can under-
stand that, can't you? You're a woman, too.

DEBORAH

Tensely.

I am making myself understand. Besides, this has nothing to do with me. It is entirely your business.

SARA

Bitterly.

Yes, business. That's the way he talked. You'd think he was making a deal for his Company. If you think I liked him insulting his wife and acting as if I was a street whore he'd picked up and was asking her price—

DEBORAH

Tensely.

Why should I think of it, Sara? It's entirely your affair.

She pauses—then strangely with an increasingly bitter vindictiveness.

But—you appealed to me as a woman, didn't you? You mean forget he is anything to me. I can. I have forgotten him several times before in my life. Completely as if he had never been born. That is what he has never forgiven. If I were in your place I would hate him, and I would revenge myself by becoming what he wished me to be! I would become it so ruthlessly that, in the end, he would feel cursed by having what he wanted! I would make him pay for me until I had taken everything he possessed! I would make all his power my power! Until I had stripped him bare and utterly ruined him! Until I had made him a weak slave with no ambition left but his greed for me! And when he had no more to pay me, I would drive him out of my life to beg outside my door! And I would laugh at him and never permit him to return—!

She stops abruptly—guiltily.

But it is really none of my business, Sara. I do not mean to interfere between husband and wife or presume to advise you.

Confusedly.

I—I don't see how I can have such vile, disgusting dreams—unless he is still thinking of us in his study, his mind still deliberately willing to poison mine.

With a flash of renewed vindictiveness.

And as a woman I still say it would be poetic justice if you destroyed him by giving him his desire! And as a woman, my pride will glory in your revenge—

Then hastily and guiltily.

I hope you understand, Sara, and do not think I am a cruel, evil mother.

SARA

With a vindictive smile—strangely.

I understand well enough. If you think there isn't a woman in me who felt exactly like that the moment I guessed what he was up to, you don't know me! And he doesn't! But he'll find out—

Then guiltily.

I don't know how I can think such wickedness—except it's what you said that he's still poisoning us.

Abruptly changing the subject.

But now tell me what he made you agree to that you've been hiding. I'll understand, whatever it is, that he did it.

DEBORAH

With a strange vengeful gleam in her eye.

Yes, we have been forgetting my part of it, haven't we? Well, it's merely this, Sara, that he begged me to give him a life alone with me again away from his office and his home.

SARA

Stares at her suspiciously.

What do you mean?

Instinctively she starts to pull her hand away from Deborah.

DEBORAH

With a trace of mockery.

Now, now. You promised to understand.

Sara controls herself. Deborah goes on matter-of-factly.

He begged me to let him keep me company in my garden every evening from now on.

Sara stiffens with hostility and then fights it back.

And, as I know how lonely I would be in the future without the children—

SARA

Eagerly.

But I've told you you'll have them back. You asked me if you could.

DEBORAH

With a taunt underlying her cool persuasive tone.

Yes, but I had forgotten then—No, Sara, you are very generous and I am most grateful, but I really will not need them, now that I have my own son again.

SARA

Gives way to a flash of jealous, uneasy anger.

Ah, and so that's what it is! I knew I shouldn't have let him go to you! I've always known if you were ever given the chance—!

She jerks her hand from Deborah's.

DEBORAH

Pleading now frightenedly, grabbing Sara's hand.

Sara! You promised to remember! But it's my fault. I'm afraid I sounded as if I were taunting you. Forgive me. I really didn't mean—The truth is—I didn't want him in my garden ever again. I hated him for forcing his way in. But then he lied and made me hate you. He tricked me into remembering the past with him. He made himself appear like a little boy again, so forlorn and confused and lost in himself—needing my love so terribly! So I couldn't help but consent. Surely, as a mother, you can understand that, Sara!

SARA

Has controlled herself—tensely.

I do, Deborah. I've sons of my own and I know how I'll long to have them back after they've left me.

DEBORAH

With a sort of taunting satisfaction.

Then you have no objection, Sara?

SARA

Defensively.

Why should I? You're his mother. You've a right. And I'll have my own sons all to myself now. I'll have him all day at the office. No, you're entirely welcome.

With a strange bitter vindictiveness.

And when I think of the way he swindled me into letting him go to your garden—and of all he's done today to make us hate each other—I tell you, as woman to woman, I hate him [so much] that if I was in your place I'd give him his wish, and I'd let him go back and back into the past until he gets so lost in his dreams he'd be no more a man at all, but a timid little boy hiding from life behind my skirts! Or, better still, no more than a nursing baby with no life or hunger of his own outside me! And I'd dandle him on my lap and laugh at his mad cries for liberty!

Then abruptly ashamed and uneasy.

But those are evil thoughts he's putting in my mind. I'd never think them myself.

DEBORAH

With a strange bold manner.

There is no need to be ashamed before me, Sara. I admit that has occurred to my mind, too–in the garden when I hated him for in-truding—After all, if he will insist on trespassing in the past—!

She gives a soft, gloating little laugh.

Yes, I do not think we have anything to fear, Sara. Between us we can soon force him to realize how foolish he was to destroy the peace and harmony of our house. In a very short time, he will feel torn apart and driven quite insane between us, and he will beg us on his knees to restore that peace and not punish his wickedness anymore, but forgive him and take him back into our home again!

SARA

Vindictively.

And won't I laugh to see him beg!

DEBORAH

We will both laugh.

They laugh softly together.

And this, I think, will be his last rebellion. He has fought for liberty before and was beaten. He must be very tired. After this defeat, I believe, he will scream with fear if anyone ever mentions the word freedom.

Then urgently.

But we must keep on understanding each other! We must never forget our purposes are identical. We must trust each other and remain united in spirit, friends and allies, and never let him make us hate each other! Let us swear that again, Sara!

SARA

I swear I won't!

DEBORAH

And I swear!

She smiles contentedly and pats Sara's hand.

That's settled, then. Now I think we can safely forget him and be as we have been on so many other nights—simple and contented and at peace with each other and with life.

SARA

Smiling.

I'd like nothing better, and it's a help to have him out of the room so we don't have to wonder what he's thinking to himself.

With a change of tone to that of the doting mother.

Tell me about the children when they were with you in the garden, like you always do.

DEBORAH

Smiling fondly.

Of course I will.

Then she pauses, trying to remember—finally she admits guiltily.

I can't seem to—I'm afraid I have entirely forgotten, Sara.

SARA

Piqued—resentfully.

You've always remembered before.

DEBORAH

Reproachfully.

Now! I know I have, but—A lot of things have happened since then to disturb my mind.

SARA
Contrite in her turn.
Ah, don't I know.
Then uneasily.
And they're still happening. Even if he is locked in his study. I can still feel his thoughts reaching out—

DEBORAH
With a little shiver of dread.
Yes, I, too—
There is a pause during which they both stare straight before them. The expression of each changes swiftly, mirroring what is entering their minds, and becomes sly and evasive and gloatingly calculating. Their clasped hands, without their being aware of it, let go and draw apart. Then each sneaks a suspicious, probing glance at the other. Their eyes meet and at once each looks away and forces a hypocritically affectionate, disarming smile. Deborah speaks quickly and lightly.
How quiet we are. What are you thinking, Daughter?

SARA
Quickly and lightly.
Of how foolish men can be, Mother, never content with what we give them, but always wanting more.

DEBORAH
Lightly.
Yes, they never grow up. They remain greedy little boys demanding the moon.

SARA
Getting up from the sofa.
I'll get my sewing, to keep myself occupied, and come back to you.

DEBORAH
Yes, do. And I will read my book.
Sara goes slowly toward her old chair at left-front of table. Deborah's eyes remain fixed on her and abruptly her expression changes to one of arrogant disdainful repulsion and hatred and she thinks.
You vile degraded slut!—as if I could ever believe your lies again!—as

if you needed encouragement from me to become the vulgar grasping harlot you were born to be!—but I am glad I encouraged you because that is the one sure way to make him loathe the sight of you—in the end he will know you for what you are and you will so disgust him that he will drive you out of his life into the gutter where you belong!—you are too stupid to see this—but I see!—and I will see to it he sees!

SARA
Having come to the chair, fiddles around unnecessarily gathering up her sewing things, keeping her back turned to Deborah while she thinks.
She must think I'm the greatest fool was ever born if she hopes I'd ever trust her again—as if he'd waste his time in her garden every evening humoring her crazy airs and graces if she hadn't begged him to!—but let her look out, what tricks she'll be up to to take him from me—I'll keep what's mine from her if I have to drive her into the asylum itself!
A pause. She stands motionless, her back to Deborah. Both their expressions change to a triumphant possessive tenderness.

DEBORAH
Thinking.
Then my beloved son will have no one but me!

SARA
Thinking.
Then my Darling will have only me!
She turns, making her face smilingly expressionless and goes back toward the sofa.

CURTAIN

Act Four, Scene One

SCENE

Same as Scene One of Act Three—Simon's private office. Changes have been made in its appearance. A sofa has been added to the furniture. Placed at front, center, it is too large for the room, too garishly expensive and luxurious, its blatant latest-stylishness in vulgar contrast to the sober, respectable, conservatism of the old office of Simon's father. It offends the eye at once, as an alien presence. It has the quality of a painted loud-mouthed bawd who has forced her way in and defied anyone to put her out.

Other changes are a mirror in an ornate gilt frame hanging over Sara's high desk at right, rear, and tacked on the right wall beside her desk is a large architect's drawing in perspective of a pretentious, nouveau-riche country estate on the shore of a small private lake with a beach in the foreground and a wharf with small pleasure craft moored to it. A road leads back from the wharf up an elaborately terraced hill to an immense mansion, a conglomerate of various styles of architecture, as if additions had been added at different times to an original structure conceived on the model of a medieval, turreted castle. At rear, on one side of this edifice, are imposing stables. Surrounding these buildings on three sides are woods that have been cleared and made into a park.

It is an early morning in midsummer of the following year, 1841.

Sara is discovered seated on the high stool before her desk, working with a ruler and drafting instruments on a plan. A marked change is noticeable in her appearance. Her body has grown strikingly voluptuous, and provocatively female. She is dressed extravagantly in flamboyant clothes, designed with the purpose of accentuating her large breasts, her slen-

*der waist, her heavy rounded thighs and buttocks, and revealing them
as nakedly as the fashion will permit. Her face has a bloated, flushed,
dissipated, unhealthy look with dark shadows under her eyes. There is
something feverishly nervous and morbidly excited about it. Its prettiness has been coarsened and vulgarized. Her mouth seems larger, its full
lips redder, its stubborn character become repellently sensual, ruthlessly
cruel and greedy. Her eyes have hardened, grown cunning and calculating and unscrupulous. There is a stray suggestion in her face now of a
hardened prostitute, particularly in its defiant defensive quality, that of
one constantly anticipating attack by a brazen assertiveness which con-
cedes a sense of guilt. Her manner varies between an almost masculine
curt abruptness and brutal frankness plainly an imitation and distortion
of Simon's professional manner, and a calculating feminine seductiveness
which constantly draws attention to her body.*

*The door from the bookkeeper's room at right, is opened noiselessly and
Joel Harford enters, closing the door behind him. He is the same in appearance, retains the cold emotionless mask of his handsome face. But
there is a startling change in his manner which now seems weak, insecure and furtive, as though he were thrown off balance by some emotion
he tries to repress, which fascinates and at the same time humiliates him.
For a moment he stands glancing about the room vaguely, his gaze avoiding Sara. She is conscious of his presence but ignores him. Finally his eyes
fasten on her and, seeing she is apparently absorbed in her work, he stares
up and down the curves of her body with a sly, greedy desire.*

SARA
*Suddenly explodes angrily in a snapping of nerves, slamming her rule on
the desk and turning on him, her voice stridently domineering as though
she were rebuking a servant.*
Don't stand there gawking! What do you want? Speak up!
But before he can do so she goes on more angrily.
How dare you come in here without knocking? You know Simon's
orders! And I've ordered you! You better remember, if you want to
keep your job!
Then controlling her anger—curtly.
Well? What is it?

JOEL

Has cringed for a second, then immediately has regained his cold poise.
Mr. Tenard, the banker, is in the outer office. I thought, considering
his position, I had better announce him myself.

SARA

With gloating scorn.
His position, is it? His position now is under Simon's feet, and my
feet, as he very well knows!

JOEL

He states he had a letter from you making an appointment with
Simon.

SARA

That's true. I wrote him at Simon's dictation. What Simon wants of
him I can't see. We've taken his bank from him. He's stripped bare.
Then with a cunning greedy smile.
But he must have something we want, or Simon wouldn't waste time
on him.
Curtly.
Well, you see Simon's not here yet. Tell Tenard to wait.

JOEL

Making no move to go—emotionlessly.
My brother seems to be late every day now.

SARA

Betraying an inner uneasiness by forcing a too-careless tone.
Ah, he's taken to paying your old mother a morning visit in her garden as well as in the evening. She's failing rapidly in her mind, poor
woman, growing childish and living altogether in her dreams. Simon
thinks he ought to humor her all he can so she won't take leave of
her senses altogether.
Abruptly, forcing a laugh.
And what if he is late? He knows, the way he's trained me, I can take
care of anything here as well as he could.

JOEL

With an undercurrent of spite.

As long as you don't mind his keeping *you* waiting.

SARA
Stares at him — defensively.
Just what do you mean by that?

JOEL
Betraying an inner jealous excitability, his eyes unconsciously fixed on the sofa — sneeringly.
I—I am not unaware why you are so insistent about my knocking before I—intrude.

SARA
Watching him, her face lighting up with a cunning satisfaction — her expression very like a prostitute's now as she smiles seductively and mockingly.
So that's what's bothering you! Well, that's my business.

JOEL
His eyes fixed fascinatedly on her now.
Your business! Yes, I quite realize you are—what you are.

SARA
Plainly enjoying this, moves her body seductively — teasingly.
And what am I, Joel Darlin'?

JOEL
Trying to take his eyes from her.
I—I am fully aware of the means you have used in the past year to get my brother to sign over his interests one by one to you.

SARA
You don't think my love is worth it?

JOEL
Stammers.
I would not use the word love—

SARA
Teasingly.

Why wouldn't you? You're a sentimental fool, I'm afraid, Joel. What else is love, I'm asking you?

Suddenly she looks guilty and repelled—hastily.

No! That's Simon's idea, not mine!

JOEL

I suppose you pride yourself you have cunningly swindled him?

He laughs gratingly.

But it's the other way round. It's you who have been swindled!

SARA

Angrily.

That's a lie!

Scornfully.

You fool, you! Do you think, after all he's taught me, I haven't learned to get all I'm worth to him?

JOEL

Ignoring this—sneeringly.

All this imposing edifice of power and greed he has built so unscrupulously—which you have him to put in your name—what is it in fact but a house of cards? You know he has been gambling more and more recklessly in the past year. It was bad enough before you came here, but since he started playing Napoleon to show off his genius to you, he has abandoned all caution! Debt has been piled upon debt! If you had to pay the debts on the properties he has made over to you tomorrow—there would be nothing left! His position, and yours, depends entirely upon the myth he has created of his invincibility, his uncanny luck, that his touch turns everything to gold! But once let the slightest doubt arise, and his enemies see his true position—and their opportunity to revenge themselves—and strip you of everything you possess.

SARA

With forced defiance.

Let them try! They couldn't! He'll always beat the world!

Then abruptly—frightened and shaken.

Oh, I know, Joel! Sometimes, I go mad worrying! But I can't stop him. And when he's with me, I think what he thinks. I can't help it!

JOEL

Ignores this—with a strange air of being fascinated by the danger.
I tell you there is danger every second. It would take only a rumor.
A whisper spoken in the right ear. This banker who is waiting. How
he must hate Simon. If he had the slightest inkling—

SARA

Fascinatedly.
I know.
Then frightenedly.
Joel! You sound as though you'd like—
Imploringly.
You wouldn't—!

JOEL

Jerking himself back to his pose—coldly.
I? You insult my life-long loyalty to the Company. Do you believe
everyone is like you and Simon, devoid of all probity and honor?
Then with almost a smirk.
Besides, you forget I still own an interest—which is not yet for sale,
although I might consider—
Hastily.
I'm merely pointing out that you had been swindled.
Sneeringly.
But you would realize [it] if you spent more time examining the true
value of his gifts and less on designing your impossible Irish-Castle-
in-Spain.
He indicates the plan on the wall scornfully.

SARA

Furiously.
Impossible, is it? We'll see! That's one debt I'll make him pay—the
debt the Harfords owe my father's daughter!
Abruptly changing to a scornful curt tone.
I'm a fool to listen to your silly gab. I ought to know well enough by
this to laugh at you, the way Simon does, for an old stick-in-the-mud
always prophesying ruin and—!
Harshly.

Get back to your work! You're wasting my time and I'm sick of you!
She turns back to her desk.

JOEL

*Stands staring at her, then moves mechanically to the door at right and
is about to open it when suddenly he turns—angrily.*

I do protest! I own an interest; it is my right. I protest against you and
my brother turning this office—my father's office—into a brothel
room for your lust! Everyone is getting to know—to smirk and whisper! It is becoming an open scandal—a filthy public disgrace! I—

*He stammers to a halt—his eyes fixed on her in helpless fascination. She
has turned to him and again there is the look of a smiling prostitute about
her face.*

SARA

Smiling and moving her body seductively—teasingly.

Now, Joel, Darlin', you shouldn't look at me like that, and me your
brother's wife.

She laughs provokingly.

JOEL

Fighting with himself—stammers.

I do not understand you. I do not see why you should laugh—like a
common street woman. My brother's wife should have more modesty. I was only looking at your new dress and admiring it. Simon
buys you a new dress every week now. Is that part of the bargain?
You should not let his greed turn his wife into a low woman whose
beauty is for sale! I protest!

*He swallows as if he were strangling and tears his eyes from her teasing
gloating ones—he stammers.*

No, no! I do not mean—I ask your pardon for saying such things. It
is not like me at all. The truth is I have changed in the past year. I do
not recognize myself. I disgust myself. It is the atmosphere of disgusting greed here which has become so vilely intensified since you
came. I no longer recognize this as my father's office—or myself as
my father's son. Something has happened to make me greedy, too.
So please forgive and overlook—

SARA

Her prostitute air gone—pitying and frightened.

Oh, don't I know? Haven't I changed, too, so I don't know myself. Don't I disgust myself, at times. But it's not me. It's Simon. It's what he wants. I've got to be what he wants. He makes me want to be what he wants!

Controlling herself—simply.

I forgive you, Joel. And please forgive me.

JOEL

Gently.

I? Of course, Sara. And thank you for your kindness and understanding.

Dully.

I'll go back to my work now.

He turns to the door but again, with his hand on the knob his eyes fix on her body and grow greedy and he stammers.

I only wish to say—I've quite decided to sell my interest in the business—that is, to you, if you would care to consider—

He stops—Again the prostitute leer has been called back to her face. She laughs teasingly. He wrenches open the door and flings himself into the bookkeeper's room, slamming the door behind him.

SARA

Looks after him, smiling to herself with a cheap vanity.

Who'd think it of him? So stuck-up and full of don't-touch-me airs! One of the high and mighty Yankee Harfords! And now I've got him under my feet, begging! He'd pay all he's got! I could strip him bare—and cheat him in the bargain—pretend when I'd really give him nothing!

She chuckles.

The fools of men! It's too easy for us to cheat them! They want to be cheated so they can cheat themselves!

She stares in the mirror at herself admiringly—coquettishly in brogue.

Who'd have dreamed it Sara Melody—you in your beauty to have such power over bright and mighty men! By the Eternal, as my father used to swear, I think you could take what you wanted from any one of them! And if he is a poor slave of a bookkeeper, he's a handsome man, and he owns an interest—

She suddenly shivers with repulsion and tears her eyes from the mirror strickenly—in a guilty whisper.

God forgive me! Me, to have such thoughts! Like a dirty whore smiling at men in the street and showing her leg! What's happened to me. A year ago and I'd never have dreamed such a thought, not even in sleep, but now it seems natural—to be a part of me—

She stares around her frightenedly.

It's being here so long, working as his whore, with no life except in his greed—with my children running wild at home as if they had no mother—while I sit here like a miser counting gold, making plans for the grand estate I'll have, or dreaming of my mills and my ships on the sea and my railroad that he's paid me for using my body like a dirty whore's—he's made me think that life means selling yourself, and pride is to get the highest price you can, and that love is lust— it's only lust he wants—and he's made me feel it's all I want and if I didn't have that hold on him, I'd lose him!—she'd take him back with her entirely—

Then with angry defiance.

She'll never! He may forget me when he's with her but once I've got him here, I've only to kiss him and he forgets she's alive! And what if I was having thoughts about Joel? It was only what every woman thinks at times in her heart—was any one of us ever content with one man?—who didn't feel she was worth more—that she'd been swindled by marriage—who didn't want every man to want her to prove her worth to herself, who didn't feel, if she was free, she could get more for herself—

Vindictively.

Let him look out how he comes here late and keeps me waiting his pleasure, like a slave, or I'll show him I can have what I want without him, and get my price for it, too.

She laughs spitefully—then suddenly tears her eyes from the mirror and shrinks into herself with horrified disgust.

Ah, you dirty whore, you! Oh, God help me! I must be going daft— as daft as that mad old witch in her garden.

Then with increasing anger.

And who wouldn't be daft, going home every night to that hell with her? Never a moment's peace—hating her and feeling her hate me—watching every move she makes and knowing she's watching me—knowing it's a duel to the death between us—if she'd only leave me alone!—if she'd only be content with what's hers and not try to steal what's mine!—but she's bound she'll get him away from me, and make him drive me out in the street—

With threatening hatred.

But by God, he can't! And I won't stand much more from her!—She's driving me too far—a little more and my hate will have no pity left! I know her weakness and her fear of going crazy—I'll drive her into the asylum where she belongs, the mad old fool! She's making this life too small for the two of us! One of us must go—and by the Powers it won't be me!

Then hastily.

But let's pray I won't need to, and I can get rid of her the way we planned. Now Simon has the bank I'll make him stop wanting more and let the profit add up. I'll pay off the debts, and we'll sell out and I'll build the estate and I'll pay her a pension to stay alone in her garden.

Trying to reassure herself.

Yes, it won't take long—I'll soon be rid of her.

Then distractedly.

If he'll only let me!— If I'll only let myself not want more and more!

She jumps from her stool and paces around in a nervous panic.

Why doesn't he come?— I can't bear life without him with me!—What makes him so late?— That mad old witch keeps him dreaming in her garden to make him late on purpose to torment me!

In a fury.

And he knows it! He lets her do it!—Well, I won't wait, my fine Simon! Not alone! I've stood enough from you! I'll call in Joel to keep me company!— I'll change entirely to the whore you want me to be, and we'll see how you like that!

She is moving towards the bookkeeper's room when the door from the rear is opened and Simon comes in. He has changed greatly, grown ter-

ribly thin, his countenance is ravaged and pale and haggard, his eyes deep sunken. There is, however, a strange expression of peace and relaxation on his face as he enters, a look of bemused dreaminess in his eyes.

SARA
With a cry of hypocritical happy relief, rushes and throws her arms around him and hugs him passionately.
Oh, Darling! I love you so!
Then her tension snapping, she bursts into sobs and hides her face against his shoulder.

SIMON
Looks startled and bewildered as if only half awakened from a dream—pats her shoulder mechanically—vaguely.
There, there.
He stares around him, thinking and frowning, as though not quite realizing yet where he is or how he got there.

SARA
Stops crying instantly at the tone of his voice—jerks back, holding him by the shoulders, and stares into his face—frightened and pleading.
Simon! You sound—!
Forcing a joking tone.
For the love of heaven, don't you know where you are or who I am?

SIMON
Trying to force himself from his day dream—vaguely placating.
Of course, Sara. Don't be silly.
Then he relapses and smiles with a bemused pleasure and speaks dreamily.
Do you know, this morning, talking with Mother, I suddenly remembered something I had never remembered before. Nothing important. Just an incident in her garden long ago. The astonishing thing is that she says I wasn't more than a year old at the time. And yet it appeared as clear as if it were yesterday—or was happening again this very morning. Nothing important, as I've said. Childish and meaningless. But it gave me a feeling of power and happiness to be able to recall the past so distinctly.

SARA

Stares at him—frightened and resentful.

Simon! Wake up! You're here with me!

She kisses him fiercely.

Come back to me! To hell with her crazy dreams! I love you! I'm your wife and you're mine!

She kisses him again.

Can't you feel how I love you? Tell me you love me.

SIMON

With a start, awakes completely. His expression changes and becomes tense with desire and he presses her body to his and kisses her passionately.

Sweetheart! You know I want you more than life!

SARA

With a sudden revulsion of feeling, pushes back from him—desperately.

No! Please! I want love—

Then forcing a laugh.

But you'll be making fun of me for being a sentimental fool!

She throws herself in his arms again—passionately.

Oh, I don't care what I am as long as I have you!

SIMON

Passionately.

My dear beautiful mistress!

He tries to take her to the couch.

SARA

Breaks away from him. The common prostitute calculating look is back in her face now. She laughs tantalizingly.

Oh, no, you don't! You've a lot of business to attend to. I'll have no laziness. You've got to earn me, you know! You wouldn't want me if I gave myself for nothing, and let you cheat me! Not you! I know you. You'd think I was a stupid fool not to have learned more from your teaching and example, and your doing your best to train me.

SIMON

Laughs with amused admiration.

You've been a very apt pupil. You'll soon give your master cards and spades.
Teasing derisively.
What do you want me to pay you this time, Beautiful, Insatiable One? You have about all I possess already.

SARA
Greedily.
Well, there's the bank we've just smashed and got control of.

SIMON
Laughingly.
Oh, so that's it! I might have known. In fact, I anticipated and have had the papers drawn. But, of course, I won't sign them until after—

SARA
Mockingly.
Aren't you the cautious one! Are you afraid I'd cheat you? But how do I know you mightn't refuse to sign after—?

SIMON
Laughingly.
Oh, I might like to, but you know I haven't the power anymore. You've taken that from me, too! Your beauty has become more desirable to me than a thousand banks stuffed with gold!
He tries to draw her to him—passionately.
Darling One! Haven't you learned by this time that my greatest happiness is to prove to you—and to myself—how much you are worth to me?
He tries to kiss her.

SARA
Evading his embrace—coquettishly.
No, I said. Later.
She kisses him tantalizingly.
But here's a kiss to bind the bargain.

SIMON
But I have to run down to the mill today. As you know there's been

some discontent about our lowering wages and the hands are sending a deputation to ask me to reconsider.

SARA
Her face hardening—commandingly.
You put your foot down on that! Fire them! There's plenty to take their place, and starving will teach them a lesson.

SIMON
I agree with you. The Company needs every penny of profit from the mill it can possibly extort.
Then smiling.
But about our bargain. You said later, but I can't get back until late afternoon just in time for my evening visit with Mother. So—

SARA
Harshly domineering.
So you'll forget her and only remember me!

SIMON
Struggling to resist—strangely the musing, dreamy expression showing in his face.
But I remember I promised her—

SARA
Harshly.
You'll forget her, I'm saying!
Then moving her body with coarse suggestiveness—with a prostitute's calculating seductive air.
Isn't having me worth that to you? If it isn't, I'll have to find some other man who values me higher.

SIMON
Hungrily.
No, no! Anything you ask!

SARA
Triumphantly, almost sneeringly.
That's better!

Then resentfully and going on with an increasing show of jealous, bitter anger.

And that reminds me, I've a bone to pick with you. You were late again this morning on account of seeing her. I had to sit here alone—waiting and worrying—You let her keep you to make me wait. She did it on purpose to spite me! Ah, don't make excuses for her. Don't I know the hatred and jealousy and the designing greed behind her acting and pretending and her airs and graces of a great lady! It's you she makes a fool of, leading you back to her in the past before you were mine, twisting you around the fingers of her dreams, till you're as mad as she is! But she doesn't fool me! I see through her greedy scheming. And I warn you she'd better watch herself or I'll get to the end of my pity!

SIMON
His expression has changed during her speech to one of gloating satisfaction. He smiles teasingly.
What? Don't tell me you're becoming jealous again, Sara?

SARA
With forced scorn.
Jealous of that ugly old witch, who's old enough to be my mother!

SIMON
Smiling.
Then you mustn't act as if you were. To hear you one would think you feared my poor little old mother as a beautiful dangerous rival.

SARA
Sneeringly.
Her! A skinny wizened hag no man would look at twice!

SIMON
Curtly—in command now.
Very well, then. Why do you talk nonsense?
Sharply matter-of-fact.
We've had this out many times before, Sara. I've explained until I'm tired that I think it advisable, for our own sakes if not for hers, to humor her in any way I can, even if it involves my wasting valuable

time—and, if you like, playing the fool myself. You appear to cherish the absurd idea that it is a fascinating happiness for me to sit in a garden with a woman, whose mind is far gone in second childhood, and be forced to watch her greedy spirit, starved by her life-long fear of life, groping in the past and clutching at the dead.

Dryly.

I assure you I can think of many more enjoyable activities—

He stares at her desirously—with a smile.

Such as being here with you in my arms, Beloved One.

SARA

Gratefully.

Darling!

SIMON

With a return to his matter-of-fact tone, shrugging his shoulders.

But, after all, I must not complain. Sometimes she amuses me. Sometimes it is restful in her garden. You do not begrudge me a little rest, I hope. Anyway, she is my mother. I owe her some consideration. And someone has to humor her and keep her from being too much alone in her fantastic mind, or we would have a lunatic on our hands.

SARA

I've told you before I'm willing to have her have the children for company again, instead of you, and you ought to make her agree—

SIMON

Curtly and resentfully.

Nonsense. I would never permit—She does not want your children now that she has—

Abruptly changing the subject—pleasantly.

But I'll admit, you have reason to complain of me for being late. I have no right to cheat you of time that belongs to you and the Company. I promise in future I'll remember not to humor her into leading my mind so far back that I forget—

Hastily again, going to his desk with his most alert authoritative executive air.

Well, I'll make up for lost time. Tenard is here, isn't he?

She nods.
You can tell Joel to have him sent in.

SARA
Her manner that of an efficient obedient secretary.
Yes, Sir.
She opens the door at right, sticks her head in and speaks to Joel—then comes back to the desk opposite Simon and waits for orders.

SIMON
Looks at his watch.
I'll have time to dispose of him before I catch my train. You can go back to work on your plans for the estate.
She turns back toward the desk at right, rear. He glances at the plans— flatteringly, with an undercurrent of mockery.
By the way, my congratulations on the additions you have made since I last examined it.

SARA
Pleased.
I'm glad you like them.

SIMON
Now that you'll soon possess a bank, too, you can afford to add still more.
He smiles—teasingly.
I am sure in your dreams you have already thought of more.

SARA
With a greedy little laugh.
Oh, trust me, I can always think of more!
She stares at the plan—with a strange dreaminess and exultance.
I'll make it the grandest, most beautiful mansion that ever a woman's dream conceived as a house for his pride and her love for her [husband]!* Ah, won't it be a beautiful life, when I can sit back at my ease there, in the castle of my dreams, in my own house, without a care in the world, with long nights of deep sleep, not turning and twisting in nightmares like I do now, with never a debt, knowing the

---

*Carlotta has left a blank here after "her love for her." I inserted "husband" as a logical choice.

banks are crammed with my gold, watching my sons grow up hand-some rich gentlemen, having my husband and my lover always by me and all of him mine with no will or thought or dream in his heart or brain but the great need to love me!

SIMON

Stares at her back—quietly with a mocking irony tinged with a bitter, tragic sadness.

There is a poem by Doctor Holmes you should read sometime—for added inspiration.

He quotes from "The Chambered Nautilus."

Build thee more stately mansions, O my soul,
As the swift seasons roll!
Leave thy low-vaulted past!
Let each new temple, nobler than the last,
Shut thee from heaven with a dome more vast,
Till thou at length are free,
Leaving thine outgrown shell—

He pauses—then his gaze turned inward, he murmurs aloud to himself, as Sara continues to stare with fascinated, dreamy longing at the plan, not paying any attention to him.

You must have that engraved over the entrance. And Mother should put it over the magic door to her summerhouse. And I, on the ceiling of this Company's offices—in letters of gold!

He sneers self-mockingly—then slowly with a sinister determination.

But I will be soon! Oh very soon, now! Either by one way or the other—rid forever of either one or the other—thanks to either Sara or Mother!

He starts guiltily and speaks with a hastily-assumed casualness to Sara.

I am glad to see, Sara, that you have very properly ignored my stupid muddle-mindedness in remembering childish verses here. I should save such nonsense for my dutiful honoring of my poor old mother.

SARA

Oblivious to him, staring at her plan, her tone becoming more and more coarsely greedy.

Stables full of thoroughbred hunters and fast trotters! Me the great lady, full of airs and graces, riding in my carriage with coachman and footman, through the castle park, or out past the lodge down the road to the city, with the crowds on the street staring, their hearts eaten with envy, and the shopkeepers bowing and scraping, and me gazing down my nose at them, and at the whole pack of the meek, weak, timid, poor poverty-stricken beggars of life!

Vengefully.

No one will ever dare sneer at my origin then, or my poverty! By the Eternal God, I'll spit in their faces and laugh when they thank me kindly for the favor!

She chuckles viciously—then abruptly her expression changes to one of guilty shame and she exclaims confusedly.

No! I don't mean it! God forgive me, what makes me say such evil, spiteful things? They're not in my dream at all! All I want is a safe home for our love—and peace!

SIMON

Rebukingly gently but firmly.

Now, now! No backsliding into cowardly sentimental remorse, Beautiful Mistress. Remember what I've impressed on you so often in the past year. This office is no garden of dreams. It is a battlefield of reality, where you must face the fact of yourself as you are—and not as you dream you ought to be—where one eats or is eaten. It is silly to be ashamed of the undesirable fact that the humiliation of the conquered is part of the conqueror's pride in victory.

SARA

Has turned to stare at him fascinatedly—murmurs mechanically.

Yes, I suppose—but—

There is a knock on the door at rear. At once her attitude becomes that of the efficient secretary.

That must be Tenard, Sir. Shall I let him in?

SIMON

A strange, calculating gloating comes into his face.

No. I've just had an idea, Sara. Let Tenard wait outside the door for awhile like the ruined beggar he is. It will put him in a more uneasy, receptive frame of mind.

He gets up from his chair.

Come and sit in my place. I want you to handle Tenard, while I watch. You have learned a great deal in the last year. I am immensely proud of your rapid progress.

SARA
Uncertainly.
I'm glad, Simon.

SIMON
Now I'd like to see you put your knowledge into practice. Prove that, no matter what happened to me, you are fully competent to direct the destiny of this Company to a befitting conclusion.

SARA
Uneasily.
What could happen to you?

SIMON
Shrugs his shoulders—carelessly.
Who knows? All men are mortal. There is always death.

SARA
Frightenedly.
Don't say it, Darling.

SIMON
In same tone.
Or sickness, accident. Who knows? Life is a gamble and Fate a master sharper where stacked cards and loaded dice can cheat the cleverest swindler.

SARA
Frightenedly.
Don't talk like that.

SIMON
Or I might simply go away—for a long, much-needed rest.

SARA
Flaring up—with frightened jealous anger.
Ah, I know who put that in your mind! And I know she'd stop at

nothing now to get you away with her! Not even if she had to drive you as mad as she is!

SIMON

Nonsense! Your jealousy is becoming an insane obsession. What has that poor childish old woman got to do with it? All I meant was I might sometime want to leave you in charge. You've bought the Company, anyway, so—

SARA

Frightenedly.
You'd leave me—?
Then coarsely self-confident, with her prostitute's seductive smile.
I'd like to see you try to want to! Don't you know I've bought you, too?
There is another knock on the door but neither heeds it.

SIMON

Stares at her body—struggling with himself—stammers yearningly.
Yes, I know—and it's my greatest happiness to belong to you—to escape myself and be lost in you—I'll pay anything!

SARA

Laughs softly—triumphantly seductive and coarse.
That's my Simon! That's the way I like you to talk—about life and love—and not about death, or madness like trying to leave me.

SIMON

Starts toward her—lustfully.
Beloved!
There is another knock on the door, sharp and impatient. It penetrates and breaks the spell. Simon tears his eyes from her and at once his manner becomes curtly business-like—dryly.
I think our friend is now sufficiently fearful and humiliated. Sit here, Sara. I am confident you can soon show him his place.

SARA

Comes to the desk—smiling gloatingly.
Yes, under my feet, isn't it?
She laughs softly and sits down in Simon's chair.

But I don't even know why you had him come, Simon. We've ruined him. He has nothing left we want, has he?

SIMON

Yes. A few years of his life. He's past his prime but he's a capable banker and can still be useful to us. Not as he is now, of course. He is too full of old-fashioned ethics and honor. We know that because it made him so open to attack and so easy to ruin. But he can be made to forget all that and become an obedient servant, if you can discover his weakness and then use it without scruple. You will find a couple of notes I made on the pad about his present circumstances. The rest I leave in your capable hands, My Beautiful. Just bear in mind that the end you desire always justifies any means and don't get life confused with sentiment, as you used to.
He laughs, moving away from her to her desk, at right, rear.
Pretend to yourself he is I begging for your favors and you cannot fail to swindle him successfully and get what you want.
There is another, banging knock on the door. He calls curtly.
Come in!

The door is opened and Benjamin Tenard enters. He is a tall, robust, full-chested man in his sixties with a fine-looking Roman face, his clothes expensively conservative. He has the look of success, of financial prosperity still stamped on him from long habit. It is this facade which makes the sense one immediately gets that he is a broken man inside, insecure, bewildered and frightened, all the more pityingly acute. His face as he enters is flushed with humiliated pride.

TENARD

Begins to protest insultedly to Simon.
See here, Harford! You made an appointment with me, not I with you! Yet I am allowed to cool my heels in your outer office and then stand outside your door knocking and knocking like someone—!

SARA

Breaks in in a pleasantly indifferent [tone] without any hint of apology.
Sorry to have kept you waiting, Mr. Tenard. It was necessary.
He turns to stare at her in surprised confusion not having noticed her at first.

TENARD
I—I beg your pardon, Mrs. Harford. I did not see—

SARA
Nodding at the chair opposite her.
Won't you sit down?

TENARD
Uncertainly, glancing at Simon.
Thank you.

SIMON
Smiling with cold pleasantness.
It's all right. Your appointment is really with my wife. She has full authority to act for me. So if you will pardon me, I have some important work to do here.
He nods at the plans on Sara's desk, turns his back on Tenard, sits down, and during the scene between them pretends to be concentrated on the plans. Tenard comes and sits in the chair opposite Sara.

SARA
After a quick glance at the pad—smiling coolly—as she goes on, her tone and manner become more and more an exact mimicry of Simon's executive manner.
I presume you wonder why I wished to see you, Mr. Tenard. Just as I was wondering why you ever consented to come—under the circumstances.

TENARD
Humiliated and guilty.
You mean because your husband is responsible for ruining me?

SARA
Smiling coldly.
Simon does nothing without my consent, Mr. Tenard. I thought that was the cheapest way to take possession of your bank.

TENARD
Unable to keep hate and a look of horror entirely from a glance at her.

Yes, I have heard rumors that you advise him. I could not believe a woman—

Then almost frightenedly as if he is afraid he is prejudicing her against him—avoiding her eye and forcing a smile.

I bear no grudge. All is fair in war. I realize that. Perhaps, I considered the methods used not quite ethical—

With increasing suppressed bitterness.

—not to say ruthless and unscrupulous. There are some who would describe them in even stronger terms.

SARA

Curtly.

I am not interested in moral attitudes. You owned something I desired. You were too weak to hold it. I was strong enough to take it. I am good because I am strong. You are evil because you are weak. Those are the facts.

TENARD

Gives way for a second to outraged indignation.

An infamous credo, Madam!

Then hastily almost cringingly.

I—I beg your pardon. You may be right. New times, new customs— and methods.

Forcing a laugh.

I suppose I am too old a dog to learn new tricks of a changed era.

SARA

Smiling coldly.

I hope not—for your sake, Mr. Tenard.

TENARD

Stares at her stupidly.

Eh? I don't believe I understand—

Hastily forcing a good-natured, good-loser air.

But, as I said, I have no hard feelings. That's why I consented to come here—to show you I bear no grudges.

SARA

Not smiling now—her face hardening into a ruthless mercilessness.

Let us be frank and not waste my time. I know your true reason for coming. You are ruined. You have had to sell everything. You haven't a dollar. But you have an old mother, a wife, a widowed daughter with two children, all of whom depend upon [you] for support. You have applied to various banks for a position. None of them want you. You are too old. The evil reputation of recent failure prejudices them against you. One or two have offered you a minor clerk's job—out of contemptuous pity, like a penny of charity tossed to a beggar.

TENARD
With humiliated anger.
Yes, damn them! But I—

SARA
Goes on as if he had not interrupted.
Which your pride refused. Moreover, the wage would have been insufficient to support your family except in a shameful poverty to which they are unaccustomed. You were afraid that, suffering the humiliation of such poverty, your mother, your wife, your daughter, would begin to blame you and to feel a resentful contempt for your weakness.

TENARD
Staring at her fascinatedly—blurts out in anguish.
And hide it! That would be the worst! To feel them hiding it—out of pity.

SARA
But there was one last desperate hope. You heard I had not yet chosen anyone to manage your old bank for me. You came here hoping against hope that the reason I had sent for you—
She pauses—then smiles with cold pleasantry.
I am pleased to tell you that is the reason. Mr. Tenard, I do offer you that position.

TENARD
The strain snapping, he gives way pathetically and brokenly to relief and gratitude.

I—I don't know how to thank you—I apologize for having mis-
judged you—
Hastily.
Of course, I accept the position gladly.

SARA
Coldly.
Wait. There are conditions. But before I state them, let me say that
any sentiment of gratitude on your part is uncalled for. I am not
doing this for your sake or your family's. What happens to you and
yours is naturally a matter of entire indifference to me. I am solely
concerned with what is mine, or what I wish to make mine.

TENARD
Uneasily—forcing a smile.
You are—brutally frank, at least, Mrs. Harford.
With growing apprehension.
What are your conditions?

SARA
Smiling pleasantly.
I warn you your pride will probably be impelled to reject them. At
first. But I ask you to bear in mind that pride is a virtue only in the
strong. In the weak it is a stupid presumption.
Her face and voice hardening.
The conditions are that you agree to obey every order mechanically,
instantly, unquestioningly, as though you were the meanest worker
at the looms in my mills, or a common sailor in my ships, or a brake-
man on my railroad.

TENARD
Humiliated but forcing a reasonable tone.
You can rely on me, I have been the head of a business myself. I know
the desirability of prompt obedience.

SARA
I can offer you a salary that will enable you very moderate comfort
for your family, and so continue to purchase in part, at least, their
former love and respect.

TENARD
Stammers confusedly.
I—I thank you—

SARA
I am saying these things because, in order to avoid all future misunderstanding, I want you to face the cost of my offer before you accept.

TENARD
In a panic to get this ordeal over and run away.
I understand. But you need not—I have no choice, I accept.

SARA
Cruelly insistent.
There is still the matter of your old-fashioned ideals of honor in business dealings to consider. I hope you appreciate from your recent experience with my methods that, as my employee, you will have to forget all such scruples. You will be required to conduct my bank business with the entire ruthlessness as to the means used of a general in battle. The end I desire to accomplish must justify any and every means to you. Where it is necessary, you must faithfully do things which may appear to your old conceptions of honor like plain swindling and theft. Are you willing to become a conscious thief and swindler in your own eyes?

TENARD
At last insulted beyond all prudent submission—stammering with outrage.
I—You must be mad, Madam—You dare—But I cannot answer a woman—I know it must be your husband who—A woman would never—
He springs to his feet and turns on Simon in a fury.
Damn you, Sir! You blackguard, do you think I have sunk to your level? I'll see you in hell first! I'd rather be a dog! I'd rather starve in the gutter.
He strides to the door at rear.
That's my answer to your infamous offer, Sir.

Simon has not turned, gives no sign of hearing him. Tenard grabs the handle of the door.

SARA

Suddenly bursts out in a strange rage as if he had touched something deep in her and infuriated her—lapsing into broad brogue, forgetting all her office attitudes—glaring at Tenard with savage denunciation.

Arrah, God's curse on you for a man! You and your pride and honor! You're pretending to love your women and children and you're willing to drag them down with you to suffer the bitter shame of poverty, and starve in the gutter, too!

TENARD

Stares at her torturedly.

It's a lie! They would never wish me—

Then all at once he seems to collapse inside. He nods his head in a numbed acquiescence, forcing a vacant smile.

Yes, I suppose, entirely selfish—no time to remember self. Thank you, Madam, for reminding me of my duty. I wish to say I see your point about policy of bank—only practical viewpoint—business is business—

He forces a choked chuckle.

Must remember the old adage—sticks and stones—and poverty—break—but names don't hurt. Let who will cry thief! I accept the position, Madam—and thank you again—for your—charity!

He wrenches open the door and flings himself into the hall, slamming the door. Simon gets off his stool and comes to Sara with a smile of approval.

SIMON

Well done! You disposed of him as well as I could. I'm proud of you.

SARA

Her expression is changing. There is a look of dawning horror in her eyes. She forces a smile—mechanically.

I'm glad you're proud. But it was you—what you wanted me—

SIMON

Oh, no. Don't play modest now.

He pats her cheek—playfully.

That last touch finished him, and that was all your own. I had calculated he would leave, indignant and insulted, but be forced to come back after he'd faced his women again. But your method was far cleverer.

He pats her shoulder.

SARA

Staring before her—mechanically.

Yes, I didn't leave him one last shred of his pride, did I?

She suddenly breaks—with a sob.

Oh, the poor man! God forgive me!

Abruptly she turns on Simon—with rising bitter anger.

It wasn't I! It was you! You—Ah, don't I know what you're trying to do, make a cruel greedy whore of me, so you can go back and sneer with her at what a low, common slut I am in my heart!

Revengefully.

But I won't let you! I'll go to Tenard! He'll be crazy to revenge himself now! I've only to give him a hint of the true condition of the Company to turn him loose to destroy you! And then where would you be, you and your Company? You strutting with pride, playing—you're a little Napoleon! You'd not have a penny! And I'd be free to take my children and go to the old farm and live like a decent, honest woman working in the earth!

She suddenly collapses, sobbing, hiding her face in her hands.

I can't go on with this! I won't!

SIMON

Who has listened, watching her with an impatient frown—pats her shoulder perfunctorily—curtly.

Come now, Sara. I know you've just been under a severe strain. But that's no excuse to talk so absurdly.

He sits down opposite her—curtly.

That nonsense about your ruining the Company. Don't you realize it's your Company now?

SARA

I realize you've swindled me, paying me with things loaded down with debts, if that's what you mean.

SIMON
Smiling.
Ah, now you begin to talk like yourself again.
Rebukingly.
Such nonsense, Sara! As if you were a woman who would deliber-
ately ruin herself for the sake of anything. And there are your chil-
dren to be considered. You would hardly ruin them.

SARA
Shakenly.
No.

SIMON
Scornfully.
You go to that old farm, where there's only my old cabin and a ruin
of a farm house. A farm that hasn't been cultivated since God knows
when. You would have to work like a slave for a bare living, with your
pride tortured by the shame of poverty!
He laughs.
Don't tell me you can imagine yourself contented living in a potato
patch with your bare feet in the earth like a common peasant!

SARA
With a shiver of repulsion.
No. I'd hate to sink to that after all my high dreams.

SIMON
Exactly. So don't talk silly. As for your fears about the Company, you
sound like Joel playing Jeremiah.
Jokingly.
You are not complaining about the way I manage your properties, I
hope. Haven't I reorganized your railroad in two years so that now
it is one of the best run small roads in the country?

SARA
Yes. But the debt—?

SIMON
I'm amazed to hear you worrying about debts. It's unworthy of your
father's daughter. He never let debts bother him.

SARA

Suddenly smiling, with a proud toss of her head—boastfully.
True for you! He let them whistle for their money and be damned!
Then hastily and guiltily.
But I'm not like him. I—

SIMON

With a strange tense excitement.
Of course, you are right in thinking there is constant danger—that
a whisper, a hint of the truth, a rumor started among the many defeated enemies who have such good reason to envy and hate you!

SARA
Defensively.
Reason to hate me?

SIMON
Smiling.
Well, do you imagine Tenard loves you, for example?

SARA
Confusedly.
But it was you—

SIMON
Ignoring this, goes on tensely.
There's no question about the danger. It's like walking a tightrope
over an abyss where one false step—

SARA
Frightenedly.
Oh, I know! It's driving me crazy! I can't sleep, worrying!

SIMON
But you mustn't look down, for then you grow confused and the
temptation seizes you to hurl yourself—Don't you think I know by
long experience how that impulse fascinates you, how terrible the
longing is to make an end of suspense and gain forgetfulness and
peace at any cost—the passionate yearning to destroy oneself and be
free!

SARA
Frightenedly.
Darling! Don't think of it! Don't make me think—

SIMON
I know only too well how tempted you are to whisper and start the
rumor of the truth among your enemies—

SARA
No! I'd never! I was only talking!

SIMON
To throw the burden of responsibility and guilt off one's shoulders,
to release oneself from the cursed treadmill of greed! Not to have to
go on! To be able to be still, or to turn back to rest!
He is staring before him with a fascinated yearning.

SARA
Frightened, grasping his arm.
Darling! Please don't stare like that! It makes you look so—strange
and crazed—you frighten me!

SIMON
Controls himself—with a smile.
Oh, come now, there's nothing crazy about using your enemies' revenge to give you your heart's desire! That seems to me a very cunning, Machiavellian scheme—as ironically amusing as the end of one
of Mother's old, fantastic fairy tales. Except, of course, this would
be a happy end.

SARA
Flaring up angrily.
Ah, I know it's her puts all this craziness in your head. Wouldn't she
laugh with joy to see me ruin myself and lose all I have in the world!
But I'll never let her drive me to that! So don't you talk to me of the
temptation, when you know I was only joking when I said—

SIMON
I? I was only warning you against it. You must not be weak. You must

be courageously and ruthlessly what you are! You must go on to more and more!

SARA

Protests miserably.

No. I don't want to. I've enough.

Pleadingly.

Oh, Simon Darling, won't you stop and be content now you've got the bank? Won't you let the profit add up, and not make more debts to buy more, but pay off what you owe? And as soon as the debts are paid and we're safe, we'll pension off your mother, and give her the house to live alone in, where she'll have no one to hurt but herself, and I'll build my estate and have a home of my own for my husband and my children—

She presses against him with a calculating, wheedling seductiveness.

and best of all, for my lover I'm madly in love with.

SIMON

Ignoring this last—curtly.

No. You know you cannot do that now. Not unless you wish to ruin yourself. It would be fatal for you to withdraw from the Company the large amount of capital needed to build such a large estate. The battle for this bank has strained your resources to the breaking point. A dollar in cash is worth a hundred to you now. No, you can't stop now. You must go on.

SARA

Distractedly.

No! I won't! I can't! I've come to the end!

SIMON

As if she hadn't spoken.

You must keep your eyes fixed on the final goal of your ambition. Force yourself not to look down. Keep your whole mind and will concentrated on what must still be accomplished before your Company can be out of danger, safe and absolutely self-contained, not dependent on anything outside itself for anything, needing nothing but itself. Until that is done, how can you enjoy any true security or freedom within yourself—or any peace or happiness. Surely you must see that clearly, Sara?

SARA
Pitifully confused.
I—I don't know—I know I want peace and happiness in your love.

SIMON
Goes on in the same tone.
You still have to have stores to retail your cotton goods. Your own plantations worked by your own nigger slaves. Your own slave ships and your own slave dealers in Africa. That will complete the chain on the end. You see how that will protect you, don't you?

SARA
Impressed in spite of herself and beginning to be greedily fascinated.
Yes, I do see. I'm not such a fool about business after all your training. And, of course, I'd like to feel absolutely safe, and that no one had a chance with what was mine.
Then tensely desperate.
But Darling—I'm so worried—

SIMON
Goes on the same.
On this end, the stores are the last possible link—
Then with a strange laugh.
Of course, it would be the crowning achievement if I could conceive a scheme by which the public could be compelled to buy your cotton goods and only yours—so you would own your own consumer slaves, too. That would complete the circle with a vengeance! You would have life under your feet then, wouldn't you? Beautiful Greedy One—just as you have me!
He laughs, his eyes glowing with desire, and hugs her.

SARA
Her face lighting up with a responsive passion—laughingly.
Yes, I'd like that. I'd be satisfied then. So see that you find a way to do it!
Then with proud admiration.

And leave it to you, I'll wager you will! There's no stopping you, once you want anything! Haven't I always said you've the strength and the power to take anything from life your heart wished for!

SIMON
Teasingly, hugging her.
With such an insatiable mistress to inspire me, how could I dare be weak? It is your heart which has done the wishing, and I could not respect myself unless you were proud of me.

SARA
Passionately.
And I am proud! I've the grandest strongest lover that was ever owned by a woman!
She kisses him ardently.
Darling!

SIMON
Passionately.
Sweetheart!
Then with an abrupt return to his strange, obsessed excitement.
So don't let me hear any more of your timid worry about danger. What if there is danger? It lends spice to life! What if it is a tremendous gamble, with the cards stacked by the fate within you, and the dice loaded? Your father's daughter should be proud to be a born gambler and love the risk for its own sake! I'll bet he would have found his greatest happiness in staking his soul with the devil against the world on the turn of a card!

SARA
Excitedly, with a proud toss of her head.
Wouldn't he, though! Didn't he ruin himself gambling, the estate and all he possessed in life, and never blinked an eye or lost the sneer on his lips! He was a great gentleman! And he'd keep that same sneer if he played the devil, for he'd know if the devil won he'd gain only what he owned already, and he'd be laughing up his sleeve how he'd cheated him!
She laughs with gloating amusement.

SIMON

Stares at her—with a strange smile.

Yes, I have come to know that same exultant laughter at myself.

Abruptly, with a complete change to a curt business-like matter-of-fact tone.

Well, that's settled. You will go on.

He glances at his watch.

And now I'll have to go and catch my train.

He starts for the door. She gets in his way.

SARA

Seductively.

Leaving me without a kiss? When I'm making myself all you want me to be?

She suddenly embraces him with a passionate possessiveness.

Never mind! Be cruel to me! Be anything you like! I'm dirt under your feet and proud to be! For there's no price in life too great to pay to keep you mine! If it's a whore you love me to be, then I am it, body and soul, as long as you're mine!

She kisses him fiercely.

I love you so, Darling! I want you! I can't bear you to leave me now! But you'll come back here, won't you? I'll be waiting and longing—

SIMON

Kisses her passionately.

Yes! I swear to you! Nothing could keep me from—

SARA

With uneasiness—pleadingly now.

You won't forget me like you did this morning, and go to keep your engagement to visit her? You'll remember you promised me you'd forget her and let her wait.

SIMON

Vindictively.

Of course! Let the cowardly old witch wait until Domesday! It will serve her right to be alone in the twilight she dreads so with her idiotic superstitious terror of the haunted summerhouse! I am sick and tired of beseeching her to have the courage—

*He stops abruptly and his expression changes to bitter, angry resentment
—harshly accusing.*

What are you trying to do, eh? I had forgotten her! Why do you make
me remember? Damnation, can't I be free of her even here in your
arms? Why do you think I pay such an outlandish price to keep a
mistress? You seem compelled to remind me, to put her back in me!
That is the one kind of swindling I refuse to tolerate from you! What
trick are you up to? Have you made a secret bargain with her to play
one another's game? She never lets me forget you long in her garden.
She pretends to be jealous of you, just as you pretend—But, by God,
though you may hate each other, I know you hate me more and have
determined to drive me out and get rid of me! But you had better
not go on with your plot, because I warn you—it will be I who—
He checks himself, his eyes gleaming with a wild threat.

SARA
Staring at him—in a panic of dread.
Simon! Don't look like that! What's happened to you?
Suddenly resentful and angry herself.
God pity you for a fool! Have you lost your senses, to say such crazy
blather! Bargain with her, is it? Play her game for her? When I hate
her like hell itself! When my one wish about her is to drive her away
forever where she can never come back to steal what's mine—

SIMON
Staring at her—with a cold calculating sneer.
So you boast here behind her back, but with her you're afraid of her!

SARA
It's a lie! I, afraid of a poor old—

SIMON
Tauntingly.
Do you think I've stopped watching you together in the house at
night. You're afraid she might prove to be the stronger if it came to
a final decision. So you still pretend to be her friend.
Slowly.
I will believe your boasting, Sara, when you prove you want me to
be yours enough that you have the courage to—

In a burst of strange deadly hatred.

Are you going to let her come between us forever? Can't you rid our life of that damned greedy evil witch?

SARA

Stares at him with dread—but with a fascinated eagerness too—in a whisper.

You mean you want me to—

SIMON

With a change to a lover's playful teasing—pats her cheek.

I want you to do anything in life your heart desires to make me yours. You should know that by this time, Beloved. God knows I have paid you enough to prove it to you!

He laughs and kisses her.

I must catch my train. Goodbye until this afternoon.

He goes out, rear. She stands looking after him, the same expression of horrified eagerness on her face.

CURTAIN

Tao House
December, 1938

Act Four, Scene Two

SCENE

Same as Scene Two of Act Three—the corner of Deborah's garden with the summerhouse. It is around nine o'clock the same night. There is a full moon but clouds keep passing across it so that the light in the garden is a dim, pallid, ghostly grey, in which all objects are indistinct and their outlines merge into one another, with intermittent brief periods of moonlight so clear one could read by it, in which the geometrical form of each shrub and its black shadow are sharply defined and separate. Their alternating lights are like intense brooding moods of the garden itself, and under the spell of either it has more compellingly than ever before the atmosphere of a perversely magnified child's toy garden, unnatural and repellently distorted and artificial.

Deborah is discovered pacing back and forth along the path between the pool in front of the summerhouse and the door to the street in the wall at right. Her manner is pitifully distraught, nervous, tense, frightened and desperate. One feels she is fighting back complete nervous collapse, wild hysterical tears. Yet at the same time she is a prey to a passionate anger and her eyes smoulder with a bitter, jealous fury and hatred. A great physical change is noticeable in her. Her small, immature, girlish figure has grown so terribly emaciated that she gives the impression of being bodiless, a little, skinny, witch-like, old woman, an evil godmother conjured to life from the page of a fairy tale, whom strong sunlight would dissolve, or a breath of reality disperse into thin air. Her small, delicate, oval face is haggard with innumerable wrinkles, and so pale it seems bloodless and corpse-like, a mask of death, the great dark eyes staring from black holes. She is dressed in white, as ever, but with pathetically obvious touches of calculating, coquettish feminine adornment. Her beautiful white hair is piled up on her head in curls so that it resembles an Eighteenth Century mode. Her withered lips are rouged and there is a beauty-spot on each rouged cheek. There is a pitiful aspect about her of an old portrait of a bygone age come back to haunt the scene of long-past assignation.

DEBORAH
Distractedly.

God, how long have I waited like this—hours!—hours since supper even—watching, their prying eyes sneering—mocking, snickering under their breath, exchanging smiles—but frightened, too—she has told them to beware of me, I am a little crazy—then after supper out here again—waiting again—waiting, waiting!—why do I?—what makes me make myself?—why don't I go in the house?—hide in my room and lock the door—why do I stay here and hope?—Oh, how can he be so cruel?!—how can he do this to me?

She suddenly stops and listens tensely—eagerly.

There—footsteps—someone coming up the street! It must be he at last!

She rushes over and pulls open the door in the wall at right and looks out in the street—then closes it again—dully.

No one—

Bitterly.

Except Life, perhaps, who walks away again now—again forgetful I am still alive—

She turns away from the door.

How many times now have I run to open the door, hoping each time—

Flaring into sudden anger.

How dare he humiliate me like this! a common, vulgar, money-grubbing trader like his father!—I made his father respect my pride—I humiliated him—You had better beware, Simon!—if you think I will bear your insults without retaliating!—

Then trying pitifully to reassure herself.

No, no, I must not blame him—he has been detained at the mill by something unforseen—

With angry scorn.

Ah, how can you make excuses—lie to yourself when you know the truth—he deliberately forgot you—he is even now lying in the arms of that slut, laughing with her to think of the pitiable spectacle you make waiting in vain!

In a fury.

Ah, if I were sure of that. I would have no more scruples!—I would make him go in the summerhouse instead of protecting him from his insane desire—that would revenge me for all his insults!

As she is speaking the moon comes from behind a cloud and shines clearly on the summerhouse door. She stops and stares at it fascinatedly—then turns away hastily with a shiver of dread.

No!—I could not—he is my beloved son who has returned to me—and he will come here soon—he loves me—he would never deliberately wound—he knows how lonely I am—that his visits here are all of happiness and peace that is left me—all that remains to me of life—if he took them from me, I!— But he will explain it is not his fault, he was unavoidably detained— But if he had been detained at the mills—that does not explain why she has not returned home either—he must be with her!—

Distractedly.

Ah, how can I blind myself—as if I did not know she has turned his office into a brothel bedroom—she is vile and unscrupulous—she uses her one superiority—her body—plays upon the only feeling he has for her—makes herself a whore to keep her hold on him!—anything to keep him from me!—but he shall not!—I can be unscrupulous, too—he thinks I will always be afraid—the fool!—she doesn't realize I have but to take his hand, as he wishes, and lead him from her life forever!—

She has again stopped by the summerhouse and is staring fascinatedly at the door. Then again she tears her eyes away with a shudder—desperately.

Oh, why can't she leave me alone!—why does she force me to hate her so terribly—I am afraid of what her hate is making me become —I know so well the scheme she has in mind to get rid of me—to drive me insane—she deliberately goads me!—tempts me—it is horrible to be compelled to constantly resist—it exhausts my mind, my will—

She shudders—then with a sudden change to a scornful gloating.

What a stupid animal—can't she see that in the end her hate will give me the courage[*] I need—that something in me hopes that she will succeed—but, of course, she hopes I would go alone—

She laughs sneeringly.

Oh no, my dear Sara, I would take what is mine with me!

Her eyes are fixed on the summerhouse door again. The moon passes behind a cloud and the light grows dim. She turns away frightenedly.

No! I could not!—I could not—and there is no need—I have beaten her already—I have taken him from her—as I always knew I could if she gave me the opportunity—

She laughs with arrogant scorn.

What a fool she is to imagine she could match me in intrigue—I who have spent years of my life dreaming of power I might wield—I have been too subtle for her—I have used even her strength against her—encouraged him to make a whore of her—to feel himself [devoured] and[†] enslaved—until now he sees her as the filthy slut she is—his one desire is to escape her—soon she will disgust him so, he will drive her out of my house into the gutter with her brats—meanwhile, I have led him back, step by step, into memory, into the past, where he long to be—where he is my child again—my baby—where my life is his only life—where he is safe beyond her grasping claws!

Her face has taken on a soft, dreamy ecstatic look—exultantly.

My beloved son and I—one again—happily ever after—safely hidden from life in our old dreams!

Her eyes fasten on the summerhouse door—abruptly frightened—she turns away to stare about the garden uneasily.

If he would only come!—I am afraid alone in this garden at night—slowly as night [descends] it becomes strange—somber and threatening—it seems to be evil—it becomes Nature again—a Nature my arrogant whim had distorted into ridiculous artificial forms—an enslaved Nature, ground under, thwarted and sneered at—in the day it pretended to be humbly resigned—but as dark comes it strains at its chains like a black slave and longs for revenge and freedom—I feel the bitter, poisoned hatred of each amusingly humiliated shrub.

---

[*] The typescript reads "courage of," followed by a space. I have deleted the word "of."
[†] After "himself" I have replaced a space with the word "devoured," a word often used by O'Neill in this sense.

She shivers.

And something in my nature responds—pities—hates—would help it escape—to possess me—within its evil embrace I would forget fear and pity—I would have no mercy for those who sneer and deride—
She pauses—then with increasing bitterness and suspicion.

Why do I lie and tell myself it is I who have led Simon back into the past, when I know it is he who has forced me to carry out his evil scheme of revenge—
Protesting frightenedly.

No!—how can I have such a mad suspicion—I should be glad—it proves how he loves me—how much he needs my love—
Suspiciously again—sneering at herself.

Love? You know he is incapable of love—love is a passion of the soul—that greedy trader lost his soul long ago when he left me—now he is as soulless as his father—lust is the only passion he feels now—no, do not let him deceive you into believing it is love for you that impels him—what is it, then?—hate?—the hate for me she has put in his mind?—a conspiracy with her to drive me from his life—to imprison me here alone—driving me back farther and farther within myself—until he finally tricks me into unlocking the door, taking his hand—and at the last moment he will snatch his hand away, push me inside alone with that mad woman I locked in there—to be possessed by her again—never to come out—
The moon again comes from behind a cloud and shines on the summer-house. She gives a dreadful little laugh.

And then, of course, it would be so simple to have me locked up in an asylum—
Furiously.

Yes!—I see through your scheme, Simon!—I can see you now, lying in her arms, laughing as you gloat together! But take care! I am not some stupid merchant you swindle!—I am not impressed by your ridiculous posing as a little Napoleon!—nor am I that poor dull-witted peasant you cheat and make a whore of—you will find I will outwit you—I will be the one to snatch away my hand and leave you alone in there with that old mad Deborah who will have no scruple—and you beat the walls, screaming for escape at any cost!

She suddenly stops, trembling with horror at herself, and presses her hands to her head torturedly.

Oh, God have mercy,—I must stop thinking—if I go on like this, there will be no need for anyone outside me to—I will drive myself in there!

She paces back and forth distractedly, glancing with dread around the garden.

This garden has become horrible. I am afraid of myself here—Oh, if my son would only come!—he is not coming!—why don't I go in the house?—no, I must wait!—he promised me—he has been detained —I must be patient—find some way to pass the time—not think of horrible impossible things—I am still mistress of my mind—I can still dream, if it pleases me—I remember when I waited for him at the cabin that afternoon, I passed the time pleasantly in dreaming— and when I opened my eyes he was there—

Determinedly.

I can do that again. I will!

She sits on the stone bench at right-rear of the pool, closing her eyes, her face grows tense as she concentrates her will, deliberately hypnotizing herself into a trance. A pause. Then she relaxes slowly and murmurs dreamily.

The gardens at Malmaison—the summerhouse—the Emperor—

Her dream becomes disturbed and puzzled and uneasy but she only half awakes.

No—I do not wish this—it is not the same—not Versailles and the King—the Emperor Napoleon?—how strange—I had thought I hated him—Father's silly confusing him with God—and Simon pretending he is like—I always wanted to live in a time before he lived —and now I see that was very cowardly of me—to deny him—so silly to run and hide like a little bashful girl—

Sinking happily into dreams.

The Emperor kisses me—"My Throne, it is your heart, Dear Love, and I—"

While she is saying this last, Sara slinks in noiselessly along the path from the house on the left. She looks worn out and dissipated, with dark circles under her eyes, her hair dishevelled, her dress wrinkled and awry, like a prostitute the morning after a debauch. She stands regarding Deborah with a cruel mocking leer of satisfaction.

SARA
To herself.
Ah, I knew what my keeping him away would do to her! She's like I hoped she'd be! I'll have only to goad and taunt and make game of her now to drive her over the edge where she'll never find the way back! And it's what Simon wants, too, to be rid of her. It's what he asked me to do!

DEBORAH
In her dream, her face lighting up with love.
At last you have come, Sire. My poor heart was terrified you had forgotten I was waiting.

SARA
In spite of herself, her eyes grow pitying.
No. God forgive me. The poor creature! I couldn't—not yet—not unless it's the only way to save him from her madness.

DEBORAH
Laughs softly and seductively, rising to her feet.
Yes, give me your hand and let us go within, Sire, where we will be hidden from the ugliness of life—in our Temple of Love where there is only Beauty and forgetfulness!
She holds out her hand and clasps that of her royal dream lover and turns toward the door and slowly begins to ascend the steps.

SARA
With a gloating eagerness.
She's going to do it herself! I won't need to! I've only to let her alone! And that's what Simon wants.

DEBORAH
I have the key here, Sire. I have worn it lately over my heart.
She reaches down inside her bodice and pulls out a key on a cord around her neck—hesitates frightenedly—then unlocks but does not open the door.

SARA

Eagerly but at the same time frightenedly.

She's unlocked it! Nothing will stop her now! I've only to mind my own business. Why did I come here? I don't like seeing it, when I could prevent her. But it's what Simon wants—and I want!

DEBORAH

With a little shiver, holding back, forcing a little smile.

I—I confess I am a little frightened, Sire. So foolish of me—but—
Pleadingly.

Oh, swear to me again you would not deceive me—that it is love and forgetfulness!

SARA

Struggling with herself.

She's frightened! She knows even in her dream! Ah, though I hate her more than hell, I pity her now! But why should I? It's little pity she'd have for me if she saw her chance—

DEBORAH

Forcing a determined, exalting tone.

But even if it were hell, it will be heaven to me with your love!
She puts her hand on the knob.

SARA

Fiercely.

Yes, go to hell and be damned to you and leave Simon alone to me!
Then just as Deborah is turning the knob she springs toward her.
Stop! Let go of that door, you damned old fool!
Deborah starts and half-awakens with a bewildered cry, pulling her hand from the door, and stands dazed and trembling. Sara reaches her side. She is angry at herself for interfering now and takes it out on Deborah, grabbing her by the shoulders and shaking her roughly.
Wake up from your mad dreams, I'm saying! I've no patience to humor your daftness.

DEBORAH

Whimpering with pain and fright like a child.

Let go! You are hurting me! It isn't fair! You are so much stronger! Simon! Make her let me alone!

Sara has let go of her. Deborah stares at her fully awake now. She makes a shaken attempt to draw herself up with her old arrogance.

You! How dare you touch me!

SARA

Shamefacedly.

I'm sorry if I hurt you, but I had to wake you—

DEBORAH

With vindictive fury now.

Oh, I'd like to have you beaten! Lashed till the blood ran down your fat white shoulders!

SARA

Bitterly resentful.

Divil a doubt you would! And that's the thanks I get for stopping you!

DEBORAH

How dare you come here!

SARA

Angrily.

To hell with your airs and graces! Whose property is it, I'd like to know? You're the one who has no right here!

DEBORAH

Oh!

SARA

But the only reason I came was because I took pity on you, knowing you'd be kept waiting out here all night, like an old fool, if I didn't tell he'd come home with me and forgotten all about you.

DEBORAH

Then—it is true. He did go back to the office, instead of—He went back to you! You made him, with your filthy—

SARA
Tauntingly.
Made him? You don't know the strength of his love for me! I couldn't
have kept him from me, if I'd wanted!

DEBORAH
You came here to tell me—so you could gloat! You vulgar common
slut!

SARA
Goadingly.
And I've more to tell you. He's paid the last visit here he'll ever pay
you. He swore to me on his honor, lying in my arms, he never wanted
to see you again, he was sick of wasting time humoring your craziness!

DEBORAH
In a fury of jealous hatred, making a threatening movement toward her.
You lie! He would never—He will come! Oh, you despicable filthy
harlot!

SARA
He'll never come here again, I'm telling you! So don't be dreaming
and hoping!
Then angrily.
A filthy harlot, am I? Well, I'm what he loves me to be! And it's not
for you to call names, my high and mighty lady, or to give yourself
airs. What were you in your crazy dreams just now—what have you
always prided yourself you could be if you had the courage—but the
greatest whore in the world!

DEBORAH
Shrinking back to the foot of the steps as if she'd been struck—guiltily.
No, no! Only in a silly fancy—to amuse my mind—to wile away
the time—How dare you insult me by thinking I could ever really
wish—It's because you have the vile disgusting mind of a common
street woman. You judge everyone by yourself.

SARA
Roughly scornful.

Arrah, don't be talking! You don't fool me!

Jeering derisively.

I'll say this for you you have grand tastes! It used to be King Louis of France, no less, you had for your man! But now it's the Emperor Napoleon, God pity you! My, but aren't you the fickle, greedy one! You've never enough!

She laughs with coarse cruelty.

DEBORAH

Shrinking back up the steps as Sara keeps coming nearer to her—distractedly.

Don't! Don't! Oh, how dare you laugh!

SARA

With cruel mocking insistence.

It'll be the Czar of Russia next! Aren't you the beautiful evil woman with all the kings and rulers of the earth, that are or ever was, down on their knees at your feet!

DEBORAH

Shrinking back to the top step—stammers distractedly.

Don't! Don't! Let me alone!

SARA

Following her.

Begging you to let them sleep with you!

With savage contempt.

When out of your mad dreams you're only a poor little wizened old woman no common man on the street would turn to look at, and who, in the days when the men did want you, didn't have the blood or the strength to want them but ran and hid in her garden.

DEBORAH

With a pitiful, stammering, hysterical laugh.

Yes! So ridiculous, isn't it? So pitiful and disgusting and horrible!

Distractedly.

Don't! Don't remind me! Don't make me see!

Wildly.

I can't endure myself! I won't! I'll be free at any cost! I—

She turns and grabs the knob of the door.

SARA

Instinctively makes a grab for her and pulls her away—covering her guilty fear with a rough anger.
Come away from that!

DEBORAH

Struggling.
No! Let me go!

SARA

Angrily.
You will, will you?
She picks Deborah up in her strong arms, as if she weighed nothing, sets her down before the bench at right and forces her down on it—angrily.
Sit there and be quiet now! I've had enough of your tricks! If you think you'll make me have your madness on my conscience, you're mistaken!
Deborah crumples up and falls sideways face down on the bench and bursts into hysterical sobbing. Sara speaks with a grim satisfaction.
Ah, thank God, you can cry. Maybe that will bring some sense back in your head, and you won't be calling names that make me lose my temper and force me to do things to you I don't want to do except as a last resort if you keep on.
Her tone becomes more and more persuasive as Deborah's crying gradually spends itself.
But I don't think you'll want to keep on now. Not after what happened today—him keeping you waiting here and making an old fool of you! And I've told you the truth, he swore he'd never come to you again. It was part of the price I made him pay for me when he came back from the mills. Well, do you mean to tell me, in the face of that, you'll go begging him to visit you? You've got more pride in you than that, I hope. And anyway, it would do you no good. He'd only refuse you. He'd laugh at you again. He's mine now, I tell you! He's paid me everything he has. He has nothing left but me. He has no life except in my love. And I love him more than ever woman

loved a man! I'm mother, wife, and mistress in one. He doesn't need you. You're out in the cold. You're beaten.

Deborah is still now and listening tensely but she does not raise her head. Sara goes on almost wheedlingly.

Listen to me. The real reason I came here was to have a sensible talk with you, and ask you to face the truth that I've won and you're beaten. You're finished and well you know it! Well you know a moment ago I could have driven you in there where the only door out leads to an asylum! I didn't because I hoped you'd be sensible and not make me do it! I hoped you'd admit you were beaten and give up.

Almost pleadingly.

Won't you own up now that it's no good going on with your mad schemes? If you'll swear to stop, I'll stop too and make peace with you. And I'll give in on my side to make it fair with you. I'll give the children back to you to keep you company and stand between you and your dreams, and you'll be as contented as you were before. And I won't hate you. You know I don't like your forcing me to hate you, don't you?

She pauses. Deborah remains still. Sara's anger rises.

Well? Haven't you a tongue in your head? It's you, not me, ought to beg for peace! I've made you a decent offer, and it's your last chance.

DEBORAH

Abruptly straightens up and stares at her with hard revengeful eyes—with a mocking smile.

You are even more stupid than I thought. Don't you know your begging for peace is a confession of how insecure you are in your fancied victory? I am convinced now that you realize that any time I choose I can take Simon away with me!

SARA

Frightenedly.

You mean, into madness, with you?

Savagely.

I swear by Almighty God I'll murder you if you try that.

DEBORAH

Coldly disdainful.

And get your children's mother hanged?

SARA
Taken aback.
I'll do it a way no one will discover!

DEBORAH
Coldly contemptuous.
Simon would know. Do you think your husband would love a wife
who had murdered his mother?

SARA
You think he wouldn't? I tell you, he'd thank me for it! If you knew
how he hated you now for trying to make him hate me! He begged
me today to get rid of you, so he and I could be free!

DEBORAH
Shakenly.
You lie! He loves me! It's you he hates! You have become vile and
disgusting to him! He loathes your foul flesh, your filthy, insatiable
greeds! He has implored me to drive you out of life into the gutter
from which you sprang! Or if that takes too long, he has hinted I
might find some subtle way that might never be suspected, to poison
you!

SARA
Shakenly.
Ah, it's the evil liar you are! He loves me! He'd never! But I know
it's in your mind and I'll take good care what I eat or drink from
now on!

DEBORAH
Suddenly gives way to a horrified realization.
Sara! Oh, no! For God's sake, how can you think I—?
Then her face hardening again—defiantly.
I refuse your offer of peace. I do not trust you. How could I trust
you? I trusted you once. Besides, even if your begging for peace did
not clearly reveal to me how weak you are, your stopping me from
opening the door would. You could really have won then but you did
not have strength. You are weakly sentimental and pitiful. You can-

not be ruthless. You are feeble with guilty scruples. You will always defeat yourself at the last.

Scornfully.

You fool! Do you think, in your place, I would ever have stopped you? I would have laughed with joy! I could watch you lashed to death, with the blood running down your gross white back, and never raise a finger to save you!

Arrogantly.

Pah! What a fool I have been! It is you who are doomed by your weakness to inevitable defeat. I am the stronger as I always knew I would be, if given the opportunity.

SARA

Angrily.

So that's your answer, is it? That's what you think? That's my thanks for—

Vindictively.

You old lunatic, you'll see if I have any pity on you the next time!

DEBORAH

Haughtily—as if addressing a servant.

I see no reason for prolonging this tiresome interview. You have no business in this garden. Will you be good enough to return to the house where you belong and attend to your children. I know my son is waiting for an opportunity to see me alone.

SARA

Angrily, turning toward the path off left.

I'll go, and be damned to you! I've come to the end of pity!

With cruel vindictiveness.

He's waiting hoping to hear I've found you locked inside there and we can get the asylum to take you away!

DEBORAH

Her will beginning to crumple under this attack—distractedly.

Oh, no! You are lying! Not my beloved son! He couldn't!

SARA

Jeering savagely.

I'll be sorry to disappoint him but I'll promise him you're near the end and it won't be long before we're free!

She starts to go.

DEBORAH
With a pitiful frightened cry.
Sara! No!
She runs to her wildly and grabs her arm—stammering with terror.
Don't go! Don't leave me alone, here! I—I'm afraid! Please stay! I—I'll do anything you ask! I'll admit you've won! I'll make peace! I'll promise anything you want! Only—don't leave me here! I need your strength or I'll—
She throws her arms around Sara and begins to sob hysterically.
Oh, how can you be so cruel to me?

SARA
Has stared at her at first suspiciously and resentfully—then gloating triumphantly but moved in spite of herself—finally, as Deborah weeps, she is overcome by pity and soothes her as she would a child.
There, there now. Don't be frightened. I'm here. I'm strong enough for the two of us. And it's all over now. We won't destroy each other anymore. You'll have the children back. You'll be happy and contented. You know I didn't want to be cruel to you.

DEBORAH
Brokenly.
I know. And you know I didn't.

SARA
Gently.
Come in the house with me now. You must go to bed and rest. It's a wonder if you haven't caught your death already, chilled by the night and the dew.

DEBORAH
Exhaustedly—with humble affectionate gratitude.
You are so generous and kind and warm. I know that in my heart so well. How could I have forgotten? How could I have longed so horribly for your death—the one friend I have ever possessed, the one

person who has ever understood my pride. I am really so humbly grateful, and yet—How could I be so vile and evil?

SARA
Soothingly.
Ah well, wasn't I just wishing you locked up in an asylum? I'm worse than you. But it's over now. We've made peace. We'll forget.
Urging her.
Let's go in the house now. You're trembling. You've taken a chill. Come.

DEBORAH
You are so thoughtful and good.
Sara begins to lead her off left. Abruptly she stops—with dread.
No. We're forgetting he is there, Sara. We must wait. We can't face him yet. We would be too weak. We must stay here together, trusting each other, until we get back our old strength to defy him as one woman. The strength his evil jealous greed has corrupted and destroyed!
Desperately.
Yes, it is he! He! Not us! We have been driven to this!

SARA
Resentfully.
Ah, don't I know how he's driven me!

DEBORAH
Her desperation angry.
He! He! He! Only he! We saw that so clearly when he first started to goad us into this duel to the death! We swore to each other that we would constantly bear in mind it was he, not us. In him, not in us! We saw our danger if we ever let him make us forget that.

SARA
I know! But, in a few days he'd made us forget! He made us deceive each other and hate and scheme—

DEBORAH
Yes! Devote our lives to destroying each other! In meek obedience

to his whim! Oh, what weak fools we have been! How could we be so blind and stupid!

SARA

Because we loved him so much! And didn't he know that, the sly schemer, and use it to have his own way!

DEBORAH

We could have defeated him so easily! We would have been so much stronger! He would have had no more strength than a little boy or a baby! We could have kept him absolutely dependent on us, with no life except within our life.

SARA

And he'd have been happy and content, not destroyed with hunger and mad with greed like he is now.

DEBORAH

Yes! He would have been supremely happy and utterly contented with nothing but our love. But no! It wasn't enough! He had to play the great self-liberator, the conquering Napoleon, of others, with his women, too.

SARA

With resentful contempt.
Arrah, he's like all the greedy fools of men, never knowing when they're well off.

DEBORAH

If we had carried out our determination to remain united we could so easily have curbed his insane rebellion against happiness. He would have had to beg us to restore our peace to him. But instead we let him revive a dead hate of the past to start us clawing and tearing at each other's hearts like two mad female animals he had thrown in a pit to fight for his love—while he stands apart and watches and sneers and laughs with greedy pride and goads each on in turn to murder the other!

SARA

With bitter anger.

And when only one is left living, he knows she'll be so weakened by the long duel he can easily make a slave of her who'll never have strength to claim her body or soul her own again!

While she is talking, unnoticed by them both, Simon appears behind them, entering from the path at left. He does not make his presence known but stands staring at them. He is in a state of terrific tension, and there is a wild look in his eyes, cunning, calculating and threatening and at the same time baffled and panic-stricken.

DEBORAH

Yes, that is what he is trying to accomplish, of course—use one to rid him of the other.

SARA

Or both to be rid of both!

She laughs bitterly.

Ah, wouldn't he strut and puff out his chest before the mirror then, boasting what a great little independent man he was, if he were free of the two of us!

DEBORAH

Sneering bitterly.

Yes, he would be finally convinced then he was a reincarnation of Napoleon! Yes, I hadn't thought of it before but now I see that must be his most ambitious dream.

Her face hardens cruelly.

It would serve him right if we turned the tables on him, Sara. We could have the strength now as we are united again as one woman.

SARA

Fascinatedly.

You mean, throw him in the pit—to fight it out with himself?

DEBORAH

For our love—while we watched with gratified womanly pride and laughed and goaded him on!

SARA

Eagerly—but with hesitant dread, too.

Until—

DEBORAH

Yes, Sara. Until at last we're finally rid of him.

With tense hatred and longing.

Oh God, think of how simply contented we could be alone together with our children—grandmother and mother, mother and daughter, sister and sister, one woman and another, with the way so clear before us, the purpose and meaning of life so happily implicit, the feeling of living life so deeply sure of itself, not needing thought, beyond all torturing doubt and sneers and question, the passive "yes" of self-possession welcoming the peaceful procession of demanding days!

She pauses—then a bit guiltily.

I hope you do not think it evil of me that I can find it in myself to wish he were not here.

SARA

Fascinatedly.

No—there have been times at the office when I—

DEBORAH

He has taught us that whatever is in oneself is good—that whatever one desires is good, that the one evil is to deny oneself.

Tensely.

Again, it is not us but what he has made us be! So on his head—

SIMON

Speaks with a tense quiet casualness.

You are mistaken, Mother.

They both whirl on him with startled gasps of terror and cling to one another defensively. Then as he advances, they shrink back to the edge of the bench at the right rear of pool, keeping the pool between them and him. He goes on with the same tense brittle quiet.

You are hiding from yourself again, Mother. And Sara seems to have caught the cowardly habit from you. It is stupid of you to blame me. It is not on my head but in your hearts. I have merely insisted that you both be what you are—that what you are is good because it is fact and reality—that the true nature of man and woman, to which we have hitherto given the bad name of evil because we were afraid of it, is, in a world of facts dominated by our greed for power and possession, good because it is true. And what is evil, because it is a lie, is the deliberate evasive sentimental misunderstanding of man as he is, proclaimed by the fool, Jean Jacques Rousseau—the stupid theory that he is naturally what we call virtuous and good. Instead of being what he is, a hog. It is that idealistic fallacy which is responsible for all the confusion in our minds, the conflicts within the self, and for all the confusion in our relationships with one another, within the family particularly, for the blundering of our desires which are disciplined to covet what they don't want and be afraid to crave what they wish for in truth.

He smiles a thin tense smile.

In a nutshell, if you will pardon the seeming paradox, all one needs to remember is that good is evil, and evil, good.

As they have listened, the faces of the two women have hardened into a deadly enmity.

DEBORAH
Tensely and threateningly.
Do you hear, Sara. We must not forget.

SARA
In the same tone.
No, we owe it to him to be what he wants.

SIMON
His tense quiet beginning to snap.
But I did not come out here to discuss my meditations on the true nature of man.

He pauses—then the strain breaking, his voice trembling, he blurts out in violent accusation.

I—I was trying to concentrate my thoughts on the final solution of the problem. I have been forced to the conclusion lately that in the end, if the conflicting selves within a man are too evenly matched— if neither is strong enough to destroy the other before the man himself, of which they are halves, is exhausted by their struggle and in danger of being torn apart between them—then that man is forced at last, in self-defense, to choose one or the other—

DEBORAH
Starts—staring at him uneasily.
To choose, Simon?

SARA
Echoing her.
To choose, Simon?

SIMON
To throw all his remaining strength to one and help it to destroy the other. That appears to me now to be the one possible way he can end the conflict and save his sanity before it is too late.

DEBORAH
Beginning to be cruelly gloating now.
You hear what he's confessing, Sara?

SARA
Echoing her tone.
That we've been too strong for him, and he's near the end.

SIMON
As if he hadn't heard.
Before my mind is torn and clawed to death between them and devoured!

DEBORAH
Gloatingly.
Yes, he is much nearer the end than I had thought.

SARA
In same tone.
Yes, we've only to wait and we'll soon be free of him.
She chuckles.
Well, I should have known he hadn't much strength left to go on with! If you knew how I've beaten him at the office! I've stripped him clean, Deborah! I got the bank from him today. He's ruined and finished! He's nothing left to offer me! And if he hopes, after all he's taught me, that he can cheat me into giving something for nothing, he's a bigger fool even than I think him!

She laughs.

DEBORAH
Smiles gloatingly.
Oh, I have guessed, Sara. I have been with you in spirit and been proud of you in my imagination! I have helped you all I could by urging him to encourage your greed.
Then almost boastfully.
But I should have guessed how near the end he is through my own experience with him, Sara. If you could see how I have led him farther and farther away, back into the past, until now all I have to do is say one word, or even have the thought in silence, and our great man-conquering Napoleon becomes a stubborn, nagging, begging little boy whose only purpose or ambition in life is to possess the happy ending of an old silly fairy tale!
She laughs and Sara joins in her laughter.

SARA
Staring at Simon—mockingly.
Well, well, you're a great one for teaching us that everyone is for sale and it should be a woman's pride to get the highest price she can, but I'm thinking in the end it will be us who have taught you about high prices!

DEBORAH
Mockingly.
Yes, I am sure he will have learned that a woman's pride costs more than he could ever afford to pay without going bankrupt.

SARA
Scornfully resentful.
So he'll choose, will he, the great man? Like a master picking which of two slaves he'd like to own! But suppose they don't choose to let him choose?

DEBORAH
Echoing her tone.
Yes, it would be very stupid of them, when all they have to do is to wait together and stand apart and watch while he destroys himself

and sets them free. Encourage him to do so, even. Goad him on with their laughter.

She laughs softly and Sara laughs with her.

SIMON

With an abrupt change to his matter-of-fact tone.

I don't know what you're talking about, Mother. I attempt to explain an abstract problem of the nature of man, and you and Sara begin talking as if you, personally, were directly concerned in it!

He chuckles dryly.

An amusing example of the insatiable ambition of female possessiveness, don't you think?

Curtly.

Never mind. It is my fault for being such a fool as to discuss it with you. I know the one problem that interests you.

He becomes angrily excited.

God knows I could hardly be unaware of it tonight! I heard you from my study quarreling out here, clawing and tearing at each other like two drunken drabs fighting over a dollar bill! God, it becomes disgusting! You might at least have the decency to confine your revolting greedy brawls to the house! Do you want to create a public scandal, screaming where all the neighbors can hear, cursing and threatening to murder each other!

DEBORAH

Quietly.

We were not screaming. You could not possibly have heard us in your study. I am afraid what you heard were the voices of your own mind. You were dreaming your old dream of liberty for men, perhaps, and listening to your hopes.

SIMON

With angry excitement.

That's a lie! I heard you as clearly as if I were here! I could not concentrate my thoughts on the final solution of the problem, listening to your screaming hatred! It seemed there would never be a moment's peace in my life again—that you would go on with your horrible duel, clawing and tearing each other, until my mind would be ripped apart!

He checks himself uneasily—quickly, trying to adopt a tone of confident scorn.

I heard you, I tell you. So don't attempt to evade your guilt by saying I imagined it. Are you trying to insinuate I am going insane? Ridiculous! You will find you were talking louder than you realized. Hatred seldom remembers to keep its voice decently lowered. And then when you finally did become quiet, there was no peace—It was the stillness that follows a shriek of terror, waiting to become aware—I was afraid one of you had killed the other. I thought when I came here I would find only one—

DEBORAH

Staring at him—cannot control a shrinking shudder.

We know—you have been hoping—

SARA

With a shudder.

Ah, God forgive me!

SIMON

Wildly.

Well, I might have been hoping. Suppose I was? Do you think I can endure living with your murderous duel forever—always between you—a defenseless object for your hatred of each other—rent in twain by your tearing greedy claws? No! I tell you there comes a point where the tortured mind will pay any price for peace!

He suddenly breaks and sinks on the bench at left of pool, his head clutched convulsively in his hands—brokenly.

Why can't you stop? Why won't you make peace between you? I will do anything you wish! Is there no love or pity left in your hearts? Can't you see you are driving me insane?

He begins to sob exhaustedly—the two women sit together, as one, on the other bench, staring at him. Their first reaction is one of victory. But there is no satisfaction or triumph. They are exhausted and without feeling.

DEBORAH
Dully.
We have won, Sara.

SARA
Dully.
Yes, Deborah. He admits he's beaten.
They stare at him. He remains still, his head in his hands. Suddenly, their faces, as one face, are convulsed by pitying, forgiving maternal love.

DEBORAH
Our poor boy! How could we be so cruel!

SARA
Our poor darling! How could we feel as we were feeling about you!
Then, as one, they spring to their feet and go to him, separating, one coming round one side of the pool, the other round the other. They kneel at each side of him, putting an arm around him, hastening to tenderly console and comfort him.

DEBORAH
There, there! Our beloved son!

SARA
Our husband! Our lover!

DEBORAH
You mustn't cry, Dear. You break our hearts when you cry.

SARA
There's nothing need frighten you now. We've forgiven you.

DEBORAH
We love you again.

SARA
You'll be hidden safe and sound in our love, where no one can hurt you.

DEBORAH
Yes, it's so silly of you to be frightened, Dear. Couldn't you see as soon as we came here we had made peace between us?

SARA

And now you're at peace in our peace, don't you feel that, Darling?

SIMON

*Raises his head, a confused, dreamy wondering peace in his face—
dazedly.*
Yes. It is very restful here. I am very grateful to you for life.
He turns to Sara.
I love you, my mother.
He turns to Deborah.
I love you, my—
*He stops guiltily—then springs from their arms to his feet, stammering
distractedly.*
No, no! I could not live in such confusion!
*Keeping his back to them, as they remain kneeling, he adds with a sneer-
ing mockery.*
As for this peace of yours, if you think I can be taken in by such an
obvious sham—
*The two women spring to their feet. Both cry as one with anguished de-
spair:* "Simon! Don't!" *and each grabs one of his arms and clings to
it. Simon trembles with his effort to control himself. He speaks with a
hurried acquiescence.*
I ask your pardon. My mind is still extremely confused. It is such an
unexpected shock—to find Sara here where she never intrudes—and
then to hear of your confusing reconcilement—But it was very evil
of me to doubt and sneer—particularly as I love you both so deeply
and it is my dearest wish for my women to live in harmony and I
may enjoy love and peace in my home!

SARA

With happy relief.
Darling!
She hugs his arm.

DEBORAH

Dear!
Then teasingly.
And here's the kiss you cheated me of a moment ago.

She kisses his cheek.

SIMON
Smiles pleasantly.
Thank you, Mother.
Then with a too-pleasant, natural affectionate air.
Well, all is forgotten and forgiven then, and I start a new happy life within your united love, is that it?

DEBORAH
Gaily tender.
Oh yes, Dear! And we will make you so happy! Won't we, Sara?

SARA
Gaily tender.
Indeed we will! He won't know himself!

SIMON
Pleasantly.
I am sure I will not. Let us sit down and rest for a moment together then, shall we, in this garden so hidden from the ugliness of reality, where it is always so restful—
Then, as they are about to sit, he suddenly exclaims.
Ah, what a fool I am. I had entirely forgotten the object of my coming here. It had nothing to do with your quarrel, which, as you say, must have been merely my imagination. I came to remind you, Sara, it's the children's bedtime and they are waiting for your goodnight kiss. They were a bit hurt, I might add. It isn't like their mother to forget.

SARA
Guilty—rebuking herself.
Ah, the poor darlings. Bad cess to me, how could I forget—

SIMON
With a calculating insistence.
You'd better take a good look at Honey. Unless I'm mistaken, he's getting a cold. It seemed to me he was a bit feverish.

SARA

Worriedly.

Ah, the poor lamb, and me out here gabbing—

She starts off the path at left, then hesitates.

You're coming in?

DEBORAH

Quickly.

Yes, of course—

SIMON

Quickly.

Yes, it's too damp and chilly. We'll go in, Mother. But you better run ahead, Sara, and see Honey.

SARA

Worriedly.

Ah, I hope he's not going to be sick. I'll—

She hurries off, left. Simon turns and stares at his mother.

SIMON

With a sneering chuckle.

Well, you must admit I got rid of her very successfully, Mother.

DEBORAH

Staring at him—smiles gloatingly.

Yes, I felt that was what you were doing. She is such a stupid, trust-ful—

Then tensely.

No! You are making me say that! I—

SIMON

Ignoring this.

She will be occupied fussing over Honey and getting them all to bed. She will not notice we have remained out here.

DEBORAH

Stiffening—coldly.

I am not remaining here.

SIMON
Ignoring this.
It will give us an opportunity to be alone.

DEBORAH
Tensely.
I do not wish to be alone with you. I am going in and help her with
the children. I am going in! At once!
*She takes a step towards left, stiffly, as if by a determined effort of will
staring at him with a fascinated uneasiness. He reaches out and takes one
of her hands and she stops, trembling, rooted to the spot. She stammers.*
You—you may do as you please. It is not my affair—
Her tone becomes taunting.
if you choose to stay out here alone in the darkness—and make an
idiot of yourself—dreaming childish make-believe—like a silly little
boy—you, a grown man!—if you could only see yourself!—what
a ridiculous comic figure!—a Napoleon who believes in fairy tales
and marches to Moscow in search of a magic door—the Emperor
whose greatest ambition is to invade and capture a summerhouse in
his mother's garden and conquer spider webs and the dirt and mould
of old dreams and the forgotten ghost of an absurdly vain and selfish
and cowardly woman who longed to escape—
She forces a sneering laugh.
But I—I am sick and tired of humoring you, as one would a half-
witted child. I am finished with your romantic nonsense. I have
talked it over sensibly with your wife and she agrees with me that my
permitting you to come here was a great mistake. It has benefitted
neither of us. It only encourages you in your most cowardly weakness
of character—your ignoble fear of a man's responsibilities in life—
your streak of sickly-mindedness and unbalanced fantasy. And, for
my part, your visits have bored me to exhaustion! Furthermore, my
grandchildren will keep me company again now, and I shall have no
time to spare for you.
With a sneering smile.
Of course, perhaps they might consent to humor you by letting you
take part in their games, but I think it would be bad for you to encourage your morbid childishness. No, on second thought, I will not

permit that either. I forbid you to ever come to this garden again! Do you hear me, Simon?

SIMON
Frowning—with a touch of impatience.
I have heard you talking, yes. But I know you were not really addressing me, but attempting to cheat your own mind. So I paid no attention—

DEBORAH
Uneasily.
Ah.
Tensely.
Will you kindly let go my hand? I wish to go in and join Sara.

SIMON
Quietly.
You know you do not, Mother. What has your rare and fastidious, dreaming poet's soul in common with that mating and begetting female animal who is all material greed?

DEBORAH
Stares at him, her eyes lighting up with satisfaction.
Ah! You see what she really is at least, do you? Haven't I always told you she was nothing more than a common, vulgar—
Abruptly.
No! no! She is a finer woman than I! She is sweet and generous and kind! Why do I let you twist my mind! And you—it is despicable of you to speak like that about a woman who has been such a good wife to you and who loves you so deeply and unselfishly.

SIMON
Sneeringly.
You are speaking of my mistress, I think. But I owe her nothing. She made me pay two-fold the value of every pound of flesh—

DEBORAH
Disdainfully.
What did you expect? She is a natural born—
Then catching herself—jeeringly.

It serves you right! I am very glad she—I told her to make you realize, in the only terms you could understand, what a woman's love is worth!

SIMON
Taunting in his turn.
Oh, I am not grudging her her price. She is very beautiful. No one could have a more desirable mistress!

DEBORAH
Tensely—tugging to pull her hand away.
Let me go! You have become gross and filthy! The touch of your hand disgusts me!
With an abrupt change of tone—sneering jealously.
And you are a blind, besotted fool to call her beautiful! She has youth and health and a certain peasant prettiness, but that is all. She has thick ankles and fat hips and rough dish-washing hands. She—
Violently.
No! You cannot make me think ill of her and enviously criticize her beauty—

SIMON
You are quite right about her repellent fleshiness. I have been so conscious of it lately I have almost screamed with repulsion each time I touched her.

DEBORAH
Her eyes lighting up with vindictive triumph.
Ah, so at last—Oh, I knew it in the end—
Fighting with herself.
No! How dare you disdain the wife who loves you, as if she were a low prostitute you had bought and then grown tired of and were planning to discard—

SIMON
Yes, I have grown tired of her. I have had enough of her. All I want now is to get rid of her forever.

DEBORAH
Eagerly.

Simon! Do you really mean—
Struggling with herself again.
No! You are lying to save your face! You do not fool me! It is she
who is tired of you. Good heavens, what woman wouldn't be disgusted with the greedy, soulless trader in the slave market of life you
have become—the vulgar tasteless lustful owner of goods—the cotton mill Napoleon! It is Sara who had had enough and now is planning to get rid of you! Planning with me! I shall help to find the most
effective means—I shall advise her never to go to your office again.
Why should she waste her youth and beauty now you have nothing
left to offer her!
Vindictively.
We will give you the freedom you used to dream about! We will
laugh when we find you begging on the street of every woman who
passes a little pitying love to save your soul from starvation! And
finally, the solitary soul you used to be so proud of in yourself as a
mark of unique, superior distinction will come cringing and whining and pleading to our door and implore us to open and take you
back in to our love again—at any price!
*She laughs jeeringly—then with an abrupt change to a strange remorse-
ful pity.*
No—forgive me—I do not mean to be cruel and laugh—But you—
Then eagerly.
Simon! Is it true you are really planning to get rid of her now?
Savagely.
Ah! Haven't I prophesied to your office that the time would come
when you would feel so devoured and degraded and enslaved by vice
that you would loathe her and drive her out in the gutter where she
belongs!

SIMON

No. Driving her out in the streets to ply her trade is not the way
to escape her, Mother. She would stand before the door soliciting—
begging for love. It would be her revenge to never allow me to forget
the past. She would still live in my life, greedily possessing it.

DEBORAH
Furiously.

Ah! What a contemptible confession of weakness and cowardice! Have you no pride nor shame that you can admit yourself such a weak, will-less slave?

SIMON
She would still be beautiful and desirable.

DEBORAH
A base slave to a vulgar common trollop! And you call yourself my son!

SIMON
I cannot tell you how sick I am of being a fool who keeps a whore in luxury and power and watches helplessly while she swindles and ruins him. But what can I do when her beauty [arouses] my desire?
Tensely.
Oh, if you knew how desperately I long to escape her and become again only your son!

DEBORAH
Deeply moved—stammers.
I—I know. Dear—I know that must be true because—I have longed so desperately myself—
Then abruptly with a distracted suspicion and resentment.
Oh, how can you lie like that? How can you be such a hypocrite? Do you think I can believe—you have any feeling for me whatever—except scorn and hatred—when you deliberately kept me waiting here hour after hour—deliberately ignored and humiliated—spat in the face of my pride—my love—while you lay in the arms of that low slut and laughed with her to think of me here listening to each footstep on the street, thinking each time—excusing you, and lying to myself—hoping against hope, like a swindled, defrauded fool!
She glares at him with hatred.
Ah, how I hated you! How I cursed the night you were conceived, the morning you were born! How I prayed that you would die and set me free from the intolerable degrading slavery—
She stops, appalled—stammers.
No! I don't mean—I couldn't mean—
Brokenly.

Forgive me—but—Oh Simon, how could you be so horrible and cruel to me!

Then ashamed of her abjectness—her pride forcing a pitiful attempt at a belittling tone.

But how ridiculously emotional and dramatic I sound! So absurd! I fear there must be a great deal of truth in the accusation you always make that I am always acting an unreal part! The truth is I did not much mind your not coming. I was annoyed. Naturally, I do not like absent-minded people who forget appointments. But I was also very glad to be alone for a change, and be relieved of the strain of humoring your fantastic childish whims and morbid yearning with the past. I was free to be myself. It was a pleasure to sit here in my own mind and dream—

She checks herself—sharply.

I would like to go in the house now and join Sara. Will you kindly let go of my hand?

SIMON

Staring into her eyes—slowly and compellingly.

I wish you to sit here beside me, Mother, and let me explain—

DEBORAH

Stares back fascinatedly—with confused eagerness.

Yes, I knew you'd explain when you came. I kept telling myself, he will explain and I will see it was not his fault and forgive him.

She sits on the bench beside him as if his will drove her down.

SIMON

Quietly.

I realize how hurt you must have been, but I thought you would understand it was not I. It was she who insisted I must deliberately forget and return to her instead.

DEBORAH

Tensely.

I know! I knew that must be true! I know my Simon would never—

Then bitterly.

But that doesn't excuse you! You deliberately consented!

SIMON

With tense quiet.

What could I do? She is so beautiful and she demanded it as part of her price. And you must remember that there with her, my life lives in her life, and hers in mine, and I am her Simon, not yours. So how could I wish to remember you?

DEBORAH

Tensely—making a futile movement to rise.

And you think that excuses—I will not listen!

SIMON

Ignoring this.

Just as here with you now, as always in the past before she intruded, my life lies in your life, and yours in mine, and I am your Simon and my one longing is to forget she is alive.

DEBORAH

Immediately eagerly tender.

Yes, Dear, I want you to forget.

SIMON

Goes on in the same tone of tense quiet.

You know her true nature well enough to realize it was she who made me laugh with her in her arms to think of you waiting here like an old fool—

DEBORAH

In a deadly fury.

Yes! I could hear her! The infamous harlot! And to think I just let her deceive me into making peace! But there will be no peace as long as we both remain alive! I will make her pay! Oh, how terribly I hate her! How terribly I wish that she would die! That someone would murder—

She stops frightenedly.

SIMON

In same tone of tense quiet.

I am glad you see there is no possibility of getting rid of her as long as she is alive.

He pauses.
If she were dead, of course—
Insinuatingly.
If someone stumbled and fell against her when she was starting to descend the steep front stairs, it would be obviously an accident if—

DEBORAH
In a shuddering whisper.
Simon!

SIMON
Yes, I agree that is too uncertain.

DEBORAH
Stammers in confused horror.
Agree? But I never—!

SIMON
Poison would be certain. And no one would ever suspect anything but natural illness in an eminent, wealthy family like ours.

DEBORAH
Simon! Good God in heaven, have you gone mad?

SIMON
With a cold impatience.
No. Quite the contrary. I am being extremely sane. I am alive as it is behind our hypocritical pretences and our weak sentimental moral evasions of our natural selves. I am facing the truth. I am dealing with the facts of things as they are. I am not frightened by the bad names we have called certain acts, which in themselves, are perfectly natural and logical—the killing of one's enemies, for example. Our whole cowardly moral code about murder is but another example of the stupid insane impulsion of man's petty vanity to swindle himself into believing human lives are valuable, and related to some God-inspired meaning. But the obvious fact is that their lives are without any meaning whatever—that human life is a silly disappointment, a liar's promise, a perpetual in bankruptcy for debts we never contracted, a daily appointment with peace and happiness in which we wait day after day, hoping against hope, listening to each footstep,

and when finally the bride or the bridegroom cometh, we discover we are kissing Death.

SIMON

DEBORAH
No! Stop!

SIMON
Or, obsessed by a fairy tale, we spend our lives searching for a magic door and a lost kingdom of peace from which we have been dispossessed by a greedy swindler.

DEBORAH
Suddenly taunting.
Ah, if you are going to start harping on that childish nonsense—

SIMON
And when we find it we stand and beg before it. But the door is never opened. And at last we die and the starving scavenger hogs of life devour our carrion!
With sudden strange fury.
No, by God, it shall not happen to me! What has been taken from me, I take back!

DEBORAH
Terrified.
Simon! Don't look like that! You frighten me!

SIMON
Quietly again.
So, let us not be sentimental and vain about the value of others' lives to us, Mother. Of our own lives to ourselves. Regarded sensibly, we should all have clauses in our wills expressing gratitude to, and suitably rewarding anyone who should murder us. The murderer, I think, possesses the true quality of mercy.
He chuckles sardonically.
So, although I know how you have always, at any cost, escaped confronting facts—

DEBORAH
With strange scorn.

You are a fool! As if I did not once think exactly as you have been thinking. I used to sit alone in there in disdainful self-contemplation
She looks at the summerhouse.
and make my mind face every fact until my thoughts beat with broken bleeding hands at the walls of my brain and I longed to escape by any door—
Stops abruptly—staring frightenedly at the door.
But I do not wish to remember that dead woman!

SIMON
As if she hadn't spoken.
You must at least admit it—your right in self-defense to kill the enemy who plots to destroy. Surely you cannot be blind to the fact that Sara's jealous hatred has reached a pitch now where she will use any means whatsoever to get rid of you.

DEBORAH
Eagerly.
Yes! I know!
Struggling with herself.
No! It's a lie! She would never—

SIMON
And you must acknowledge that in your mind you have murdered her countless times. So I cannot see why the thought should make you shudder now.

DEBORAH
Confusedly.
Yes, I confess I have dreamed—But those were dreams. Now it becomes real—when you put it in my mind. It begins to live in my will. It is born. It begins to me, to direct itself toward a consummation, like a destiny!
Struggling with herself.
No! I will not let you put it in my mind!
With wild desperation.
But you have! It is there now! It will go on! I cannot stop it! And one day soon I will be hating her young body and her pretty face, and

I will follow her to the top of the stairs—! Or I will remember the gardener keeps arsenic in the cellar for killing vermin—!

Deliberately jumping to her feet.

No! I couldn't—I couldn't! It is your thought, not mine! How can you think your mother—You are horrible! How could I have born such a cruel, evil monster into the world! You terrify me! You are insane! I am afraid to be alone with you!

Pulling at her hand.

Let me go! I will call Sara!

She calls.

Sara! Sara!

SIMON

Keeps hold of her hand—quietly.

She cannot hear. She is too busy devouring her children.

He pulls her gently back—quietly.

Come. Sit down, Mother. What have you and I to do with her—except to plan together how we may be free of her?

Persuasively.

I am sorry if I frightened you by forcing you to confront your desire to murder her.

DEBORAH

Weakly letting herself be pulled down beside him.

No! Not my wish! Yours!

SIMON

I did it to make you realize what must inevitably happen soon. That the hate between you has reached a crisis—that one life can no longer contain you both without being torn apart and destroyed!

He suddenly bursts out with a terrible intensity.

I tell you I have reached the end of the tether! I cannot go on! One of you must cease to live in me! It is you or she! Can't you see I am trying to make clear to you that I have chosen you?

DEBORAH

Her face lighting up with a passionate joy.

You mean—you really mean— Oh, I know! I knew in the end I could not fail! Oh, my son! My beloved son!

Then frightened.
But not murder— You must not murder—promise me you will
not—

SIMON

No. There is another way for us to be free.

DEBORAH

Ah! Oh, I will do anything, if you will not compel me to murder!
What—?

SIMON

We will leave her here. We will go together so far away from the
reality that not even the memory of her can follow to haunt my
mind. We will go back where she never existed. You have only to open
that door—
His eyes fasten on the summerhouse door with a fascinated longing.

DEBORAH

Stares at it with dread and longing herself—forcing a belittling tone.
Now, Dear, you mustn't start harping on that fantastic childish nonsense again!

SIMON

*Ignoring this—gets to his feet—holding her hand, his eyes on the door—
eagerly.*
But we must hurry, Mother. She will come back before long. She will
try to keep me within her greed. She will open her arms to me. She
is very beautiful. She will make me believe her lust is love.

DEBORAH

Her face hardening—gets to her feet.
No! I am willing to pay any price to save you from her, and if this is
the one possible way, so be it!
*She takes a step toward the door—then her eyes fixed on it, she recoils,
shuddering, stammers.*
No! Wait!

SIMON

His eyes on the door—fascinated.

I have waited ever since I was a little boy. All my life since then I have stood outside that door in my mind, begging you to let me re-enter that lost life of peace and trustful faith and happiness! I cannot wait any longer, Mother. And you cannot wait. You must choose between me and yourself. You once chose yourself and drove me out, and that has happened since [then].* Now you must either choose to repudiate that old choice, and give me back the faith you stole from me, or I will choose her!

DEBORAH
No!

SIMON
I will choose her! And then there will be no choice left to you but to run and hide within yourself in there again, and dream yourself into the madhouse to escape yourself!

DEBORAH
Horrified.
Simon! For God's sake, how can you say such things to your mother who loves you more than life! As if you wished—

SIMON
I wish to be free, Mother!

DEBORAH
Anguished.
Oh! You can admit that to me!

SIMON
Free of one of my two selves, of one of the enemies within my mind, before their duel for possession destroys it. I have no longer any choice but to choose. Either you and all the life of dreams, in which love is spirit, of which you are the living symbol in my mind—or her and all the world of reality in which flesh is fact, and love is the body's lust. To belong wholly to either is my one possible escape now. *He adds grimly.*

---

*The typescript reads "since began." I have substituted "since then" to retain the logic of the thought.

Or would you prefer I should go insane—and so be rid of me again?

DEBORAH
Shuddering.
No! Oh, how can you say—! You must be insane already or you wouldn't—

SIMON
I am waiting, Mother—for you to open that door, and give me back what was mine—my kingdom of the spirit's faith in life and love that your greed for yourself dispossessed me from!

DEBORAH
Bitterly.
So it was all my doing, was it? You have changed your tune! You have always boasted your love of liberty and the natural rights of man left of its own free will!
She sneers tauntingly.

SIMON
You are speaking of something my pride was forced to choose long after I had been driven out in spirit. Naturally, to keep my self-respect—to go on living at all—I had to pretend I had found more worthy objects for my dreams—and, to the outside world to which you exiled me, a more unselfish object for my love, someone who would be mine, and not I, hers!

DEBORAH
Her eyes gleaming with satisfaction—tauntingly.
And how Sara has turned the tables and cheated you, poor boy! How common prettiness has but to smile and pretend desire for your desire and you begin begging on your knees!
She laughs.
I must warn you to take care, Dear. Your pride is making the most humiliating confessions for a Napoleon among men! Why, I begin to think now you were to have no life at all that did not hide within a woman's life—that you have never loved liberty at all but hated and dreaded it!
She laughs mockingly.

SIMON
Coldly.
You are compelling me to choose her.
He lets go her hand.
Very well. I shall go to her. Do not attempt to follow me in the house.
I shall lock you out as you once did me. You will stay here alone until
you do what you must do to escape. I have no doubt you will find
happiness in a foolish dream as a King's courtesan! And I shall be
free to be Sara's—body and soul. Goodbye, Mother.
He turns to go.

DEBORAH
Grabs his hand—pleading frantically.
No! For God's sake, don't leave me alone here! I will do anything
you ask!
*She leads him a step towards the door—then falters again and begins to
argue desperately as if she were trying to convince a child.*
But—it is all so silly and childish—so absurd and perverse—and revolting—for you, a grown man—a great man of worldly affairs—to
remember—to make into a literal fact—an old fairy story—a passing fantasy of my brain—I made up in an idle moment to amuse you
and make you laugh.

SIMON
With bitter hatred.
You know that is a lie, Mother! To make me realize you hated your
love for me because it possessed you and you wanted to be free! To
hurt me, to taunt me, to laugh at my love, to force me from you back
into myself! That's why you told it!

DEBORAH
Weakly.
No! How can you think I could be so cruel to my beloved little boy?
Then defensively.
But even if what you accuse me of is true, surely I had a right to own
my own life!

SIMON
Ignoring this.

You know I knew who you meant by the evil enchantress and that I was the exiled Prince!

DEBORAH
Defensively.
You are being ridiculous. That was your old selfish demand that I might not even dream of myself without including you!
Trying to argue again—desperately.
But surely you see how idiotic it is to connect the door and that silly tale, which has no existence except in your fanciful imagination, with the actual wooden door of a common old summerhouse—the one we see so clearly in the moonlight now! Why that—that really is insane, Simon.

SIMON
Tensely.
I know very well it is a wooden door to an actual summerhouse— in the reality outside us— But I know, too, as you know, that in the deeper reality inside us, it has the meaning our minds have given it.

DEBORAH
Your mind has given it one meaning, but in mine it has an opposite—you think it is the door to some fantastic dream of Heaven, but I remember the hell—

SIMON
Ignoring this—obsessedly.
It exists in our minds as a symbol of our destiny, a door through which you drove me out of your love when you became evil and greedy for a false freedom. Surely you see that is what you meant in your symbolic fairy tale?

DEBORAH
No! No! It was merely a humorous fantasy—a capricious whim! I meant nothing!

SIMON
In same tone.
The actual door there is a necessary concrete symbol. Your opening it and leading me inside will be the necessary physical act by which

your mind wills to take me back into your love, to repudiate your treachery in driving me out of your heart, to deny the evil ruthless woman your dreams of freedom made you and become again your old true self, the mother who loved me alone, whom alone I loved!
He smiles at her with a sudden awkward tenderness.
So you see it is all perfectly rational and logical in my mind, and there is nothing insane about it, Mother. The kingdom of peace and happiness in your story is love. You dispossessed yourself when you dispossessed me. Since then we have both been condemned to an insatiable, unscrupulous greed for substitutes to fill the emptiness, the loss of love we had left within us.
He stares obsessedly at the door again.
But you have only to open that door, Mother—which is really a door on your own mind—

DEBORAH
With a shudder.
I know!—and I know only too well the escape it leads to!

SIMON
Pats her hand—tenderly persuasive, but his eyes are fixed on the door.
Forget those silly fears, Mother. They came after. We have gone back before they existed, or the woman who dreamed them existed. Just as we are now back in a life before Sara existed in me and I in her. We have got rid of her.

DEBORAH
Eagerly.
Yes! I will pay anything to do that to her!

SIMON
We are back here in your garden on the day you told me that story.
He pauses—then turns on her with a bitter vindictive condemnation.
You knew I knew what you meant me to know! I have never forgotten the anguished sense of being suddenly betrayed, of being wounded and deserted and left alone in a life in which there was no security or faith or love but only danger and suspicion and devouring greed!
Harshly.

By God, I hated you then! I wished you dead! I wished I had never been born!

DEBORAH
DEBORAH

With an obviously fake air of contrition thinly masking a strange, cruel satisfaction.

Did you, Dear? I am sorry if I hurt you. It is true I hoped you would guess what I meant. You were such a stubborn greedy little boy, so inquisitive and pryishly possessive. I could feel your grasping fingers groping toward every secret, private corner of my soul. I had come to the point when I even preferred Joel because I was utterly indifferent to him, where at times I hated you and wished you had never been born. So I had to do something to warn you, and I thought a fairy tale would be the most tactful way—

Abruptly her expression changes to one of horror for herself—distractedly.

No! I never meant—! You put it in my mind! It's insane of you to make me confess such horrible things! And how can you admit you hated your mother and wished her dead!

SIMON

Contritely stammers.

I—Forgive me, Mother!—I did only because you—

Then passionately.

All I ask is that you go back and change that—change the ending—open the door and take me back—and all that has happened since, which you began that day, will be out of memory, forgotten! There will be only love and faith and trust in life—the old greedless security and content with what we have! There will be only you and I! There will be peace and happiness to the end of our days! Can't you believe me, Mother? I tell you I know!

DEBORAH

Shakingly—staring at the door fascinatedly.

Oh, if I could, Dear! If I only could believe, how willingly I would go! If you knew how I have loved you, how desperately I have longed to have you back, to take you from her, to know you were mine alone, to be nothing but your mother, to live and forget myself, to live solely in your life, to make any sacrifice of self with happiness, exultantly in self-fulfillment, to dream no dream except to love you more and more!

Passionately.

Yes! I think I believe now—believe that if the mind wills anything with enough intensity of love it can force life to its desire, create a heaven, if need be, out of hell!

With a strange triumphant laugh.

Yes, taking you with me, I would have no fear of insanity, for all is fair in love, and love would make it sane.

SIMON

Strangely.

Yes, we need not concern ourselves with the bad names men have given to things they fear or do not understand.

He laughs harshly.

Good God, if the reality of hoggish greed and dog eat dog and lust devour love is sane, then what man of honorable mind would not prefer to be considered lunatic!

With sudden urgency.

Come, Mother! Let us leave this vile sty of lust and hatred and the wish to murder! Let us escape back into peace—while there is still time!

DEBORAH

With forced eagerness, mounts the first step.

Yes, let us hurry, Dear—before I can think—

Then stops—desperately.

But I must warn you—I could never forgive myself if I did not warn you once more of the danger—

SIMON

Scornfully proud.

Danger? Don't you know Sara has made me a greedy gambler who loves danger and the greatest possible risk? What do I care if the fate in there has stacked the cards and loaded the dice? I promise you I will outswindle it and steal our happiness and love from under its nose!

Boastfully.

What I want I have the power to take, and will always take! You forget they do not call me a Napoleon of trade without my having proven my right to the title!

DEBORAH

Hangs back resentfully now—almost jeeringly.

You had better not boast of your power to enslave, for I warn you you may bitterly regret your daring if you find it is, in truth, the evil enchantress of my fairy tale who waits there to enslave you in her arms! If I remember the mad woman I locked in there, she must have chosen madness long ago, because she was entirely ruthless and unscrupulous, a daring courtesan who takes what she wants by any means she can, even madness. She will not recognize you as her son! She never had a child. Her pride would have made her kill herself before she would ever have shared herself, or seen her beauty grow bloated and misshapen, with an alien's possession! Her arrogance would never put her life in bondage to another's life, or create another she would be forced to love as she loved herself! She has loved herself alone! She has remained free! You will be no more than another man to her—that is, no more than a slave to her every whim and caprice—like the King before she discarded him to make a fool of Napoleon whom her poor weakling of a father confused with God and himself!

She stops abruptly—guiltily confused—and stammers stupidly.

I—please do not mind me—I do not think I know what I was saying—

SIMON

Has turned on her sneeringly.

I should hope not! You remember how I had to laugh at you the time you boasted to me of that preposterous romantic evil dream about yourself! You, my poor little, old mother!

He gives a taunting, sneering chuckle.

DEBORAH

Stung—with furious hatred.

How dare you—!

Then with a sudden change to an ominous gentleness.

But I see. You are so cunning to get your own way by any means, aren't you, Dear—like Napoleon? You were clever enough to see that while love might make me hesitate, for your sake, hate would give me the necessary courage to be quite ruthless in thinking only of winning a final victory over her.

She laughs softly, turns abruptly and goes up the remaining steps—tenderly.

Come, Dear. Mother is only too glad to do anything you ask her to now.

SIMON

Strangely.

We will go far back before that laughter existed, Mother. You will not know you ever heard it, then, or that I ever laughed. There will be peace and unity. We shall have gone back beyond separations. We shall be one again.

Suddenly in a panic.

But hurry, Mother! Hurry! I hear someone coming! It must be she! But I will run away from her now and hide in my mind back there in our past together. She will be a stranger!

DEBORAH

Begins to assume an air of a cruel ruthless gratification.

Let her come! It will add strength to my hatred! And it will be a pleasure to have her witness my final victory! Now I have decided, I am stronger than she ever dared to be!

She moves so that she stands protectingly before Simon, her right hand on the knob of the door. Sara comes hurrying in from the left. She is in a panic of apprehensive dread. When she sees them both still outside the summerhouse, this changes to rage against Deborah.

SARA

To Deborah.

You liar! You thief! You black-hearted traitor! I should have known better than to leave you—But God be praised I'm back in time!

DEBORAH

Jeering quietly.

Yes. You are just in time—to bid us farewell!

SARA

Frightened—forcing a commanding tone.

Simon! Come here to me away from that door! Do you want to lose
what little wits you've left, playing her crazy games with her?

*But Simon appears not to have heard her, or to have noticed her coming.
He keeps behind his mother turned sideways to Sara, his eyes fixed fascinatedly on the door.*

DEBORAH

Addressing him over her shoulder, her eyes on Sara.

My love, you no longer remember this woman, do you? You will not
permit a vulgar, common slut to intrude and delay our departure.

SIMON

*Starts and turns his head to stare at Sara without recognition over his
mother's shoulder. His face has a strange, mad, trance-like look. He murmurs obediently.*

No, Mother.

He addresses Sara with a sharp arrogance.

Who are you? What do you want? How dare you trespass here and
start making a disgusting scene? Do you think my mother's garden
is the parlor of a brothel?

SARA

Shrinks as if she'd been struck—strickenly.

Simon! Don't speak like—

SIMON

By what right do you presume to call me by my first name? I do not
know you.

Strangely.

It is true you remind me of a mistress I once bought to amuse myself
observing her greedy attempt to swindle me of myself. But it was I
who swindled her by paying her with counterfeit appearances. Then
when her lust began to bore me, I deserted her and went off with
another woman, an old lover in my childhood.

He adds hastily.

Whom I loved with a great pure love, a spiritual love of the mind and the soul, rare and beautiful, her ethereal passion, a love belonging to fantasy and dreams!

SARA
Trembling.
Simon! It is mad you are!

SIMON
Disdainfully—as if he were addressing a servant.
Begone! Before I summon the police!
Pointing to a door in wall at right.
That door leads to the street where you belong. Go back and ply your trade there. Your body defiles the pure atmosphere of my mother's garden.

SARA
Pitifully.
Darling! It's I! Your Sara!

DEBORAH
Gloating—haughtily.
You have my son's orders!
Then to Simon.
But I think, Dear, it might be simpler for us to leave her now.

SIMON
Eagerly.
Yes, Mother. Let us go!

DEBORAH
Exultantly.
Yes! I can now! I am as strong as I ever wished to be in any dream! I will take what my whim desires from life, and laugh at the cost!
She laughs and with an abrupt movement jerks open the door behind her so it stands back against the wall. Simon gives a gasping eager cry and leans forward, staring into the darkness inside. But Deborah does not turn to it but remains confronting Sara.

SARA
Wildly.

No!
Rushes up and grabs Deborah's skirt and falls on her knees before her.
For the love of God have pity, Deborah!

DEBORAH
Starts.
Pity?
Then angrily.
Would you remind me of pity now, you scheming slut?

SARA
Pleadingly.
Remember I had pity on you!

DEBORAH
You lie! I will not remember! I have forgotten pity.
She kicks at Sara viciously.
How dare you hold me! Let me free!

SARA
Pleadingly.
I'm asking your pity for him, not for me! You love him! You can't do this!

DEBORAH
Scornful.
You weak sentimental fool! Love is proud, not pitiful! It takes what it desires!
Hastily.
You dare to speak of pity! You, the harlot whose greed is devouring him and driving him insane! It's because I love him that I must save him from your destroying lust! So let go!
She kicks her skirt from Sara's hand and half turns to the door, grabbing Simon's arm.
Come, Dear! Quick! Let us go where we cannot hear her lies about love and pity!

SIMON
With a crazy eagerness.

Yes! The door is open! I feel our old peace and happiness waiting to welcome us! Take my hand, Mother!

SARA

Wildly, grabbing Deborah's skirt again.

No! Wait! Listen! Deborah! I give up! I admit I'm beaten now! I'll pay you any price you ask, if only—

DEBORAH

Triumphantly.

Ah! So you admit—I always knew that in the end—

Then with arrogant disdain.

You have the impertinence to believe there is anything you possess that I could be so low as to desire? You flatter yourself!

SIMON

Turns his head a little from staring inside the summerhouse—dazedly and uneasily.

Sara? Sara? Who? Who are you talking to, Mother? What is she trying to make me remember? How could I? This is long before any other woman. There is only your love. I do not need her. Make her leave us alone, Mother!—so we can go back to peace.

DEBORAH

Cruelly scornful and at the same time uneasy.

Yes, I will not listen to her pleading lies! We will go—

SARA

In anguish.

Simon! Darling! It's her madness in there! It's the asylum!

DEBORAH

Shakenly—fighting back fiercely.

You lie! Our minds will compel it to be our dream! Our love can make a heaven even in hell if we are together—if we are one again!

She half turns to Simon but keeps her eyes averted from the doorway.

Do not listen to this low, vulgar harlot, Dear! What could she know of the transfiguring power of the mind, or the miraculous power of the spirit, she whose soul is a pound of greedy flesh!

She reaches out her hand which he clasps eagerly.

Here is my hand, Dear! Come!

She tries to [   ] determinedly—to rush in with her eyes shut, leading him.

SARA

Distractedly—throws herself forward and flings her arms around Deborah's legs—pleading wildly.

For the love of God! For the love of your son, Deborah! You can't! And don't you see there's no need now! You can have him back without—I'm telling you I'll give him up to you! I'll go away! I'll leave him to you! I'll never trouble you again! You'll be rid of me! And that's all you've wanted, isn't it? So, for the love of God, stop—!

DEBORAH

Stares at her, her face lighting up eagerly, but unable to believe her ears.

You really mean—you will give up—go away—never again intrude or trespass—on what is mine?

SARA

I will—for love of him—to save him. You can have him all to yourself again. I know I can trust your love for him, once I'm out of the way, to protect him from himself—and from your own mad dreams. And I know, when he has only you to love, he'll forget me, and he won't be destroyed and torn between us within himself.

DEBORAH

Eagerly.

Yes! I swear to you I will protect and make him contented and at peace with life.

Complacently.

After all, I am his mother, and I would give my life for him.

Relaxing with a smile of triumph.

Ah!

Then immediately with suspicious anger.

You're lying! This is all another of your cunning tricks! Do you still think I trust you?

SARA

Dully.

No, Deborah. I'm beyond tricks now. I'm finished.

DEBORAH
Smiles down at her with contemptuous gloating.
You must be utterly beaten, then—more beaten than I ever hoped you could be! Evidently, I gave you credit for more strength and pride than you possess!
Sneeringly.
But I think I see! You've swindled him out of everything he owns, except what you find you cannot steal—what is mine—himself! So now, having got all you can, he's useless to you and you'll discard him like the unscrupulous slut you are, and go soliciting a new victim! Is that it?
She sneers insultingly. A strange angry hostility is creeping into her attitude as if, now she had won a complete victory, she was beginning to feel it was a defeat.

SARA
Dully.
No. I'll sign all that over to you. I don't want it. All I'll keep is the old farm, so I'll have a home for my children, and can make a living with them. I'll take them there tomorrow.
She gets to her feet slowly and exhaustedly.

SIMON
Who has remained tense and motionless, staring fascinatedly into the darkness inside the summerhouse—in a boyish uneasy whisper, tugging at her hand.
Why are you waiting, Mother? We mustn't wait—or it may be too late! You will get afraid again.
But neither woman seems to hear him.

DEBORAH
Sneering more insultingly.
You are welcome to the farm. I am glad you at last realize what you are and where you belong. A stupid peasant tilling the soil, her bare feet in the earth, her gross body stinking of sweat, a dumb brainless, begetting female animal with her dirty brats around her!
Jeeringly.

But what becomes of your grand estate, and the ridiculous Irish dream castle in Spain?

SARA

Resignedly—without resentment.
That was foolishness. I'm done with that, too.

DEBORAH

Sneeringly.
What virtuous Christian resignation! How shamelessly abject and humble you are!

SARA

Quietly.
If I'm humbled, it's by myself and my love, not by you.
With a flash of pride.
And I'm proud of that. For, if I'll never rise to owning a grand estate now, I've risen in life now in the only way that counts, above myself, which is more than you'll ever do! I can wish him happiness without me, and mean it! Yes, and I can even wish you to be happy so you can make him happy, and mean that, too!

DEBORAH

For an instant moved in spite of herself—stammers gratefully.
I—thank you, Sara—you are generous and fine—
Then in a burst of sneering hostility.
You lie! You cannot fool me! This is all cheap acting, and the role of sacrificed, unselfish love is absolutely fake to your true nature!
Jeeringly.
The truth is what I have always known! You are incapable of love! I alone really love him because I would rather see him dead—or kill him myself!—than give him up to another woman!

SARA

Quietly.
You don't believe that. You know no woman could love a man more than when she gives him up to save him!

DEBORAH

With strange repressed fury.

I know—I begin to see your scheme—the trick behind—with your superior self-sacrificial airs—you want to show me you—to make me feel vile and contemptible—

SARA
Quietly and exhaustedly.
No. I've told you I'm beyond scheming. I'm too—dead.
Dully.
I'll leave you now, Deborah. I'll get the children up now and take them to a hotel where he can't find us. You keep him out here until I'm gone. That's the best way, to get it over and done now. You can explain in any way you think it best for you and him. But make it strong that I'm sick of him, and I'm getting another man and I never want to see him again. Give him a good excuse to give himself to forget me. That's all he needs to bring him peace with you alone.
Then giving Simon a worried look.
And look out you bring him back to his senses right away now. It isn't good for him to stay long—so far away in the past as you've taken him.
She turns to go off left—brokenly, without looking at him.
God bless you, Simon, Darling, for all the joy and love you gave me, and give you peace and happiness!

SIMON
With a sort of bewildered anguish.
Mother! Someone is calling me! I'll have to go! I cannot remain back here much longer! Hurry, Mother! Hurry!

SARA
Goodbye, Deborah.
She starts to walk away.

DEBORAH
Stammers weakly.
No—Sara—
Then fiercely.
Goodbye and good riddance! Get out! Go! Leave me alone! I hate the sight of you!
Then brokenly.

No, Sara—forgive—wait—I want to say—my gratitude—want to tell you—you are beautiful and fine—so much more beautiful—fine—than I—

Then bursting into a jealous fury, glaring at her with hatred.

Ah, God damn you. You low, scheming trollop! Do you think I don't see through you? All this hypocritical sentimental posing! Your false self-sacrificial airs! You the noble loving woman! I am the evil one who desires her son's life! Whose greed does not scruple to use any means—base and utterly ignoble—cruel and insatiable. You dare insult me so!—humiliate and put me to shame before my son!—my beloved son—You dare to boast before him you love him more than I, his mother, who, ever since the day I bore him, would gladly give my life for his happiness! As if a low lustful creature like you could even imagine the depth of the love I have for him, let alone feel it! And yet you have the vulgar effrontery to pretend—

In a fresh burst of savage passion.

You liar! But I'll prove to you who is the final victor between us, who is the one who loves him most!

She turns to face the darkness within the doorway.

SIMON
With an eager cry.
Mother! At last! Hurry! She is coming to take me!

SARA
Frightenedly.
Simon!

DEBORAH
Pulls her hand violently from his.
No! Alone!

SIMON
Despairingly—grabbing at her hand.
Mother!

DEBORAH
Flings his hand away—with a strange boastful arrogance.
Alone, I said! As I have always been. As my pride and disdain have

always willed I be!—hating the vile sordid ugliness of life—choosing to keep my spirit pure and untouched and unpossessed!—my soul my own!—at any cost—at any sacrifice—

Looking at him now with repulsion.

Go away! Do not dare to touch me! What are you to me! I am my own! Ah, how could I have ever been so weak as to allow you to intrude on my dream and involve me in a filthy sordid intrigue with a greedy, money-grabbing merchant and his peasant slut of a wife! I, if I had been born in a nobler time, could have had the love of a King or an Emperor!

To Simon with hatred.

You—get back to the greasy arms of your wife where you belong!

With extraordinary strength she gives him a push in the chest that drives him off balance and sends him spinning down the steps to fall heavily and lie still by the stone bench at left of pool.

SARA

Flings herself on her knees beside him and raises his head.

Simon!

He stirs and moans feebly.

DEBORAH

Turns and stops on the threshold, confronting the darkness—with a self-contemptuous laugh.

To think you were afraid, Deborah! Why, what is waiting to welcome you is merely your last disdain!

She goes in quietly and shuts the door.

SARA

Oblivious to her going.

Darling! Are you hurt bad?

She feels his body.

I can't find anything broken—but I heard his head hit—

SIMON

Suddenly raises his head and stares at the door and mutters stupidly the unhappy end of the fairy story.

So the Prince waited before the door and begged for love from all who passed by.

He falls back in her arms in a faint.

SARA
Frightenedly.
Simon! Merciful God! Speak to me, Darling!
In a panic she puts her hand over his heart — relieved.
No, he's only fainted.
She chafes his wrists.
Maybe it's best. He'd be trying to get in there.
She stops rubbing his wrists and turns to stare at the summerhouse — in an awed horrified whisper.
God help me, she's done it.
With admiration.
Ah, it's a great noble lady you couldn't help proving yourself in the end, and it's you that beat me, for your pride paid a price for love my pride would never dare to pay!
She shudders — then with growing intensity.
But I swear to you now, Deborah, I'll try to keep up my end of the bargain and pay back all I can. I see now the part my greed and my father's crazy dreams in me had in leading Simon away from himself until he lost his way and began destroying all that was best in him! To make me proud of him!
Brokenly.
Ah, forgive me, Darling! But I'll give my life now to setting you free to be again the man you were when I first met you — the man I loved best! — the dreamer with a touch of the poet in his soul, and the heart of a boy!
With a strange almost masochistic satisfaction.
Don't I know, Darling, the longing in your heart that I'd smash the Company into smithereens to prove my love for you and set you free from the greed of it! Well, by the Eternal, I'll smash it so there'll be nothing left to tempt me! It's easy. It needs only a whisper of the true condition to Tenard, pretending I'm a fool woman who takes him into her confidence, now he's in the Company.
With a gloating smile.
I can hear the revenge in his heart laughing, rushing out to tell all our enemies and combine with them to pounce down and ruin us!

Well, they can't take the old farm anyway, and we'll live there, and the boys will work with me, and you'll never have to lift your hand again, but you can spend your days in your old cabin where you first were mine, and write poetry again of your love for me, and plan your book that will save the world and free men from the curse of greed in them!

She pauses guiltily.

God forgive me, I'm happy at the mere thought of it, and it's no price at all I'll be paying to match yours, Deborah, if I'm happy!

Then with an abrupt change to practical calculation.

That reminds me, before I start the whisper, I'll get all the Company's cash from the banks and put it in her name, along with this house, with Joel to take care of it, so she'll have enough and plenty to keep her here, with her garden, and the comfort and riches and luxury that's due the great Princess on her grand estate she'll be on in her dream till the day she dies!

While she has been saying this last, the door of the summerhouse has slowly opened and Deborah has appeared. She now stands on the top of the steps. Her eyes have a still, fixed, sightless, trance-like look, but her face is proud, self-assured, arrogant and happy, and she looks beautiful and serene, and many years younger.

DEBORAH

In a tone of haughty command.

Be quiet! Who is talking? How dare you come here? Who are you?

SARA

Starts and stares at her—in an awed whisper.

Ah, God pity her, the poor woman!

DEBORAH

Coming down the steps—As she does so, Sara gets to her feet, letting Simon's head rest back on the grass.

Answer me!

A look of recognition comes over her face—with a regal gracious condescension.

Ah, you are the Irish kitchen maid, are you not? I remember you—

SARA

An impulse of angry insult flashes in her eyes—but immediately she controls this, whispering pityingly to herself.

Poor creature! She's hidden herself in her dream forever!

DEBORAH

Approaching her, erect and arrogant and graceful, her head held high.

What are you doing in the Palace grounds at this hour, poor peasant? Do you not know there is a terrible punishment for trespassing in my domain?

SARA

Humoring her—bobs her an awkward servant-girl curtsy and speaks humbly.

I know I have no right here, My Lady. If you'll be kind enough to forgive me, I'll never intrude again.

DEBORAH

This garden is the Emperor's gift to me. He is very jealous of my privacy.

Then with a cautious backward glance at the summerhouse.

Sush, we must not wake him.

With a soft gloating little laugh.

But he sleeps soundly. My love is too great for him. It devours him. In my arms, he is so weak—so like a little boy, the Great Napoleon! So small, compared to my great love! He will give me the world, and still it will be too little!

Then suddenly—sharply and suspiciously.

Why are you silent? Do you dare to doubt me?

SARA

Humbly.

Indeed I don't, Your Majesty.

DEBORAH

Reassured and pleasant.

I am not Majesty, my poor woman. Of course, if it were my whim— He would gladly divorce his wife, who is a stupid, common woman, quite unworthy. But I tell him marriage is a trader's bargain. It corrupts love which shall be always beautiful and free.

Then with a condescending kindliness.

But you would not understand that. You have not told me why you are here, poor peasant. You came to keep an assignation with your lover, I suppose. Doubtless some groom from my stables. You peasants are such animals. But never mind. I am disposed tonight to be lenient toward all lovers, for love's sake. I forgive you.

SARA

With another curtsy.

Thank you, My Lady.

Then impulsively.

I wanted to ask you to forgive me, Deborah.

DEBORAH

Wonderingly.

Deborah? Who is Deborah?

Her eyes fall on Simon. She starts—then indifferently.

Who is that lying at your feet? Your lover? Is he dead? Did you murder him for love of him? Oh, do not be afraid. I understand everything a woman's love could possibly compel her to desire. I know she can even kill herself to prove her love, so proud can she be of it.

SARA

Quietly.

I am sure you know that, My Lady.

She stares at Deborah and suddenly her face is convulsed with a look of horrified suspicion and she grabs her by the arm and stammers.

For the love of God, Deborah, tell me you're not just pretending now—for love of him, to save him and set him free! That would be too great a price—I couldn't let you—!

DEBORAH

Trembles and seems about to collapse—avoiding Sara's eyes, falteringly.

I—I do not understand you—You must not—!

Suddenly she is the arrogant grand dame again—with haughty anger—snatching Sara's hand off her arm.

You forget yourself. Do not presume to touch me. Your presence wearies me. I must go back to the Emperor. See that you take your lover away at once and never return here.

SARA

Stammers.

Yes, My Lady.

Confusedly to herself.

No, no—I'm a fool. She's really gone forever in her dreams! But— Tell me this, are you happy now? Ah,—My Lady?

DEBORAH

Smiles condescendingly.

You are impertinent. But I forgive it, because I *am* happy. And I wish you may be happy with your lover, too.

Haughtily.

But now farewell, good woman.

She holds out her hand arrogantly.

You may kneel and kiss my hand.

SARA

A flash of insulted pride comes to her eyes and for a second she seems about to retreat angrily—then impulsively she kneels and kisses her hand.

Thank you for your great kindness, My Lady.

Deborah turns from her to ascend the steps. Sara adds huskily.

And God bless you.

DEBORAH

Ascending the steps, looks back, with a smile of gracious understanding amusement.

Why, thank you, good woman. I think that I may say that He has blessed me.

She goes in the summerhouse and closes the door behind her.

SARA

Stares after her—miserably.

I wonder—I wonder—Oh, God help me, I'll never be sure of the truth of it now!

Simon groans and stirs and looks up at her.

SIMON
Murmurs stupidly.
Mother. Hurry. Let us go. Peace and happiness.

SARA
At once forgetting everything but him.
Yes, Darling. We'll go. Come on. Raise yourself.
She bends and puts her arm around his shoulder to help him.
That's it.

SIMON
Dazedly—like a little boy.
I fell and hit my head, Mother. It hurts.

SARA
I'll bathe it for you when we get in the house. Come along now.
She turns him into the path leading off left and urges him along it.

SIMON
Dazedly.
Yes, Mother.

SARA
With a fierce, passionate possessive tenderness.
Yes, I'll be your mother, too, now, and your peace and happiness and all you'll ever need in life!
They disappear off left.

CURTAIN

Tao House
Dec. 30, '38

Epilogue

SCENE

Same as Act One, Scene Two, Simon's old cabin by the lake on the farm. It is a late afternoon of a fine day in early June of the following year, 1842.

There is a great change in the cabin and little clearing from the abandoned, neglected appearance it had in the first act scene of 1832. The grass, a fresh green, has been cut and the paths across it from the woods at left to the door of the cabin, and from the door down to the shore of the lake, off right, are clearly defined. The windows of the cabin are washed and clean, with their frames a newly painted white. The chinks in the logs have been caulked, the chimney patched up with fresh mortar. The bench against the wall of the cabin has been painted green.

Sara's and Simon's youngest son, Owen Roe "Honey" Harford, is discovered, squatting on his heels on the grass before the bench, playing a game with a jackknife, flipping it from his fingers to make it stick in the ground. He wears only an old shirt and a pair of short pants. Both are dirty. So are his sunburned, freckled face, his hands and bare legs and feet. He is going on nine and a half now, is big for his age, stout and healthy. His face is typically Irish with blue eyes, dark curly hair, and he has a marked resemblance to his mother. His expression is happy and good-natured. He has a charming ingratiating grin and a sparkle of sly, droll humor in his inquisitive eyes. As he plays he sings softly Thomas Moore's "Believe me if all those endearing young charms." He has a fine voice, clear and pure.

His brother, Jonathan, next to him in age, a year and a half older, comes in from the path at left. Although older he is smaller than Honey, under-

sized, thin and wiry, with a large head out of proportion with his body. His face is long, with a big nose, and sharp intelligent grey eyes, and straight mouse-colored hair. He is dressed much the same as Honey but his clothes are clean, as are his face and hands and legs. He gives one the impression of being older than his years, full of a tense nervous vitality, but remarkably self-disciplined and sure of his own capabilities. Between these two younger brothers the relationship is one of close affection with Jonathan the leader, a bit bullyingly superior and condescending, and Honey an admiring satellite, but not so admiring he does not poke constant fun at him.

JONATHAN
Stops just inside the clearing and attracts his brother's attention.
Ssstt!
Honey looks up. Jonathan beckons and Honey goes to him without stopping his song. Jonathan asks in a low voice.
Is he still there?

HONEY
What d'you think? I'd have gone after him, wouldn't I if he'd left.
He starts singing again.

JONATHAN
Scornfully.
He could sneak out and you'd be too lazy to catch him.
Scowling.
Shut up that music, can't you?

HONEY
Derisively.
Now? I sing good. You're jealous because you can't keep a tune! Anyway, Father likes it. Once when I stopped he called out to keep on.
He glances back at the cabin.
I think he's asleep now. I peeked in the window and he's lying down.

JONATHAN
Anxiously.
Did he know you all right? I mean, really know he was your father?

HONEY
Eagerly.
Sure! He talked like he used to—before he got sick. And the way he was talking to himself he remembers this place, and when he used to live here, and everything.

JONATHAN
Relieved.
That's fine. Gosh, I hope he'll be all right now, for keeps!
With a trace of bitterness.
It's been no fun having him out of his head for so long, acting like a kid, and us having to pretend to him he was our brother.

HONEY
Yes. It's been crazy.
Then guiltily—loyally.
But he couldn't help it. It was brain fever. Mother says brain fever always does that to people.

JONATHAN
Guiltily.
Who's blaming him? He's my father, too.
Abruptly changing the subject.
Mother just got back from the funeral. Ethan told her how Father seemed to wake up all of a sudden and knew all of us in the potato field this morning, and asked for her, and how we'd lied and told him she'd gone to the city shopping. She burst out and started to cry she was so happy. She sent me down to tell you to keep him here. She'll be down as soon as she's changed her clothes. She doesn't want him to see her in mourning. She doesn't want him to know Granny's dead yet.

HONEY
I'm glad Granny's dead. Aren't you? She was a crazy old fool. I got to hate her.

JONATHAN
Frowning.
So did I. But we ought to forget that now.

HONEY
Stubbornly.
I won't. She hated Mother. I don't see why Mother had to go to her
funeral, or why she never let us say a word against her.

JONATHAN
Sharply.
That's Mother's business.
Then practically.
Anyway, what's the use of thinking about it now.

HONEY
Grinning.
I won't anymore.
In brogue.
The divil take her!
*He turns away, carefree, and begins to sing again—then stops abruptly,
looking around him.*
Let's go for a swim, as soon as Mother comes. Gosh, I like it out here.
I don't mind being poor, do you?

JONATHAN
Scornfully.
You like it? Yes, you do! When you don't have to work!

HONEY
Well, who wants to be a farmer? You don't. Neither does Ethan. Nor
Wolfe either, even if he pretends not to care.

JONATHAN
Seriously.
No, I don't want to be a farmer. And I won't be any longer than I
have to. There's no money in farming. You can't get ahead.
Determinedly.
And I'm going to get ahead.

HONEY
I'm going to own an hotel and run a livery stable. I love horses. And
renting rooms and hiring out carriages, that's easy.

JONATHAN
Scornfully.
Something easy! That's what you always want!

HONEY
Grins.
Sure! I'll get mine!
Then after a glance up the path.
Here comes Mother.
He dashes over and sits on the bench as if he were dutifully keeping guard. A moment later Sara enters. She wears a cheap calico working dress and is barefooted. Her fair complexion is tanned and her fine figure is strong, firm and healthy. She looks younger and at the same time older. Younger in that her face is no longer haggard, lined and tense. Older because of the look of resigned sadness in her eyes and the streaks of white in her black hair. Just now, however, her face is lighted up by an excited hope that is afraid that it is too good to be true.

SARA
In a whisper to Jonathan as she enters.
He's in the cabin?

JONATHAN
Nods.
He's asleep.

HONEY
Comes over toward her—virtuously.
I never stopped keeping guard over him one moment, Mother.

SARA
Mechanically.
That's a good boy.
Then a bit disappointedly.
Asleep, is he? I'd best let him sleep then. He's so weak. I was hoping he'd—It's hard to wait, wondering if he'll know me.

HONEY
Can I go swimming now—me and Jonathan?

SARA

Welcoming his interruption, surveys him critically.

You can. But you'll go up to the house first and get soap to take with you, and you'll use it! Look at you! You can get more dirt on you in an hour than two pigs could in a week! Look at your clothes, too! And to think I ever dreamed of making you a gentleman!

She gives him an affectionate pat and push.

Get along with you. Go up to the field first, and you and Johnny help Ethan and Wolfe finish the row they're doing. Tell them they can stop work after that and come swimming. We all have a right to take a bit of a holiday and give thanks to God, if your father is getting well—

She gives a longing look toward the cabin, but uneasy, afraid her hope may not be true. The two boys start eagerly off left. Suddenly she has a thought—guiltily.

Wait. Did you remember, like I asked you, to say a prayer for your grandmother's soul at the time of the funeral?

They hang their heads and avoid her eyes. She says sadly.

I see you didn't.

To herself.

Poor woman! I was the only one really to mourn her. I kept my distance at the cemetery, with my veil on my face so none would know me. Ah, if she ever knew in her dreams what I've suffered, with him all mixed up and lost in his mind, calling me Mother, as if I was her, and forgetting he'd ever had a wife, she'd feel she was the one who'd won in the end after all.

HONEY

Fidgeting impatiently.

Can we go now, Mother?

SARA

Starts—then sharply.

You can't till you've said the prayer. You had no right to forget. Get down on your knees, now!

As they hesitate sheepishly—peremptorily.

You hear me!

They flop down self-consciously. She goes on argumentatively.

Just because we have no faith in it doesn't mean it mightn't be true.
No one knows. And it does no harm. It's a mark of respect. Say a
prayer now.
The two boys exchange looks. They feel silly and giggly.

JONATHAN
We've forgotten. What'll we say, Mother?
She starts and hesitates, looking confused.

HONEY
With an impish grin.
You don't remember any either, Mother.

SARA
Hastily.
Say God rest her in peace, and that'll do.

JONATHAN AND HONEY
Burst out in mechanical chorus.
God rest her in peace.

*They bound to their feet with relief that the absurd business is over. As
they do so the door from the cabin is opened and Simon appears. He is terribly emaciated, pale and hollow-eyed, as though he had passed through
a long and devouring fever. His eyes have a groping and bewildered stare.
His clothes, the same as he wore in Act Four, are clean and well kept, but
wrinkled now as though he had slept in them. He stands in the doorway,
fixing his eyes on Sara, clinging weakly to the door frame for support. The
boys see him at once and start. Sara guesses from their faces and whirls
around. She tries to speak but is terrified to risk it, and only her lips move
soundlessly.*

SIMON
With a great gasp of relief and longing.
Sara!
He takes a weak, faltering step toward her.

SARA
With a happy cry.
Simon!

She rushes to him.

Darling! Oh, thank God you know me!

She throws her arms around him and hugs him to her. The two boys give them an embarrassed, and yet happy look and then dart away up the path.

SIMON

Stammers brokenly.

My love! I was so afraid I had lost you!

SARA

Tenderly—with a trembling smile.

Lost me, is it? You couldn't. I'd never let you—not in this life—nor in death, neither! But you know I love you!

Protestingly.

Sit down. Here like we used when we first knew love—me on the bench and you on the grass with your head on my lap.

She sits on the bench and he obeys mechanically, sitting on the grass, his arms around her hungrily and clingingly, his head on her lap. She goes on in a blissful, tender, emotional croon.

There now. Don't talk for a while. Just rest and be happy, Darling.

SIMON

Lets himself relax for a second, closing his eyes.

Yes, Sweetheart.

Then he jerks awake—pleading almost hysterically.

No! You must tell me. At once! I want to know! I've been lying in there trying to remember—how I got here—why?—when?—what happened?

SARA

Bullying him soothingly.

Now, now. Be quiet, and I'll tell you. There's nothing to be worried about. You've been sick with brain fever you got from working too hard and worrying too much about the Company—and I brought you here to get well. And now you are well, Darling.

SIMON

Dazedly.

Brain fever? Yes—that would explain—
Frightenedly.
But—

SARA
Pulling his head back.
Sush now, I tell you. Everything is all right. All the doctors said it
was the most natural thing for you to lose your memory for a while.
It's the way the sickness takes everyone that gets it.

SIMON
Beginning to be relieved.
Is it?
Forcing a smile.
Well, I've come out all right, haven't I?
Pleading again.
But please tell me everything, Sara. I feel, so strange—as if part of
me were lost—or had died.
He shudders.
It's a horrible feeling.

SARA
Sush, be quiet and I'll tell you every bit of it.
Then she hesitates and casts a worried look at him—calculatingly.
But maybe it would be simpler if you told me first the last thing you
remember.

SIMON
With frowning concentration.
The last? I have one clear memory. It came to me when I was lying
in the cabin. The last thing I can remember was one day at the office
I had an appointment with the directors of the bankrupt railroad to
sign a final agreement forcing them out and taking it over.
A look of bitter self-disgust comes to his face.
Damned hog and fool that I was!

SARA
With a deep breath of relief.
So that's the last you remember!

Then quickly.

Ah, don't be blamin' yourself, Darlin'. That was all my fault. I was always egging you on. I was never content. Nothing would do me but you must become a Napoleon of business. It was me was the greedy fool, Darlin'. With my dream I got from my father's boasting lies that I ought to rise above myself and own a great estate. But that's dead and gone and I'm cured of it, so don't worry.

SIMON

Obviously comforted by this—protests weakly.

No, you're not to blame. I had the same greedy streak in me.
Then almost accusingly.

But it was true you were the inspiration. I was so afraid you couldn't be proud of me unless I kept on—

SARA

Ah, don't talk. I'm prouder of you now you're all mine again than ever I've been since the day I first met you.
She kisses him tenderly.

But now tell me what else you remember of that day.

SIMON

Frowning.

I remember you came in. I was surprised because you hadn't been there for a long time.

SARA

Stares at him.

Ah.

SIMON

Forcing a smile.

You had seemed to become entirely wrapped up in the children and to have forgotten me. I confess I felt a bit jealous. So what was my delight to have you tell me you felt guilty for neglecting me, and lonely, too, and you wanted us to be again as close as we were in the old days, and you asked if I'd give you the job of my confidential secretary.

SARA

Gives him a strange look—slowly.

Ah, you remember I asked you that, do you?

SIMON

With a smile.

Yes, I remember it distinctly, and how happy it made me.

SARA

Forcing a laugh.

Well, God be praised. You're well again when you can remember that so clearly.

SIMON

Uneasily again.

But—I can't remember a thing after that. How long ago was that Sara?

SARA

Hesitating apprehensively.

Well, maybe longer than you'd think. Only bear in mind it's only natural, the doctors say, that with brain fever you forget not only the time you're sick but a long time before it—sometimes years.

She hesitates—then blurts out.

That day at the office was five years ago.

SIMON

Frightenedly.

Five years! Good God!

SARA

Hastily.

Now, now! Don't be worried! I'm telling you the truth when I say there's nothing in those years you'd miss remembering if you knew.

SIMON

Excitedly.

I must know everything, Sara. All that happened!

SARA

With an evasive teasing tone.

You're a great one for asking to know everything and have all, aren't you? But my memory's not that good. I've forgotten a lot since I brought you here on the farm to get well—here where the spell of the sun and the earth is in me and life is clear and simple. And right now with you in your right senses and me in mine, it's hard to remember it ever happened, except as a dream in my mind, a nightmare.

As he stirs uneasily, she forces a joking tone.

But what I remember clear as day is the one important thing, that you and I kept as much in love as ever, and more than ever! You're glad to hear that, I hope.

SIMON

Smiling tenderly.

I know that without remembering, Dear. Nothing could ever change that.

SARA

No, it couldn't. And nothing ever will. Another thing worth remembering is that your sons grew into the fine lads they are now, that you can be proud of.

SIMON

I am, Sara. I was so proud of them today in the field when I first—awakened from my nightmare—and saw them.

Then excitedly.

But what else? Tell me! The Company? Do I have to go back?

SARA

With a certain savage satisfaction and at the same time bitterness.

Ah, don't let the damned old Company bother you. It went bankrupt and the creditors stripped us clean. We've not a thing in the world except this farm. We're as poor as Job's turkey. You're free as you always wanted to be in your heart. We're back where we started with only our love for riches!

Hastily.

And it's more than enough! It's the greatest treasure in the world!

SIMON

Stares before him—with a dreamy exultance.

Yes, it is, Sara. Love! Freedom from greed! This is a happy awakening for me, Sara. I confess I always hoped something would turn up to release me from the soul-destroying compulsion to keep on enslaving myself with more and more power and possessions.

SARA
Smiling tenderly—but with an undercurrent of pitying scorn for his weakness.
Don't I know it? I could almost hear your heart dreaming it at times.

SIMON
That's why I gambled as I did. But my cursed luck kept me winning when I wanted to lose. Many a time I was tempted to deliberately ruin the Company. But I was afraid you would think me a coward and never forgive me.

SARA
Roughly tender.
Then get that idea out of your head right now. Don't have it in our new life that's beginning. It shows how little you know me. If you'd read my heart, as I'd read yours, you'd seen I wanted to be free as much as you.

SIMON
Gratefully—kissing her hand.
Sweetheart! Forgive me! What a fool I was! If I'd known—

SARA
Proudly.
And I proved it! It was I who smashed it! Oh, it couldn't have gone on long after you took sick. But I didn't wait. I used old Tenard to do it for me. You'd have laughed to see the crafty way I fooled him. I'd learned a lot about men from you, working in your office, and watching the fools come in and try to hide their greed and fear and the price tag of their souls hanging in their eyes!

SIMON
Bewilderedly.
Tenard? The banker? What had he to do?

SARA

You took his bank from him.

SIMON

I? But what did I want with his bank? Good God, wasn't I burdened enough already?

SARA

You wanted to give it to me because I wanted it. You don't know how greedy I get. Haven't I told you I egged you on? I alone was to blame. You did everything for love of me.

SIMON

Eagerly.
Yes, now that you've said it yourself, that is the real truth of it, Sara.

SARA

A bit mockingly.
It is. It's the best excuse in the world for you. So forgive yourself, do you hear? And I'll make up to you by doing everything I can for the rest of life to keep you free and happy.

SIMON

Oh, I know I'll be happy now, Sara. I never really wanted to leave here, you know. It was a great mistake your insisting I go into business. Because I was bound to fail in the end. It really isn't in me to succeed. It's a damned sordid hog's game.

SARA

I know, Darling. You're a gentleman and a poet at heart, and a lost child in a world of strangers. I'll never ask you to succeed again. With the boys helping me you'll have a living here, at least, and you needn't ever lift your hand. You can be in your dream of a world free of greed where men are good, and write the books you planned here in the old days. And maybe write a poem of your love for me once in a while, as you used. And there will be a song of happiness in my heart, knowing you're happy, even when I'm digging praties in the field, with my bare feet in the earth like a poor ignorant bog-trotter. *She starts—then adds proudly.*

I mean, like the common woman I am, and my mother was, whose one pride is love.

SIMON

Pats her hand tenderly.

You're the finest woman on earth.

Then weakly, even reluctantly assertive.

But don't think I will spend all my time on my back writing poetry. I can do my share of work in the fields. Of course, I'm too weak now. But later I'll be strong—

SARA

Bullying him.

You won't. You've done enough. You'll do as I say! You're mine, now!

SIMON

Gratefully—resting his head on her breast.

Yes, yours, Sweetheart. Everything in and of me yours! That is my heart's whole desire now!

Again weakly assertive.

But don't think I'll let you and the boys support me. I'll at least do enough work on the farm to earn—

SARA

Oh, an hour now and again, for the exercise, like a gentleman's hobby. I'll let you do that. But it will be a long time before you're strong enough. So rest now and don't think of it, but be at peace.

She cuddles his head against her. He closes his eyes.

SIMON

Vaguely and drowsily.

I seem to remember I tried to find relaxation from the grinding daily slavery to the Company by engaging my mind in some study of the duality of man's nature. Did I, Sara, or is that just a dream?

SARA

Uneasily.

Just a dream, Darling. You were too worried about business to have time. Anyway, you've got too much sense to waste thought trying to solve the old puzzle of life that there's no answer to, except an answer of death that's no comfort except to those who have lost love.

SIMON
Vaguely.
No, it's silly. There's no duality in me, I know. At least, not now.

SARA
After a pause—unwillingly as though her conscience forced her to speak.
There's something you haven't asked me—about your mother.

SIMON
Vaguely and drowsily—and indifferently.
That's true, I had forgotten. But I think the reason is I have a feeling that Mother is dead. She is, isn't she?

SARA
Blurts out.
Yes. She's dead.

SIMON
Indifferently.
I think I can picture what the rest of her life was without your telling me. I remember what a doting, contented old grandmother she had become. I imagine she grew more and more wrapped up in the children, and more at peace with herself, and was quite happy and reconciled to life—and to death—by the time she died. Isn't that true?

SARA
Tensely.
Yes. That's what happened to her. Exactly.

SIMON
Indifferently.
I'm glad. All that Mother ever needed was some unselfish interest that would take her away from her childish daydreaming and give her the courage to live in reality. It was fortunate for her you were generous enough to give her the opportunity by sharing the children

with her and becoming her close friend—I remember how grateful she was to you. I hope she remained so to the end.

SARA
Tensely.
I—I'm grateful to her.

SIMON
Drowsily.
I remember it was such a pleasure to me to find you two get on together so well. I had been afraid—But why speak of that now, when it all worked out so happily.
Sara smiles a twisted bitter smile over his head.
I was glad for her own sake, particularly. Your friendship meant so much to her. Poor Mother, she was always such a lonely, isolated woman.

SARA
She was, and she was proud to be, no matter what it cost her. She was a great lady.

SIMON
As if something in her voice frightened him—uneasily.
She—Mother *was* happy when she died, wasn't she? Wasn't she, Sara?

SARA
Tensely.
No woman could be happier. She had all the love her heart dreamed of.
Then hastily.
But don't think of the dead, Darling. It's bad luck with our new life starting. Think only of me, and my love for you, and that you're safe and at peace in it, at last!

SIMON
Drowsily smiling.
I am only too glad to, Sweetheart. That's all—I ever want to remember.
A pause—more drowsily.

I feel so sleepy. Your breast is so soft and warm—forgive if I—
He falls asleep.

SARA
Stares down at his face with a fierce, brooding tenderness—then speaks to herself with a strange intermixture of maternal admiration and pride, and a bitter resentment.
Ah, sleep, my Darlin'. Sleep on my breast. It's yours like the heart beating inside it! Rest in peace. You're home at last where you've always wanted to be. I'm your mother now, too. You've everything you need from life in me!
She chuckles to herself bitterly and admiring.
But ain't you the craftiest, greediest man that ever walked the earth, God forgive you, to keep on and never let anybody beat you, not even yourself, but make life give you your own stubborn way in the end! But don't think I'm complaining, for your way is my way! Yes, I've made even that mine, now!
She laughs softly with a strange gaiety. The four boys enter from the path at left, on their way to the lake, led by Ethan and Wolfe. The two latter look the same as in Act Three, Scene Two, except that Ethan is taller and heavier, and Wolfe taller and still slender. As their eyes fall on their father and mother, they are all embarrassed, look away, and quicken their pace to hurry past them down the path to the lake off right. Sara speaks.
SuSSH! Quiet now. He's asleep.
They disappear off right. Her eyes follow them. She speaks aloud to herself dreamily, her thought with her sons now—proudly.
Fine boys, each of them! No woman on earth has finer sons! Strong in body and with brains, too! Each with a stubborn will of his own! Leave it to them to take what they want from life, once they're men! This little scrub of a farm won't hold them long! Ethan, now, he'll own his fleet of ships! And Wolfe will have his banks! And Johnny his railroads! And Honey be in the White House before he stops, maybe! And each of them will have wealth and power and a grand estate—
She stops abruptly and guiltily—self-defiantly.
No! To hell with your mad dreams, Sara Melody! That's dead and done! You'll keep your hands off them if you have to cut them off to

do it! You'll let them be what they want to be, if it's a tramp in rags without a penny, with no estate but a ditch by the road, so long as they're happy! You'll leave them free, do you hear, and yourself free of them!

She looks down at Simon's sleeping face on her breast—with a brooding, possessive, tender smile.

After all, one slave is enough for any woman to be owned by! Isn't it true, my Darling?

She laughs with a gloating, loving, proud, self-mockery—then bends and kisses him softly so as not to awaken him.

CURTAIN

Tao House
Sept. 8th '38

Eugene O'Neill (1888–1953) was born in New York City, the son of James O'Neill, a popular actor, and Mary Ellen Quinlan. During his childhood years he lived mainly in hotels with his family, following the tours of his father's company; the only permanent home the young O'Neill knew was a summer cottage in New London, Connecticut, which later became the setting for *Long Day's Journey into Night*.

As an adolescent, O'Neill attended eastern preparatory schools and then Princeton University for one year until he was expelled. During the next five years he worked as a gold prospector, a sailor, an actor, and a reporter.

O'Neill began writing plays in 1913, and by 1916 his one-act play *Bound East for Cardiff* was produced in New York by the Provincetown Players, a group he had helped found. In 1920 his full-length play *Beyond the Horizon* was produced in New York and won O'Neill the first of his four Pulitzer Prizes. During decades of extraordinary productivity, O'Neill published 24 other full-length plays. After receiving the Nobel Prize for literature in 1936, he completed several masterpieces of the modern theater, including *A Touch of the Poet, More Stately Mansions, The Iceman Cometh, Long Day's Journey into Night,* and *A Moon for the Misbegotten*. O'Neill died in Boston in 1953.